Contents

BTEC FIRST

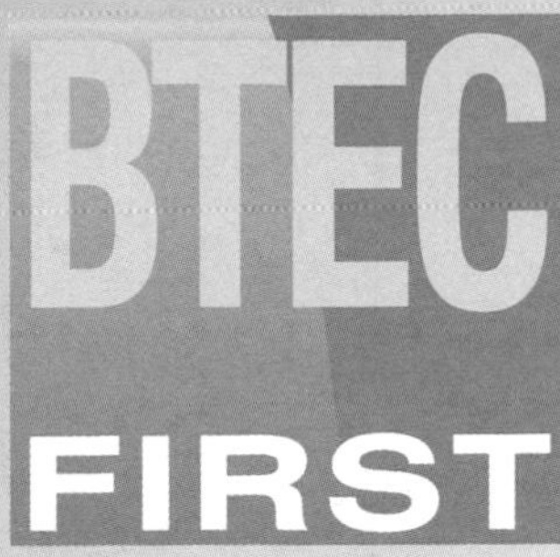

Children's Care, Learning + Development

Sandy Green

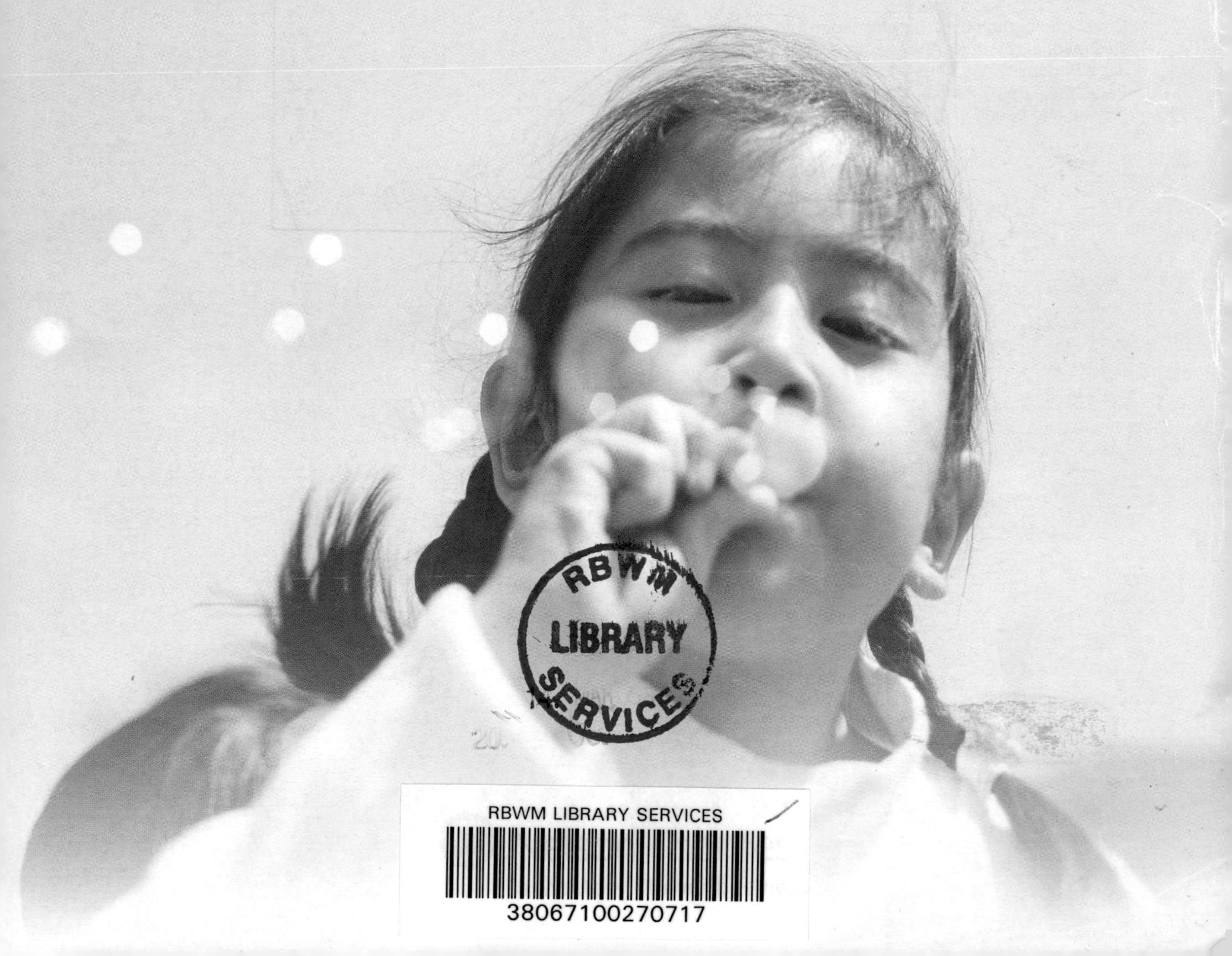

Published in 2007 by:
Nelson Thornes Ltd
Delta Place
27 Bath Road
CHELTENHAM
GL53 7TH
United Kingdom

07 08 09 10 / 10 9 8 7 6 5 4 3 2 1

A catalogue record for this book is available from the British Library

ISBN 978 0 7487 8408 0

Cover photograph by © Bloomimage/Corbis
Illustrations by Pantek Arts Ltd. Archive illustrations by Jane Bottomley and Angela Lumley
Page make-up by Pantek Arts Ltd, Maidstone, Kent
Printed and bound in Great Britain by Scotprint

Introduction

Early years practitioners work with children in a variety of care and education settings, in schools, nurseries, pre-schools, crèches and hospitals, and in the home as childminders and nannies. There are also opportunities within after-school clubs and play schemes. This is an exciting time to be an early years practitioner as there is greater interest than ever before in supporting children in the earliest years, both from society and from central government. Greater numbers of parents now work full time, necessitating care placements for their children from babyhood. Opportunities to support children within the classroom have also increased, as inclusion is the accepted preference for many children with an additional need. Career progression is increasing with qualifications at levels 3, 4 and 5, including Foundation level degrees.

If you enjoy begin with young children and are enthusiastic about training and development then this course will introduce you to an interesting and challenging career, providing you with opportunities to learn about all the key areas and supporting you within a range of settings to help you gain practical experience.

How do you use this book?

Covering all 8 units of the 2006 specification, this book has everything you need if you are studying BTEC First Certificate or Diploma in Children's Care, Learning and Development. Simple to use and understand, it is designed to provide you with the knowledge and understanding you need to gain your qualification. We guide you step by step toward your qualification, through a range of features that are fully explained over the page.

Which units do you need to complete?

There are 8 units available for BTEC First Children's Care, Learning and Development. For the BTEC First Diploma in Children's Care, Learning and Development you are required to complete 5 core units and 1 specialist unit.

Core Units	Specialist Units
Unit 1 **Understanding Children's Development**	Unit 6 **Supporting Children's Play and Learning**
Unit 2 **Keeping Children Safe**	Unit 7 **The Development and Care of Babies and Young Children Under Three Years**
Unit 3 **Communication with Children and Adults**	Unit 8 **Providing Support for Children with Disabilities or Special Educational Needs**
Unit 4 **Preparing and Maintaining Environments for Childcare**	
Unit 5 **Professional Development, Roles and Responsibilities in Childcare**	

Is there anything else you need to do?

1 Talk to other child carers about their work and listen to their guidance and advice on practice, qualifications and personal development.
2 Take time to observe others working with children, noting how they approach and respond to them. These observations will help you understand how to respond yourself.
3 Take whatever opportunities you can to gain experience working with children in different settings and of different ages. This will broaden your understanding and practical skills and help you identify where to start your career once qualified.
4 Keep yourself up to date with current thinking and ideas by reading the many magazines and journals especially for the early years.
5 Never be afraid to ask for help or advice when you need it.

We hope you enjoy your BTEC course – Good Luck!

Turn over now for your guide to the features of this book.

Features of this book

Understanding Children's Development

This unit covers:

- Understanding the growth and development of children
- Understanding the role of observation of children's development in the workplace
- Knowing how to observe children's development
- Understanding the importance of planning in supporting children's needs and development

This unit gives a clear overview of child development. Having knowledge and understanding of development is fundamental to working with children as this will help you to plan for them appropriately, and to respond to and meet their needs as fully as you are able.

Knowing how to observe children is also important and clear guidance on carrying out observations and the role of observation in the workplace is discussed here. It should always be remembered that the stages of development set out in this unit are averages, and therefore many individual children will differ from them, some being more advanced in one aspect of development, but still moving towards the averages in others. The averages give a framework for practitioners and medical professionals to monitor any concerns against. Examples of developmental averages can be found on p.00.

grading criteria

To achieve a **pass** grade the evidence must show that the learner is able to:	To achieve a **merit** grade the evidence must show that, in addition to the pass criteria the learner is able to:	To achieve a **distinction** grade the evidence must show that, in addition to the pass and merit criteria, the learner is able to:
P1 describe the principles, stages and sequences of growth and development in children	**M1** describe the developmental differences of children in the different age groups	**D1** compare the development of a child that you have observed with the expected development of a child of this age
P2 outline the physical, intellectual, emotional, social and communication development of children 0–3 years, 3–7 years, 7–12 years and 12–16 years	**M2** explain the potential effects of four factors on the growth and development of children	**D2** describe the strengths and possible weaknesses of the plan to support the development of the observed child
P3 identify the range of factors that affect children's growth and development including the role of maturation	**M3** explain the steps undertaken to ensure the effective and appropriate observation of children	
P4 describe the role of observation of children's development	**M4** suggest a plan to support the development of a child you have observed	
P5 observe and record the physical, intellectual, emotional, social and communication development of a child		

Learning Objectives
At the beginning of each Unit there will be a bulleted list letting you know what material is going to be covered. They specifically relate to the learning objectives within the 2006 specification.

Grading Criteria
The table of Grading Criteria at the beginning of each unit identifies achievement levels of pass, merit and distinction, as stated in the specification.

To achieve a **pass**, you must be able to match each of the 'P' criteria in turn.

To achieve **merit** or **distinction**, you must increase the level of evidence that you use in your work, using the 'M' and 'D' columns as reference. For example, to achieve a distinction you must fulfil all the criteria in the pass, merit and distinction columns. Each of the criteria provides a specific page number for easy reference.

Understanding Children's Development UNIT 1

activity
GROUP WORK

With a partner, compile a list of both local and national support groups. Keep this in your professional practice file. You may find it helpful to be able to offer such information to the families you work with.

Activities are designed to help you understand the topics through answering questions or undertaking research, and are either *Group* or *Individual* work. They are linked to the Grading Criteria by application of the D, P, and M categories.

case study 1.1

Justin

Justin is fifteen. He is of slight build and as yet shows little sign of the onset of puberty. His best friends, Steve and Callum, are now both taller and broader than he is, and Steve is already shaving. Justin would like a new jacket as he feels out of place in his old school coat, when his friends are wearing more up-to-date styles. Justin's parents refuse to buy him anything new as they know he is likely to have a growth spurt very soon. Justin starts turning down opportunities to go out in the evenings and at weekends, spending more and more time on his own.

Case Studies provide real life examples that relate to what is being discussed within the text. It provides an opportunity to demonstrate theory in practice.

activity
INDIVIDUAL WORK

1 What are the main issues here?
2 How might this be affecting Justin's self-confidence?
3 How might this affect Justin in his relationship with his current friends?
4 How might this affect Justin in his relationship with his parents?
5 Is this likely to affect Justin in forming new friendships or relationships?
6 How could the situation for Justin be helped?

An **Activity** that is linked to a Case Study helps you to apply your knowledge of the subject to real life situations.

keyword
Attachment An emotional bond that develops between a baby and their carer

It is agreed by modern day theorists that children need a secure **attachment** (a two-way relationship of pleasure and tenderness) with their main carers, not just with their mother, as was thought to be the case in the past by theorists such as John Bowlby (1907–90). Theorists agree that the carers' ability to respond to a child is the most important factor in influencing the attachment process. The quality of the 'bond' is what counts, and children make multiple attachments, having a different sort of attachment to different carers.

Keywords of specific importance are highlighted within the text in blue, and then defined in a 'keyword' box to the side.

Refer to p.00 for socialisation theory

Links direct you to other parts of the book that relate to the subject currently being covered.

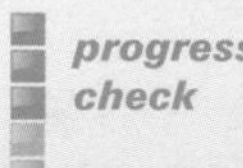

progress check

1. Explain the terms 'growth' and 'development'.
2. What are the primitive reflexes?
3. Explain the difference between primary and secondary sexual characteristics.
4. At what age is bowel and bladder control usually attained?
5. What conditions are needed to achieve emotional security?
6. What do the terms 'attachment' and 'bonding' mean?
7. Why are boundaries important to children?
8. Explain the ABC behaviour strategy.
9. What is social learning theory?
10. Outline three theories of language development.

Progress Checks provide a list of quick questions at the end of each Unit, designed to ensure that you have understood the most important aspects of each subject area.

References and suggested further reading

Baston, H and Durward, H (2001) *Examination of the Newborn. A Practical Guide*, Routledge
Bee, H (1992) *The Developing Child (6th edn)*, Allyn & Boston
Brain. C and Mukherji. P (2005) *Understanding Child Psychology*. Nelson Thornes.

Websites
www.babycentre.co.uk
www.pampers.com

Information bars point you towards resources for further reading and research (e.g. websites).

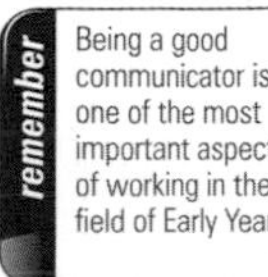

remember
Being a good communicator is one of the most important aspects of working in the field of Early Years.

Remember boxes contain helpful hints, tips or advice.

Acknowledgements

A huge thankyou to my family and friends who continually show interest and provide love, support and encouragement. A special thank you to Sally Foster for her contribution to Unit 8.

Dedication

To my mum, Peggy Powton. A much loved lady who will never be forgotten.

Photo credits:

Andrew Ward/Photodisc 41 (NT), p.332 (top); Barbara Penoyar/Photodisc 16 (NT), p.18 (all top, bottom middle); Bubbles Photolibrary, p.207, p.216, p.217; Bubbles Photolibrary/Jacqui Farrow, p.191; Corel 138 (NT), p.186; Corel 637 (NT), p.18 (bottom left and right); Craig Holmes/Alamy, p.297 (top); David Young Wolff/Alamy, p.250; Indiapicture/Alamy, p.192; Jack Hollingsworth/Photodisc 45 (NT), p.7 (top); John Birdsall, p.206; Jules Frazier/Photodisc 61 (NT), p.338; Mark Longhurst/Rex Features, p.252; Mother and Baby Picture Library, p.7 (right); Nicola Sutton/Photodisc 41 (NT), p.249; Photodisc 76 (NT), p.226; Russell Illiq/Photodisc 41 (NT), p.232; Sally & Richard Greenhill Photolibrary, p.7 (left); Science Photolibrary, p.283 (both), p.369 (both); Steve Allen/Brand X RW (NT), p.185 (both); Vernon Leach/Alamy, p.73.

Every effort has been made to contact copyright holders and we apologise if any have been overlooked.

Understanding Children's Development

This unit covers:

- understanding the growth and development of children
- understanding the role of observation of children's development in the workplace
- knowing how to observe children's development
- understanding the importance of planning in supporting children's needs and development.

As an understanding of how children develop is fundamental to working with children, the unit begins with an overview of child development and looks at the factors affecting growth and development. This knowledge will enable you to plan appropriately and respond to and meet children's needs to the best of your ability.

Observation has an important role in early years work, and you will look at why observations are undertaken and at a range of methods.

Planning is essential when supporting children's needs and development, and in the final part of the unit you will be introduced to this aspect of the early years worker's role.

grading criteria

To achieve a **Pass** grade the evidence must show that the learner is able to:	To achieve a **Merit** grade the evidence must show that the learner is able to:	To achieve a **Distinction** grade the evidence must show that the learner is able to:
P1 describe the principles, stages and sequences of growth and development in children	**M1** describe the developmental differences of children in the different age groups	**D1** compare the development of a child that you have observed with the expected development of a child of this age
P2 outline the physical, intellectual, emotional, social and communication development of children 0–3 years, 3–7 years, 7–12 years and 12–16 years	**M2** explain the potential effects of four factors on the growth and development of children	**D2** describe the strengths and possible weaknesses of the plan to support the development of the observed child

grading criteria

To achieve a **Pass** grade the evidence must show that the learner is able to:	To achieve a **Merit** grade the evidence must show that the learner is able to:	To achieve a **Distinction** grade the evidence must show that the learner is able to:
P3 identify the range of factors that affect children's growth and development including the role of maturation	**M3** explain the steps undertaken to ensure the effective and appropriate observation of children	
P4 describe the role of observation of children's development	**M4** suggest a plan to support the development of a child you have observed	
P5 observe and record the physical, intellectual, emotional, social and communication development of a child		
P6 describe the process of planning to support children's development		

Understanding the growth and development of children

keyword
Development
The changes that take place as an individual grows.

Principles

Development is holistic; each aspect of a person's development interconnects with other aspects.

This unit looks at the main areas of development:

- physical development
- emotional development
- social development
- moral development
- communication and speech development
- intellectual and perceptual development.

> **remember**
> A child may be more advanced in one aspect of development but still moving towards the averages in others.

It also examines the influences of prior experiences, both positive and negative, and looks at factors that can affect development, before, during and after birth.

As you study development, you will look at the rate and sequences of change that take place within the body of an average child. Although children develop at different rates, the order of development is usually the same.

It should always be remembered that the ages given for the stages of development set out in this unit are averages, and that there will be individual variation: some children develop faster than average, others more slowly. The averages provide a benchmark for practitioners and medical professionals against which they can monitor children if there are any concerns.

Refer to pages 9–15 for examples of developmental averages.

> **keyword**
>
> **Growth**
> Increase in size, height, weight, and so on.
>
> **Screening**
> The process of examining a whole population to identify who is showing signs of a disease or may be predisposed to develop it.
>
> **Health**
> The state of well-being.

Growth

Growth and development have different meanings. Growth is most easily defined as the changes in the body that are measurable. This includes height, weight, skeletal frame and shoe size. Each of these measurements can be reproduced on a graph or table and form part of the **screening** programme (the checking of a child's growth and development) that monitors most children in developed countries. In the UK, measurements are usually plotted on a graph called the centile (or percentile) chart. These charts are found in a child's **health** record book.

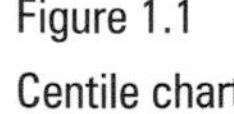

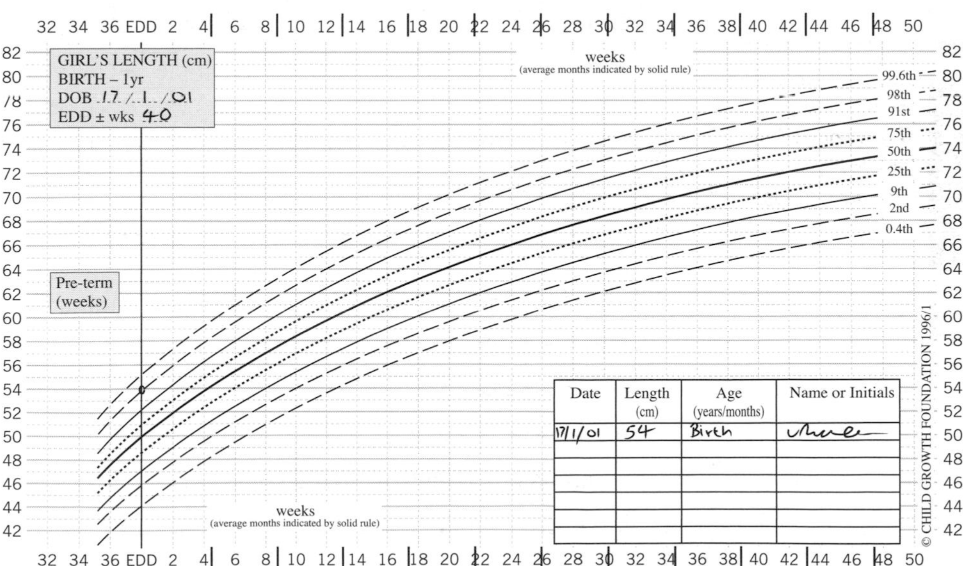

Figure 1.1
Centile chart

For more examples of centile charts, see Unit 7, pages 287–289.

Ongoing screening

Screening programmes continue throughout life. In children they include:

- neonatal screening, during the first month (particularly the first 14 days)
- infant screening, at six weeks, eight months and around 18 months
- childhood screening, pre-school, together with ongoing assessments as necessary.

These screening programmes help to ensure that children are growing and developing as expected, and they also help to identify some of the conditions that are not obvious at birth.

Refer to Unit 8, pages 347–369, for an overview of a range of conditions affecting development.

keyword

Fontanelle
The area of an infant's skull that allows flexibility during the birth process.

Development

Development is concerned with the changes that occur within the body as it grows, for example, the closing of the **fontanelles** on an infant's skull and the ossification of the skeleton (whereby the cartilage in a newborn infant is gradually replaced by bone).

See page 8 and Unit 7, page 281, for more about the fontanelles.

remember

Developmental norms are simply a guideline; most children are slightly ahead or behind in some or all areas of development. It is also important to note that developmental norms do not accurately reflect all races and cultures.

The increase in physical abilities is developmental (e.g. gaining head control, sitting, crawling, standing and, finally, walking); so are the development of the nervous system and the patterns of organ and tissue development that mark, for example, the onset of puberty and reproduction.

Development is often uneven, while remaining sequential, so different areas may be more advanced than others. For example, a child's physical skills may be very advanced, whereas their language is less well developed.

It is important that everyone working with young children understands what are considered to be the 'normal' expectations of a child's development. Knowing what is considered normal will give you a benchmark, enabling you to identify if a child's development is delayed or impaired in any way. *Normative development* and *developmental norms* are the terms most often used in this context.

Stages and sequences

Figure 1.2
The continuum of life – from infancy to late adulthood

Milestones of development

During an average lifespan, each person moves through a range of developmental stages, containing developmental **milestones**, for different aspects of development. In this book, the stages are categorised as follows:

- the prenatal stage, from conception to birth
- the neonatal stage, from birth to one month
- infancy, from one month to one year
- the toddler, from one to two years
- early childhood, from two to five years
- middle childhood, from five to 12 years
- adolescence.

However, the book focuses predominantly on the development of children up to the approximate age of eight years, as this is the age range mostly associated with the BTEC First Children's Care, Learning and Development programme.

keyword
Milestones
Significant events linked with stages in development.

Physical development

An early aspect of physical development is seen in the **primitive reflexes** of newborn infants.

Later, the child develops motor skills (locomotor skills and non-locomotor skills) and skills for manipulation.

- Locomotor skills involve the body moving forward in some way (e.g. walking, running and hopping).
- Non-locomotor skills describe the physical movements that take place while stationary (e.g. bending, pulling and pushing).
- Manipulation involves actions using dexterity (e.g. throwing and catching a ball, threading cotton reels and placing one brick on top of another).

keyword
Primitive reflexes
Automatic responses seen in newborn infants that are not generally observed in older children and adults.

See page 8 and Unit 7, page 284, for more about the primitive reflexes.

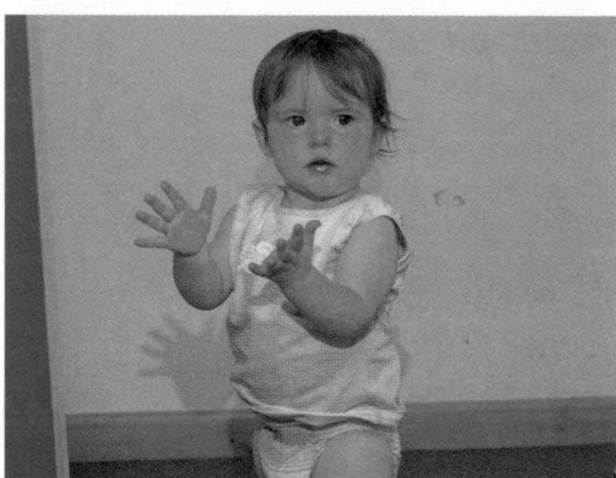

Figure 1.3
Different types of physical activity

Physical skills, which can be gross (large) or fine, include movement and balance. Movements can be either precise or casual and can involve the whole body or just one part of it.

activity
1.1
INDIVIDUAL WORK

Using the illustrations above as examples to start you off, write a list of as many activities as you can think of that provide opportunities for the following:

- precise movements
- carefree (casual) movements
- general movements
- balance.

You might find it helpful to refer to Unit 6, pages 243–254, for ideas for activities.

Development becomes increasingly more complex, and children acquire more difficult physical skills as it progresses. The maturational changes can be described as moving:

Figure 1.4

A child can hug a large teddy bear before they can fasten their clothing

- *From the simple to the complex*. A child learns simple actions, such as learning to stand, before learning the more complex actions involved in walking.
- *From cephalo (head) to caudal (tail)*. Physical control starts at the head and gradually develops down through the body. For example, head control is attained before the spine is strong enough for an infant to sit unsupported, and sitting unsupported is achieved before the child is able to stand.
- *From proximal (near to the body) to distal (the outer reaches of the body)*. A child develops control of actions near to the body before they develop control of the outer reaches of the body. For example, a child can hug and carry a large teddy bear (arm control) before they can fasten their clothing (finger control).
- *From general to specific*. Generalised responses give way gradually to specific ones. For example, when recognising a favourite carer, an infant shows the generalised physical responses associated with excitement, but in the same situation an older child would make the specific facial response of smiling.

Early physical development

At birth the infant will sleep most of the time, mostly waking for feeds and nappy changing and often falling asleep during these **routines**. Gradually, sleep patterns change, and infants remain awake for longer periods.

keyword

Routines
Set procedures that should meet the needs of all concerned.

All babies are born with dark eyes; permanent eye colour is not established until much later on.

The extremities (feet and hands) are often bluish in colour owing to poor circulation of blood in the earliest days.

Posture and motor skills

Immediately after birth, many infants naturally curl into the foetal position with their heads to one side.

Limbs are kept partly flexed and are hypertonic (have tension), and movements tend to be jerky. The head and neck are hypotonic (weak) and, as neck muscles are undeveloped, there is no head control, so full support of the head and neck area is needed whenever the infant is handled.

Figure 1.5 A baby in the foetal position

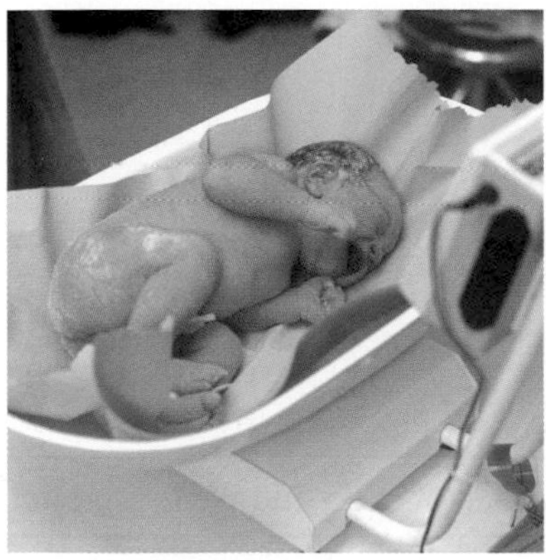

Figure 1.6 A baby in flexed pose

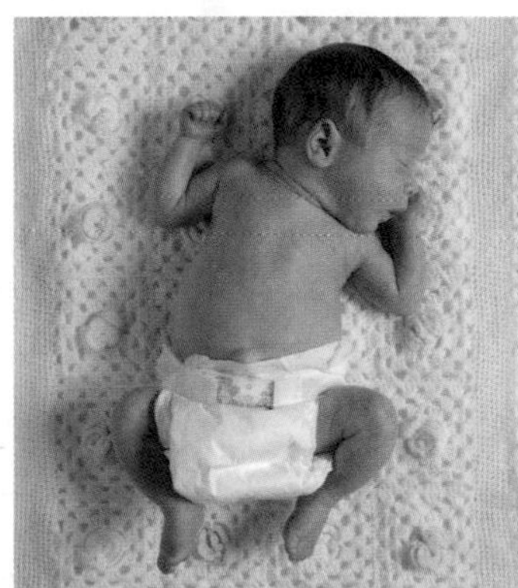

Fontanelles

There are two fontanelles. The posterior fontanelle is a small triangular area near the crown, which closes within a few weeks of birth. The anterior fontanelle is near the front of the head and is diamond shaped. It usually closes over by 18 months of age and pulsates at the same rate as the infant's heartbeat. Fontanelles are areas of the skull where the bony plates of the skull meet. They enable some movement of the skull during the birth process.

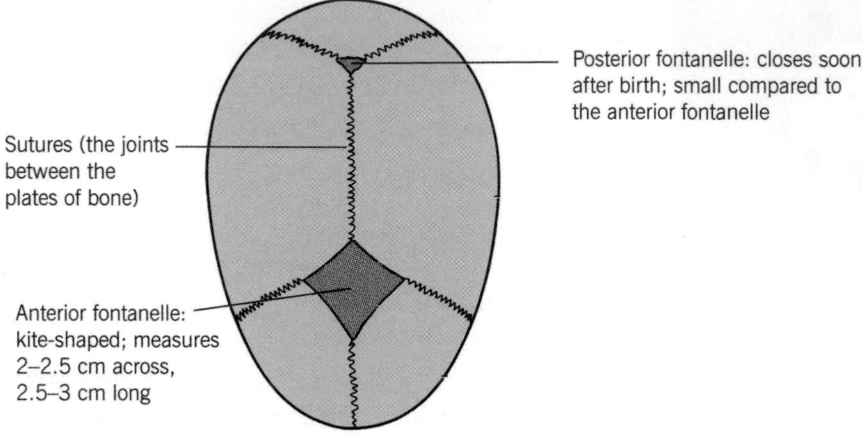

Figure 1.7
The fontanelles on a baby's skull

Birth marks

There are various types of birth marks; most are neither serious nor permanent. Examples include port wine marks, strawberry naevi (haemangioma), 'stork bite' marks, Mongolian blue spots and congenital melanocytic naevi (CMNs).

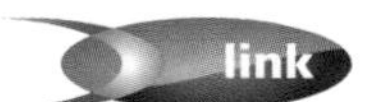

Refer to Unit 7, page 283, for a fuller discussion of birth marks.

Reflexes

Primary **reflexes** can be defined as 'automatic body reactions to specific stimulation' (Bee, 1992, page 105). These reflexes are:

> *keyword*
> **Reflex**
> An involuntary response to a stimulus, for example blinking.

- blinking
- rooting
- the sucking reflex
- the palmar grasp
- the plantar reflex
- stepping reflex
- the moro reflex
- the startle reflex
- the asymmetric tonic neck reflex.

The primary reflexes are explained and illustrated in Unit 7, pages 284–286.

Some reflexes stay with us for life, for example blinking, but some are lost after the first few weeks (the primitive reflexes). The presence of reflexes is an indicator of how well an infant's nervous system is functioning (their neurological well-being). As the brain gradually takes over the body's responses, the primitive reflexes disappear. If the primitive reflexes are retained for longer than is usual (they usually start to diminish at around six weeks), it may indicate that there is a developmental problem that requires investigation.

All infants are usually assessed by a doctor at six weeks of age.

The senses

The hearing of a newborn baby is very sharp, whereas their vision is initially limited and their eyes are not always fully co-ordinated.

A section in Unit 7 focuses specifically on newborn babies and sets out a useful summary of their senses in the earliest days and weeks. Refer to Unit 7, page 286, for an overview of the senses: hearing, vision, touch and smell.

Milestones of physical development

Infancy (one month to one year): a summary of physical skills

Gross motor skills

- Movements remain jerky and uncontrolled.
- Head lag gradually decreases and head control is usually achieved by five months.
- Rolling over is first seen between four and six months (from back to side), and then from front to back by about eight months.
- Reaching for objects begins at about four months with the ability to pass toys from hand to hand seen from about seven months.
- At four months, the infant discovers their feet and manages to sit with support.
- Sitting alone commences at about seven to eight months, with greater balance gradually developing.
- Crawling can start from six months (commando crawling); traditional crawling is seen from about eight months. Some infants bear-walk or bottom-shuffle.
- Some infants miss out the crawling stage and move straight to pulling themselves up on furniture at around eight to 10 months.

Figure 1.8
Crawling and bear-walking

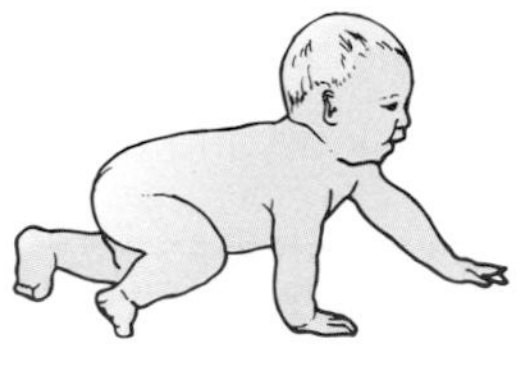

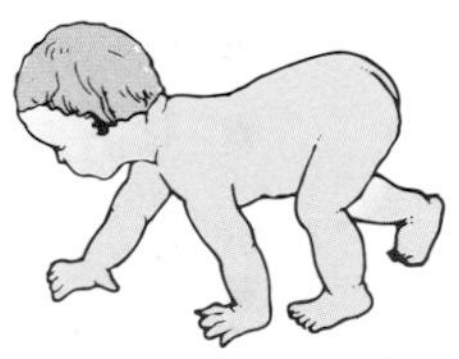

- Standing alone can occur any time from 10 months but is more usual at around a year, when balance is generally more established.
- Walking is normally achieved by 12–16 months.

Fine motor skills

- Hand and finger movements gradually increase, from the grasping of adults' fingers in the earliest months, through to playing with own fingers and toes, and handling and then holding toys and objects from three to four months.
- Everything is explored through the mouth.
- At about seven months, the infant will try to transfer objects from one hand to the other with some success. Pincer grasp (index finger and thumb) is emerging.
- By about 10 months, pincer grasp is developed.
- The infant will pick up small objects.
- Toys are pulled towards the infant.
- Pointing and clapping are deliberate actions for most infants by 10–12 months.
- Controlled efforts are made when feeding, with some successes.

Figure 1.9
Toddler walking

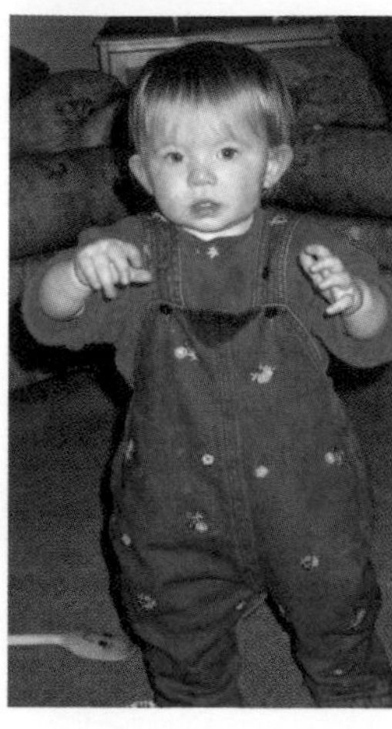

Toddler (one to two years): a summary of physical skills

- Standing alone is achieved but toddlers are unable at first to sit from being in a standing position without help. They begin to let themselves down in a controlled manner from about 15 months.
- When walking, hands are held up for balance and the infant's steps are uneven; they have difficulty in stopping once they have started.
- They can creep upstairs on hands and knees quite safely (not advisable without an adult supervising).
- They begin to kneel.
- By 18 months, walking is usually well established, and the arms are no longer needed for balance. The toddler can now back into a small chair and climb forwards into an adult chair.
- Squatting when playing is now common.
- They can usually walk upstairs holding an adult hand.
- Manipulation skills (the ability to use hands and fingers in a controlled manner) are developing. Pages of books can usually now be turned quite well, and pencils can be held in a clumsy (primitive) grasp.
- By two years, the child can usually run safely, starting and stopping at will.
- They are able to pull wheeled toys, with some understanding of direction.
- They are usually able to control a ball to throw forwards.
- They are able to walk up and (usually) down stairs, holding on and two feet to a stair.
- They cannot yet kick a football without falling into it, as they lose their balance when they kick their foot forward.
- They cannot usually pedal a tricycle.

Figure 1.10
Clumsy (primitive) grasp

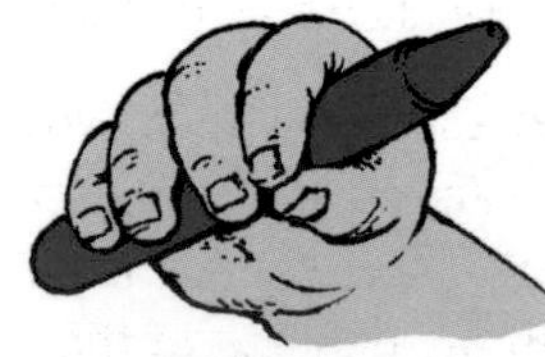

Child (two to five years): a summary of physical skills

- Walking up stairs alternating the feet is usually achieved by three years. Going securely up and down on alternate feet is seen by three and a half.
- At two and a half, a child can kick a football gently; by three years with force.
- Pushing and pulling of large toys is achieved by two and a half.
- Locomotor skills (e.g. movement forwards and backwards) improve rapidly during this stage of development.
- Use of pedals is often achieved by three years, and a child can steer around corners.
- Balance gradually improves, and by four years a child can usually stand, walk and run on tiptoes, and navigate skilfully when active.
- From three years, ball skills increase: catching, throwing, bouncing and kicking.
- Manipulation skills improve.
- Scissor control is developing, and greater pencil control is achieved by three years.
- By four years, threading small beads and early sewing is achieved.
- Adult pencil control is usually present by four years.

Child (five to 12 years): a summary of physical skills

The emphasis is now on practice and further development of the physical skills already gained. There will be improvements in large motor skills, for example in how fast a child can run, their stamina when playing group games, and their ability to climb and manoeuvre more difficult objects, in more challenging circumstances. The child's ability to balance also improves (e.g. hopping, skipping and climbing).

Hand–eye co-ordination develops, allowing a more adult level of control when writing, drawing, sewing, and so on, and there is greater skill in ball games and in activities involving manual dexterity.

Puberty

Puberty is a physiological stage that can cross middle childhood and adolescence. For girls, the **pre-pubescent** stage can begin from nine years onwards, but it is mostly associated with adolescence. Height develops rapidly here with the thigh bone growing at a faster rate than the rest of the body.

> *keyword*
> **Pre-pubescent** Before the onset of the development of secondary sex characteristics, such as periods, body hair and breast development in girls.

Adolescents: a summary of physical development

Early adolescence is marked by a variety of changes, including the adolescent growth spurt, maturation of the reproductive system, and the development of secondary sexual characteristics. These changes are collectively known as puberty.

For girls, the most important change is the onset of menstruation (periods). Girls can start menstruating from as early as 10 years, but ages vary considerably, up to 15 or 16. Ethnic group, heredity, exercise levels and health can all influence individual biological timings. Breast development starts with the budding of the breasts, followed by enlargement, until full breast maturity is reached with the formation of the areola. Once menstruation has begun it usually continues for approximately 35 years, only being interrupted by pregnancy.

Table 1.1 Sexual characteristics: girls

Primary sexual characteristics (formed before birth)	Secondary sexual characteristics (develop during puberty)
■ Vagina ■ Uterus ■ Ovaries ■ Fallopian tubes	■ Breast budding preceding full breast maturity ■ Pelvis widens (in preparation for childbirth) ■ Pubic hair develops ■ Axillary (underarm) hair develops ■ Ovaries start to produce eggs ■ Onset of menstruation

In boys, puberty starts a little later (girls are on average two years ahead of boys in their development during this stage of life). The first sign of puberty in boys is usually pubic hair growth, followed by a slight increase in the size of the scrotum and testes. The texture of the scrotum changes, and when the penis develops it firstly increases in length and then in breadth. Deepening of the voice also occurs during this phase of development.

Both boys and girls have a tendency for oily skin throughout adolescence, leading to skin problems such as acne.

Table 1.2 Sexual characteristics: boys

Primary sexual characteristics (formed before birth)	Secondary sexual characteristics (develop during puberty)
■ Penis ■ Testes ■ Scrotum ■ Seminal vesicles ■ Vas deferens	■ Pubic hair develops ■ Axillary hair develops ■ Chest hair develops ■ Facial hair develops ■ Deepening of the voice (voice 'breaks') ■ Penis increases in size and length ■ Testes grow and begin to produce sperm ■ Ability to ejaculate

To summarise:

- By 18 years of age, puberty is usually past, and the genitals and reproductive ability of both boys and girls are fully mature.
- Overall physical strength and stamina are increased.
- Shoulders broaden and full height is reached.
- Body image is important.

- Eating disorders are not uncommon, with severe disorders such as anorexia nervosa causing secondary amenorrhea (the absence of menstruation).
- Secondary amenorrhea can also be linked to high levels of exercise and is quite often noted in athletes, gymnasts and dancers.

Milestones of social and emotional development

Social development includes interactions, play, personal care and learning social expectations; emotional development includes self-esteem, feeling secure, and expressing and controlling emotions, for example tantrums.

Infancy (one month to one year): a summary of social and emotional development

- The first social smile is usually seen by six weeks.
- Smiling is first confined to main carers and is then in response to most contacts.
- The infant concentrates on carers' faces.
- Pleasure during handling and caring routines is seen by eight weeks, through smiles, cooing and general contentment.
- Expressions of pleasure are clear when gaining attention from about 12 weeks and in response to the main carers' voices.
- Social games, involving handling and cuddles, elicit chuckles from four to five months onwards.
- Infants enjoy watching other infants.
- Sleep patterns begin to emerge from about four months onwards, although these will continue to change.
- From about nine or 10 months, the infant may become distressed when the main carer leaves them and temporarily lose their sense of security and become wary of strangers. This is a normal stage in development.
- Playing contentedly alone (**solitary play**) increases by one year, but the reassuring presence of an adult is still needed.

keyword
Solitary play
Playing alone, a normal stage of development in young children.

Figure 1.11 Baby looking to the side

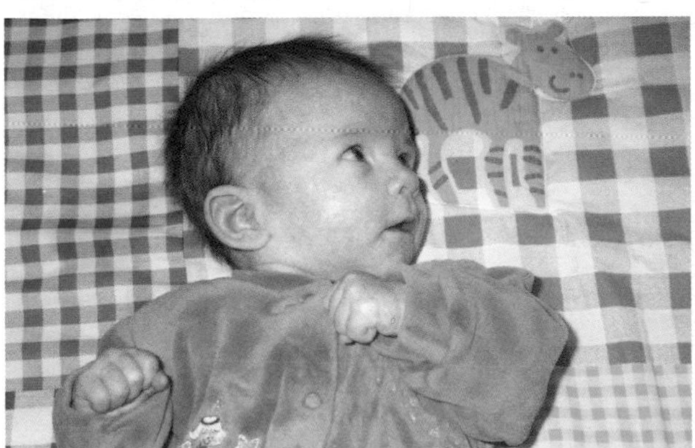

Figure 1.12 Toddler playing

Child (one to two years): a summary of social and emotional development

- By about 15 months, infant will usually indicate a wet or soiled nappy.
- Infant co-operates with dressing, for example holding up arms for a jumper.
- They are dependent on an adult's presence for reassurance.
- They experience frustration at not being able to achieve their aim (e.g. putting two bricks together), which leads them to discard toys in anger.
- By 18 months, the child is usually very successful at feeding self with a spoon.
- Infant is confident when handling a cup but does not put it back down (gives it to adult).
- The infant removes hats, shoes, etc. but can rarely replace them.
- They make urgent vocalisations when making a demand.
- Bowel control is sometimes attained by 18 months and is usually attained by two years.
- By two years, there is **parallel play**.
- Children can be rebellious and resistive and get frustrated when trying to make themselves understood.
- They can easily be distracted from their tantrums at this age.
- It is both common and normal to have no idea of sharing and no understanding of the need to defer their wishes.
- Child follows adult around and needs reassurance when tired or fearful.
- By two years, child can usually put on hat and shoes and can reposition a cup on a surface.

keyword
Parallel play
The stage of play when children play alongside other children without interacting.

Child (two to five years): a summary of social and emotional development

- At two and a half, tantrums are common when needs are thwarted. A child is less easily distracted from them now.
- Child is very resistive of restraint, for example when having a hand held in a busy shop.
- Mostly, the child still watches others or plays in parallel; they may occasionally join in briefly.
- By four years, children can eat skilfully and can dress, wash and clean their teeth (with supervision).
- This is generally a more independent age; many children want to try things on their own.
- Child co-operates with others but can also be uncooperative if wishes are refused.
- Child can be very strong willed.
- At five years, behaviour is noticeably more sensible and controlled.
- Child understands sharing and turn-taking and the need for fair play.
- **Co-operative** play is constant at five years.

keyword
Co-operative play
The stage of play when children play with each other, sometimes taking on simple roles or making simple rules for their games.

- Child chooses own friends and plays well.
- Child is very protective towards younger children, pets and distressed playmates.

Child (five to 12 years): a summary of social and emotional development

- Co-operative play is frequent and sustained.
- Gender awareness is strong.
- Co-operative play is mostly with same-sex peers.
- Individual friendships are very important.
- Children make definite decisions about their friends.
- Parents are less openly important, but their continued support is needed.

Adolescents: a summary of social and emotional development

- Forming relationships becomes of great importance.
- Interest in the opposite sex develops.
- Sexual identity becomes an important focus.
- Confusion regarding sexuality is common.
- Forming own self-identity can at times be difficult.
- Mood swings and hormone imbalance can cause emotional upheaval.
- Peer pressure is intense and can cause difficulties in maintaining beliefs.
- Depression is common at this stage.

In adolescence, forming relationships is important.

case study 1.1 Justin

Justin is 15. He is of slight build and as yet shows little sign of the onset of puberty. His best friends, Steve and Callum, are now both taller and broader than he is, and Steve is already shaving. Justin would like a new jacket as he feels out of place in his old school coat, when his friends are wearing more up-to-date styles. Justin's parents refuse to buy him anything new as they know that he is likely to have a growth spurt very soon. Justin starts turning down opportunities to go out in the evenings and at weekends, spending more and more time on his own.

activity INDIVIDUAL WORK

(a) What is the main issue here?
(b) How might this be affecting Justin's self-confidence?
(c) How might this affect Justin in his relationship with his current friends?
(d) How might this affect Justin in his relationship with his parents?
(e) Is this likely to affect Justin in forming new friendships or relationships?
(f) What could be done to help Justin in this situation?

Peer pressure

During adolescence, peer pressure becomes increasingly important. No one likes to be different or outside the main crowd; and it can be hard for individuals to maintain their moral thinking and beliefs in the face of pressure to conform to the activities of a social group.

Peer pressure can lead individuals into situations that they know are wrong, causing inner conflict. This, in turn, can affect their self-esteem and personal value.

Peer groups are important in that they can have a significant effect on attitudes as well as actions, both positively and negatively. Dealing with negative peer pressure becomes easier as the individual gains in self-confidence and develops a clear sense of right and wrong.

Moral development

keyword

Boundaries
Rules that guide behaviour and ensure consistency.

Culture
Beliefs, customs and values of people from a similar background.

Religion
A person's belief in a god or gods.

Role model
A person who is considered to be setting an example to others.

Moral development involves learning what is right or wrong, good or bad. Children need moral guidance. There are close links between moral development and social development: a child's understanding of socially acceptable behaviour is a factor in their ability to build successful relationships. Developing an understanding of what is right and wrong and of sharing is important and is helped by having well-defined **boundaries** within the setting, together with a positive approach to addressing problems that arise. Valuing other **cultures** and **religions** is essential in our multi-cultural society; equality should be both recognised and respected. Acquiring self-value helps us to cope with peer pressure, to stand firm and maintain our beliefs, and moral conduct.

Your task in helping and supporting moral development is as a **role model**, and by setting clear boundaries regarding what is acceptable within the setting. It is also important that the adults within the setting are prepared to challenge unacceptable actions or talk, both with the children and with other adults.

Table 1.3 Kohlberg's six-stage theory of moral development

Level 1 Pre-conventional morality (based on external authority)
Stage 1 Child acts to avoid unpleasant consequences (punishment)
Stage 2 Child acts to gain rewards. You should behave fairly and honour deals
Level 2 Conventional morality (based on judgements about the expectations of others)
Stage 3 Child wishes to please others and be thought of as 'nice' – a 'good boy' or 'good girl'
Stage 4 Child respects social rules. It is good to uphold the law and do one's duty
Level 3 Post-conventional morality (based on self-chosen ethical principles)
Stage 5 Involves recognising rules or laws may be unjust, and so can sometimes be broken
Stage 6 Reasoning is based on universal principles which show profound respect for life

(Adapted from Cullis *et al.*, 1999, p. 118)

Each person develops their own moral code, which they strive to live by. The moral reasoning of young children is initially defined by obedience in order to avoid punishment, whereas later on it becomes important to them to uphold certain rules, because they feel that it is expected of them (conventional morality). The final stage of moral reasoning is only reached when the individual understands that at times rules need to be broken in order to achieve justice and they develop a respect for the 'universal value and dignity of human life' (Cullis *et al.*, 1999).

Self-concept and personal identity

keyword

Self-concept
An understanding of our own identity that includes how we are seen by others.

As part of their social and emotional development, children develop a **self-concept**, i.e. a sense of self-awareness and personal identity, and a sense of security. It entails their learning to understand how they, and also others, feel and learning how to express how they feel to other people. It is much easier for children to explain how they feel physically than how they feel emotionally, and adults should be aware that very young children will often generalise their physical feelings as, perhaps a 'tummy ache', when really the source of discomfort is elsewhere.

Emotions can be both positive and negative and, at times, very intense. There should be opportunities for children to express their feelings within the safety of play. They need to know that it is OK to have strong feelings and that adults sometimes have them too.

activity
1.2 INDIVIDUAL THEN GROUP WORK

(a) Draw up two columns; head one 'positive emotions' and the other 'negative emotions'. Look at the emotions listed below and write each in the appropriate column, according to whether you think it is a positive or a negative emotion.

happiness curiosity anger sadness love suspicion
eagerness excitement guilt disappointment fright frustration
anxiety sorrow fear hate pleasure jealousy
contentment laughter delight distress

(b) In a small group, discuss the choices that you made for (a).
Then, as a group, tackle (c) and (d).

(c) Which emotions are most common in young children?

(d) Would any of these emotions concern you in a young child? If yes, which emotions and under what circumstances would you be concerned?

Figure 1.13
A range of emotions can be seen on children's faces

Responding to and encouraging the expression of feelings

Play is an ideal way for children to be able to express their feelings safely, in an atmosphere of support and understanding. A well-planned early years setting will offer opportunities for the physical expression of emotions, for example anger or frustration, through the use of malleable materials such as clay, dough or plasticine. Alternatively, emotions can be expressed through physical activity such as woodwork, ball games and activities involving large motor skills.

Relevant storybooks, role play and opportunities for creativity can sometimes help children to cope with emotions such as sadness, confusion and jealousy. As an adult working with children, you should give children the time to talk, to ask questions and to chat about what is troubling them.

In early years settings, it is up to the adults to encourage the development of positive self-esteem and self-confidence. Children need to feel happy with themselves as a person and to have an understanding of how they can achieve their intended 'aim', and they need to have a degree of control within their lives, being able to take the lead, to initiate ideas and to make choices and manage their environment. It is important that adults consult children about the things that will affect them, giving them age-appropriate choices where possible.

If children have positive feelings about themselves, they are more likely to be able to cope with stressful situations than if their self-esteem is low. It is part of the role of early years workers to observe children and note changes in their behaviour. It is also part of your role to identify new children who need help in enjoying and benefiting from what the setting offers them.

Professional Practice

- Promoting self-confidence in young children includes helping them to understand and accept that at times they will win and at other times they will lose, and most regularly they will need to share and take turns.
- As children get older, they should be given more opportunities to develop this understanding and acceptance.

Conditions for secure emotional development

Figure 1.14
The conditions for secure emotional development

keyword

Emotional disturbance
Is evidenced by behaviour that causes concern and needs professional intervention (when serious or long term) or sensitive handling by parents and carers (for temporary or common problems such as tantrums).

The figure above shows what, ideally, is needed for a child to be secure emotionally. Sadly, there are many children whose lives do not provide these conditions for them. This can, at times, lead to **emotional disturbance**.

Emotional disturbance

Many children go through periods of mild or temporary emotional disturbance, which are not usually serious, and with careful handling are overcome quite quickly. Temper tantrums in toddlers and mood swings during adolescence are examples of such phases. These are normal stages of development and are of no real concern. Less frequent and more worrying signs of emotional disturbance which would cause concern are:

- a child becoming withdrawn and insecure, clinging to a familiar adult and lacking confidence
- a child displaying anti-social behaviour to draw attention to themselves
- extreme anxiety and phobias
- physical habits such as excessive hair chewing or nail biting, which can at times indicate a lonely or neglected child
- tummy upsets, tics and skin irritations, which can sometimes be signs of emotional disturbance.

remember Tummy upsets and skin irritations are mostly caused by viral or bacterial infection.

Severe emotional disturbance can result in a halt in development or the child's returning to an earlier stage (regressing). Emotional disturbance can be triggered for many reasons, such as:

- physical neglect, where a child's nutritional, clothing or medical needs are not met
- emotional neglect, where a child receives little or no praise, comfort, encouragement, etc.
- when parents are unable to understand a child's needs, perhaps through their own limited understanding
- when parents have not learned how to show love, leading, for example, to lack of close physical comfort
- when parents are immature and not ready or able to cope with a child's needs and actions
- lack of consistent parenting, where no clear boundaries are given to children regarding their behaviour
- lack of consistent day care, for example where children are passed from carer to carer with no regular routine
- when no secure **attachment** has been formed between the child and another person
- bereavement, for example loss of a parent or a significant person in a child's life
- violence in the home, for example either receiving, witnessing or being affected by violence
- the arrival of a new baby, triggering feelings of jealousy and the feeling of being unwanted
- when a child is not ready to cope with a new situation, for example starting nursery or school
- body image issues, such as disability or physical disfigurement.

keyword **Attachment** An emotional bond that develops between a baby and their carer.

keyword
Bond
The close relationship formed between a child and one or more of the child's main carers.

Attachment and bonding

According to modern-day theorists, children need a secure attachment (a two-way relationship of pleasure and tenderness) with their main carers, not just with their mother, as theorists, such as John Bowlby (1907–1990), had argued previously. It is now agreed that the carers' ability to respond to a child is the most important factor in influencing the attachment process. The quality of the '**bond**' is what counts; children make multiple attachments, having a different sort of attachment to different carers.

The attachment process can be hindered when there is a barrier between the infant and the carer. This may be caused by separation at birth due to factors such as illness or prematurity. Lack of eye contact in a visually impaired infant or carer is another barrier. What is clearly seen is that a child who has been able to form a strong bond to a parent or carer is usually more secure emotionally than a child who has no secure attachment at all.

Separation and loss

When infants are around nine months old, they suddenly become reluctant to be with unfamiliar adults; this is a normal stage of development. If separated from their parent or carer at this stage, the child is fretful and looks for them. Children who are securely attached to their parent or main carer will gradually lose their anxiety with strangers and develop a sense of independence. Children who are not so well attached tend to be less willing to explore and investigate their environment.

keyword
Social learning theory
The theory proposing that children learn by observing and copying the behaviour of others; this theory was supported by Albert Bandura's Bobo doll experiments.

Social learning

In social learning children observe and copy the actions of others. An example of research into social learning is described below.

Social learning theory

Possibly the most well-known example of social learning theory derives from the research carried out by Albert Bandura (1965), who used a film with three different endings to see how children could be affected by what they had seen. The film involved an adult hitting and shouting at a Bobo doll. Three groups of children were each shown one version of the film.

Group 1. The first film ending showed the adult being rewarded for hitting the doll.

Group 2. The second film ending showed the adult being punished for hitting the doll.

Group 3. In the third film, nothing happened to the adult after they hit the doll.

After they had watched their particular version of the film, the children in all three groups were given Bobo dolls to play with and were observed by the researchers. The children who had seen the adult rewarded for hitting the doll also showed a higher tendency to hit the doll. This study could not claim evidence of a direct cause and effect, but its results certainly suggest that the children in Group 1 may have been influenced by observing the rewarding of negative behaviour.

remember
As an adult working with children you need to think about the messages that you are giving them. These messages have a direct impact on the social learning of the children in your care. Messages can be portrayed by actions, words, attitudes and non-verbal behaviour. They can be positive or negative.

Social learning theorists believe that children learn moral behaviour by observation and imitation. Refer back to the section on moral development on page 16 to remind yourself about other explanations.

Communication and speech development

The main way in which humans communicate with each other is language; this involves facial expressions, tone of voice, body posture and expression of meaning through the use of words or symbols.

Language is:

- *Rule governed*. Grammatical rules are present in each language (syntax).
- *Structured*. There is a system of speech sounds (phonology).
- *Symbolic*. Words have meaning, building into phrases and so on (semantics).
- *Generative*. It is the basis of the sharing of knowledge (pragmatics).

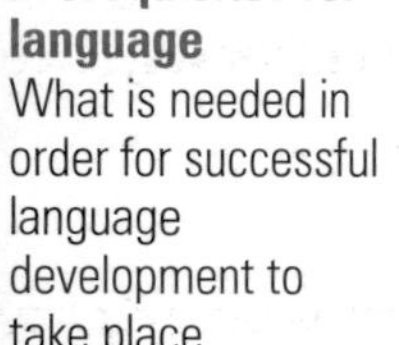

Prerequisites for language
What is needed in order for successful language development to take place.

Prerequisites for language

There are a number of **prerequisites for language**. Language development is affected by other areas of our development: not only are the physical abilities of vision, hearing and speech vital, but there are also social and intellectual prerequisites, such as an understanding of the benefits of communicating with others. Otherwise, it can be difficult for language to develop normally. Children learn the basis of their culture through communication, observing how others act and interact. Through this they develop an understanding of themselves and how they fit within their peer and social groups (this is known as 'goodness of fit'). This process is described as socialisation.

Refer to Unit 5, page 182 for more about socialisation.

Psychologists believe that language plays an important part in all aspects of human development, with some theorists arguing that language is the basis of learning. In an important debate on the origins of language, people have asked the questions: 'Is language dependent on thought?' or 'Is thought dependent on language?'

Theories of language

There are a number of different theories about how language develops. These are summarised briefly below.

Association theory

According to association theory, children gradually build their language by associating words with what they see, for example learning that a tree is a tree, a dog is a dog, and so on. This works well up to a point, but does not take into account all aspects of language, for example those words used to describe feelings or emotions.

Behaviourist theory

Behaviourist theory argues that a child's language development is shaped by the responses given to them by the adults in their lives. Positive reinforcement (i.e. reward) encourages the child to repeat a specific sound over and over again. For example, when a child makes the sound 'Dadada'', the mother will be likely to reward that sound by saying, 'Yes, Dada will be home soon'. However, if the child makes the sound 'Nununu', the mother may well make no response, as it has no specific meaning within the English language, and that sound will eventually be lost to the child.

Biological theory

Biological theory states that infants are born with an inbuilt programme for language, which Noam Chomsky calls the infant's 'language acquisition device' (LAD). He considered that the device enables children to absorb the language they hear, decode it and develop an understanding of its rules and grammatical structures.

Maturational theory

Maturational theory states that, as long as children are exposed to language, they will simply pick it up as their development progresses in other ways, i.e. as they mature.

Interactionist theory

According to interactionist theory, children's language reflects what they have experienced and what they understand. Many of the most respected developmental theorists agreed with this theory, including Jean Piaget, Lev Vygotsky and Jerome Bruner.

Other research

Research has shown that hearing children born to deaf parents are able to learn words from the radio, television, and so on, but they need to be actively involved in conversation with other people in order to develop their understanding and use of grammar. For some such children, speech therapy soon results in a sudden improvement in their language structure, bringing them up to the level of language development expected for their age.

Stages of language development

As with every aspect of development, children develop language at differing rates within a normal range. The process of language development can be divided into 10 basic stages, which are as follows:

1. non-verbal communication/expression
2. speech-like noises
3. controlling sounds, using mouth and tongue
4. imitating sounds
5. first words

6. development of vocabulary (50 words is usual at two years)
7. putting words together to form simple phrases and sentences
8. use of grammar
9. use of meaning
10. using language to develop other skills, for example, early literacy.

Table 1.4 The sequential development of language

Age	Understanding	No. of words	Type of words	Average length of sentence
3 months	Soothed by sound	0	Cooing and gurgling	0
6 months	Responds to voice	0	Babble	0
1 year	Knows own name and a few others	1	Noun (naming word)	1 word
18 months	Understands simple commands	6–20	Nouns	1 word
2 years	Understands much more than they can say	50+	Verbs and pronouns (action + name)	1–2-word phrases
$2\frac{1}{2}$ years	Enjoys simple and familiar stories	200+	Pronouns: I, me, you Questions: What? and Where?	2–3-word phrases
3 years	Carries out complex commands	500–1000	Plurals Verbs in present tense Questions: Who?	3–4-word phrases
4 years	Listens to long stories	1000–1500	Verbs in past tense Questions: Why? Where? How?	4–5-word sentences
5 years	Is developing the ability to reason	1500–2000	Complex sentences with adult forms of grammar	

The development of speech sounds in the English language

Speech sounds are made up of consonants and vowels. The approximate sequential development of consonants in the English language is shown in Table 1.5:

Table 1.5 The sequential development of consonants in the English language

Age	Consonants
At age 2 years	m, n, p, b, t, d, w
At $2\frac{1}{2}$ years	k, g, ng (as in sing), h
$2\frac{1}{2}$–3 years	f, s, l, y
$3\frac{1}{2}$–4 years	v, z, ch, j, sh
$4\frac{1}{2}$ years onwards	th (as in thin), th (as in the), r
Double consonants, such as sp, tr and fl and also the sounds r and th, can develop as late as $6\frac{1}{2}$ years in some children	

Consonants

Consonants are known as 'closed' sounds because to produce a consonant sound there is an obstruction to the airflow, caused by parts of the mouth coming into contact with each other or almost touching.

Try saying the word 'book'. To pronounce the 'b' in 'book', the lips need to come into contact. Now try the word 'sand'. To pronounce the 's' in sand, the tip of the tongue has to touch the ridge just behind the top front teeth. These are examples of how the obstructions are made.

Vowels

The basic vowel sounds are a, e, i, o and u, but there are other vowel sounds too. These include the double sounds such as 'ee', 'oo', and so on. Vowels are 'open' sounds. There is no obstruction to the airflow during pronunciation; each sound differs according to the position of the mouth:

- If the lips are spread widely, the sound 'ee' is produced.
- If the lips are rounded, the sound 'oo' is produced.
- Vowels can be long sounds, as in the word 'more'.
- They can also be short sounds, as in the word 'pack'.
- There are simple vowels such as 'o' as in pot, 'u' as in put, and 'a' as in pat. These are simple because once the mouth is set in position it does not need to alter in order to produce the sound.
- There are also more complex vowel sounds such as 'oy' as in the word 'boy' and 'ow' as in the word 'cow'. With these sounds, a change in mouth and/or tongue position is necessary for the full sound to be made.
- All vowels in English involve the vibration of the vocal cords.

Syllables and words

Speech sounds combine together to form syllables. A syllable is made up of a combination of consonants (c) and at least one vowel (v). There can be up to three consonants before a vowel and up to four consonants after a vowel in the English language.

Examples of syllables are:

- be = cv (1 consonant and 1 vowel)
- and = vcc (1 vowel and 2 consonants) and so on ...
- plot = ccvc
- strip = cccvc
- tempts = cvcccc.

The more consonants there are in a syllable, the harder it will be for a child to pronounce.

Words
Syllables, in turn, combine to form words. Some words will have just one syllable, for example 'cat', 'dog' and 'hen'. These are called monosyllabic words. All other words have more than one syllable and are known as polysyllabic words. Even in adulthood, some people have difficulty in pronouncing some polysyllabic words.

case study 1.2

Daisy

Daisy plays contentedly alone and is often seen briefly imitating everyday activities in her play, for example having a cup of tea or combing her doll's hair. She responds to simple instructions such as 'Please fetch your coat, Daisy'. She only rarely takes toys to her mouth now.

activity
INDIVIDUAL WORK

(a) How old do you think Daisy is likely to be?

(b) What else would you expect to see with regard to Daisy's development?

(c) How well developed would you expect Daisy's language to be?

Language as a means of communication

Language is essential for communicating our needs, expressing our feelings and extending our experiences beyond our own environment by interacting with other people. These interactions enable us to develop our understanding further and to learn new skills. Spoken language is our most important means of communication and is strengthened by facial expression, tone of voice and body language.

remember Being a good communicator is one of the most important aspects of working in the field of early years.

Language disorders and delayed speech

Concerns about language development would include the following:

- lack of non-verbal communication with parents and carers in the early weeks
- significant feeding difficulties (speech therapists can often be involved at this early stage)
- lack of vocalisation from three months onwards
- no babbling from eight to nine months onwards
- lack of verbal responses to play
- vocalisation that is completely out of line with the developmental norms.

Language disorder

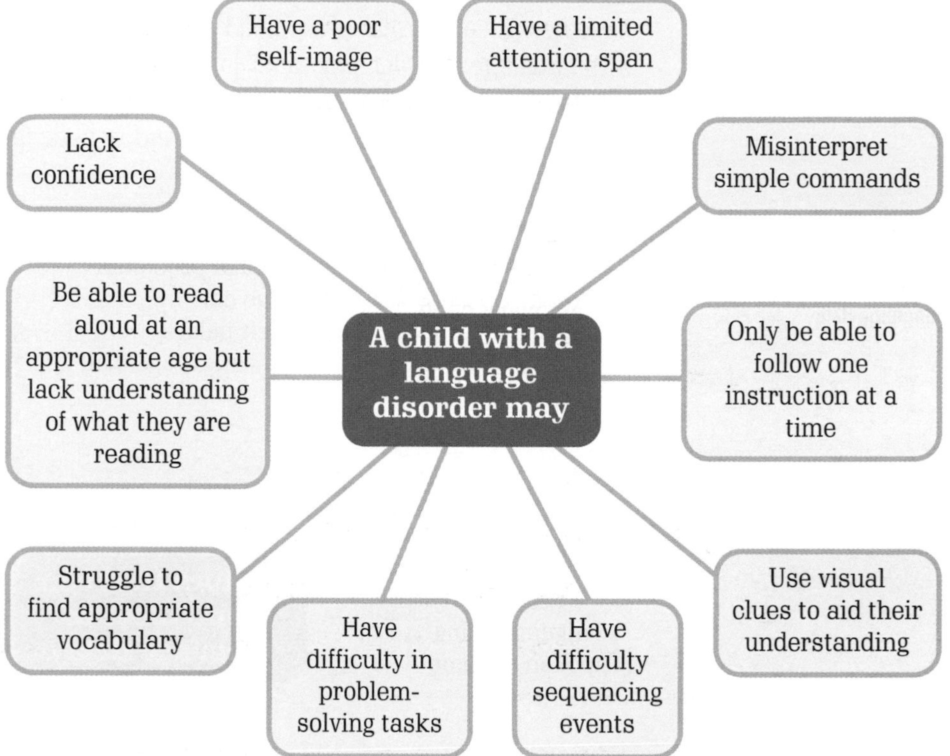

Figure 1.15
Children with a language disorder

> *keyword*
> **Language disorder**
> A problem that may cause difficulties in speech and communication.

When expressing themselves, a child with a **language disorder** may:

- have difficulty in finding appropriate words
- use words in a confused order
- have difficulty in giving explanations
- use confused grammar
- miss out grammatical word endings
- confuse sounds within individual words.

From reading the above, you will appreciate that language disorder can also affect other aspects of a child's learning and development.

Factors that can affect language include medical problems such as glue ear. This is a condition of the middle ear in which sticky mucus is formed and is unable to drain away through the Eustachian tubes in the normal way. If it becomes severe and is left untreated, the condition can lead to permanent hearing loss.

A cleft lip and palate can affect speech. A child born with one or both of these physical conditions will automatically be referred to a speech therapist, to ensure that the most appropriate feeding positions are established right from birth.

Language delay

Language delay means that the child's language development is slow and they have not achieved what is expected according to the developmental norm. As with language disorder, any significant delay would be monitored and a referral made to a speech therapist as appropriate. As shown in Figure 1.16, environmental, medical, social, cultural and genetic factors can affect language development.

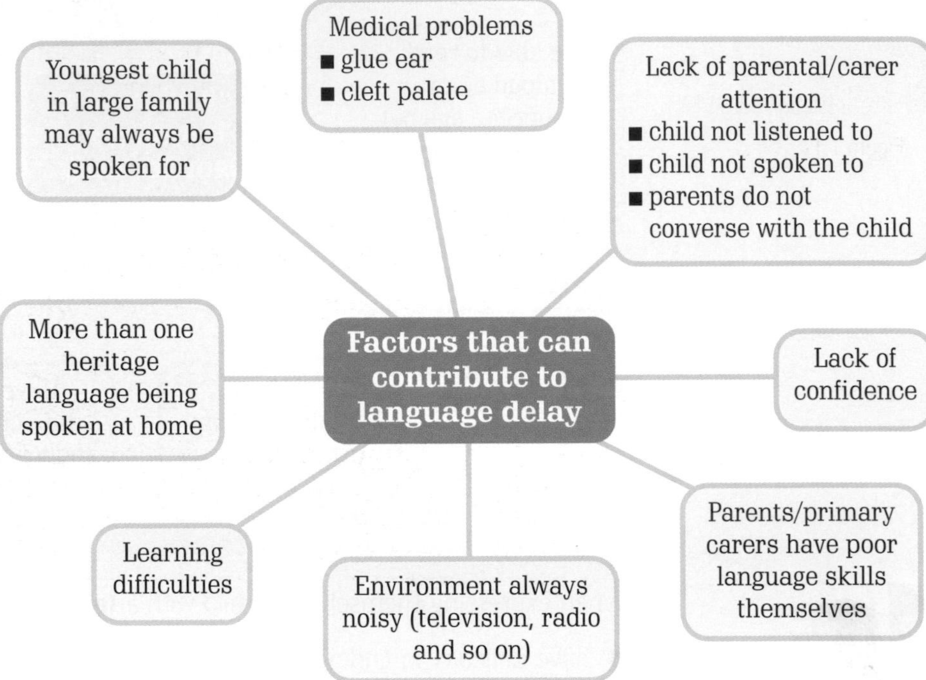

Figure 1.16
Factors that contribute to language delay

keyword

Dysfluency
Being unable to speak words fluently, stammering. This is a common (temporary) occurrence in young children.

Dysfluency

Many children have phases of unclear speech but they do not all need to be seen by a speech therapist. A common occurrence is **dysfluency**: the child hastens to say something and stumbles over their words in their eagerness and excitement.

There may be hesitation as a child tries to express themselves; in this case, the dysfluency is likely to be associated with attempting to use a more complex language structure. Speech therapists refer to this as 'normal developmental dysfluency'; it does not usually need professional intervention.

When conversing with a dysfluent child, it is important to give them time and attention to make the effect of the dysfluency as minimal as possible. The following is a checklist for communicating with a dysfluent child:

- Do speak steadily and clearly yourself.
- Do give the dysfluent child your full attention.
- Do avoid interrupting the child whenever possible.
- Do focus on 'what' they are saying and try to ignore the dysfluency.

- Do not ask the child to repeat what they have said, or to start again.
- Do not tell the child to 'take a deep breath' before they speak.
- Do not tell the child to 'slow down'.
- Do not ask the child to 'think it through' before they speak.
- Do not allow discussion of their dysfluency in their presence.

activity 1.3 GROUP WORK

Watching television can have both a positive and a negative influence on communication and learning in young children.

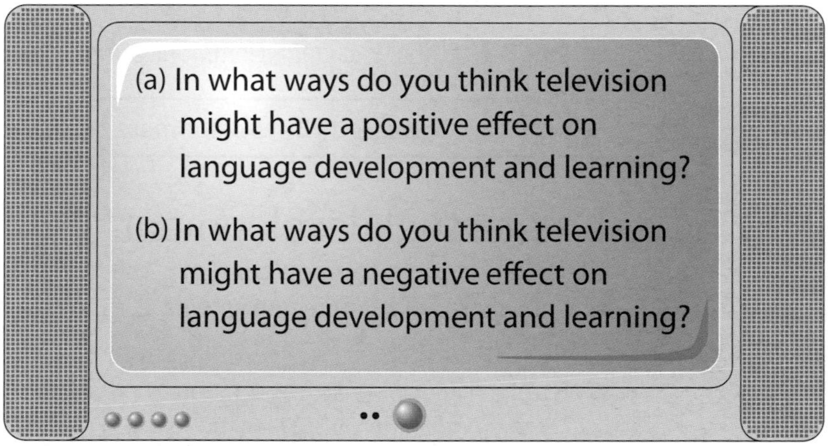

Figure 1.17

(a) In what ways do you think television might have a positive effect on language development and learning?

(b) In what ways do you think television might have a negative effect on language development and learning?

Self-expression

Opportunities for self-expression occur through speech and conversation, art, music and role play. Children who have not as yet acquired the words that they need to make themselves understood fully, for whatever reason, will benefit from experiencing a variety of these options. This includes children for whom English is not the first language, children with limited hearing, and those in the younger age groups.

Professional Practice

- Children need opportunities to express themselves in a range of different situations.
- Body language, hand movements and facial expressions are important too.

Signed language

Signing is used by deaf people, those whose hearing is impaired, people with certain forms of disability and by many people communicating with them. Signing involves facial, hand and body movements. A number of different forms of sign language are in use; each is a language in its own right, with its own rules with regard to grammar and how the words are put together. Examples include:

- sign language
- Makaton
- bliss symbols
- cued speech
- Braille
- **PECS** (Pictorial Exchange Communication System).

keyword
PECS
Picture Exchange Communication System, a system for signing language.

Refer to Unit 3, pages 128–130, for more on these languages.

Intellectual development

Milestones: birth to one year

- The infant's main source of learning is to explore orally (with their mouth) throughout most of the first year.
- By about four months, recognition of an approaching feed is demonstrated by excited actions and squeals.
- By nine to 10 months, the infant understands that an object exists even if it has been covered up. For example, the child will pull a cover off a teddy that they have seen hidden, in order to 'find' it again.
- The understanding of simple instructions or statements begins from about nine months, and this is clearly evident by one year (e.g. 'Wave bye-bye to Daddy').

Milestones: one to two years

- Toddlers of this age are very curious, and they investigate everything they can.
- They are interested in all that happens around them.
- A precise pincer grasp (index finger and thumb) is seen now.
- They enjoy putting objects into containers.
- They take toys to their mouth less often now.
- They enjoy activities that involve fitting objects together (e.g. simple construction toys or a 'build-up' clown).
- They will place an object on another – a two-object tower.

Milestones: two to three years

- From two years, children rarely take toys to mouth.
- Brief imitation is seen of everyday activities (e.g. the feeding of a doll).

Figure 1.18
A busy toddler

- They are usually content to play alone.
- Simple role play is demonstrated.
- They can build six to eight objects into a tower.
- They can follow simple instructions (e.g. 'Fetch your shoes, please.').
- They can complete simple jigsaw puzzles.
- They can draw vertical and horizontal lines.

Milestones: three to five years

- Children of this age can usually draw a person with the main details.
- Role play is frequent and detailed by five years of age.
- Floor play is very complex (e.g. cars, train sets, farms).
- Understanding of time linked to routine is emerging; for example, they begin to understand that they will be picked up from pre-school after the singing has finished.

Milestones: from five years onwards

From around age five, co-operative play becomes very involved, with considerable role play requiring accuracy and detail. Much time is taken up in planning who will take on which role and who will do what. Children increasingly develop the skills to add up, subtract, put in order, and read and write. The basis of all these skills has been built through the activities supported by the Foundation Stage curriculum.

Examples of activities related to the Foundation Stage curriculum are set out in Unit 6, pages 243–254. You may find it helpful to refer to that section now.

Children now develop from Piaget's pre-operational stage to the concrete operational concept of thinking. In addition to learning to read, they develop the ability to add up, subtract and order, as long as they can relate the problem to real events or objects.

For a description of Piaget's pre-operational and concrete operational stages, see page 34.

By about the age of 11, an average child has a vocabulary of 11,000 to 12,000 words. Children of this age are usually fluent readers with substantial reading stamina. On the whole, girls tend to read more than boys.

Milestones: adolescents

As children reach adolescence:

- The emphasis is on learning and developing career options for the future.
- Understanding of abstract concepts has developed.
- Colloquialisms and 'peer' talk are frequently displayed.
- Conflicts arise, particularly with parents and figures of authority.
- Family **values** are frequently challenged.
- Moral reasoning becomes important.
- More sophisticated problem-solving skills are required as greater independence is attained.

keyword

Values
Moral standards.

Perception

Perception is the organisation and interpretation of information received from the senses; it helps us to understand what is happening both to us and around us. Certain conditions within us can influence our level of perception. For example, our brain may choose for us not to 'see' something that is likely to make us anxious and filters it out. Perception is also affected by selective attention, which occurs if we are fully focused on one thing and simply do not notice something else happening close by. Expectation also affects what we perceive. For example, two people will not necessarily see the same things when seemingly watching the same sequence of events. Their brains may have focused on slightly different aspects of what was in front of them.

keyword

Perception
The organisation and interpretation of information received from the sensory organs; gaining insight or awareness.

Refer to Unit 7, page 293, for information on early sensory development. This will help you to understand the different sensory experiences that give us the feedback on which perception is based.

activity 1.4 INDIVIDUAL WORK

(a) Look at the following illustrations. What do you see?

(b) Ask others what they see. Did they see the same as you, or different?

Figure 1.19 Visual images

You will find that you can only see one image at a time, and may not see the second image until it is pointed out to you.

Perception in infants

Much research has been carried out into the perceptual abilities of young babies. For example, Gibson and Walk (1960) devised a piece of equipment that they called a 'visual cliff' to investigate depth perception in infants. The infants were first placed on the 'visually safe' side of the table (a chequered floor) and were encouraged to crawl across the surface above the 'visually unsafe' cliff (clear glass) towards their mothers. Out of 27 infants aged six to 12 months (who had gained a degree of mobility), only three crawled across the surface. The remaining 24 showed a marked reservation with regard to crossing from the 'safe' to the 'unsafe' area of the visual cliff's surface, even though they would be moving towards their mothers, who would normally be a safe haven for them.

Under the age of six months, it is clearly not possible to investigate depth perception in the same way, owing to infants' lack of mobility. However, Campos *et al*. (1970), monitored the heart rate of infants when placed first on one side, and then on the other of the visual cliff. At just 55 days (approximately eight weeks) the heart rates were different, indicating that even at this young age a degree of depth perception is present. Under eight weeks of age, depth perception did not appear to have developed.

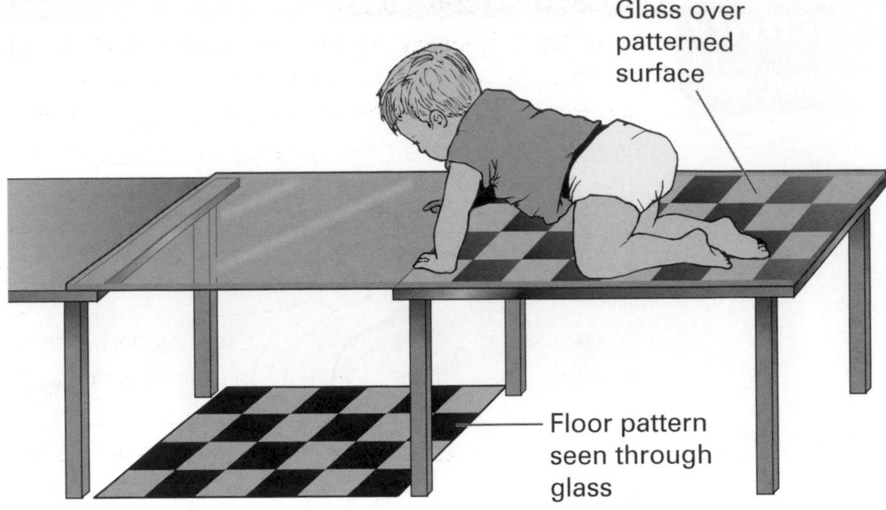

Figure 1.20
The visual cliff experiment by Gibson and Walk

Refer to Unit 7, page 296, for more on infant perception.

Thinking

Many theorists have been interested in how children think and learn and the connection between the two. You will probably have heard of at least some of them. The following section will briefly outline the thoughts of Jean Piaget, Lev Vygotsky and Jerome Bruner.

Piaget (1896–1980)

Piaget believed that children's interactions with their environment formed the basis of their development of thinking and problem-solving abilities. He proposed that there are four main stages of **cognitive** (intellectual) **development**:

1. sensorimotor stage (birth to two years)
2. pre-operational stage, divided into the pre-conceptual stage (two to four years), and the intuitive stage (four to seven years)
3. concrete operations stage (seven to 11 years)
4. formal operations stage (11 years onwards).

keyword

Cognitive development
The development of knowledge through thinking and problem solving.

activity 1.5 PAIR WORK

(a) With a partner find out what you can about each of Piaget's proposed stages.

(b) At which stage are the children at your placement?

Vygotsky (1896–1935)

Like Piaget, Vygotsky believed that children learn through active involvement. In addition, he considered the role of the adult to be especially important, with adult input being central to children's learning. Vygotsky believed that children could often understand more than they demonstrate in free play. He suggested that they show greater understanding of some concepts if helped to try out new ideas by an adult, thereby achieving more through the involvement of a sensitive adult (one who supports, but does not direct or take over the planning, etc.), than if left to play alone. The difference between the child's actual development and the level that they could potentially achieve with additional support from the adult is called the 'zone of proximal development' (ZPD); it is a well-known concept in early years work.

Refer to the target child observation on page 53. This gives a useful example of the ZPD.

Bruner (1931–)

Bruner, who was influenced by Vygotsky's ideas, uses the term 'scaffolding' to describe how the adult supports the learning of the child by giving them manageable amounts of information, enabling them to solve a problem or to achieve more than they would otherwise have done. Bruner believes that scaffolding contributes to a child's learning.

He considers that there are three modes (types) of thinking that develop sequentially in children:

- *Enactive thinking*. Information is recorded mentally and linked to physical activity; this type of thinking is mostly associated with infants under one year.
- *Iconic thinking*. Mental images are linked to the senses; this type of thinking is mostly associated with children aged one to seven years.
- *Symbolic thinking*. A range of representative forms, such as language and number, are used to demonstrate learning. This type of thinking is mostly associated with children aged seven onwards.

activity 1.6 INDIVIDUAL WORK

Can you think of an example for each of Bruner's modes of thinking?

Professional Practice

- Areas of development are not independent of each other. They affect each other in various ways. For example, a child with hearing problems will be unlikely to develop clear and grammatically correct speech as easily as a child who has perfect hearing.
- Similarly, a child who has not developed an understanding of social skills such as sharing or turn taking is less likely to be socially accepted by their peers and may therefore be hindered in developing friendships.

Factors affecting growth and development

Growth and development can be affected in many ways and by a variety of factors.

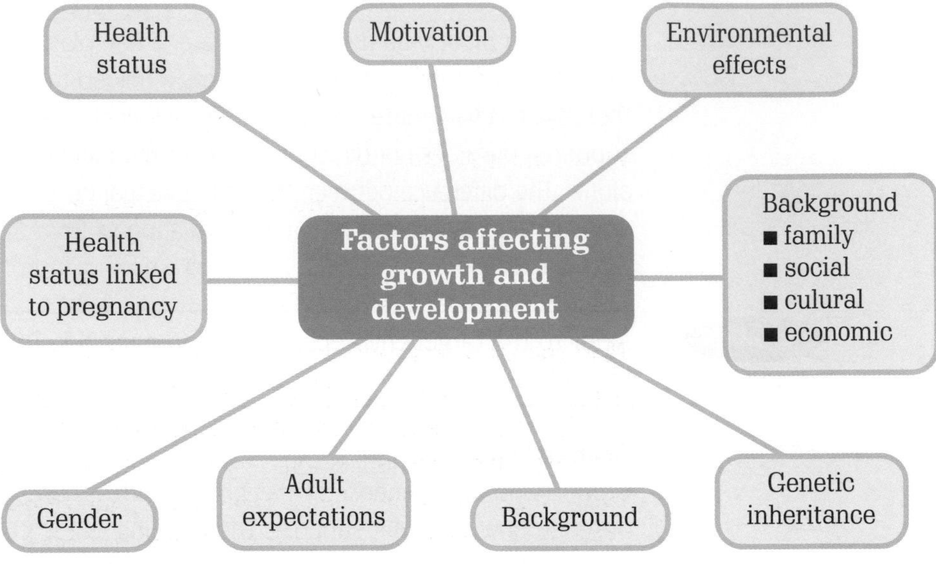

Figure 1.21
Factors affecting growth and development

Let's start by thinking about each of these in turn:

Motivation

We all do better if we are feeling motivated. Motivation is linked to being interested in what we see, hear, feel, etc. going on around us and, clearly, there is a direct relationship between being motivated and being stimulated to learn. This highlights why it is important to provide a range of developmentally appropriate activities for children that take into account their current interests and offer them new **challenges** in order to help their development to progress fully.

> *keyword*
> **Challenge**
> An experience that will help develop a skill or aspect of learning.

Adult expectations

If, as an adult, we do not expect very much from the children in our care, they are unlikely to develop as fully as if we were more encouraging. However, there is a great difference between encouragement and pressurising children to learn and to achieve. At times, too much pressure is put on children, as parents or carers try to push them on at a pace that is too fast for them. This is often called 'hot housing'. Children in this situation are likely to rebel against learning or reach 'burn out' at an early age. A balance is needed, and learning opportunities should be targeted appropriately.

Health status

Healthy children will usually have all the energy necessary to benefit from the range of opportunities open to them. A child with a health problem may miss opportunities through prolonged periods of illness; they may need more rest, or may be restricted by appointments and medication needs. This can affect both growth and development. Owing to the health status of the mother, some children's health problems started before they were born.

Health status linked to pregnancy

Any woman planning to have a baby needs to consider the factors affecting the development of the foetus:

- diet
- level of exercise
- smoking habits
- alcohol consumption
- use of drugs (prescribed as well as recreational)
- social life
- stability in her relationship.

Planning for a pregnancy in advance can enable a woman to give up smoking or using drugs before conceiving, and reduce or eliminate her intake of alcohol. It can give her time to assess if her relationship is stable, and for her to begin to eat a healthier diet, eliminating foods that are not considered to be completely 'safe'. If a woman knows that she is unprotected against rubella (German measles) it is wise for her to be vaccinated, but she should then avoid becoming pregnant for at least three months after having the vaccination. Any unprotected pregnant woman should try to stay clear of children who might have the rubella virus, particularly in the first 12 weeks of pregnancy, as contracting the virus may seriously damage her unborn child.

Women with long-standing medical conditions or disorders should consult their doctor before planning a pregnancy, to ensure that any medication they need to take regularly will be safe for the developing child. Doctors may need to make changes to the woman's medication, either because it could harm the foetus or because it could make conception more difficult to achieve.

Table 1.6 Foods to avoid in pregnancy

Food	Possible outcome
Soft cheeses	Listeria, which can cause miscarriage
Paté	Listeria, which can cause miscarriage
Raw eggs	Salmonella, which causes food poisoning
Raw meat	Toxoplasmosis, which is a mild infection in adults but can cause serious harm to an unborn child

Folic acid

In recent years taking a supplement of folic acid has been recommended for women from before conception, up until 12 weeks into the pregnancy, as this contributes to the optimal (best) development of the baby's central nervous system, helping to prevent the occurrence of problems such as spina bifida.

For an overview of this condition refer to Unit 8, page 358.

Environmental effects on foetal development

Infants are not only affected directly by the environment into which they are born and raised but can also be affected by environmental influences before birth. For example, antenatal development can be influenced by alcohol, smoking, and illegal and (some) prescribed drugs.

Alcohol

Foetal alcohol syndrome (FAS) results from the mother continuing to consume alcohol, usually in considerable amounts, throughout her pregnancy. In 1991, researchers declared it to be the leading cause of 'mental retardation' in the US. FAS affects the development of the infant, causing delay, deformities and learning difficulties. Pregnant women are now advised against drinking alcohol altogether, as even a moderate amount can carry a risk to the infant and judgement can become impaired by alcohol, leading to accidents.

Smoking

Smoking (tobacco as well as illegal substances) affects birth weight due to the release of nicotine and other substances into the body. It can also lead to learning difficulties. There is a suggestion that infants born to smokers are at a higher risk of being affected by sudden infant death syndrome (also known as SIDS and cot death) and of developing respiratory conditions later on. Passive smoking is thought to contribute to respiratory problems in infants and older children, and also to glue ear.

remember

Cough and cold remedies are also drugs and should be treated with the same caution as any other medication. A pregnant woman should always check the suitability of such remedies with the GP or a pharmacist before taking them.

Drugs

Any non-essential drug should be avoided during pregnancy. Illegal drugs, such as crack cocaine, cause low birth weight and developmental delay, and babies who are born addicted suffer withdrawal symptoms after birth and are in great distress. Many of these babies suffer all-round developmental problems and some develop epilepsy.

Prescribed drugs are only issued to pregnant women with extreme care, as some have been known to cause deformity and developmental problems. Most notoriously, the drug Thalidomide caused severe limb deformity in some children born in the 1960s. The mothers of these children were prescribed the drug in good faith to combat severe vomiting during pregnancy.

Genetic inheritance

keyword

Genetic inheritance Features passed down to an infant from their parents; this may involve the passing on of a condition or disorder through the genes of one or both parents.

Genetic inheritance is an important influence on our overall development as a person; it refers to aspects of ourselves that we cannot change, for example our sex, and the rate at which we grow, develop and age. Genes influence how tall a child grows, what sort of bone structure they have, and whether they have a thin, wiry build, or are short and stocky, heavy framed, frail and petite, etc. Genes also decide skin type and hair colour and can influence whether the individual is likely to be predisposed to suffer from certain health problems, for example heart disease, in later life. Sometimes, the genes that are passed on cause certain conditions and disabilities.

Genetic counselling is available to help parents weigh up the genetic risk of their having a child with an inherited disorder; it can be obtained through a referral from the couple's GP.

Illustrations of genetic inheritance can be found in Unit 8, page 347. You may find it useful to refer to this now to boost your understanding. For examples of genetic disorders, see pages 348–349.

Screening in pregnancy

Some conditions can be identified during pregnancy by antenatal screening. Specific tests are offered to some women depending on circumstances. For example, older mothers or women with a family history of certain inherited disorders will be offered additional screening.

Antenatal tests include the following:

Blood tests

Routine tests on blood can screen for low iron levels, venereal disease and rubella (German measles). Low iron levels may need boosting by supplements, and venereal disease will be treated as appropriate. A pregnant woman who is not immune to rubella will be advised to avoid contact with the infection during the early months of her pregnancy.

Ultrasound scan

An ultrasound scan is a procedure usually carried out at around 20 weeks' gestation to note the development levels and measurements of the foetus. Measurements are taken of the main bones, such as the femur (thigh bone), the head circumference is noted, and the heart chambers are carefully examined. Further scans are done if considered necessary by the midwife or obstetrician.

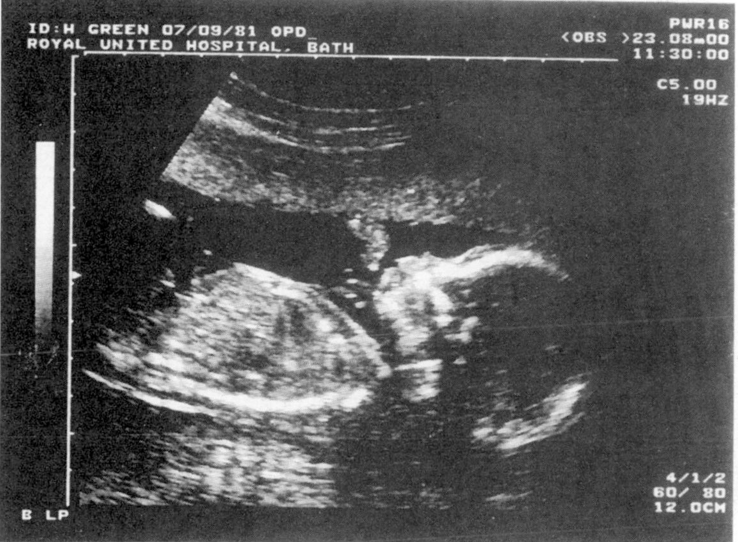

Figure 1.22
A scan of a 20-week foetus

The foetus shown above is developing within the normal range. The measurements and examinations made included the:

- thigh bone
- head circumference
- spine
- heart chambers
- brain
- amniotic fluid.

The outcome showed that the foetus (now named Jasmine) was developing well within normal limits, as Jasmine's mother's pregnancy was at 19+3 weeks, according to her dates, and the outcomes were as follows:

- bone development 19+5 weeks
- head circumference 19+5 weeks
- amniotic fluid 19+1 week.

Serum alpha-fetoprotein (SAFP)

This test is used to identify the possibility of the foetus having the condition spina bifida. It is carried out at 16 weeks' gestation and is offered to women who are considered to be at risk.

The triple blood test

This triple blood test takes into consideration the mother's age and measures the levels of human chorionic gonadotrophin (HCG), serum alpha-fetoprotein (SAFP) and the placental hormones (oestriols). The combined outcome gives an assessment of the risk of the foetus having conditions such as Down's syndrome. It is offered to women in the high-risk group, usually mothers over 35 years.

Amniocentesis

This test checks for chromosomal disorders, such as Down's syndrome. It usually takes place between 16 and 18 weeks' gestation and involves the sampling of the amniotic fluid from the amniotic sac, while the pregnant woman is linked up to an ultrasound machine. There is a slight risk of miscarriage occurring with this procedure.

Chorionic villi sampling (CVS)

This CVS test involves the removal of a tiny amount of tissue directly from the placenta. It is usually carried out between eight and 11 weeks' gestation and can help to identify a range of inherited disorders, but, as with amniocentesis, it carries a small risk of miscarriage.

Refer to Unit 8, page 350, for information about Down's syndrome.

Gender

Boys and girls should have the same opportunities. Although at times children play quite stereotypically with, for example, boys favouring construction and physical play and girls favouring quieter, caring games, surrounding children with non-stereotypical images helps them to understand that their gender should not limit what they enjoy, learn and achieve.

Background

The type of family unit a child is born into will also have an impact on their development. Poverty, low income, unemployment and social exclusion influence the conditions in which the child lives and all affect health. A child who lives in a spacious home with access to fresh air and opportunity for regular exercise is likely to be healthier and to develop better in some respects than one who lives in cramped conditions with no safe place to play or meet their friends.

A higher incidence of infection and respiratory disease is also found in children who live in poverty or in poor conditions, and a higher level of depression is often found in their parents. Parents who are depressed are often less interested in, and responsive to, their children and less likely to provide stimulation for the children.

Parents' access to facilities such as shops, day care and leisure facilities is often dependent on employment and earnings. Unemployment can be socially excluding: families may feel unable to keep up with their former peers, or may remove themselves from their previous social circles because of a fall in self-esteem. Disability may also lead to isolation or social exclusion if, for example, there is lack of access, lack of transport or insufficient carers.

remember

According to social learning theory, children learn social roles by observation and imitation.

Cultural differences may be seen in the level of support within families and through the degree of support given by the more extended family. In some cultures, the bulk of day-to-day family care falls predominantly to the women in the family and only the men work outside the home. Such gender issues can affect how children perceive themselves and what they consider they are able to do or not do and, subsequently, their development.

Environmental effects

Poverty is an economic issue that has implications for the environment and therefore for children's health, for example diet may be poor because of low income. Poor lighting in the home, lack of suitable heating in winter and lack of safety precautions such as stair gates, cooker guards, etc. increase the likelihood of accidents in the homes of families on lower incomes.

Poor air quality and traffic pollution can affect health, as can lack of play and exercise space, through living in cramped conditions.

If the parents are depressed, their dependency on smoking and alcohol may increase as these can become comforts. Smoking exposes the children to cigarette smoke (passive smoking), and the lethargy that can follow alcohol use and depression may increase isolation.

Agencies working for and with children and young people

There are many agencies that support the health care of children and young people. Early support for the care and development of babies or children alongside their parents is often available within Sure Start centres.

For older children and young people needing advice on personal care, contraception and pregnancy, organisations such as the Brook Street Bureau provide excellent support.

There are also groups, agencies and societies that support specific conditions and illnesses, for example the Sickle Cell Society and Mencap.

activity 1.7 GROUP WORK

Compile a list of local and national support groups to be kept in your professional practice file. You may find it helpful to be able to offer such information to the families with whom you work.

keyword

Discrimination The unfair treatment of an individual, group or minority, based on prejudice.

The effects of disability or sensory impairment

Clearly, a disability or a sensory impairment is likely to have a considerable effect on how an individual develops. When working with children your role will be to ensure that every child has the level of support that they need to take up the opportunities available to them. If a child's needs are not supported, they are likely to be further disadvantaged, which can be a form of **discrimination**.

The effects of discrimination

Discrimination, whether due to culture, religion, disability, gender or social circumstances can potentially have an impact on how fully a child is able to take up the opportunities available to children in general in their area. It is important to understand what discrimination is and to explore your own thoughts and viewpoints.

Refer to Unit 8, page 347, for discussion on how to provide support for children with a disability or special educational need and to Unit 5, page 179, for more about discrimination.

Understanding the role of observation of children's development in the workplace

Observation of children is both useful and interesting. It forms an important part of the role of all practitioners working with children and helps them to assess and meet the needs of the children they care for.

The purpose of careful observation

Figure 1.23
The purpose of careful observation

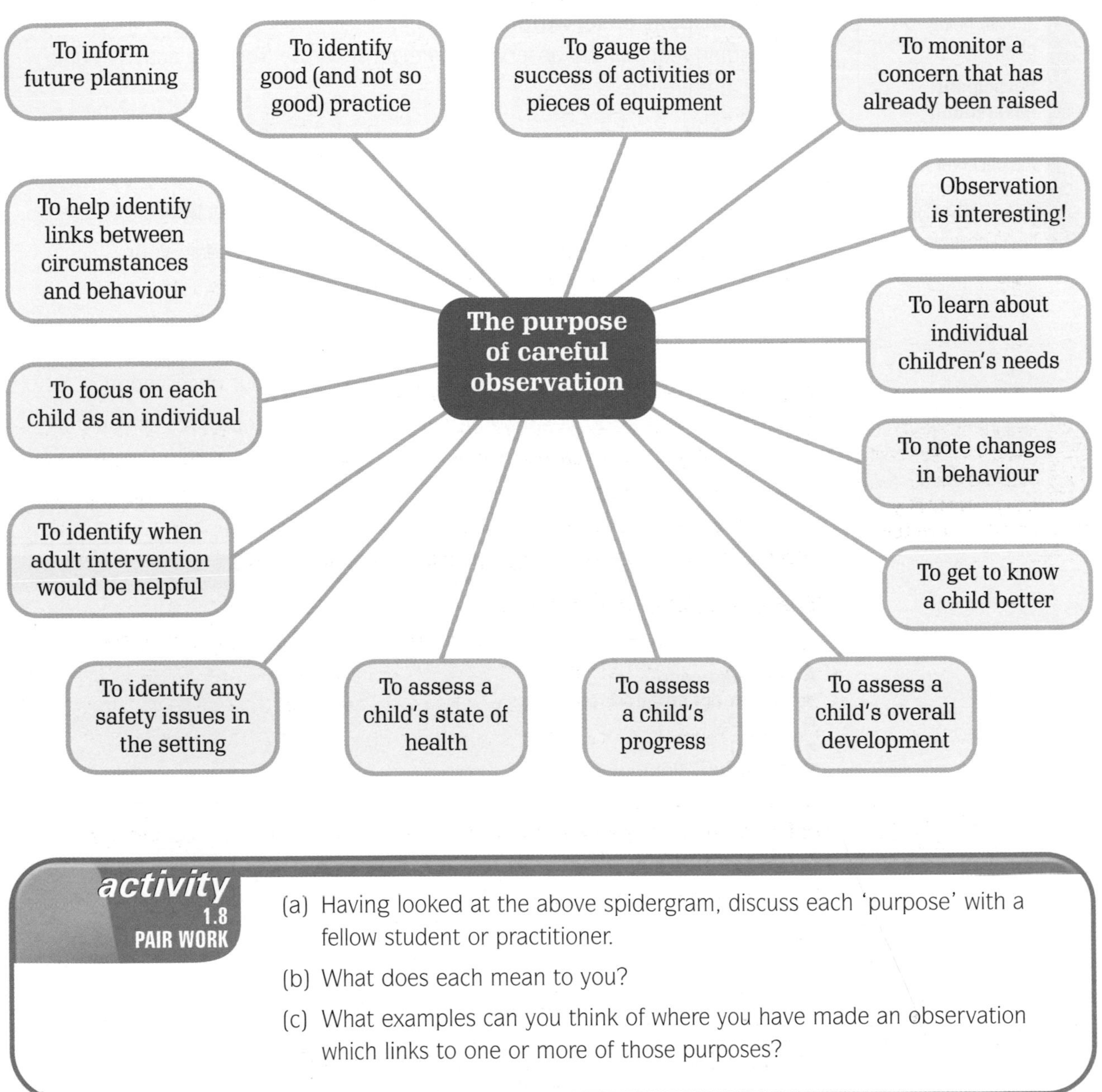

activity 1.8 PAIR WORK

(a) Having looked at the above spidergram, discuss each 'purpose' with a fellow student or practitioner.

(b) What does each mean to you?

(c) What examples can you think of where you have made an observation which links to one or more of those purposes?

Methods of recording observations

There are many methods of observing children. The aim is always to select the best method for the type of behaviour or situation that you intend to observe and to be aware of the advantages and disadvantages of each. Table 1.7 sets

keyword

Non-participant observation Observation where the observer does not actually interact with the person or activity being observed.

Participant observation Observation where the observer is involved with the person or activity being observed.

out the most usual range of methods used when observing individual children or small groups.

It is important to distinguish between **non-participant** and **participant observation**.

Non participant observation

This method requires the observer to remain separate from the activity being observed; therefore:

- It is ideal for an inexperienced observer who can note down what is happening without the distraction of being involved in the activity.
- Non-participation may help the observer to be more objective.
- Non-participation means that most techniques can be used.

However:

- You may find it difficult to take time out from planned activities or care routines to sit away from the action and undertake your observation.
- Children may not do or say what you were hoping to observe, or you may simply not be in the right position to see and hear what is of interest to you.

Table 1.7 Observation techniques for use with individuals and groups

Individual	Group
■ Written record ■ Target child ■ Event sampling ■ Time sampling ■ Movement and flow charts ■ Checklist ■ Sociogram ■ Child study (longitudinal)	■ Target child ■ Sociograms ■ Movement and flow charts

Participant observation

As the name suggests, the observer takes part in the activity while observing; therefore:

- The participant observer can give instructions to a child in order to observe the type of behaviour that is desired.
- This method may be more effective in terms of time available for observations, as less time is spent waiting for spontaneous events to happen.

However:

- It may be difficult to capture all that is happening if the observer is involved.
- Not all methods are suitable for participant observation, particularly if a narrative of an episode is required.

- Children may be influenced by the pressure of the situation or the presence of an unfamiliar adult, or their behaviour may be altered because of a desire to please the adult observing them.

Checklists or tick lists are useful methods of recording behaviour during the observation, as are Post-it notes and quick jottings.

Naturalistic observation (using a written record)

This is likely to be one of the first methods of observation that you use. It is useful as it needs no specific preparation: you simply have to be able to make a written record, writing down as clearly (and concisely) as you can what you are observing. It can, however, be repetitive and longwinded to write the record out neatly afterwards. As children are so active, you may find that with this method you miss out on recording some of what they are doing.

This method:

- is ideal when beginning to observe children
- is useful when time is short as it is usually only possible to use the method for short periods of time
- can provide 'open' data
- helps the observer to practise **objectivity** as the point is to record what the observer sees and hears, without interpreting (at this stage)
- gives the observer the opportunity to make a structured or unstructured observation and is ideal for capturing snapshots of a child's interests and abilities
- can require intensive concentration to capture details and is not suitable for lengthy observations.

keyword

Objectivity
Observing without any prejudgement or bias.

Example of an unstructured written observation

Sarah, Fliss and Abi are in the role-play corner with Megan (student). Sarah and Fliss are leaning over the cot; Megan is standing at the entrance to the role-play corner and Abi is sitting at the table. Sarah says, 'I want to go shopping. Shall we take our babies out with us?' Fliss says, 'All right, can Megan come with us?' and moves to the back of the role-play corner where she pulls out the pushchair and puts her baby doll into it. Sarah walks over to Fliss and pats the baby doll on the head. She then picks up a shopping bag and hands this to Megan, saying, 'You can buy the food for dinner'. Abi is now standing at the side of the bookcase, looking at the other girls. Megan asks Abi, 'Do you want to come shopping?' and then she helps her to find another pushchair for her doll. Megan and the three girls then come out of the role-play corner, and Sarah and Fliss walk in front of Abi and Megan.

Movement and flow charts

These enable you to monitor the movements of a particular child; they are also sometimes called 'tracking' observations. The simplest way to produce a movement and flow chart is to produce a rough sketch of the setting, noting where each activity is positioned, and then track the child's movements, adding in the times and duration of use at each activity.

A movement and flow chart:

- can be helpful in matching a child's needs to the learning and play opportunities provided in a setting
- allows staff to observe a child's particular interests over a specified time period
- can produce data that are difficult to analyse unless the chart is clearly laid out
- provides 'closed' data
- limits spontaneity because the observer will need to have previously drawn a template plan of the area where the observation takes place.

In the example below, the movement and flow chart tracks Jenny's movements.

Summary of Jenny's movements:
Jenny arrives at Little Lambs Nursery at 8.30 a.m.

8.30 She moves straight to the drawing and writing table (8.30–8.40)

8.40 Jenny moves to the dressing up clothes (8.40–8.55)

8.55 Jenny plays outside (8.55–9.15)

9.15 She returns to the dressing up clothes to change her outfit (9.15–9.20)

9.20 Jenny enters the role-play corner (9.20–9.40)

9.40 Jenny returns the dressing-up clothes to the box (9.40–9.45)

9.45 Jenny now moves to the jigsaw puzzle area (9.45–10.10)

10.10 From the puzzles Jenny moves to the book corner (10.10–10.30)

10.30 She goes outside to play again (10.30–10.50)

10.50 Jenny now returns to the jigsaw puzzles (10.50–11.00)

11.00 Jenny plays a board game (11.00–11.15)

11.15 Jenny goes to do some drawing (11.15–11.30)

11.30 Jenny joins the whole group for a story and singing (11.30–11.50)

11.50 Jenny is collected by her dad.

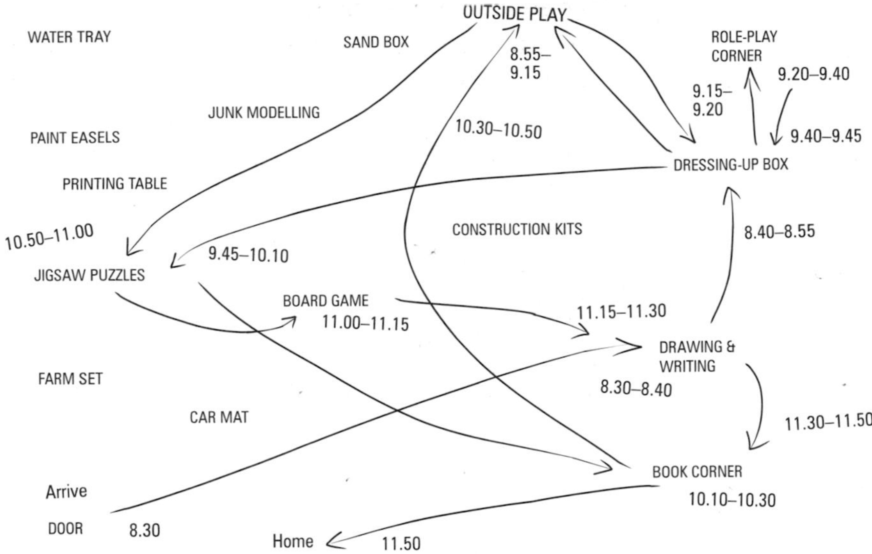

Figure 1.24
Jenny's movement and flow chart

activity 1.9 INDIVIDUAL WORK

What does the above flow chart tell you about Jenny's morning?

The example observation above would be of limited use to you without further details. To be able to see if Jenny was interacting and playing as is usually expected for her age group, you would need to know:

- Jenny's age
- for how much of the morning Jenny was playing alone
- if she interacted as a pair
- if there were times when Jenny was playing in a small group
- if there were times when she was playing in a large group
- if Jenny interacted with adults during the morning.

Without this information, it is hard to know if Jenny's experience was as positive as possible. She clearly kept herself fully occupied, but did you notice anything about her choice of activities?

At no time did Jenny involve herself in any 'messy' activities. This may not be an issue, as she may simply not have wanted to take up those opportunities on that particular day, but, if this behaviour was identified in other observations, it would be considered unusual. It would also have been useful to include details of how long Jenny has been at the setting. This too could be relevant in relation to how well she interacts with others and her confidence in involving herself in some activities.

Observations using movement and flow charts enable the setting to monitor a child's particular choices of activities and review the layout of activities to maximise use.

Time sampling

Time samples are used to observe a particular child at regular intervals throughout a planned period of time, usually on more than one day. This method can be especially useful if there is some concern about the child; perhaps they have suddenly become withdrawn and no longer seem to interact with other children. Your observation can help identify whether there is a major cause for concern, or if the child's behaviour simply needs monitoring for a short while. As you time sample, you should be as unobtrusive as possible to ensure that you obtain a true record.

By observing a particular activity at regular intervals rather than focusing on a specific child, time sampling observations can also help to identify whether activities or equipment are being under-used or used inappropriately. Time sampling can give accurate information which is easily understood, but it is a time-consuming method and takes a member of staff out of the adult:child ratio equation.

The method:

- can be used for individual children as well as groups
- collects 'open' data
- makes it easy for the observer to record the information, although clear focus on timing is needed.

However,

- help from other practitioners may be needed at times, so all need to be familiar with the aims and method
- events may be 'missed' if the activity occurs outside of the pre-set timings.

Event sampling

As with time sampling, event sampling may necessitate observations being carried out over several days or even longer. Event samples are useful when a child is displaying worrying and/or aggressive behaviour that is having an impact on their own and others' daily experience within the setting. Event sampling is a useful means of identifying whether any trigger factors initiate the unwanted behaviours. You record each time the behaviour occurs, how long it continues and whether the behaviour had been triggered by anyone or any specific situation. The advantage of this method is that data are clearly timed and recorded and easily understood but, as with time sampling, the method is also time consuming. It may also require all staff to be involved in the recording of events.

Event sampling:

- is straightforward to use
- collects 'open' data
- allows observer and practitioner to identify and understand a focus of anxiety and plan an intervention
- needs a pre-prepared template and may require the co-operation of others.

Table 1.8 Example of a record sheet for event sampling

Child's initials ______	The concern you have:				
Date	Time	Was reaction provoked?	Duration of 'incident'	Emotions/behaviour displayed	Staff observing

If an observation is undertaken to look at particularly serious cases of behaviour disturbance, the event samples may need to be shown to other professionals who become involved with the child's welfare; they may also visit the setting in order to observe and assess the child for themselves.

Target child

The target child method is one of the most widely used observational techniques. It was first developed by the Oxford Pre-school Research Project, led by Kathy Sylva, and was originally aimed at identifying which activities and situations helped children to develop their concentration. It is also useful in identifying aspects of socialisation in children and gives opportunities for noting their language, in particular when they initiate conversation.

- The method can be used for a variety of different purposes and time scales.
- Once the observer is familiar with the format and codes, it is relatively straightforward to use.

- This method can result in a narrow focus of information but is not limited to 'closed' data.
- Spontaneous use is precluded because pre-prepared templates are needed.

The target child method involves the remembering, understanding and recording of pre-coded information. These codes are recorded in a table under the following headings:

Figure 1.25
Example of a target child record table

Min	Activity record	Language record	Task code	Social code

The coding is set out minute by minute, usually for up to 10 minutes at a time. The minutes are recorded in the first column of the table.

Activity record
The activity record column is a brief comment on what is happening with the activity being used by the target child. The codes used are:

TC = target child (the child's name or initials are not used)

C = child

A = adult.

Figure 1.26
An example of an activity record

Min	Activity record	Language record	Task code	Social code
1	TC & C on car mat pushing cars on road			

Social code
The codes in the social code column (who the child is with) are:

SOL = the target child is playing on their own (solitary)

PAIR = the child is with one other person, child or adult

SG = the target child is within a small group (three to five children)

LG = the target child is within a large group (six or more children).

If the target child is playing with the same activity as others but is not interacting with them in any way (parallel play) you would write one of the following codes:

PAIR/P = the target child is playing parallel to one other child

SG/P = the target child is playing parallel to a small group

LG/P = the target child is playing parallel to a large group.

If there is an adult interacting with an activity, there would be a circle drawn around the social code (see Figure 1.27).

Figure 1.27
An example of activity and social codes

Min	Activity record	Language record	Task code	Social code
1	TC & C on car mat pushing cars on road			PAIR

Task code
The entries in the task code column (what the child is doing) include the following codes:

LMM = large muscle movement

LSC = large-scale construction

SSC = small-scale construction

MAN = manipulation

SM = structured materials

PS = problem solving

SVT = scale-version toys

IG = informal games

SINP = social interaction, non-play

DB = distress behaviour.

There are many more task codes covering the complete range of actions displayed and activities enjoyed by children. Most colleges have complete lists.

Figure 1.28
An example of task codes

Min	Activity record	Language record	Task code	Social code
1	TC & C on car mat pushing cars on road		SVT	PAIR

Figure 1.29
Example of a language record

Min	Activity record	Language record	Task code	Social code
1	TC & C on car mat pushing cars on road	TC>C 'That my car' TC> 'brmm brmm' TC>C 'Mine!'	SVT	PAIR
2	3 Cs now playing	All Cs > 'brumm brmm'	SVT	SG
3	A joins them on mat	A> 'What a lot of cars' TC>A 'Mine a red car'	SVT	SG

Language record
To record language (what the child is saying), you would simply write: TC>C, if the target child is speaking to another child, or TC>A, if they are speaking to an adult.

Uses of the target child method
The target child method can be useful for 'at a glance' monitoring of a child's social development, because a quick look at the social codes will indicate whether the child is mostly playing with others or alone. This information, together with the child's age, indicates whether they are following the social norms.

The two target child observations A and B, which follow, are good examples of how the intervention of an adult has enabled a child to improve their understanding of the activity that they are using. The sensitive input from the adult in the first example has raised the achievement of the child from what they could achieve alone, to what had been within their potential to achieve. In other words, they were able to work within what Vygotsky called the zone of proximal development.

Checklists

Assessments of children are a routine part of most early years settings and involve the regular observation of children to ascertain what they are currently able to achieve. One such assessment programme is the Sound Learning Pre-school Record System, which includes assessment records for all ages of pre-school children; the assessments, it suggests, can be completed on monthly, three-monthly or termly bases. However, it must be noted that reliance on checklists alone tends to promote a deficit model, showing what children cannot achieve rather than identifying what they can.

A checklist:

- is relatively simple and quick to use
- can be used for one child or adapted to cover or compare several children

Figure 1.30
Target child observation A

Min	Activity record	Language record	Task code	Social code
1	Dries hands & cooks tea	TC> 'All dry. Nice & dry;	DA PRE	SOL
2	Lays table, matching coloured cups, saucers etc. C arrives & sits at table. TC serves tea	TC> 'Blue… & a blue. Green… & a green', etc.	PRE PRE	SOL PAIR/P
3	Eats tea	TC> 'Yummy, Nice tea – Sausage'	PRE	PAIR/P
4	Crying child arrives C stops crying	TC>C 'Don't cry Why you cry? I'm a mummy. Don't cry. Want a sausage?' TC> 'Eat your sausage'	SINP PRE " "	PAIR " " "
5	TC washes up TC leaves home C & goes to construction table Tries to build tower (Duplo) – It is top heavy!		PRE SSC	SOL SOL
6	" " "		"	"
7	" " " Tower won't stand A joins her TC leans tower against box & grins	 A>TC 'That's a tall tower' TC>A 'It falling down. It keep falling down' TC>A 'How can you stop it falling?' TC>A 'Don't know' TC>A 'You hold it' A>TC 'I could but how will you manage when I go to get the milk?	" SSC	" (PAIR)
8	TC picks up a brick & considers	A>TC 'Could you use any of these larger bricks to help you?'	SSC	(PAIR)
9	Adds 2 bricks to bottom of tower TC went on to make two more towers	TC>A 'I can stand it. I can stand it.' A>TC 'Well done. That was a really good idea.'	SSC	(PAIR)

Figure 1.31
Target child observation B

Min	Activity record	Language record	Task code	Social code
1	Duplo – clipping yellow bricks together, then green, etc.	TC> naming the colours	SSC	SG/P
2	" " "		"	"
3	Lines bricks up in rows of 6	TC> 1 2 3 4 5 6	SSC	SG/P
4	" " "		"	"
5/6	Builds tower of single bricks, It does not balance. TC adds a larger base to tower		SSC	SG/P
7	TC builds another tower & stands the 2 towers next to each other.	TC> 'My tower won't fall'	SSC	SG/P
8	Added large bricks to the tops of towers. They remained standing		SSC	SG/P
	TC very proud of her achievement			

- can be used on subsequent occasions, as long as the date of each observation is clearly recorded
- can result in a deficit model as it only records what the child can do, not what they might be near to achieving with support or time
- requires a pre-prepared template.

For older children within the Foundation Stage, the recording codes are:
E = emerging

W = working on

C = consolidating

A = achieved.

Many early years settings, and some local authorities, have developed their own style of recording sheets. For the youngest children, these may reflect the use of the Birth to Three Matters framework; the Foundation Stage Profile may be used for the older children. Ask your current setting what they use.

Figure 1.32
Development record for older children

LEARNING AREA RECORD | **Communication, Language and Literacy (1)**

Name ____________	**Assessment date**					
D.O.B. ______	**Colour code**					

		E	W	C	A
Enjoys listening to stories, songs, rhymes and conversation between others					
Incorporates elements of what he/she has seen and heard into her/his everyday play and learning experiences					
Enjoys participating in conversations, sharing experience and ideas with others					
'Talks' to self during play and during imaginative play with figures or puppets					
'Talks' to miniature figures, or puppets, recreating conversations and experiences					
Recreates conversations and recounts experiences during imaginative and role play					
Experiments with mark making equipment such as pens, pencils, crayons, brushes, sponges, fingers, sticks					
Incorporates shapes, symbols and letters in his/her free writing					
ELG: is able to enjoy listening to and using spoken and written language, and readily turns to it in play and learning					
Explores sounds in a variety of ways such as:	sounds in the environment				
	sounds made by everyday objects				
	sounds and words made by voices				
Responds to a range of sounds by:	imitating				
	identifying their source				
	linking to make sound patterns				
Recreates words she/he hears and incorporates in own language usage					
Makes up new nonsense words e.g. rhyming nonsense words 'cap, hap, dap, zap'					
Makes observations such as 'that sounds like', 'that sounds the same as'					
Sounds out familiar letters in a simple text					
Sounds out familiar words in simple text					
ELG: Explores and experiments with sounds, words, text					

COMMENTS

Key to code:
E – Emergency
W – Working on
C – Consolidating
A – Achieved

Sociograms

A sociogram gives an 'at a glance' record of the social behaviour of a group of children. It can be used to identify friendship groups and secure pair-relationships and also for establishing when a child lacks friends within the setting. The observers should always be aware how quickly friendship groups change, particularly with children under the age of five, and, for this reason, the method has limited use. The benefit of identifying a relationship concern for a particular child is that strategies can be established to help them to integrate further.

A sociogram:

- is quite an easy technique to use
- can be used for looking at a group of children
- captures a relative 'moment in time' rather than giving a long-term perspective
- requires skilful interpretation.

Longitudinal studies

keyword
Confidentiality not passing on information inappropriately; keeping information to yourself, thereby respecting the privacy of others.

In a longitudinal study, the observation is carried out at intervals over a considerable length of time. Such studies need written parental permission before starting and involve regular visiting and observing of the child's development and progress over a pre-set period. A baby study may, for example, involve weekly visits for three months, whereas a child study is likely to require fortnightly visits for six months or more. Longitudinal studies should be approached in an objective manner, and it is important to ensure the **confidentiality** of the family.

The longitudinal approach will enable you to:

- get to know the child and the impact of their family life on their development
- understand the needs of the child more fully
- identify and record changes in the child's development
- comment on each area of development and how the rates of development vary
- chart the child's development according to a chosen screening process.

remember
A longitudinal study of a child will benefit from the inclusion of other observational methods.

The drawbacks of longitudinal studies can be that:

- visits to a child's home can sometimes feel intrusive
- family holidays, illness and visitors can sometimes affect your planning
- objective observations are not always welcomed by the parents
- a house move by the family may end your study prematurely.

Table 1.9 Comparison of methods

Method	Benefits
Written records ■ Structured ■ Unstructured ■ Snapshots ■ Individual child or baby studies ■ Open data	■ Simple to use ■ More suitable for one child ■ Short time span but can be repeated sequentially ■ Can provide detailed information about individual
Movement and flow charts (tracking) ■ Closed data	■ Can be used to match interest to provision ■ Gives a full picture of child's movements or interest ■ Clearer data if used with one child
Time sampling ■ Open data	■ Can be used for single child or group ■ Pre-set form allows easy collection of data ■ Longer recordings can be made
Event sampling ■ Open data	■ Simple to use ■ Can identify area of concern ■ Best used with individual children
Target child ■ Mostly open data	■ Simple to use when familiar with method ■ Can be used with one or more children ■ Allows observation over longer periods
Checklists ■ Closed data	■ Easy to use with one or more children ■ Can be used to compare children ■ Can be repeated at intervals
Sociograms ■ Closed data	■ Simple to use ■ Can be used with group of children

Limitations of methods

There will, of course, be limitations to any of the methods mentioned, some of which have already been highlighted. There is no one ideal method for any situation, and it is important to be aware of the differences between the methods and of the advantages and disadvantages of each one. Table 1.10 summarises the limitations of each method.

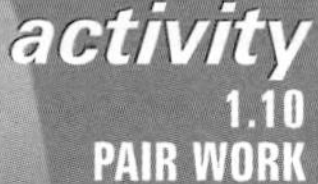

(a) With a friend, choose two observational methods and observe the same child or group of children in the same situation.

(b) Compare your findings, looking for similarities and differences.

(c) Which method gave the fuller, and therefore more useful, information?

Table 1.10 Limitations of each method

Method	Limitations
Written records	■ Difficult to use for long periods of time ■ Intense concentration needed to 'capture' all the data ■ Notes need to be written up at the time or shortly afterwards
Movement and flow charts	■ Spontaneous use is limited ■ Clear recording necessary or data can be difficult to interpret
Time sampling	■ Help from other practitioners may be needed ■ Events may be missed if they occur outside the time frame
Event sampling	■ Requires a pre-prepared template and understanding of coding categories ■ Help of other practitioners may be needed
Target child	■ Difficult to use spontaneously ■ Requires a pre-prepared template and understanding of coding categories ■ Help of other practitioners may be needed
Checklists	■ Do not allow effort or potential to be noted ■ Can result in deficit model ■ Only skills observed are assessed and much may be missed ■ Pre-prepared template needed
Sociograms	■ Capture a limited moment in time ■ Can be difficult to interpret
Longitudinal studies	■ Require careful planning of visits ■ Family may find it intrusive or may move away ■ Notes must be written up after each visit or relevant data may be forgotten

Objectivity

It is important to consider our own feelings, attitudes and values when we carry out observations of children, as these can affect objectivity if they are not taken into account. If we already have a fixed idea about a child or situation, it is possible that our observation may be clouded by what we expect to see happen. There are many reasons for only carrying out an objective observation, as Figure 1.33 shows.

(a) Think of a stereotypical judgement that could be made about a child.

(b) Discuss in a group how a child could be affected by such a judgement.

Reporting

On occasions, it will be necessary to refer a child to another professional; this could be for health, developmental, care or learning needs. As a student, if you have any concerns about a child for any reason, you should speak to your placement supervisor or to the child's key worker. It is likely that some needs would be managed within the setting, with the staff and resources already

Figure 1.33
Objective observation

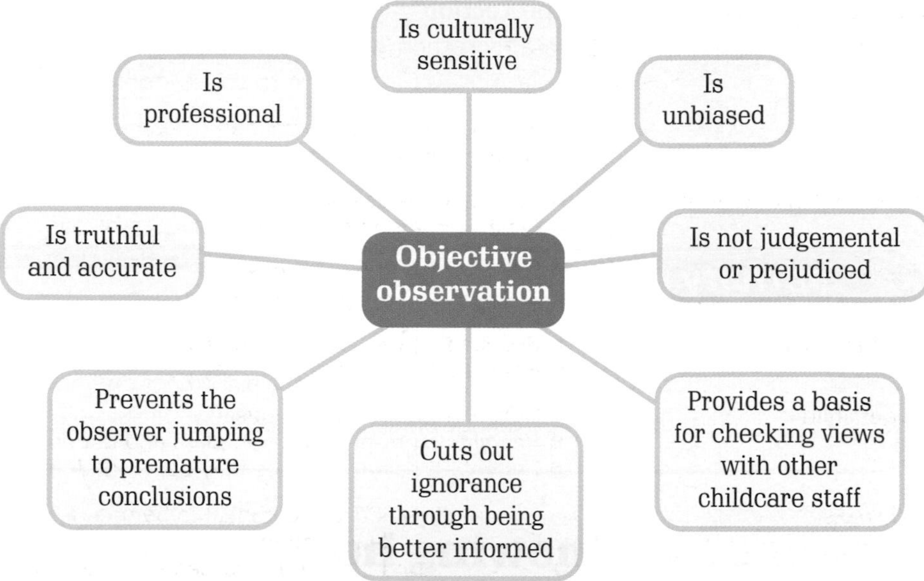

keyword
Portage
A daily home-teaching programme specified for the individual child.

available. At other times, additional or one-to-one support will be required and an extra member of staff may be brought in, or the child may have a **Portage** worker, or a specialist teaching assistant.

Refer to Unit 8, page 347, for more on supporting children with a disability or special educational need.

A child may have to be referred because of suspected neglect or another form of abuse. Each setting has a member of staff designated to make such referrals to the local child protection team. It is inappropriate for you as a student to make the referral yourself. You must always talk to your placement supervisor.

For more on child protection issues, refer to Unit 2, pages 83–94.

Confidentiality

It is expected that confidentiality will always be kept when carrying out observations. Confidentiality respects the rights of both the child and their family, and will be part of the ethos of the setting in which you work. You will need to ask permission to carry out an observation on a child and, when you record your observations, the child's identity should not be apparent to anyone who does not need to know.

A parent should be kept informed of any concerns raised about their child as a result of observations made by the setting. It is totally unacceptable for a parent to find out information, referral details, or that a concern has been raised, simply through looking at a child's records.

Data protection

The Data Protection Act 1988 covers any information kept on paper or computer. This Act is relevant to you not only as a student, in relation to the information that you use in writing up your assignments, observations and recordings, but also as a practitioner, writing observations and maintaining records on children.

activity 1.12 INDIVIDUAL WORK

(a) Research the main points of the Data Protection Act in your college library or on the internet.

(b) Talk to staff at your current placement and find out how they ensure that they do not breach the parameters of the Act.

Knowing how to observe children's development

During your training you will be asked to observe children in a range of settings and situations, carrying out a range of activities, and focusing on each of the main developmental areas:

- physical development
- social development
- emotional development
- communication and language development
- intellectual development.

Observing and noting children's physical development

When observing children's physical development, you will need to focus on how they move, i.e. their locomotor and non-locomotor skills and their ability to co-ordinate their movements. You will look at balance and spatial awareness and also at their manual dexterity and use of small equipment. For example, you might choose to observe children:

- as they play freely outside (e.g. running, jumping and hopping)
- catching and throwing balls
- riding bikes, tricycles and scooters
- scrabbling through tunnels and over humps and soft-play blocks
- climbing and balancing on climbing frames, logs, beams, etc.
- joining in parachute games
- playing ring games

- responding to music (e.g. dancing, marching, skipping, etc.)
- building with construction materials (e.g. large and small, commercial or natural)
- using malleable material (e.g. sand, water, clay, dough, gloop, etc.)
- manipulating small world resources (e.g. farms, doll houses, cars, train sets)
- holding and using mark-making instruments (e.g. pens, pencils, paintbrushes, printing blocks, etc.)
- holding books and turning the pages.

Observing and noting children's social and emotional development

When observing children's social and emotional development, you will need to focus on how they function, both alone and with others, and consider their behaviour in a range of situations and circumstances. You will look at how they interact and at how they express their feelings and emotions. You will also look at how secure they appear to be, both within themselves (self-concept) and within the care environment.

For example, you might choose to observe:

- children as they arrive in the morning and how easily they say goodbye to parents or carers
- how readily they settle into the activities of that day
- whom they talk to (adults and children)
- whether they chat freely or if it takes time for them to gain the confidence to do so
- if they have quiet times or spend time alone
- to assess if they seem to have friends
- their ability to share (e.g. resources, treats and adult time)
- their understanding of the needs of others
- how they react to conflict or obstruction
- how well they respect or challenge boundaries
- whether they join in activities voluntarily or always need encouragement
- their willingness or reluctance to try new experiences
- how well they use the social terms of greetings, requests and thanks
- how they interact within a small group, looking at their level of confidence
- how they interact within a large group, looking at their level of confidence
- how they interact with a familiar adult
- how they interact with an adult new to the setting
- how they respond to change
- how they respond in a mock emergency, such as an evacuation of the setting.

remember

In the event of a real emergency, any observation that you might be carrying out must be abandoned so that you can help with the evacuation process.

Observing children's communication, language and intellectual development

When observing children's communication, language and intellectual development, you will need to focus on how well they make themselves understood, how they play, how they use their imagination, solve problems and use their memory. You will be able to consider their level of concentration and how well they use each of their senses to gain new information.

For example, you might choose to observe:

- how well children make themselves understood, when they explain, ask questions and tell their news, both in general and at circle times
- their use of gesture, body language and facial expressions both during play and when speaking to friends, family and adults
- the maturity of their grammar and/or vocabulary
- the sorts of questions they ask and whom they ask
- how they experiment with natural materials (e.g. sand, water, clay and wood)
- how they take on the role of others through dressing up, role play and home-corner play
- how they use puppets
- if they respond with empathy to stories, discussions or distressed friends
- how they use their imagination within role play, construction, creative activities, outside in the garden, etc.
- how they persevere with jigsaw puzzles and when constructing, sorting, matching and sequencing, etc.
- their use of recall during story telling and discussions
- their ability to use description (e.g. sounds like ..., smells like ...).

Understanding the importance of planning in supporting children's needs and development

Planning

Planning will usually be linked to the relevant curriculum framework for the age of the children in the group or class and the area of the UK in which you work. These frameworks provide guidance on working and planning for the under-threes, pre-school-age children and school-age children. They not only take into account the ages and usual stages of development of the children within the parameters of the framework but also the needs and requirements of the area.

Examples of planning can be found in Unit 6, page 242, and Unit 7, page 328. You may find it helpful to refer to these now.

Observation should be used automatically to inform planning, whatever the age of the children. This not only helps to ensure that you meet each child's needs fully but also monitors the breadth of their skills, development, friendship circles and use of resources.

Participation

It can at times be difficult for a student or a new member of staff to make their views known or to feel able to offer contributions to support assessment and planning. As you become more involved with the team you work with, you will become more established and will feel better able to initiate ideas and add suggestions to what is already planned.

You should be able to contribute your ideas and suggestions:

- during team meetings
- during one-to-one meetings with your line manager
- through informal discussions with colleagues
- within in-house training sessions
- through a suggestions box, if the setting provides one.

(a) Why do you think that it is important for all staff to be able to contribute ideas to the planning and assessing of the children in their care?

(b) Should the value of a suggestion always be based on experience or qualifications? Discuss this within a small group.

Children's needs and development

Planning to meet the needs of children includes ensuring that the appropriate equipment and resources, including the relevant range of consumables, are available whenever required and in sufficient quantity.

(a) What else can you think of? Consider how and where babies play, feed and rest.

(b) Think now about rooms for older children. What will you consider there?

For example, in a baby room there should be refrigeration for bottles and foods, and sterilising equipment, changing facilities, etc.

You might find it helpful to refer to Unit 2, page 67, to remind you what is needed to maintain a safe and hygienic environment; to Unit 6, page 222, for activities and the resources needed to carry them out successfully; and to Unit 7, page 300, for the care needs of babies and toddlers.

progress check

1. Explain the terms 'growth' and 'development'.
2. Explain what is meant by the term 'primitive reflexes'.
3. Explain the difference between primary and secondary sexual characteristics.
4. At what age is bowel and bladder control usually attained?
5. What conditions are needed to achieve emotional security?
6. What do the terms 'attachment' and 'bonding' mean?
7. Why are boundaries important to children?
8. What is social learning theory?
9. Outline three theories of language development.
10. Outline the stages of language development.
11. What is perception?
12. List as many factors as you can that may affect growth and development.
13. What is the purpose of observation?
14. What is objectivity and why is it important when observing children?
15. Explain what is meant by the term 'confidentiality' and why confidentiality is so important when working with children.

References and suggested further reading

Baston, H. and Durward, H. (2001) *Examination of the Newborn: A Practical Guide*. Routledge, London.

Bee, H. (1992) *The Developing Child,* 6th edn. Allyn & Bacon, Boston, MA.

Brain, C. and Mukherji, P. (2005) *Understanding Child Psychology*. Nelson Thornes, Cheltenham.

Cullis, T., Dolan, L. and Groves, D. (1999) *Psychology for You*. Nelson Thornes, Cheltenham.

Dare, A. and O'Donovan, M. (1998) *A Practical Guide to Working with Babies*, 2nd edn. Nelson Thornes, Cheltenham.

Green, S. (2003) *Baby and Toddler Development Made Real*. David Fulton Publishers, London.

Green, S. (2007) BTEC *National Children's Care, Learning and Development, Books 1 and 2*. Nelson Thornes, Cheltenham.

Keene, A. (1999) *Child Health: Care of the Child in Health and Illness*. Nelson Thornes, Cheltenham.

Lindon, J. (2005) *Understanding Child Development: Linking Theory and Practice*. Hodder Arnold, London.

Mukherji, P. (2001) *Understanding Children's Challenging Behaviour*. Nelson Thornes, Cheltenham.

Phillips, C. (1996) *Family-Centred Maternity and Newborn Care*, 4th edn. Mosby Publishers, St Louis, MO.

Sheridon, M. (1997) *From Birth to Five Years: Children's Developmental Progress*, Revised edition. Routledge, London.

Websites

www.babycentre.co.uk
www.pampers.com
www.bounty.com
www.parentlineplus.com
www.nctpregnancyandbabycare.com

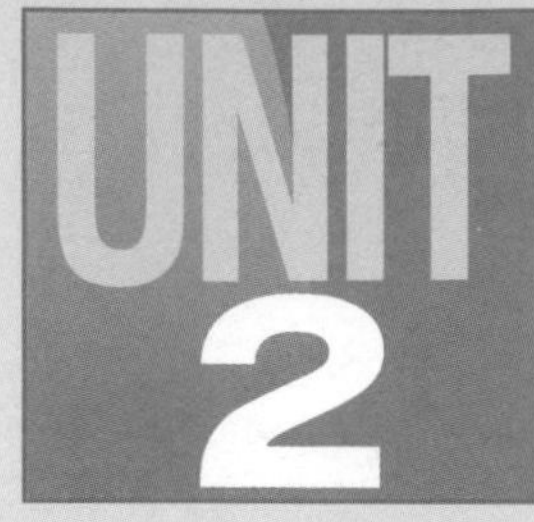

Keeping Children Safe

This unit covers:

- understanding how to prepare and maintain a safe and secure environment for children
- knowing how to support the protection of children from abuse
- understanding how to maintain the safety of children on outings
- knowing how to deal with accidents, emergencies and illness.

This unit begins with a look at the various aspects of safety that must be considered when working with children. As you read, think about the different settings with which you are familiar, noting any particularly good examples of safety practice that you have observed.

The unit then outlines different types of abuse and the signs that indicate that a child may be subject to abuse. You will learn about the legal framework and regulations that cover the way that children are protected from abuse and about how the early years setting should respond if abuse is suspected.

Outings provide opportunities to widen children's experience, but require considerable planning, particularly with regard to safety. The third section of the unit looks at safety considerations for outings.

Finally, you will learn how to respond to an accident or in an emergency and about common childhood illnesses.

grading criteria

To achieve a **Pass** grade the evidence must show that the learner is able to:	To achieve a **Merit** grade the evidence must show that the learner is able to:	To achieve a **Distinction** grade the evidence must show that the learner is able to:
P1 describe how to prepare and maintain a safe and secure environment for children	**M1** explain how to prepare and maintain a safe and secure environment for children	**D1** justify the lay-out, organisation, equipment and materials in a childcare setting known to them in terms of safety considerations
P2 outline basic hygienic principles for a childcare setting	**M2** explain the importance of ensuring that hygiene principles are carried out in a childcare setting	**D2** evaluate the ways that policies and procedures with respect to accidents, emergencies and children's illnesses ensure the safety of children

grading criteria

To achieve a **Pass** grade the evidence must show that the learner is able to:	To achieve a **Merit** grade the evidence must show that the learner is able to:	To achieve a **Distinction** grade the evidence must show that the learner is able to:
P3 state the possible types, signs and symptoms of child abuse and why it is important to follow the policies and procedures of the work setting	**M3** explain the reasons underlying the procedures to be undertaken when taking children on an outing	
P4 outline the procedures and practices that need to be adhered to when taking children on an outing	**M4** explain how policies and procedures with respect to accidents, emergencies and children's illness help to keep children safe.	
P5 outline the policies and procedures related to accidents, emergencies and children's illness in a childcare setting		
P6 undertake basic first aid procedures		

Understanding how to prepare and maintain a safe and secure environment for children

Any setting or organisation wishing to care for children must register with the local authority; exceptions are settings such as toddler groups where the parent or carer remains with the child throughout. Criteria for gaining registration are quite extensive and involve agreeing to work to a range of regulations, Acts, guidelines and care standards. These cover the setting up of the provision, and the maintenance of all health and safety practice.

Regulations are overseen by statutory authorities such as:

- Ofsted (which joined with the Social Services Inspection and Registration Units in September 2001 to offer combined inspection to all early years settings)
- Environmental Health Officers
- local education authorities

- Health and Safety Executive
- Fire service.

The aspects of provision that these oversee are shown in Figure 2.1.

Figure 2.1
Aspects of provision

Details of registration criteria are found in the *Guidance to the National Standards for Under Eights Care* (DfES, 2003). The five versions of these guidelines cover the five main categories of early years care and are:

- full day care
- sessional day care
- childminding
- crèches
- out-of-school care.

activity 2.1 INDIVIDUAL WORK

Copies of the National Standards Guidance should be available in your college library and will usually be available at your placement too.

(a) Arrange to have access to a copy (have a look at the 2005 Addendum too).

(b) Compare the similarities and differences between different settings if you can.

(c) Why do you think that National Standards are so important?

Safety and supervision

As an early years student, you will not be made responsible for any particular child or children in the event of an emergency, but you will be expected to assist others in evacuation procedures or in calming children down following an accident or incident. You will also be expected to take suitable steps to maintain your own safety, and that of others, through safe practice.

Use your observation skills to identify any potential hazards and report them to your placement supervisor. Use your initiative and remove obstacles or obvious dangers from the children's immediate environment. It is important to remember that children need to be challenged by their environment in order to learn practical and personal limitations, but if you are in doubt about something, you should ask a member of staff. It is always better to be safe than sorry.

keyword

Risk assessment The identification of potential hazards and guidance on managing the risk of accident or incident.

Each setting is required to carry out a **risk assessment** of the provision that it offers and to keep a record of the outcomes and how any identified risk is being addressed. Ask how this is carried out, how often and by whom.

The general working environment is important to safe working practice; aspects to be considered include the heating, lighting and ventilation within the setting.

Heating

- Room temperatures must be between 18–20°C (65–68°F).
- A wall thermometer should be on display and checked regularly.
- Whenever possible, radiators should be controlled by thermostats.
- Fire guards or heater guards should be fitted where necessary.

Lighting

- Natural light is important to avoid headaches and eye strain.
- Lighting must be adequate for safe working practice.
- Accidents are more likely to occur in poorly lit settings.

Ventilation

- Children and staff work best within a well-ventilated environment.
- Good ventilation lessens opportunities for cross-infection.
- Ventilation points need to be kept well cleaned, as they can easily attract dirt and a build-up of bacteria.

Lay-out and organisation

The lay-out of the setting should allow sufficient space for:

- children to play in groups
- children to use the floor
- differentiated use of the rooms for quiet activities, messy activities, active play, etc.
- displaying children's creativity, both two-dimensional and three-dimensional
- storing equipment and activities, allowing access to some items by the children
- moving safely between activities
- safe evacuation of the building in an emergency
- rearranging activities and equipment without undue disruption to the setting
- staff to oversee activities in general while involved in other areas of the room.

Furniture and fixtures

- All cupboards, shelving and any other permanent storage must be securely held in place, and any doors should close firmly and remain closed when not in use.
- Access to storage should not interrupt play or be hazardous to children playing.
- Mobile storage needs to be stacked carefully, avoiding overloading or the risk of items falling.
- Furniture should be child sized.
- Ideally, tables that can combine to extend or alter shape should be used.
- Furniture should be sturdy and be kept in good condition.

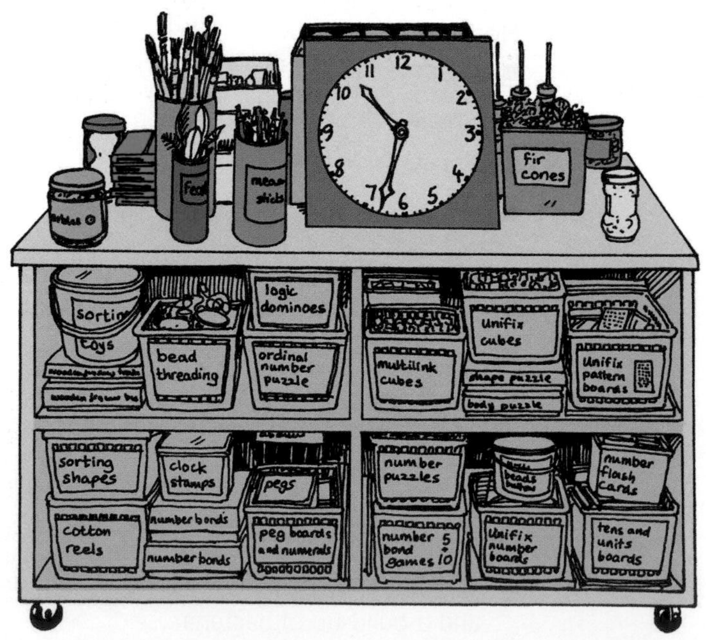

Figure 2.2
Storage should be easy to access and clearly labelled

- Wooden chairs should be checked regularly for splinters, and plastic moulded chairs should be examined for any cracks.
- All surfaces used by the children should be hygienic and in good condition.

Mobility of children

The lay-out of a setting should take into account the mobility needs of the children for whom it caters. For example:

- In baby rooms, there should be sufficient floor space to encourage mobility and floor play with staff.
- Children with a physical need may require larger spaces between activity areas to accommodate a wheelchair, walking frame or support from an adult.
- In a setting caring for a child who is blind or severely visually challenged, retaining a familiar lay-out will allow the child a degree of autonomy and independence.

keyword

Minimum space requirements Legal requirements concerning the space needed for the numbers of children being cared for in any one place.

Rooms

To ensure safe working practice it is important that no area of a building is used for more children than is safe. The regulatory bodies consider the following **minimum space requirements** to be suitable. Sometimes, a restriction is also placed on how many children can play outside at any one time. This can be due to lack of space, or to restrictions on noise if the setting is within a dense residential area.

Maximum numbers of places

No early years setting is allowed to place more than 26 children in one room except for special occasions, such as a Christmas party or a concert. This is regardless of the size of the room. A separate room is always needed for babies and toddlers, adjacent to changing and food preparation facilities.

remember

The space required does not include space taken up by fixtures and fittings.

Toilets and hand basins

- Hot and cold running water should always be available.
- Water temperatures in children's hand basins should not exceed 39°C (102°F).
- There should be a minimum of one toilet and one hand basin for every 10 children in the setting.
- Staff should have separate toilet and hand-washing facilities.

Table 2.1 Minimum space requirements

Age of child	Square feet	Square metres
0–2 years	37.7	3.5
2 years	26.9	2.5
3–7 years	24.8	2.3

Furniture

Whenever possible, furniture should be appropriately sized for the children using it. Most early years settings have low tables and chairs; the seating for staff is usually low too. Baby rooms are often furnished with beanbags for staff and low sofas to ensure that staff remain at the level of the babies in their care as much as possible.

Taking into account disability and specific needs

Any setting caring for a child with specific needs must ensure that it:

- adapts the environment adequately to meet the child's needs
- provides appropriate resources
- encourages all children within the setting to become involved with any children with a disability or specific need.

activity 2.2 INDIVIDUAL WORK

How might staff at a setting encourage children to become involved with any children with a disability or specific need?

Adapting the environment

Supporting a child with restricted mobility

A child with restricted mobility will need a greater area to move about in than a child with full mobility. Points to consider include:

- providing plenty of space between activities and tables
- allowing plenty of space for wheelchairs to turn easily
- having a table that a child in a wheelchair can use, ensuring integration with others at mealtimes as well as in play
- providing suitable seating for a child who needs additional support
- providing wedges to support a child who needs to lie on their front (prone position)
- providing a mobility stand to support a child who cannot stand unsupported
- ramps to help independence in using steps into the garden or other areas of the setting
- lifts (if setting is on more than one floor)
- wide doorways
- a large toilet to accommodate wheelchairs and walking frames
- low-level hand basins to encourage independent personal care
- handrails at child and adult heights where necessary.

Supporting a child with visual impairment

A constant lay-out will help children with visual impairment to develop confidence and personal independence. They will also benefit from:

- plenty of natural light
- plenty of space to move around
- floors clear of clutter
- raised edges on surfaces to prevent objects falling off, thereby spoiling the enjoyment of activities and making floors hazardous.

To help visually impaired children identify where they are within the setting or outside, provide:

- textured surfaces at the edge of areas, such as the sand-pit area
- bright colours or visual clues to help them identify doorways, steps and so on.

Supporting a child with an autistic spectrum disorder
The lay-out should allow you to provide opportunities for play alongside a main group, if group play appears to be overwhelming for the child.

Professional Practice

- A child with an autistic spectrum disorder likes consistency, so keep the routine as constant as you can.
- Try to minimise unnecessary noise and over-excitement.

Figure 2.3
Allow plenty of space for children with restricted mobility

Equipment and materials

Safety of toys, activities and equipment

Checks should be made at the start of every day or session to ensure that all equipment and resources are in good, safe working order. Checks should also be made during and after each session, when any damaged resources and equipment should be removed and either discarded or repaired, and any faults or concerns should be reported to the person responsible. This could be the setting supervisor or manager, a head teacher, or a caretaker of a building.

…ds … …ited on …kaging of … objects as toys, baby equipment and electrical appliances to guide consumers as to their suitability for the intended use or recipient.

All equipment used in early years settings should be made to a recognised safety standard. Table 2.2 shows an up-to-date range of **safety marks**.

Table 2.2 Safety marks

Mark	Name	Meaning
	BSI Kitemark	Indicates that a product has met a British safety standard and has been independently tested
	Lion mark	Indicates adherence to the British Toy and Hobby Association Code of Practice and ensures that a product is safe and conforms to all relevant safety information
0-3	Age warning	Indicates: 'Warning – do not give the toy to children less than 3 years, nor allow them to play with it' Details of the hazard, e.g. small parts, will be near the symbol or with the instructions
BEAB Approved	BEAB mark of the British Electrotechnical Approvals Board	Indicates that electrical appliances carrying this mark meet a national safety standard
	BSI safety mark on gas appliances, light fittings and power tools	Indicates that the product has been made and tested to a specific, safety standard in accordance with the British Standards Institute
RESISTANT	Safety mark on upholstered furniture	Indicates that upholstery materials and fillings have passed the furniture cigarette and match tests – a lighted cigarette or match applied to the material will not cause the article to burst into flames
LOW FLAMMABILITY TO BS 5722 KEEP AWAY FROM FIRE LOW FLAMMABILITY TO BS 5722	Low Flammability labels	Children's pyjamas, bathrobes made from 100% terry towelling and clothes for babies up to 3 months old must carry a label showing whether or not the garment has passed the Low Flammability Test. Either of these two labels is acceptable. Always look for these labels when choosing such garments
KEEP AWAY FROM FIRE	Keep Away From Fire label	Indicates that the garment is not slow burning and has probably not passed the Low Flammability Test. Great care must be taken anywhere near a fire or flame

Health and safety during outdoor activities

When providing outdoor play space, it is important that suitable play surfaces are used. Concrete, gravel and similar surfaces are not suitable because they do not absorb the impact if a child falls, often resulting in serious injury. A more suitable surface for general play is grass, but during dry summer months this will also become hard and unyielding.

It is particularly important that any surface under and around climbing or play equipment from which a child may fall a distance of 60 cm (2 ft) or more should be able to absorb some of the impact of the fall, reducing the risk of serious injury. Impact-absorbing playground surfaces include:

- loose-fill substances such as tree bark or sand (at least 30 cm/1 ft deep)
- 'wet-pour' rubber, which sets to form a spongy surface
- thick rubber tiles.

All surfaces should meet the safety standard BSEN 1177. They should be kept in good condition, with any damage repaired. Sand or tree bark should be raked regularly to remove any debris or animal excrement.

Good hygiene practice

Lack of good **hygiene** practice is the most common cause of spreading infection. It is important to understand and work to the standards of best practice described below.

> *keyword*
> **Hygiene**
> Good practice regarding cleanliness, handling food and personal care.

Toileting

Every effort should be made to encourage children to develop independence in the bathroom. They also have a right to privacy, within sensible boundaries of supervision. Potties should be safely and hygienically stored and cleaned thoroughly after each use.

Each setting should have a policy regarding:

- who is allowed to change babies' nappies
- who is allowed to supervise in the bathroom
- the wearing of disposable gloves
- the safe disposal of nappies, baby wipes, etc.
- the safe disposal of cleaning materials
- the sending home of soiled clothing.

Cleaning of the environment

This includes both the setting itself and the equipment and furnishings within it.

- Cleaning of the environment should take place at the end of each session, and day.
- Cleaning should also take place as necessary throughout the day.
- Carpeted floor surfaces should be easily cleanable with a vacuum cleaner.
- Washable non-slip surfaces should be cleansed with a mop, which is disinfected daily.
- Suitable anti-bacterial products should be used regularly to cleanse all surfaces.
- Toys and activities should regularly be cleaned with anti-bacterial products.

- The cleansing of surfaces is particularly important before any food preparation, cooking activities or before snack time.
- There is usually a rota of staff to ensure that the setting is kept clean and hygienic at all times.
- Staff should not be carrying out cleaning duties while still responsible for supervising children.

Cleaning of consumable materials

It is important to ensure that consumable materials are clean. For example:

- Sand should be sieved daily to remove any 'bits', and cleansed regularly.
- Any sand that has been spilt on the floor should be sieved and cleansed before being returned to the sand tray, or else be discarded.
- Outdoor sandpits should be kept securely covered when not in use to prevent fouling by animals and rubbish and garden debris gathering.
- Water should be replenished daily, and water trays should be cleaned and disinfected regularly.
- Pets should be kept scrupulously clean, following normal pet-care routines.
- Dough should be renewed regularly and stored in a refrigerator.
- Dough should be discarded and replaced following any infectious illness in the setting, to avoid repeated cross-infection.

Personal hygiene

This involves:

- regular hand washing throughout the day
- washing hands before all food preparation
- washing hands after any activity that could potentially spread bacteria, such as:
  - nappy changing
  - using the toilet
  - coughing
  - sneezing
  - nose blowing
- use of antibacterial soaps
- nails kept clean and short
- cuts and sores covered
- use of disposable gloves.

Note also that:

- Hair should be kept tied back to reduce the risk of infestation, cross-infection and general untidiness.

- Clean clothing and overalls should be worn at all times, changing as necessary for food preparation and cooking activities.
- Covering nose and mouth when coughing and sneezing should be automatic and should be encouraged in children too.

remember

If all practitioners take health and safety measures as a matter of course, this ensures that no child is treated differently, or made to feel different.

HIV and hepatitis

Good hygiene practice and use of disposable gloves when dealing with body fluids should be an automatic part of everyday life in care situations. A child who is HIV positive or who has hepatitis poses no greater risk to carers than any other child. In fact, they are sometimes more susceptible to infection from their carers owing to a suppressed immune system, so vigilance is needed to help protect them.

Provision of food and drink in any setting

All food preparation must adhere to the guidelines of the Food Safety Act 1990 and the Food Safety (General Food Hygiene) Regulations 1995.

Kitchen hygiene

This involves:

- keeping surfaces cleaned and free from bacteria
- ensuring that all surfaces used are unblemished and not chipped
- using separate cutting boards for cooked or uncooked foods
- using separate knives for cooked and uncooked foods
- keeping floors cleaned thoroughly
- washing up as dirty utensils occur, to eliminate additional bacteria growth (where possible use a dishwasher as this is the most effective method)
- wrapping all waste securely and emptying bins regularly
- regular cleaning and defrosting of refrigerators and freezers
- ensuring that the temperature of a refrigerator is kept at 4–5°C (39–41°F)
- storing cooked foods at the top of the refrigerator, raw foods below
- minimal handling of all foods
- keeping food well covered
- ensuring that use-by dates are adhered to
- ensuring that any reheated food is served piping hot
- not keeping food warm for more than a few minutes.

Legislation and regulations

As part of your understanding of health and safety you will need to familiarise yourself with the main aspects of a variety of pieces of legislation. Copies of these may be available from your college library or learning centre. Alternatively, they can be found on the internet.

keyword

HASAWA
The Health and Safety at Work Etc. Act 1974, 1999

RIDDOR
Reporting of Injuries, Diseases and Dangerous Occurrences Regulations 1995.

COSHH
Control of Substances Hazardous to Health Regulations 2002

keyword

Children Act 2004
A major piece of legislation, bringing together a range of laws to do with the rights and well-being of children; it builds on the Children Act 1989.

Relevant legislation that ensures a healthy and safe environment includes:

- Health and Safety at Work Etc. Act (**HASAWA**) 1974, 1999
- Food Safety Act 1990
- Food Safety (General Food Hygiene) Regulations 1995
- Reporting of Injuries, Diseases and Dangerous Occurrences Regulations (**RIDDOR**) 1995
- Control of Substances Hazardous to Health Regulations (**COSHH**) 2002
- Regulatory and setting requirements.

Summaries of the main points follow.

HASAWA: Health and Safety at Work Etc. Act 1974, 1999

This Act protects employees and anyone else who could be affected by a setting's procedures. It requires settings to have a safety policy and to assess, and reduce accordingly, the risk of accident or injury. There should be a written health and safety policy and a named person with responsibility for health and safety in any setting that employs more than five people.

Local authorities can (under the **Children Act 2004**, originally the Children Act 1989) ask early years settings to produce health and safety policies, irrespective of how many people are employed by the setting.

activity 2.3 INDIVIDUAL WORK

(a) Why do you think it is good practice to have a health and safety policy?

(b) Who benefits from a health and safety policy?

Professional Practice

- The setting's health and safety policy should be available for parents to read if they so wish.
- All staff and students should be asked to read the health and safety policy.

Food Safety Act 1990 and the Food Safety (General Food Hygiene) Regulations 1995

This legislation includes guidelines on both personal and general kitchen hygiene. It is relevant to all staff who handle food or drink and all settings where food or drink is stored, handled, prepared or served. Summaries of what these regulations entail are set out on page 77.

RIDDOR: Reporting of Injuries, Diseases and Dangerous Occurrences Regulations 1995

These regulations require:

- the reporting of all deaths that occur
- the reporting of any injuries that result in a child, a parent or a visitor being taken to hospital from the setting
- a telephone report to the local authority.

Reporting also applies to the death or serious injury of a member of staff. If a member of staff is injured (but not seriously) or becomes ill because of their work, the local authority should be informed in writing. There is a special form for all written reports.

keyword

Accident book
A book in which staff record all accidents or injuries that occur in the workplace.

Accident books

All settings should have an **accident book** in which they report all accidents and incidents, both large and small.

COSHH: Control of Substances Hazardous to Health Regulations 2002

Health problems such as irritation of the skin, asthma or similar conditions can occur because of the presence of certain chemicals in some substances. A range of symbols has been devised by COSHH to warn people in advance of potential hazards. Most of these substances will not be present in early years settings; however, bleach and some other cleaning products can cause irritation and respiratory reactions.

In schools, chemicals may be used within the context of design technology or art. Although many products are now 'safe', potentially harmful substances include some marbling inks and spirits for cleaning, and some spray paints and glues. These would usually only be handled by adults, but children may be present during their use. A risk assessment should be carried out by the setting and any potentially hazardous products identified. Relevant information on storage, use, and treatment following spills should be noted.

Professional Practice

- Cleaning products should not at any time be left where they can be reached by children.
- Always read the instructions for the use and dilution of any product and the importance of ventilation when using them.

Regulatory and setting requirements

The requirements for each setting regulated by Ofsted are set out in the *National Standards for Under Eights Day Care and Childminding* published by the DfES (2003). There are 14 standards that have to be met; criteria vary slightly according to the setting.

The headings for the 14 standards are as follows:

1. Suitable person
2. Organisation
3. Care, learning and play
4. Physical environment
5. Equipment
6. Safety
7. Health
8. Food and drink
9. Equal opportunities
10. Special needs (including special educational needs and disabilities)
11. Behaviour
12. Working in partnership with parents and carers
13. Child protection
14. Documentation.

activity
2.4 INDIVIDUAL THEN PAIR WORK

(a) Using a copy of the standards for full day care, identify which of the 14 are relevant to health and safety.

(b) Discuss your findings with a friend.

Adult:child ratios

It is important that there are always sufficient adults to safely supervise the number of children present. The number needed differs according to the age of the children. In practical terms, provision for older children will usually need fewer adults, but, as with early years provision, adult:child ratios often need to exceed requirements to take into account any children who have additional needs, particularly if they need one-to-one care. The nature of the activities being offered will also affect the numbers of adults needed to ensure safe practice.

There are standard recommended staff:child ratios.

Fire safety

Fire safety is also covered within the National Standards. In day care settings (including childminders' homes), the main issues are:

- accessibility of the register
- suitable places for smoke alarms
- means of escape from the building
- the type of heating and any fire/heating guards used
- the safety of all electrical appliances

Table 2.3 Standard recommended staff:child ratios

Type of setting/Age range	Ratio	Comments
Under 5 years' full day care 0 to 2 years 2 to 3 years 3 to 5 years	 1:3 1:4 1:8	Because of management and administration duties, managers or officers-in-charge should not be included in these ratios where more than 20 children are being cared for
Nursery schools and classes	2:20 (minimum)	One adult should be a qualified teacher and one a qualified nursery assistant
Reception classes in primary schools		Where 4-year-olds are attending Reception classes in primary schools, the staffing levels should be determined by the schools and local education authorities
Childminding Under 5 years 5 to 7 years Under 8 years (no more than three being under 5)	 1:3 1:6 1:6	All these ratios include the childminder's own children and apply to nannies employed by more than two sets of parents to look after their children
Day care services for school-age children Where 5- and 7-year-olds are cared for on a daily or sessional basis (i.e. care at the end of the school day and full care in school holidays) Where facilities are used by children aged over 8 years as well as under 8 years	 1:8	A higher ratio may be necessary if children with special needs are being cared for. A lower ratio may be appropriate for some short sessional facilities not lasting the full day Providers should ensure that there are sufficient staff in total to maintain the 1:8 ratio for the under eights

(Reproduced by kind permission of the Stationery Office, from *The Children Act 1989, Guidance and Regulations*, Volume 2, 7th impression, 1998.)

- the storage of any flammable materials
- means of preventing unsupervised access to the kitchen
- ensuring that fire exits remain unobstructed
- responsibility for checking fire exits regularly.

remember If children with special needs are included in the setting, a higher ratio of staff to children may be necessary, depending on the specific needs of the child or children.

Emergency proceedings

Fire is only one type of emergency that early years workers need to know how to react to. Others include:

- accidents
- suspected or actual gas leaks
- flooding
- bomb scares.

A checklist for emergencies

- Each setting should have a clear procedure for evacuating the building.
- All staff should know who and what they are responsible for on evacuation.
- All staff should know where they are to congregate following the evacuation.
- An agreed procedure for ensuring that the emergency services have been called must be established.
- The manager of the setting is likely to take charge, but consideration should be given to what happens if it is the manager who has had the accident!
- Students should not be given responsibility for evacuating children from the setting.
- As a student, you should be fully aware of what the emergency procedure involves and where you should go.
- All adults should remain calm and help to reassure the children.
- Emergency exits should be signposted with appropriate symbols.
- Emergency exits should be kept clear at all times.
- Emergency exits should be unlocked (but childproof) and be easily opened from the inside.
- Clear instructions for emergency evacuation procedures should be displayed at all times.
- All staff, students and parents should familiarise themselves with the instructions. Where more than one language is spoken in the setting, copies of the procedure should be translated accordingly.

Figure 2.4
Examples of emergency exit signs

activity 2.5 INDIVIDUAL WORK

Imagine that you have just been evacuated from the school where you are on placement. You are now in a local church hall and need to help occupy 27 reception class children until told that you can return to the classroom.

(a) What would you suggest doing?

(b) How would you calm the children's excitement or anxiety?

Knowing how to support the protection of children from abuse

Policies and procedures

Each setting or organisation will have a policy and procedures drawn up in accordance with statutory law and local authority guidance. These are important because they help to ensure that any concerns about the welfare of children are brought to the attention of the appropriate people to deal with them. Procedural guidelines also help practitioners to seek help for a child by giving them guidelines on when and how to raise their concern.

Types of abuse

Abuse can take any of the following forms:

- *physical abuse* – any harmful actions directed against a child, often resulting in bruises, burns, scalds, head injuries, poisoning or fractures
- *neglect* –the failure of the child's carers to properly safeguard the health, safety and well-being of the child, which includes their nutritional needs, physical needs and social needs
- *sexual abuse* – any involvement of a child or developmentally immature adolescent in sexual activitics, including viewing photographs and pornographic videos
- *emotional abuse* – the continuous rejection, terrorising or criticising of a child
- *bullying* –including physical and/or verbal hostility and aggression
- *harassment* – being pestered and made to feel uncomfortable, under pressure and often scared
- *potential effects of social factors such as substance abuse* – this includes neglect, sexual, physical and emotional abuse carried out by persons under the influence of abusive substances or alcohol. Involvement with these substances can also lead to self-harming.

Professional Practice

- Every local authority has a set of definitions relating to the abuse of children. It is important that you gain access to a copy of this and read it carefully. Your placement will have one.
- If you do not understand anything, ask for clarification.

Signs and symptoms of abuse

It is important to remember that all children have accidents from time to time which result in bruises, cuts and scratches. Toddlers, for example, often fall over or into low tables as they learn to walk and balance. Older children learn to ride bikes and climb trees and fences, tumbling in the process and scraping knees, grazing arms and legs, and on occasions suffering from more serious injuries such as concussion and fractures.

When you make a judgement as to whether an injury is considered to be of concern, it is essential that you consider the age and stage of development of the child and take into account the circumstances of the injury.

Physical abuse

Possible indicators of abuse are:

- bruises on the soft areas of the body (inner arms, thighs, buttocks)
- bald patches
- unexplained injuries, including bruises, burns and fractures
- bite marks – remember that a dog bite will look very different from a human bite and that an adult's bite mark is considerably larger than a child's
- finger-tip bruising on the face – this could be caused by forced bottle feeding of a baby or a young toddler
- unusually shaped bruises – consider how a child might show non-accidental bruising other than being hit with an implement such as a stick or lash
- thumb and finger-tip bruises each side of the torso, which can indicate that a child has been shaken or held forcefully
- pin-point haemorrhage in the ears, which can be caused by shaking
- scald and burn marks – an accidental scald (if, for example, a child pulls over a kettle of boiling water) will have different signs from a scald caused, say, by a cup of tea deliberately thrown (the photographs below show a very severe scalding on the leg and foot of a baby, and a burn inflicted by a cigarette burn)
- evenly spaced scald marks which can indicate the deliberate placing of hands or feet in hot water – these will often have the appearance of socks or gloves
- repeated black eyes or injuries which should start to raise alarm bells.

Figure 2.5
Severe scalding on a baby (l) and a cigarette burn (r)

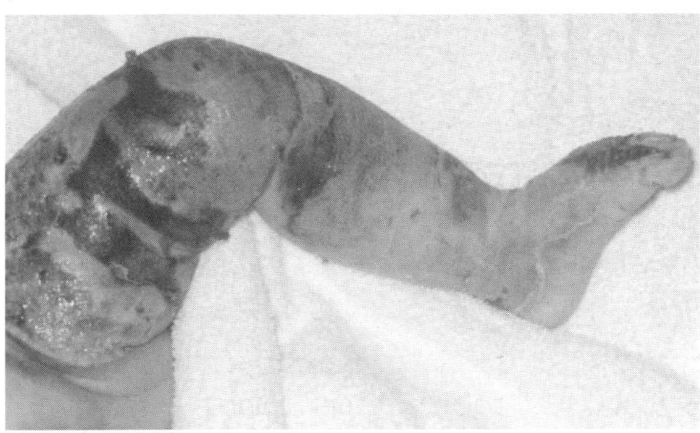

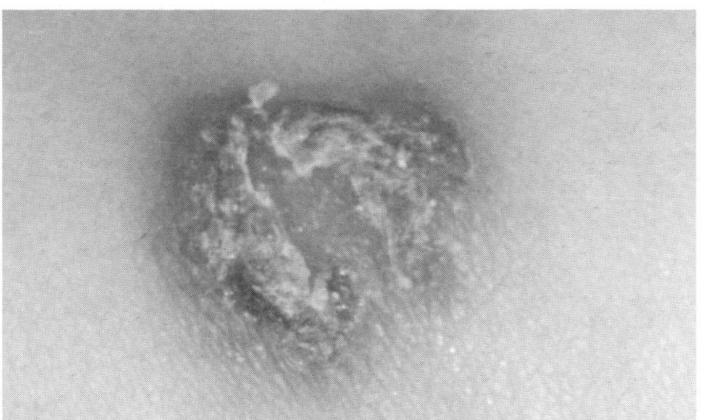

At times injuries can be misinterpreted. Examples include:

- the condition impetigo, which can be mistaken for cigarette burns
- the 'hidden' condition osteogenesis imperfecta (brittle bone disease or Lobstein's syndrome), which can be mistaken for non-accidental fractures
- Mongolian blue spot, a dark birth mark found usually at the base of the spine, occasionally seen in dark skinned babies and children. It can look like a dark bruise.

The explanation of how and when a bruise occurred can at times be important. A dark purple/black bruise is unlikely to be a week old, whereas a yellowing bruise has not just occurred.

Neglect

Neglect can stem from ignorance and lack of practical childcare skills, and it is not always intentional. This does not, however, lessen the physical effects for a child. Neglected children may show the following possible indicators of abuse. They may:

- be underweight, possibly emaciated
- be hungry, scavenge for food or wolf food down at mealtimes
- be dirty and unkempt, with poor personal hygiene
- suffer frequent minor injuries
- appear to have no regular bedtime pattern – the child may indicate that they watch late, and unsuitable, television programmes
- suffer from frequent minor infections such as colds and coughs, due to inappropriate nutrition, and subsequently become run-down
- lack experience of common childhood activities, such as looking at books and using creative materials
- be left unsupervised on a regular basis – the child may indicate this in conversation

- have parents who lack interest in the child's progress in school or nursery
- display self-comforting behaviour such as rocking and head-banging.

Sexual abuse

Sexual abuse includes:

- the use of pornographic material – showing it to children and young people or involving them in the making of it
- incest – an incestuous relationship is one which involves sexual activity between family members who are too closely related to be able to marry, for example between father and daughter or brother and sister.

Physical signs of sexual abuse include:

- bruises on areas such as the inner thighs and genitals
- soreness in the anal or vaginal areas, or in the throat
- vaginal discharge in girls
- swollen penis or discharge in boys
- sexually transmitted diseases and urine infection, sometimes found if medical examination takes place
- distress when having nappy changed (babies and toddlers)
- difficulty or reluctance to pass urine or faeces, often resulting in constipation
- difficulty in walking and in standing up or sitting down
- pain on movement generally
- poor personal hygiene
- obsession with sexual matters
- having unexplained sums of money on a regular basis (older children).

Emotional abuse

Emotional abuse accompanies all other experiences of abuse. Children quite understandably become bewildered and confused when a person whom they love or trust begins to abuse them. Emotional abuse is rarely cited as the main type of abuse in official reports, the term only being used if it is clearly defined as the only form of abuse suffered by the child concerned. This would perhaps occur if a child was cared for physically but was denied love and was constantly rejected, or was put down and ridiculed, by the abuser.

Possible indicators of emotional abuse are that the child may:

- have low self-esteem and lack confidence
- have a poor concentration span
- show developmental delay
- be fearful of new situations
- be concerned about their parents being contacted

- respond inappropriately to situations
- have speech disorders
- find it hard to build social relationships with their peers
- use self-mutilating behaviours, such as head-banging and pulling out their hair.

Bullying

Bullying can take a number of forms, but there is a common factor in that bullying causes lasting harm to children and young people, leading to self-harm, and suicide in some cases. Bullying encompasses a wide range of abusive behaviours such as physical and verbal hostility and aggression, extortion of goods or property, isolating or excluding a child from peer groups, discriminatory behaviours and many other offensive verbal and physical acts.

Possible indicators of bullying are:

- school or nursery refusal
- frequent complaints of feeling unwell early in the day
- returning home with clothes in disarray or torn and appearing hungry (suggesting that their food has been stolen)
- showing signs of emotional distress
- disturbed sleep patterns
- starting to behave in an aggressive manner to others.

Changes in behaviour

It is important to consider a child's behaviour and whether there have been any obvious changes in how a child acts. Some children will become withdrawn and quiet. They may be reluctant to go home or be fearful of certain adults.

Children who are physically abused may show signs of general discomfit; they may try to avoid undressing in front of others, or be wearing long trousers or long-sleeved tops although the weather is hot.

Neglected children often appear to be very tired and weary, from going to bed when they choose. Their concentration and attention span may be limited. Sometimes they crave adult attention.

At times, sexually abused children demonstrate sexually inappropriate behaviour and talk. They often appear to be sad and their development may regress. For example, a child may start to wet the bed again, even though they have been dry for a long time. As they get older, the child may try to confide in a trusted adult, referring to 'my friend'. Building relationships can be difficult for them, and eating disorders such as anorexia and bulimia are common, as is running away from home.

remember

Not all cases of anorexia or bulimia are linked to abuse. Such cases do, however, need to be investigated and the appropriate support offered.

Emotionally abused children learn from their abuser that they are not of value, which lowers their feelings of self-worth. They are often sad and lonely.

Support

Children can and must be taught self-protection strategies. Having the confidence to speak out when they have a problem is important, and you can help to teach them the necessary skills. Activities which encourage them to take the lead, to demonstrate, illustrate or describe something will help children grow in confidence. Their sense of self-esteem will be enhanced by being praised for the effort they have made, not just for achievement. You can also make them feel valued and worthwhile as an individual person by giving them small responsibilities.

Body awareness

Children need to understand that their body belongs to them and that no one has the right to touch their body if they do not want them to. They need to understand that this applies to everyone, except during medical treatment, when a nurse might take a blood sample or a doctor may listen to their chest. Although such procedures may be unwelcome, children have to accept that, at times, they are necessary.

A simple way of assisting young children to understand that their body belongs to them is to refer to the area of their bathing suits, explaining that the area beneath their bathing suit is private and just for them. It should not be touched by anyone except themselves. This gives the child a clear message that helps protect them, whilst still 'allowing' them to explore their own body as they wish.

Secrets

It is important that children of all ages understand the difference between good and bad secrets. Nobody wishes to take away the excitement of a secret surprise for a birthday or a celebration. These are good, happy secrets. For some children, however, the word secret is linked to abuse, with the abuser saying, 'This is our little secret. Don't tell anyone about this because ....' You must help children understand that in these situations they must tell a trusted adult.

Legal framework of child protection

The abuse of children harms their development in many ways. Abuse is always wrong and it is important that adults act to protect children if ever they are concerned about their safety.

A **legal framework of child protection** is in place, and the main aspects of law that help to protect children are those set out in the Children Act 2004. This Act has brought together all the legislation relevant to children. There are a variety of legal steps that can be taken to help keep a child safe from harm.

Police protection

A child may be taken into police protection for up to 72 hours, during which time an **emergency protection order (EPO)** can be applied for.

Emergency protection order (EPO)

An application for this short-term order can be made by anyone, and, if the order is granted, the applicant subsequently takes on parental responsibility for

> *keyword*
> **Legal framework of child protection**
> Laws and procedures to protect children and vulnerable young people.

> *keyword*
> **Emergency protection order (EPO)**
> An order of law, applied for through the courts to help protect children from harm.

the child for the duration of the order. The order is usually issued for eight days, with one extension opportunity of a further seven days. An applicant taking on parental responsibility: 'must take (but may only take) action which is reasonably required to safeguard or promote the child's welfare' (*Children Act 1989, Guidance and Regulations*, Volume 2).

This might include an assessment of the child, or decisions about how much contact or who has contact with the child.

An emergency protection order is always followed by an investigation by the local authority.

Child assessment order

A **child assessment order** can only be applied for through the courts by the local authority or the NSPCC (National Society for the Prevention of Cruelty to Children). It is applied for when a child's parents are unlikely to give permission for an assessment of their child's state of health or level of development to be made, when a concern is raised that a child is already suffering harm, or is likely to suffer significant harm. A child assessment order lasts for a maximum of seven days.

> keyword
> **Child assessment order**
> A legal order applied for in court when a child is considered to be at risk or already suffering significant harm.

Recovery order

A **recovery order** is designed to provide a legal basis for recovering a child who is the subject of an EPO, a care order (see below) or who is in police protection. It is used in situations where a child has been unlawfully taken away or is being kept away from the person who has parental responsibility for them. It also applies if the child runs away from the 'responsible' person or is considered to be missing.

> keyword
> **Recovery order**
> A legal order enabling the police to take into their possession a child who is the subject of police protection or an emergency protection order, if the child is missing, has run away, or has been abducted from the person responsible for their care.

The recovery order directs anyone who is in a position to do so, to produce the child concerned if asked to do so, or to give details of the child's whereabouts. The child will then be removed by the local authority. Police are authorised under the order to enter and search any premises as is necessary, using reasonable force.

Supervision order

On occasions a child is placed under the supervision of the local authority (for up to one year) if it is not felt that sufficient co-operation between the parents and the authority will ensure that the child is fully protected. Although the child continues to live at home, the local authority has a right of access to the child. The **supervision order** can be extended if deemed necessary.

> keyword
> **Supervision order**
> A legal order in which a child is under the supervision of the local authority, but where the authority does not have parental responsibility.

Care order

As with the supervision order, a child continues to live at home under a care order. The local authority has a shared responsibility for the protection of the child, and its decisions hold the greater balance of power in any disputes between the authority and the parents. At any time the authority can remove the child from the parents' home without the need to apply to the courts for any other order. The care order can last until the child reaches the age of majority (18 years old).

keyword

Local Safeguarding Children Board (LSCB)
A group of professionals who meet to discuss individual child abuse or protection cases.

Local Safeguarding Children Board (LSCB)
Under the Children Act 2004, each area is required to have a joint forum for developing, monitoring and reviewing child protection policies. This is the responsibility of the **Local Safeguarding Children Board (LSCB)**, formerly the Area Child Protection Committee (ACPC). LSCBs are made up of those persons who have contact with a child whose case comes before them, for example:

- social workers
- police officers
- medical practitioners
- community health team workers
- school teachers
- voluntary agencies.

An interagency approach to each case ensures that relevant information is passed on to all who need it. This means that there is an exchange of information between different professions, such as teacher, GP, police officer and social worker. This helps to reduce situations where communication breakdown can have tragic consequences.

Referral procedures
Investigations into cases of abuse or suspected abuse, or where there is a concern that a child may be at risk, are carried out following a referral. Referrals can be made to the police, social services departments or to the NSPCC. Anyone can make a referral, and the impetus to do so can follow the disclosure by a child to the individual making the referral, or their representative (early years settings and schools have a designated person who takes on this responsibility). It may also result from the concern of an individual or a group of people represented by one individual. Referrals are also made by neighbours, family members and concerned members of the public. It is always preferred if individuals identify themselves when making a referral, but anonymous referrals are also accepted and investigated as necessary.

It is a misconception that, following a referral, the 'authority' goes immediately to the family and takes away the child. This only happens on rare occasions when there has been a clear case of abuse and the child faces imminent risk of further abuse. Most cases go through a set procedure to establish if a concern is justified, to explore the concerns raised with all those who are in contact with the child, or who might have relevant information, and to establish the level of risk to the child. An example of a situation in which immediate action may be needed to remove the child to safety would be if physical violence is likely to continue or increase following the referral being brought to the family's notice. If a child is not allowed to leave voluntarily, an EPO can be obtained.

Figure 2.6
The investigation procedure in cases of suspected child abuse

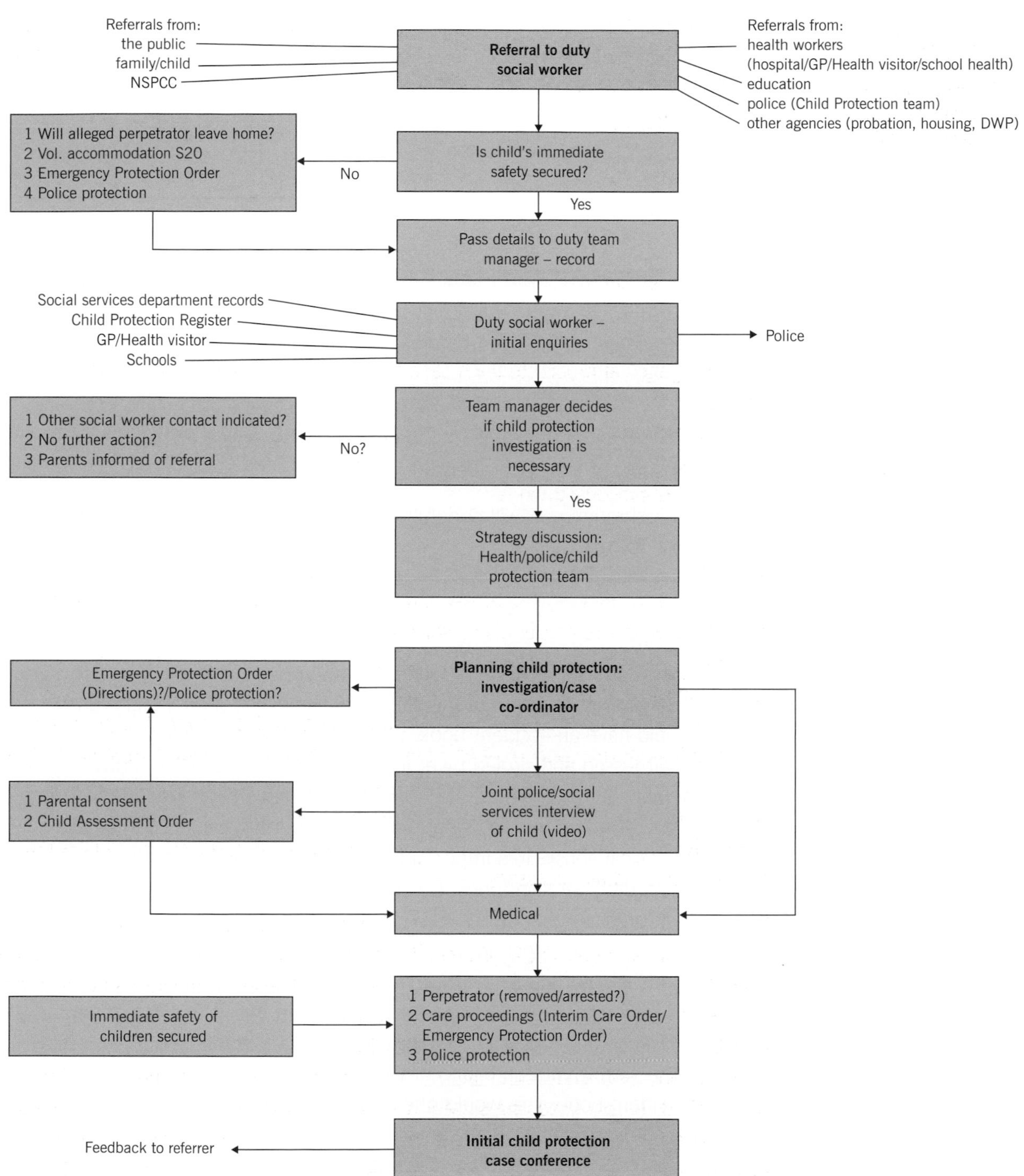

Professional Practice

- If during your placement experience you are worried about a child for any reason, you should talk to your placement supervisor or, if you do not yet feel comfortable doing this, your college tutor. They will help you explore your concerns further and take action appropriately.
- It is never appropriate simply to talk to your friends about a concern, as confidentiality is of utmost importance in all cases, and information about any suspected case of abuse should only be discussed on a 'need-to-know' basis.

activity 2.6 INDIVIDUAL WORK

Think about how you might feel if you had concerns about a child. What range of emotions would you expect to feel regarding:

(a) the child you are concerned about?

(b) the perpetrator of any abuse?

(c) the prospect of making a referral?

Thinking this through now will hopefully prepare you should you be faced with the situation for real.

Keeping records

In early years settings, clear record keeping and report writing help to provide all the details that may be asked of the setting in the event of an inquiry. Each setting should have an accident book, where all accidents and incidents are recorded, witnessed and signed by at least two members of staff. Many settings use 'body maps' to record marks and bruises that have been identified, adding a date to them. This can form a useful piece of supporting evidence in a case involving physical abuse. It is important that staff are able to identify signs and symptoms on different skin tones. Building up good relationships with parents is important in order to provide the best possible care for their child. If the setting has a policy on child protection, which states what will happen in the light of any concerns, this lets parents know that you are making the welfare of their child of paramount importance, as set down by the Children Act 2004 (the paramountcy principle). The setting's policy could include a clause stating that, if any child arrives in the setting with an injury, details of the injury will be noted in the accident/incident book. This would offer added safety for the child and for staff, avoiding the situation that on collecting their child a parent may question an injury that the child had arrived with earlier that day.

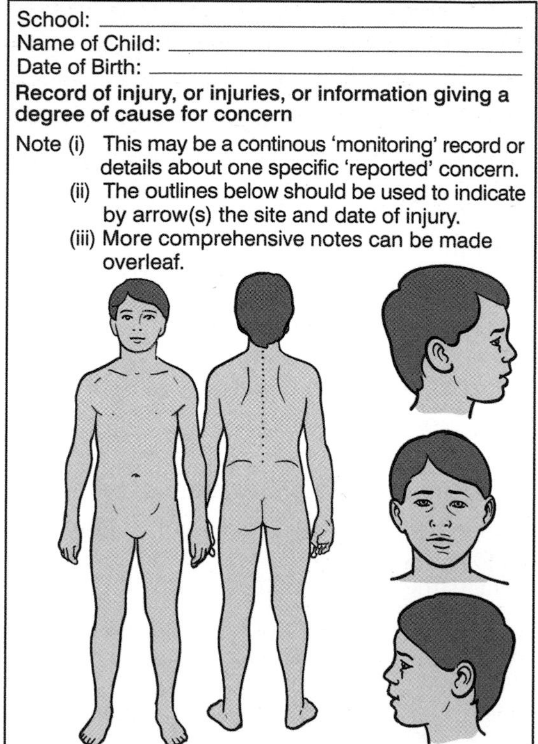

School: ______
Name of Child: ______
Date of Birth: ______

Record of injury, or injuries, or information giving a degree of cause for concern

Note (i) This may be a continous 'monitoring' record or details about one specific 'reported' concern.
(ii) The outlines below should be used to indicate by arrow(s) the site and date of injury.
(iii) More comprehensive notes can be made overleaf.

Figure 2.7
A body map

activity
2.7
INDIVIDUAL WORK

(a) Each setting should have a child protection procedure, which follows the guidelines provided by the local authority. Ask to see it.

(b) Try explaining the guidelines and procedure to another person. If you can explain them clearly then it is likely that you understand them.

(c) If the guidelines are not clear to you, ask for an explanation.

Child protection register

keyword

Child protection register
A computerised list, kept by a local authority, of children who are considered to be 'at risk'.

Child protection registers were first set up within each local authority in the mid-1970s. A child's name is put on the register if there is concern about the safety of that child or their family. At times, an unborn baby may be placed on the register, if there is a known abuser in the family.

The register contains relevant information (see below) about the child, so that the child's situation can be monitored and appropriate action taken when necessary. The child's case and inclusion on the register is reviewed regularly.

If a senior professional has a concern about a child, they can ask for a check to be made of the register for the name of that particular child or their family. These registers are now computerised and held centrally, enabling checks to be made quickly. The information is not readily given out, and professionals wishing to consult the registers have their details and authority to apply to the register checked before information is released to them.

De-registration

De-registration can only occur if:

- the original points that led to registration no longer apply
- the child reaches the age of majority (18) and is no longer termed a 'child'
- the child dies.

Contents of a child protection register

The information held on a child protection register includes:

- the child's name (and any other names they are known by)
- their address, gender, date of birth, culture and any known religion
- the name and contact details of their GP
- the name and details of their main carer
- details of any school or other setting that the child is known to attend
- if applicable, the name and details of any person who has parental responsibility for the child (if different from above)
- outline details of any court orders
- an outline of the alleged or confirmed abuse that has previously occurred
- the date the child was placed on the register
- the name and details of the professional responsible for the child's case (the child's key worker)
- the date of the proposed review of the child's situation.

Understanding how to maintain the safety of children on outings

Planning and preparation

Going on an outing is an exciting experience for most children, and for many it will be the first time they have been somewhere without their parent or main carer. Outings with children need careful planning. Those responsible need to consider:

- where to go
- adult numbers needed to meet (and preferably exceed) legal requirements
- arrangements for venues, coaches, insurance
- risk assessments
- what the adult with overall responsibility should take with them
- what individual children need to take with them.

The person leading the outing should ensure that the planned destination is suitable for the age group concerned. It is important that a risk assessment is carried out, and, whenever possible, a visit is made in advance to confirm suitability and familiarise the outing's leader with the facilities. For example, open water, free-roaming animals, dense undergrowth and woodland are potential hazards and would usually need greater levels of supervision; also, they might completely restrict children's freedom thereby detracting from their enjoyment of the outing. A venue with limited access to toilets can be problematical when the group comprises very young children.

Accompanying children on outings

It is important that adult:child ratios are adhered to:

Table 2.4 Adult:child ratios for outings

Age group	Adult:child ratio
0–2 years	1:1
2–5 years	1:2
5–8 years	1:5
8+	Usually 1:8

keyword

Parental consent forms
Forms in which parents give written permission for something, e.g. for emergency medical treatment to take place.

keyword

First aid
The emergency actions taken following an accident or sudden illness.

On any outing including under-eights, the appropriate ratios for those age groups must be adhered to, and never affected by the inclusion of older children.

The overall supervisor for the outing should:

- Have an accurate register with them at all times.
- Check the register regularly throughout the day and carry out regular headcounts.
- Check that **parental consent forms** have been returned and signed.
- Check that all accompanying adults know which children they are responsible for.
- Check that all adults understand their role and responsibilities for the day.
- Provide identification badges for young children as an 'extra' precaution in case they get separated. These must never include the child's name, just the name of the school, nursery or group.

- Ensure that a small emergency **first aid** kit goes with them.
- Ensure that children are wearing clothing and footwear appropriate for the destination.
- Ensure that hats and sun protection are worn or administered according to the setting's policy.
- Ensure that the means of contacting the emergency services is available.
- Check that any transport used meets safety requirements in relation to seat belts.

Professional Practice

- As a student you may be asked to accompany children on an outing. You would usually work with another adult in supervising children.
- Constant observation and awareness of what children are doing is vital.

activity 2.8 INDIVIDUAL WORK

(a) Why is it important not to have a child's name on their identification badge?

(b) Why are adult:child ratios higher when on outings?

(c) Why are parental consent forms important?

case study 2.1 Fatima

Fatima is planning to take her nursery and after-school club to the zoo for their summer outing. There will be 20 children between the ages of two and five years, and 10 children between the ages of five and eight years. They will be going on a coach, and taking lunch with them.

activity GROUP WORK

(a) How many adults will Fatima need to accompany her on the trip?

(b) What will she need to arrange in advance?

(c) What will she need to take with her on the day?

remember

In the event of an emergency your role will be to help calm children down, keeping calm yourself.

Emergency arrangements for outings

Figure 2.8
Emergency arrangements for an outing

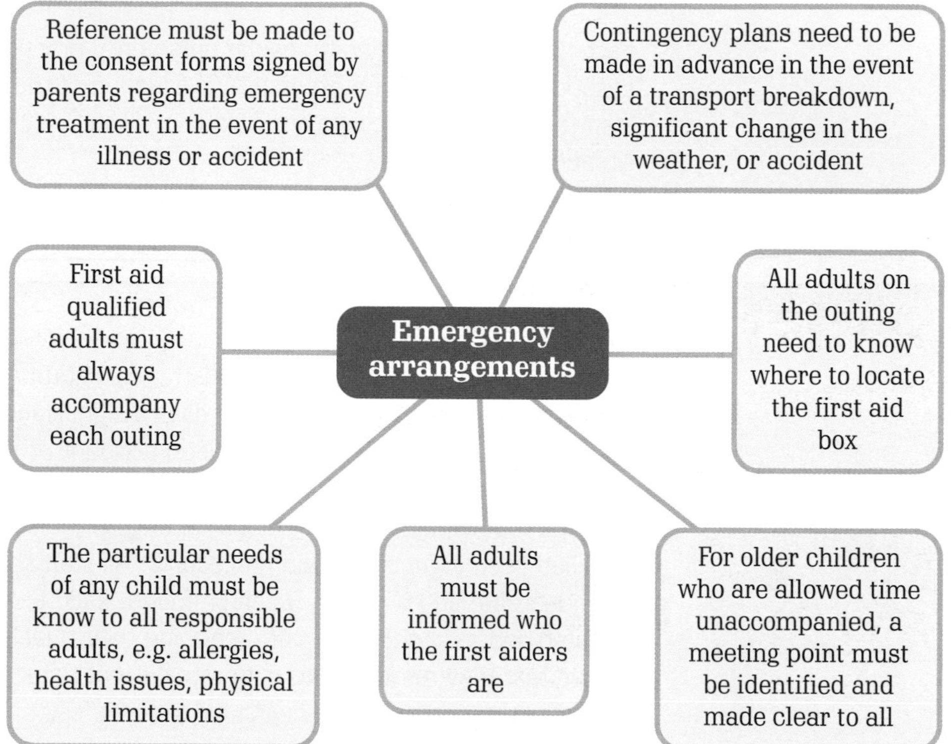

Knowing how to deal with accidents, emergencies and illness

Policies and procedures

Every early years setting or organisation that cares for or supervises children and young people of any age has a policy and procedure for dealing with each of the following:

- illness
- safety
- child protection
- emergency situations such as a fire
- missing children.

It is important that you familiarise yourself with each of these. They will set out what to do, who is responsible for what actions, who telephones a child's parents and when, who telephones for medical advice or the emergency services and when, who stays with the main group, and who is able to leave the main group to seek help or look for a missing child. As you move between placements during your course, you will be able to compare policies and procedures, noting differences and evaluating how successfully they work in practice.

Each setting will incorporate regular emergency practices into their planning, ensuring that all children experience evacuation of the premises etc. and that all staff (particularly those who are new) know what they should do in all potential situations.

Refer back to page 82 for evacuation procedures.

Basic first aid

Knowledge of first aid is essential in early years settings, as the initial actions following an accident or incident can have a significant impact on the eventual outcome. First aid limits the effects of an accident or incident through action taken to assist the recovery of the person concerned. Every early years setting is required to have at least one person on duty in the setting at all times who is qualified in emergency first aid procedures. All staff should know who these individuals are and where they can be found. Each first aider must be regularly updated and assessed externally, renewing their qualification every three years to ensure that they remain up to date with current thinking and that they can still remember and carry out basic first aid procedures.

Knowledge of what a first aid box should contain and how its contents should be monitored is also important.

Individuals working as nannies and childminders should produce a first aid box for themselves and take on the responsibility for arranging to update their first aid qualification at appropriate intervals.

The contents of a first aid box are outlined on page 108.

remember

Most people will (thankfully) never have to use the majority of the techniques they learned during their first aid training, but none of us knows when we might have to, so we need to be prepared.

Basic first aid procedures

As an early years worker, you will have to know how to cope with many differing situations, including how to:

- check for signs and symptoms
- prioritise treatment
- deal with an unconscious casualty
- use the ABC procedure
- deal with allergies and anaphylaxis
- treat minor and major injuries
- treat cuts and grazes
- treat burns and scalds

- treat fractures and sprains
- deal with poisoning
- deal with breathing difficulties
- deal with foreign bodies
- treat seizures.

Each of these situations will be covered during your first aid training. Written instruction can also be found in first aid manuals. The illustrations below should also be a useful source of reference.

remember

A first aid manual, as with all other written first aid instructions, should never be used as an alternative to attending a recognised training course in first aid.

First aid manuals

First aid manuals are produced by recognised bodies such as the Red Cross and St John Ambulance. If you are taking a first aid course as part of your BTEC First Children's Care, Learning and Development programme, your college will let you know which you will need to acquire. It is important that you always refer to the most up-to-date edition, as procedures change from time to time, based on new understanding.

Administering first aid

The table below sets out the appropriate first aid treatment for a range of accidents and incidents that may occur in an early years setting. You should familiarise yourself with each of these.

Table 2.5 Administering first aid

Injury	Signs	Action
Sprain	■ Child cannot put weight on the affected ankle ■ May limp or hop ■ Complains of pain	■ Remove the shoe and sock ■ Raise and support the foot to reduce any swelling ■ Apply a cold compress against it, wrap with cotton wool padding and crêpe bandage. ■ Rest, ice, compression, elevation (RICE) ■ Keep the ankle elevated ■ Call the doctor if the foot may be broken or take the child to the accident and emergency department at the local hospital
Fracture	■ Signs depend upon the site of the fracture: ▪ pain ▪ swelling ▪ loss of use of a limb or inability to walk or stand ▪ tenderness increased with movement	■ Call for the establishment's first aider to administer first aid depending on the site of the injury ■ Contact the parents ■ Take the child to the accident and emergency department if a fracture is suspected
Swelling	■ May occur after a fall or knock when the injured area expands ■ Compare the affected limb (arm or leg) with the other limb when a swelling will be apparent	■ Reduce swelling by holding a cold compress against it for 30 minutes ■ Rest ■ Ice ■ Compression ■ Elevation – raise and support the injured part

Table 2.5 continued

Injury	Signs	Action
Splinter	■ Sharp pain in the hand ■ Limping if in the foot ■ Close inspection will reveal the site, and a small piece of the splinter may protrude through the skin	■ Wash the area with warm water and soap ■ Use a pair of clean tweezers to remove the splinter ■ Encourage a little bleeding by squeezing the area ■ Inform parents if the splinter cannot be removed
Bruise	■ Purple-blue coloured areas on the skin – darker on black skin. They fade to yellow before disappearing 10–14 days later ■ Common sites on children are forehead, elbow, knees, and shins	■ Apply cold compress to prevent further bleeding underneath the skin ■ Bruising in unusual and unexpected areas should be investigated, e.g. armpits, back, abdomen, buttocks, inside the thighs, etc.
Cuts and grazes	■ Bleeding	■ Sit the child down ■ Wash the injured area with water and clean cotton wool or gauze – wipe away from the open wound ■ Apply direct pressure if bleeding will not stop ■ Remove any dirt and gravel carefully ■ Cover the area with a gauze dressing
Poisoning	■ Child has swallowed poisonous berries or leaves, alcohol, drugs, chemicals or bleach ■ Find out exactly what has been swallowed and how much ■ Keep containers, berries or leaves to show to the doctor	■ Comfort and reassure ■ DO NOT TRY TO MAKE THE CHILD VOMIT ■ DO NOT GIVE THE CHILD ANYTHING TO DRINK ■ Call the doctor or an accident and emergency (A & E) department ■ Contact the parents ■ Put the child in recovery position if they are unconscious
Bites	■ Irritation and pain at the site ■ Puncture teeth marks in the skin after an animal bite	■ Rinse the wound under running water for 5 minutes ■ Wash the area with soap and water ■ Cover the wound with a dry dressing ■ Check that the child is immunised against tetanus
Stings	■ Sudden cry when the sting occurs ■ May see sting sticking out at the tip of a swollen area ■ Itching ■ Irritation and pain at the site	■ Carers should remain calm as this will reassure a frightened child ■ Sting may be removed carefully if possible, avoiding pressure on the poison sac ■ Wasp sting – apply dilute vinegar ■ Bee sting – apply bicarbonate of soda ■ Apply cold compress followed by calamine ■ Observe for signs of an allergic reaction
Burns and scalds	■ Pain ■ Inflamed skin ■ Blistering	■ Put affected area under cold, running water for 10–15 minutes to cool it. This will also help to reduce pain. ■ Remove clothing when the area has been cooled (remove tight clothes before the area begins to swell) ■ Cover with a clean, soft, non-fluffy cloth, cling film is adequate. These will keep the area cool and prevent infection ■ Take child to the A & E department if the burn is larger than a 10 pence piece

Figure 2.9
Cooling a burn

Figure 2.10
Dealing with bleeding

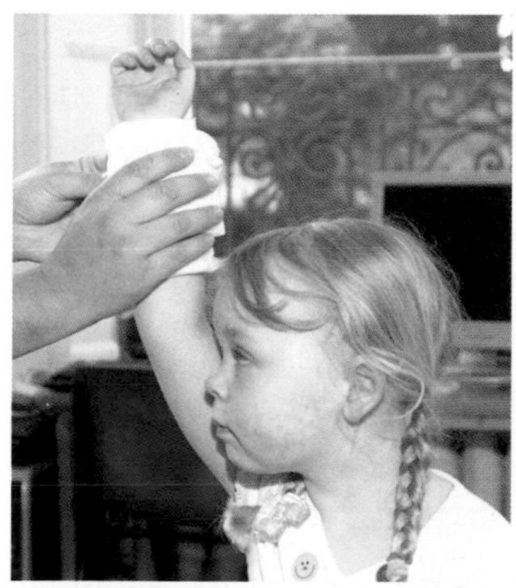

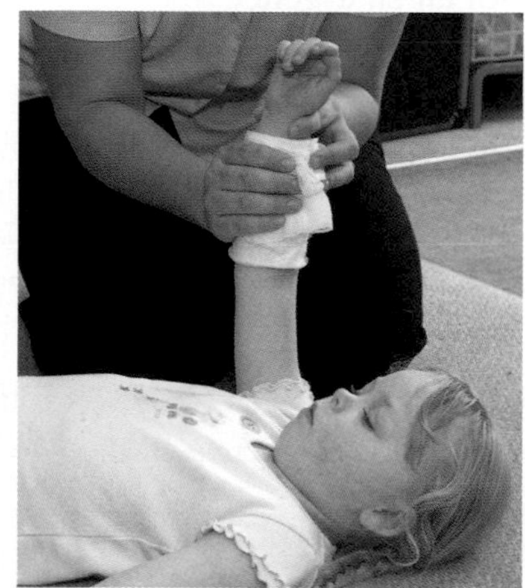

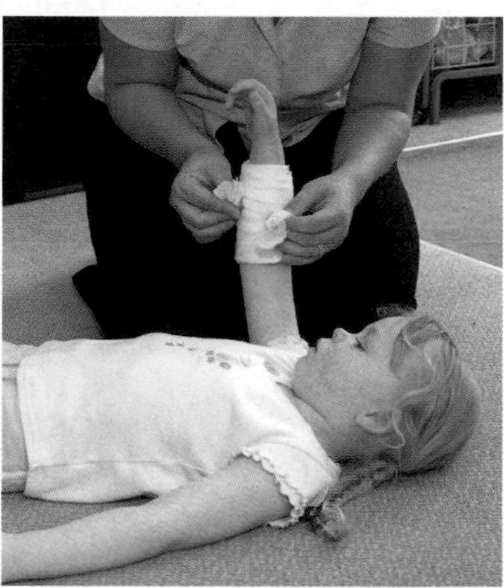

Figure 2.11
Dealing with a nose bleed

Figure 2.12
Dealing with a sprained ankle

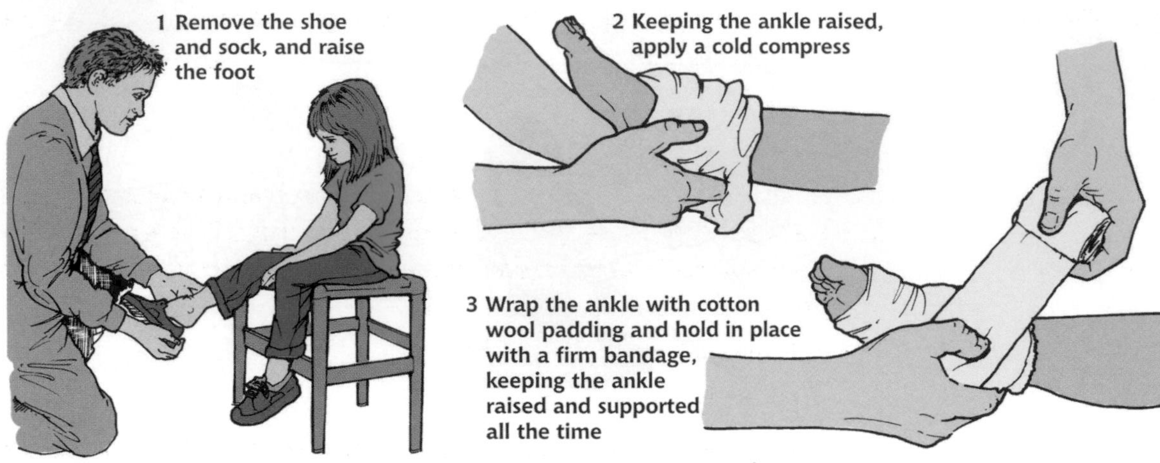

Dealing with an emergency

As children's bodies are still developing, it is not always appropriate to use the same techniques for emergency first aid for a child as you would use on an adult because you may injure the child further. In some cases, techniques designed for adults can be extremely dangerous to a young child. For example, tilting the head of a young infant back too far may actually occlude (block) the airway, rather than open it. Similarly, if too much pressure is placed on the soft tissue under the jaw when opening the airway, this may block it.

The following section offers an easily accessible overview of emergency procedures for babies and young children.

Professional Practice

- These procedures should be carried out by a qualified first aider. You will learn the techniques during your first aid training course.
- Disposable gloves should be worn when dealing with any body fluid.
- First aid procedures are constantly being updated.
- Parents need to be informed of any accident or injury.

Stage 1

- Review the situation, assessing as far as is possible what has happened.
- Decide what your immediate priorities are.
- Stay calm.
- Consider if there is anyone else who could help you.
- Professional help should be sought unless only a minor injury has occurred (if on your own, shout for help).
- Whenever possible, any other children present should be reassured and led away.

Stage 2

- Remove any dangers. You will be of little use to the casualty if you become injured yourself. Ask yourself if it is safe to proceed with first aid. For example:
  - Is the fire out?
  - Is the electricity turned off?

remember You should not be putting yourself in unnecessary danger too.

Stage 3

- Assess the casualty for any response. It must be remembered that, with very young children, inability to speak will not automatically mean that they are unconscious. They may still be in the pre-verbal stage of their development. Consider the following:
  - Is the child moving?
  - Have they opened their eyes?
  - Have they given a verbal response, a cry, moan or any other vocalisation?
  - If no response is obtained, it is likely that they are unconscious.
  - You will need to begin the ABC procedure.

The ABC of resuscitation

This section describes the **ABC of resuscitation**.

keyword **ABC of resuscitation** A sequential emergency first aid process: open the airway; breathe for the injured person; help circulation to be restored.

A stands for the AIRWAY

The airway needs to be kept clear. If it becomes blocked and the child stops breathing, they will soon become unconscious. This will eventually lead to the heart slowing down and stopping due to the lack of oxygen.

Remove any obvious obstructions from the child's mouth, but be aware that a 'blind sweep' with your finger may block the child's airway further! Ask yourself:

remember These procedures should only be carried out by a qualified first aider.

- Is the chest rising and falling?
- Is the tongue well forward?
- Can you hear breathing sounds when your ear is close to the mouth?
- Can you feel the breath on your cheek?
- If not, you will need to open the airway for the child.

To open the airway in a baby:

1. Place the baby on their back, tilting their head back slightly.
2. Use one finger under the chin to move it forwards (imagine that they are sniffing a flower and position them accordingly).
3. Look, listen and feel again for breathing.
4. If there is no change, you will need to try artificial ventilation (B in the ABC sequence).

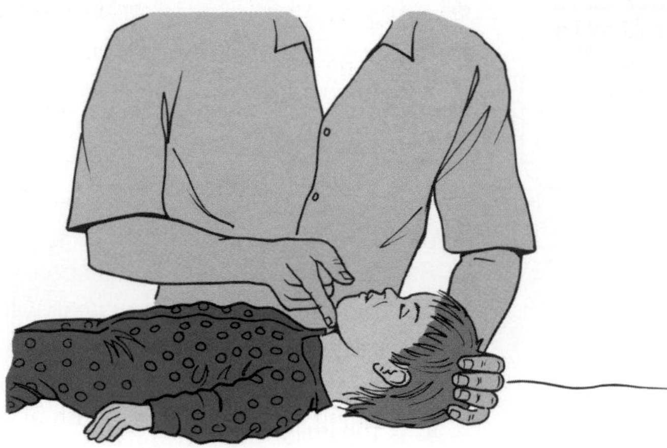

Figure 2.13
Opening a baby's airway

To open the airway in an older child:

1. Place the child on their back.
2. Place two fingers under the chin.
3. Place a hand on the forehead and tilt the head backwards, again ensuring not to tip it too far.
4. Look, listen and feel again for breathing;
5. If there is no change you will need to try artificial ventilation (B in the ABC sequence).

B stands for BREATHING

Have a look at the casualty's tummy. Can you see the child's chest moving? If breathing has stopped, you may need to do this for them. Whenever possible, send someone to call for an ambulance. If you are on your own, perform the following procedure for one minute and then go and call an ambulance yourself. If the casualty is a young baby, you may be able to take them with you and continue the breathing procedure for them.

remember
These procedures should only be carried out by a qualified first aider.

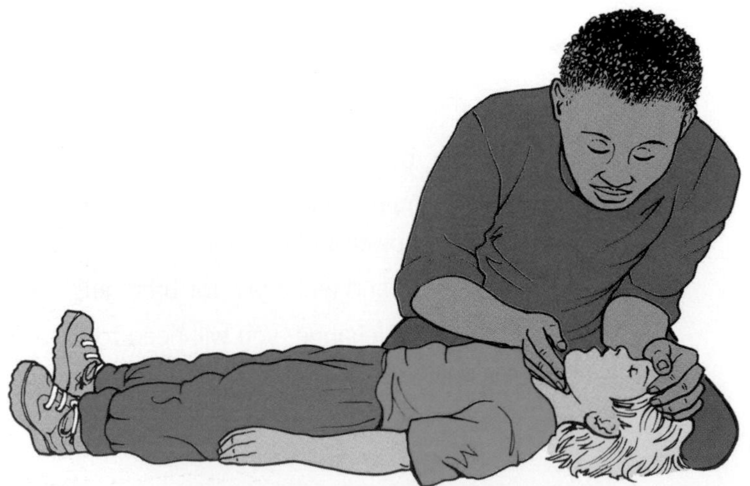

Figure 2.14
Opening a child's airway

To carry out artificial ventilation for a baby:

1. Open the airway as in A.
2. Place your lips around the mouth and nose of the baby.
3. Give five 'rescue' breaths (breaths that are hard enough to make the chest move as though the casualty had taken a deep breath for themselves).
4. Continue to blow, very gently, at a rate of 20 breaths per minute.
5. After each breath, remove your mouth and watch for the chest to fall as the air expires.
6. If, after five rescue breaths, you have not been able to establish effective breathing, re-check their mouth and head position and try again.

Figure 2.15
Artificial ventilation for a baby

To carry out artificial ventilation for an older child:

1. Open the airway as in A.
2. Pinch their nostrils together.
3. Place your lips firmly over the child's mouth.
4. As with a baby, give five rescue breaths, then
5. Blow gently into the mouth at a rate of 20 breaths per minute.
6. Again, as with a baby, remove your mouth after each breath and watch the chest fall as the air expires.

Figure 2.16
Artificial ventilation for a child

NB The updated UK Resuscitation Council guidelines state that only professionally trained health workers should check the pulse during resuscitation attempts.

> **remember**
> These procedures should only be carried out by a qualified first aider.

C stands for CIRCULATION

The circulation is the beating of the heart, which keeps the blood flowing through the body. The most usual signs of circulation are breathing, coughing or movement. If you cannot see signs of circulation, you will need to start the procedure known as chest compression.

Chest compression for a baby:

1. Place the tips of your fingers one finger's width below the baby's nipple line.
2. Press down sharply to between one-third and one-half of the depth of the chest.
3. Give five compressions per one breath, 100 compressions per minute if working alone.

Figure 2.17
Chest compression for a baby

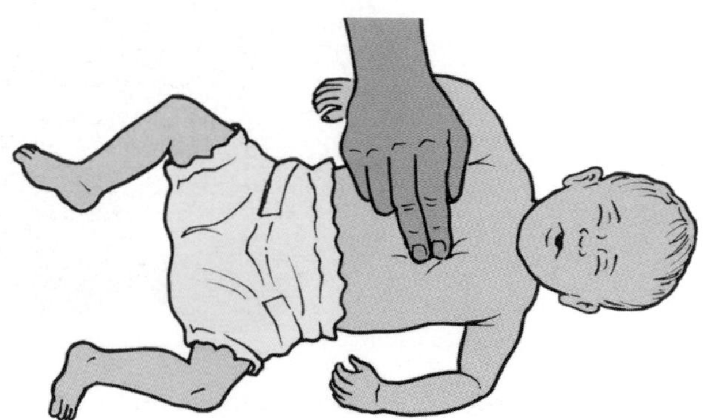

Press on lower breastbone with two fingers

Chest compression for a child:

1. Using the heel of your hand rather than your fingers, press down sharply to between one-third and one-half of the depth of the chest.
2. Work in cycles of 15 compressions per two breaths, 100 compressions per minute if working alone.

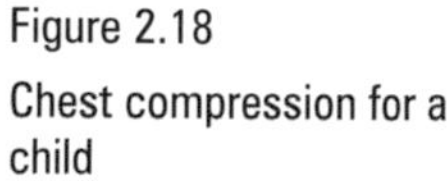

Figure 2.18
Chest compression for a child

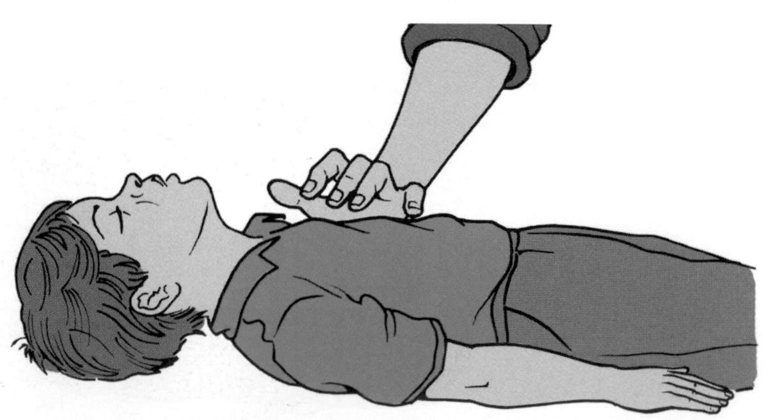

Press on breastbone with heel of hand

remember It can be dangerous to continue with chest compressions once the casualty has started to recover.

Remembering the ABC sequence will enable you to carry out procedures in the right order. The procedure needs to be continued until either the child begins to recover or professional help arrives.

The recovery position

Once a child has begun to breathe for themselves they need to be placed in the recovery position.

The recovery position for a baby

Hold the baby in your arms with their head tilted downwards to help keep the airway open.

Figure 2.19
The recovery position for a baby

The recovery position for a child

1. Ensure that the airway is open.
2. Bend the arm nearest to you at a right angle. Bring the child's furthest arm across the chest and cushion their cheek with the back of their hand.
3. Roll the child towards you. Keep the child's hand pressed against their cheek. Bend the outside knee, grasp them under the thigh and, keeping the near leg straight, pull them towards you.
4. Bend the child's top leg at a right angle to the body to keep them on their side and to prevent them from rolling on to their front. Tilt the head back to ensure the airway remains open. Check their head is still cushioned by their hand.

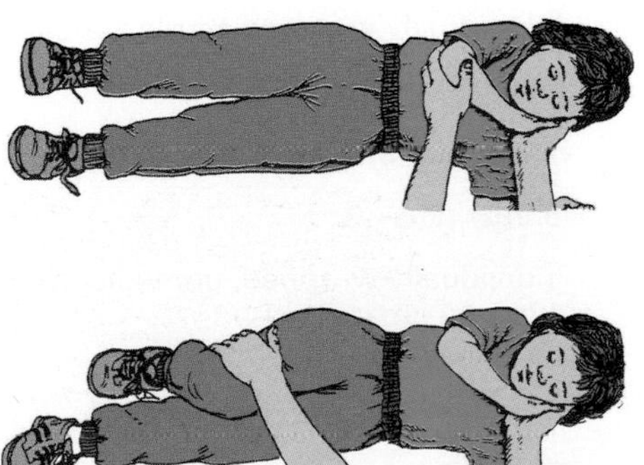

Figure 2.20
The recovery position for a child #1

Figure 2.21
The recovery position for a child #2

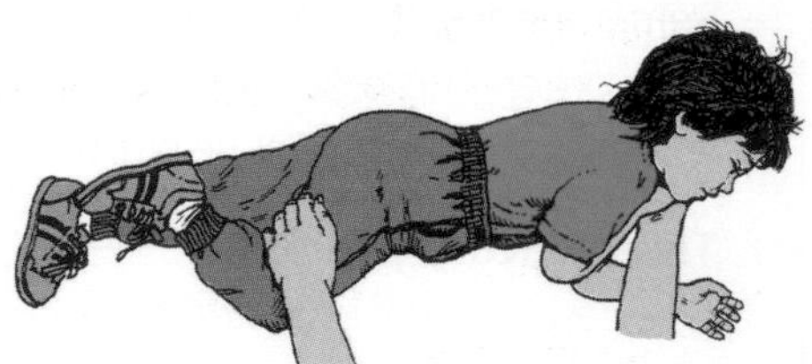

Figure 2.22
The recovery position for a child #3

Once a child has been made comfortable in the recovery position, they should be closely monitored, and reassured as necessary until professional help arrives.

First aid box

Every early years setting needs to have a first aid box. It is a legal requirement of all employers, under the Health and Safety (First Aid) Regulations of 1981. The container should be both airtight and waterproof and it should be easily recognisable – the most usual design is green with a white cross. The box should always include a guidance sheet on emergency first aid. Every setting will have different requirements according to the numbers and needs of its children and staff. The first aid box should be checked regularly and kept in good order by a specified person.

Local policy

In some local authorities there are recommendations not to use certain items, such as plasters and lotions, because of the risk of allergy in some children. Each setting needs to ensure that its first aid box is drawn up in accordance with local policy.

Parental consent forms

Written parental consent is needed with regard to emergency treatment for each child. Some parents have cultural or religious beliefs, which will mean they withhold permission for some forms of treatment.

Contents of a first aid box

An employer with 10 or more staff is required by law to include the following in the first aid box:

Table 2.6 Contents of a first aid box

Item	Number required
Individually wrapped sterile adhesive dressings (various sizes)	20
Sterile pads	2
Triangular bandages (ideally these should be sterile)	4
Safety pins	6
Individually wrapped, unmedicated wound dressings 12 × 12 cm 18 × 18 cm	 6 2
A pair of disposable gloves	1
First aid guidance leaflet	1

Additional items

An early years setting will also need to include additional items, such as:

- scissors (kept only for first aid use)
- tweezers
- several pairs of disposable gloves
- non-allergic tape
- non-allergic plasters (if used)
- bandages in various sizes
- sterile gauze
- a digital thermometer (never a glass or mercury thermometer)
- a checklist of the box's contents.

Professional Practice

- A specified person (or persons) should be responsible for checking and replenishing the first aid box regularly and after every use.
- A checklist of the minimum requirements should be kept in the box.
- A form should be kept in the box and be signed and dated after every check and each time the box has been cleaned.
- All staff should be aware of parents' wishes in the event of emergency treatment for their child.

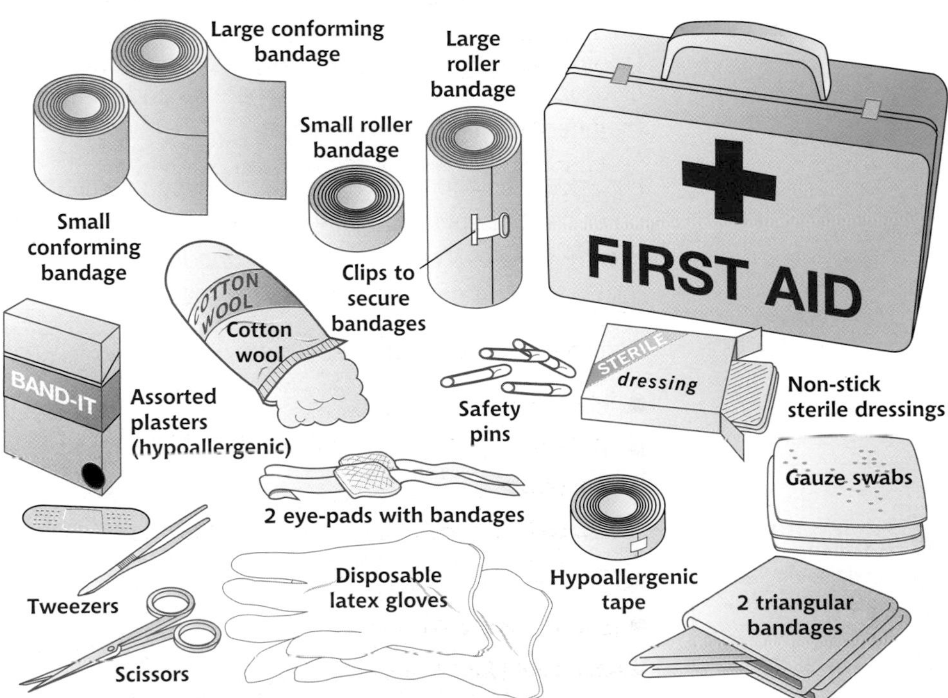

Figure 2.23
Some of the contents of a first aid box

Illness

Every early years setting has a policy and procedure for dealing with illness. It is important that you familiarise yourself with these. They will set out where children need to be taken (a separate room or screened area), who telephones a child's parents and when, and who telephones for medical advice or the emergency services. It will also cover the storage and administration of medicines.

As an early years practitioner, it is inevitable that you will from time to time have to deal with children who are unwell, with conditions ranging from minor sniffs and sniffles to the sudden onset of tummy upsets, childhood illnesses and more serious infections. It is important that you are able to recognise signs that may indicate an unwell child.

As well as crying, sitting quietly without interest in activities and the child clearly not being their usual self, signs of illness include:

- pallor – sickly pale skin tone
- fever – a raised temperature above 37.5°C
- rashes – spots, blisters and blemishes
- breathlessness – often associated with asthma and allergies.

Recognising common childhood illnesses

There are many common childhood illnesses; most last only a short period of time and, although they can be very unpleasant during the process, are not a cause for undue concern. Others, such as meningitis, are far more serious. Long-term consequences can result from some conditions, and the severity of illnesses such as measles, particularly in children who have not been immunised, should never be underestimated. By being able to identify some of the common conditions, you will help to prevent cross-infection of the condition. Prevention of cross-infection involves notifying parents and carers, and arranging to exclude the affected child from the setting.

For additional information on the following conditions, together with a range of other health issues, you may find it helpful to refer to the publication *Child Health: Care of the Child in Health and Illness* by A. Keene (see References and further reading on page 122).

Common childhood illnesses include:

- chickenpox
- rubella
- measles
- mumps
- hand, foot and mouth disease
- coughs and colds
- gastro-intestinal problems
- asthma.

remember

A serious condition that all early years workers should also know about is meningitis.

Chickenpox

What is chickenpox?

- Chickenpox is an itchy and highly contagious condition, which is spread by droplet infection (tiny droplets of moisture from the nose or mouth of another person).
- It causes spots that blister, weep and subsequently crust over.

What causes chickenpox?

- It is a viral infection called herpes zoster.
- The same virus can cause shingles in adults who have previously had chickenpox, if they are exposed to the virus a second time.

Recognising chickenpox

- Spots appear in groups, initially on the torso and then more 'groups' of spots appear anywhere on the body over several days.
- The spots turn into fluid-filled blisters, which weep and then dry after about three days.
- As the spots appear in successive groups, they will also dry up in successive groups.

Initial actions

- Comfort and reassurance are needed.
- If the initial spots appear in a day care setting, the child's parents must be contacted.
- Paracetamol is usually given to reduce the discomfort.
- Antihistamines can be useful in reducing the irritation.
- Calamine (or similar) lotion can be applied to the spots to soothe them.
- Using bicarbonate of soda in a cool bath can also help reduce the itching.

NB Paracetamol, which is given for a range of childhood illnesses, should only be given when necessary and by approved staff. If the child is allergic to it, advice must be sought regarding an alternative.

Ongoing care

- Paracetamol is usually given as needed, for example to reduce a raised temperature.
- Calamine and bicarbonate of soda may be used over a few days.
- Ensure the child has plenty of fluids and is kept comfortable.
- Cut fingernails short to avoid scratching.
- In young babies, cotton mittens can be useful.

Possible complications

- Some children have internal spots (e.g. in the nostrils, throat, vagina, anus).
- Secondary infections can occur through scratching.

- Encephalitis (inflammation of the brain) is rare but serious.
- Pneumonia (inflammation of the lungs) is also rare but serious.

Immunisation

- None is available at present, but a vaccine is currently being developed.
- It is important that pregnant women and children and adults with a reduced immunity due to conditions such as leukaemia or HIV are not exposed to the chickenpox virus.

Incubation period and potential to infect others

- The incubation period for chickenpox can be up to 21 days.
- Children are infectious for about three days prior to the first spots appearing.
- They remain infectious until all the scabs have dried over.

Rubella (German measles)

What is rubella?

- Rubella is usually only a mild condition in children.
- It involves a high temperature and an all-over rash.

What causes rubella?

- Rubella is a virus.
- It is passed on through droplet infection.

Recognising rubella

- The appearance of the rash is usually preceded by a raised temperature.
- The all-over pale rash, which usually starts on the face, does not itch.
- Glands are often swollen behind the ears and in the neck.

Initial actions

- Give paracetamol to reduce the temperature.
- Drinking plenty of fluids should be encouraged.

Ongoing care

- Avoid contact with women who are or could be pregnant because contact during the first 12 weeks can affect the foetus.
- No other special care is needed, and children usually recover quickly.

Possible complications

- In children and adults there are unlikely to be complications.
- For an infected foetus, complications can include:
    - loss of hearing or vision
    - impaired hearing or vision
    - heart deformities
    - learning difficulties.

Immunisation

Rubella vaccine is given as part of the MMR triple vaccine at the ages of 15 months and at four years.

Incubation period and potential to infect others

- The incubation period for rubella is 14–21 days.
- Children are infectious from about seven days prior to the rash appearing and until four to five days afterwards.

Measles

What is measles?

- Measles is a highly contagious virus with a distinctive rash.
- It can be a very serious condition.

What causes measles?

The virus is passed through droplet infection.

Recognising measles

- Children usually appear unwell for three to four days before the rash appears.
- Runny nose and general cold symptoms are common.
- The rash is dense, blotchy and red, usually starting on the neck and face before spreading down over the whole body.
- White spots form inside the mouth, on the cheeks (Koplik's spots).
- Eyes become sore and an avoidance of bright lights is common.

Initial actions

- Paracetamol should be given to reduce the raised temperature.
- Plenty of fluids should be encouraged.
- Children would only be visited by a GP in exceptional circumstances, but in most health authorities the child will usually be seen by a health visitor to confirm diagnosis and, if necessary, refer the child to the GP.
- Children will normally be most comfortable resting with curtains closed to reduce the light.

Ongoing care

- Give paracetamol as necessary.
- Maintain high fluid intake.

Possible complications

- Eye infections may need antibiotics.
- Ear infections may need antibiotics.
- Hearing needs to be checked within a few weeks of illness if ears were affected.
- Inflammation of the brain can occur (encephalitis).

Immunisation
Measles vaccine is given as part of the MMR triple vaccine at the ages of 15 months and at four years.

Incubation period and potential to infect others
- The incubation period for measles is eight to 14 days.
- Children are infectious from the day before the symptoms appear until four to five days afterwards.

Mumps

What is mumps?
- Mumps is an inflammation of the salivary glands, which are found in front of and below the ears.
- It can be a very painful condition.

What causes mumps and how is it spread?
- It is caused by a virus.
- It is spread by droplet infection.

Recognising mumps
- Initially children feel unwell for two or three days before the swelling occurs.
- Swelling and tenderness occur on either or both sides of the face.
- A raised temperature is usual.
- Earache is common.
- Eating and drinking can cause pain due to restricted movement of the jaw.

Initial actions
- Give paracetamol to reduce the temperature.
- Encourage the child to drink plenty of fluids (using a straw might be helpful).

Ongoing care
- Paracetamol given shortly before meals will help pain when eating.
- Easy-to-eat foods should be offered such as soup, jelly or stewed fruits.

Possible complications
- Hearing loss or even deafness can occur.
- Meningitis (inflammation of the meninges) can occur.
- Orchitis (inflammation of the testes) is a possible complication but is unusual in young children.

Immunisation
- Mumps vaccine is given as part of the MMR triple vaccine at 15 months and at four years.
- Having the condition provides the body with natural immunity.

Incubation period and potential to infect others

- The incubation period for mumps is 14 to 21 days.
- Children continue to be infectious for several days after the symptoms have appeared.

Hand, foot and mouth disease

What is hand, foot and mouth?

- This is a mild, but highly infectious condition, which is common in children of pre-school age.
- It is in no way connected to foot and mouth disease found in cattle and other hoofed animals.

What causes hand, foot and mouth?

- It is a viral condition spread by droplet infection.
- The virus is called Coxsackie.

Recognising hand, foot and mouth

- A child's temperature may be raised slightly.
- Very small blisters are often found inside the cheeks; these may ulcerate.
- Blistery spots with a red surrounding edge appear about two days after the mouth blisters on hands and fingers, and tops of feet.

Initial actions

- Give paracetamol to reduce the raised temperature.
- Give plenty of fluids; avoid anything that might irritate the sore mouth.
- Foods suitable for a slightly sore mouth should be offered.

Ongoing care

Prolonged mouth blisters may require an appointment with the GP.

Possible complications

No real complications noted.

Immunisation

There is no immunisation available for hand, foot and mouth disease.

Incubation period and potential to infect others

There is no known incubation period.

case study 2.2 Russell

Russell is six and is in the Year 2 class at your placement. He was not his usual bright and cheerful self this morning and was less active at playtime than he is usually. Russell is now running a raised temperature and has a pale rash on his face. He says that his ears hurt and his neck feels lumpy.

activity INDIVIDUAL WORK

(a) What do you think might be wrong with Russell?

(b) How should he be cared for?

(c) Might there be any long-term health problems linked to Russell's illness?

(d) If yes, what might they be?

Coughs and colds

What are coughs and colds?

- Coughs and colds can vary from the very mild to quite severe.
- They can be highly contagious.

What causes coughs and colds?

- Coughs and colds are caused by viral infections.
- They are passed through droplet infection.
- Coughs can also be part of another condition, such as bronchitis or pneumonia.

Recognising coughs and colds

- Colds usually start with a raised temperature and runny nose and eyes.
- Accompanying coughs can be dry and ticklish, or deep and chesty.

Initial actions

- Give paracetamol to reduce the raised temperature.
- Plenty of fluids should be offered.

Ongoing care

Continue paracetamol as necessary.

Possible complications

- Ear infections may require antibiotics.
- Chest infections may require antibiotics.

Immunisation

There is no immunisation for the common cold.

Incubation period and potential to infect others

Each cold virus is unique and so there is no known incubation period.

Gastro-enteritis

What is gastro-enteritis (vomiting and diarrhoea)?

Gastro-enteritis is the most common irritant of the stomach and intestinal lining.

What causes gastro-enteritis?

- It is caused by bacteria and viruses.
- It can be passed on in food due to poor hygiene during food handling.
- It can be passed by direct or indirect contact.

Recognising gastro-enteritis

Children appear unwell, lethargic and miserable before the onset of the main symptoms, which include:

- vomiting
- diarrhoea
- raised temperature
- loss of appetite.

Initial actions

- Only clear fluids (cooled boiled water) should be given for 24 hours.
- Re-hydration drinks may be used for children over the age of one year, particularly if symptoms are severe.

Ongoing care

- Breastfed babies should continue to breastfeed as usual.
- If there is no improvement, medical advice should be sought, particularly for very young children.
- Continue with clear fluids, together with 'ice-pops' to give the child some sugar.
- Light foods should be offered when appetite returns.
- Diet drinks are not considered to be suitable for children.

keyword

Dehydration
State in which the water content of the body falls dangerously low.

Possible complications

- **Dehydration** can easily occur in very young children and babies.
- If children cease to pass urine frequently, medical advice should be sought.
- Intravenous fluids may need to be given in severe cases.

Immunisation

There is no immunisation available.

Incubation period and potential to infect others

- Strict hygiene is needed to try and minimise the spread of infection.
- Gastro-enteritis often 'sweeps' through families, nurseries and schools.

Asthma

What is asthma?

Asthma is a condition of the lungs.

What causes asthma?

It is a narrowing of the airways that can be caused by a variety of 'triggers', for example:

- infections
- going out into the cold air
- cigarette smoke
- exercise.

Recognising an asthma attack

There may be:

- coughing
- shortness of breath
- wheezing
- a tightness in the chest area.

Initial actions

- It is important to keep calm in order to encourage calm in the child.
- If is a child's first attack, seek medical help.

Managing an attack

Keene (1999) sets out a 10-point plan for managing an asthma attack:

1. Reassure the child.
2. Encourage relaxed breathing – slowly and deeply.
3. Loosen tight clothing around the neck.
4. Sit the child upright and leaning forward, supporting themselves with their hands in any comfortable position.
5. Stay with the child.
6. Give the child their bronchodilator to inhale if they are known asthmatics – dosage according to the GP's instructions.
7. Offer a warm drink to relieve dryness of the mouth.
8. Continue to comfort and reassure. Do not panic as this will increase the child's anxiety which will impair their breathing.
9. When the child has recovered from a minor attack they can resume quiet activities.
10. Report the attack to the parents when the child is collected. If the child is upset by the episode the parents should be contacted immediately.

An ambulance should be called if:

- It is the child's first attack.
- After five to 10 minutes there is no improvement in the child.
- The child becomes increasingly distressed and exhausted.
- Blueness of lips, mouth or face begins to occur.

Ongoing care

There are two different types of inhalers:

- Preventers contain medicines to reduce the swelling and mucus in the airways; they are usually in brown/orange inhalers and are used on a regular basis to prevent asthma attacks.
- Relievers contain medication that dilates the airways; they are usually in blue inhalers and are used to relieve symptoms of wheezing and coughing when an attack occurs or are used prior to exercise to prevent an attack.

Possible complications

Each year a small number of children die during an attack.

Immunisation

There is no immunisation available.

Incubation period and potential to infect others

Asthma cannot be passed on to others.

Meningitis

What is meningitis?

Meningitis is an inflammation of the protective covering of the brain and spinal cord (the meninges).

What causes meningitis and how is it spread?

- Meningitis can be caused by different organisms, and can be either viral or bacterial.
- Bacterial meningitis is always the more serious type.

Recognising meningitis

- Symptoms for both viral and bacterial meningitis are similar in the early stages.
- In babies, there is usually:
  - high temperature
  - drowsiness and irritability
  - vomiting
  - crying and restless
  - the fontanelles may bulge in a very young baby due to pressure inside the skull.

- In children, there is usually:
  - headache
  - vomiting
  - averting of eyes from the light (photophobia)
  - a stiff neck (the muscles become rigid making it difficult for the neck to be moved forward towards the chin).
- Of particularly importance is that:
  - In bacterial meningitis, the symptoms will rapidly increase and the child will quickly become very ill.
  - Septicaemia may develop (infection of the blood).
  - The septicaemia rash looks like bruising appearing.
  - The septicaemia rash is flat with dark, purple or pink spots.
  - The septicaemia rash does not fade or disappear when pressed (try this with a glass).
  - The development of the septicaemia rash is an extreme emergency.

Initial actions

- Always call an ambulance if meningitis is suspected or take the child to hospital yourself if this is quicker.
- Keep the child in a darkened room until emergency services arrive.
- Reassure the child as best you can and try to reduce their temperature.

Ongoing care

- Intravenous antibiotics will be given by doctor or hospital staff.
- A lumbar puncture (in which cerebrospinal fluid is taken from the spinal canal through a fine hollow needle) is carried out to check that the condition is meningitis, and to identify the correct type of the condition.

Possible complications

- There are not usually any complications with viral meningitis.
- Bacterial meningitis can cause deafness, brain damage, epilepsy and, in some cases, death.

Immunisation

- Vaccinations are only available against bacterial forms of meningitis.
- Haemophilus influenzae type b (Hib) and meningitis C vaccines are given to infants as part of the infant screening programme.
- Meningitis C vaccine is offered to teenagers and young adults who have not benefited from the introduction of the infant screening programme.

Incubation period and potential to infect others

- The incubation for meningitis can vary between two and 10 days.

At times, local communities are screened for signs of meningitis following an outbreak. This usually involves throat swabs and prophylactic antibiotics (used as a preventative measure). On occasions, schools, pre-schools, etc. may close temporarily to avoid further risk of infection.

The immunisation programme

The most effective way of reducing the incidence of many childhood illnesses is through the immunisation programme. It needs the majority of children to be immunised for the various illnesses to be kept at a minimal level. From time to time parents become scared by articles in the media, and concerns raised by health professionals about certain immunisations, and this can cause a drop in uptake of the vaccines and therefore an increase in incidence of the illnesses concerned. This happened with the MMR vaccination in the late 1990s.

The current immunisation programme is given in Table 2.7. Each vaccination is given as a single injection into the muscle of the tight or upper arm.

Table 2.7 The immunisation programme

When to immunise	Diseases protected against	Vaccine given
Two months old	Diphtheria, tetanus, pertussis (whooping cough), polio and *Haemophilus influenzae* type b (Hib) Pneumococcal infection	DTaP/IPV/Hib and Pneumococcal conjugate vaccine (PCV)
Three months old	Diphtheria, tetanus, pertussis, polio and *Haemophilus influenzae* type b (Hib) Meningitis C (meningococcal group C)	DTaP/IPV/Hib and MenC
Four months old	Diphtheria, tetanus, pertussis, polio and *Haemophilus influenzae* type b (Hib) Meningitis C Pneumococcal infection	DTaP/IPV/Hib MenC and PCV
Around 12 months	Haemophilus influenza type b (Hib) and meningitis C	Hib/MenC
Around 13 months	Measles, mumps and rubella (German measles) Pneumococcal infection	MMR and PCV
Three years four months to five years old	Diphtheria, tetanus, pertussis and polio Measles, mumps and rubella	DTaP/IPV or dTaP/IPV and MMR
Thirteen to eighteen years old	Tetanus, diphtheria and polio	Td/IPV

Source: Department of Health, Crown copyright 2006.

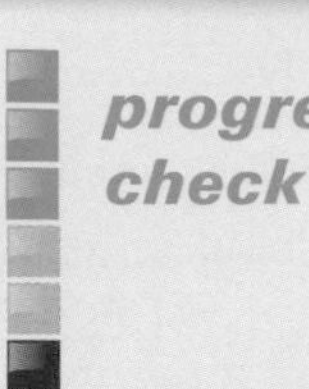

progress check

1. Explain what is meant by good hygiene practice.
2. What does HASAWA stand for and what is its purpose?
3. What does RIDDOR stand for and when is it needed?
4. What does COSHH stand for? Give an example of something that COSHH would cover.
5. What is meant by the term 'abuse'?
6. State examples of the signs and symptoms that can indicate abuse.
7. What is an emergency protection order?
8. Who might be involved in a Local Safeguarding Children Board (LSCB)?
9. When and how is a child protection register used?
10. Explain the ABC resuscitation procedure.
11. How would you identify chickenpox?
12. How would you identify measles?
13. How would you help a child who is having an asthma attack?
14. How would you check for the meningitis septicaemia rash?
15. When is the MMR immunisation given and what does it protect children against?

References and suggested further reading

Children Act 1989 Guidance and Regulations, Volume 2, 7th impression, 1998. The Stationery Office, London.

Dare, A. and O'Donovan, M. (2000) *Good Practice in Child Safety*. Nelson Thornes, Cheltenham.

DfES (2003) *National Standards for Under Eights Day Care and Childminding*. DfES/DWP, Nottingham.

Green, S. (2007) *BTEC National Children's Care, Learning and Development*. Nelson Thornes, Cheltenham.

Hobart, C. and Frankel, J. (2005) *Good Practice in Child Protection*. Nelson Thornes, Cheltenham.

Keene, A. (1999) *Child Health: Care of the Child in Health and Illness*. Nelson Thornes, Cheltenham.

Meadows, R. (1993) *ABC of Child Abuse*, 2nd edn. BMJ Publishing, London.

Parker, L. (2006) *How to Avoid Illness and Infection*. David Fulton Publishers, London.

Parker, L. (2006) *How to Do a Health and Safety Audit*. David Fulton Publishers, London.

Parker, L. (2006) *How to Keep Young Children Safe*. David Fulton Publishers, London

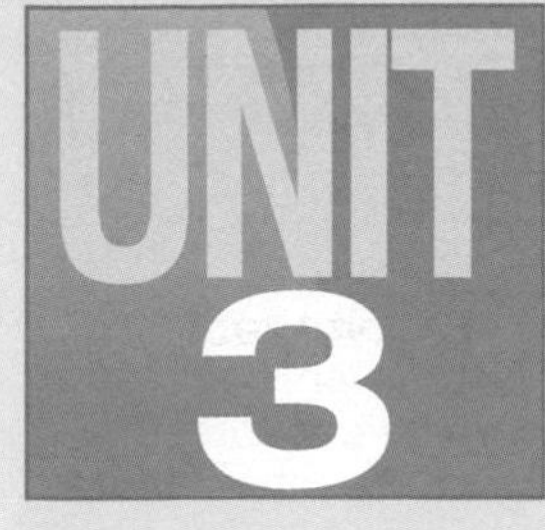

Communication with Children and Adults

This unit covers:

- understanding the key features of effective interpersonal communication
- understanding how to interact and communicate with children
- understanding how to interact and communicate with adults.

Communication involves the giving and receiving of information, both verbally and non-verbally. Effective communication is essential to building a positive relationship with children, colleagues and parents and is therefore central to good practice.

The unit starts by examining the features of effective communication, including how to impart information and how to listen effectively. You will learn about possible barriers to communication and how these can be overcome.

The development of a child's self-esteem can be affected by the way that carers interact with them; you will read about the importance of allowing children to express themselves and about the need to tailor your communications to the child's developmental stage.

Finally, the unit looks at ways of maintaining good communication with parents and how to overcome potential difficulties. As some of what you hear when working with children will be confidential, you will examine the implications of confidentiality for the early years setting and for you as a student.

grading criteria

To achieve a **Pass** grade the evidence must show that the learner is able to:	To achieve a **Merit** grade the evidence must show that the learner is able to:	To achieve a **Distinction** grade the evidence must show that the learner is able to:
P1 describe the key features of effective interpersonal communication	**M1** explain the key features in promoting effective communication and overcoming difficulties	**D1** evaluate the interactions/communications carried out with children and adults
P2 outline the difficulties that may arise in communication and how these may be overcome		

grading criteria

To achieve a **Pass** grade the evidence must show that the learner is able to:	To achieve a **Merit** grade the evidence must show that the learner is able to:	To achieve a **Distinction** grade the evidence must show that the learner is able to:
P3 describe how communication can be used to promote self-esteem	**M2** explain the differences and similarities between interacting and communicating with children and adults	**D2** justify the ways in which children were given encouragement to express themselves in the interactions undertaken
P4 demonstrate understanding of how to interact and communicate with children	**M3** explain how self-esteem can be promoted in interactions with adults and children	
P5 demonstrate understanding of how to interact and communicate with adults	**M4** explain why it is important to have a policy with respect to confidentiality and the sharing of information in a childcare setting	
P6 describe a policy in a childcare setting that concerns confidentiality and the sharing of information		

Understanding the key features of effective interpersonal communication

keyword

Interpersonal skills Communicating with others in a positive (with good skills) or negative (with bad skills) manner.

Communication The means of passing and receiving information.

Your ability to communicate is directly linked to your **interpersonal skills** (how good you are at getting on with other people and your sensitivity to their feelings and needs). An individual with good interpersonal skills is able to identify when **communication** is not effective, by noting the responses of the person with whom they are communicating, and is both willing and able to adjust their approach accordingly. This flexibility is important, as within all settings there is a variety of relationships both to develop and maintain.

Figure 3.1
Relationships within the setting

activity
3.1
INDIVIDUAL WORK

(a) Make a note of the different sorts of relationships that you might have with a parent, child or colleague.

(b) Note the main aspects of each relationship, for example your relationships as a team member.

(c) Each relationship will involve certain expectations. What might these be?

All families vary in structure and situation. You should be aware of any personal bias or preconceived ideas that you might have about families because this can have an impact on the way in which you interact with them. It is important that you work with families in a non-judgemental way, responding equally and positively to all, respecting their rights and ensuring that your attitude and use of language is always appropriate.

Professional Practice

- Parents are placing their child in your care. They will want to know that they can trust and rely on you.
- Other staff and outside professionals will expect a certain level of knowledge and understanding from you, together with practical skills relevant to your experience and training.
- Children will simply want you to be there for them, to play, interact, care for and take an interest in them.

keyword
Non-verbal communication The messages that are given through body language and facial expression.

Verbal and non-verbal behaviour

There can be both verbal and **non-verbal communication**.

Verbal communication

Communication differs according to the person with whom you are talking. The tone used when talking to a young baby will most likely be quite different from that used between you and your peers; and the length of a pause will differ according to the communication-skill level of the person with whom you are speaking.

Figure 3.2
Verbal communication

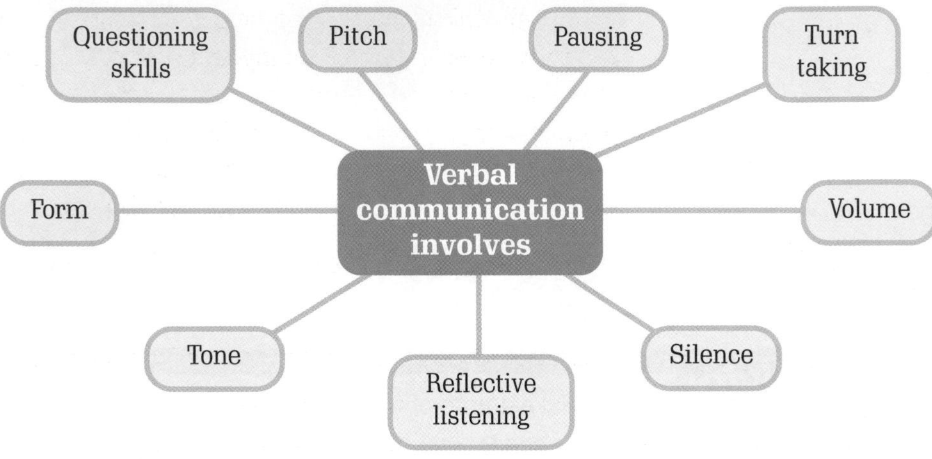

Refer to Unit 7, page 337, for information on 'motherese'.

Non-verbal communication

keyword
Custom Usual practice.

Non-verbal behaviour can tell us a great deal about how a person is feeling. It is important to remember that there are different cultural practices. For example, eye contact is an important aspect of communication for many people, but it is unacceptable between some people within some cultures. Whenever possible, research the **customs** of all the children in your care to ensure that you do not offend or cause embarrassment.

Figure 3.3
Non-verbal communication

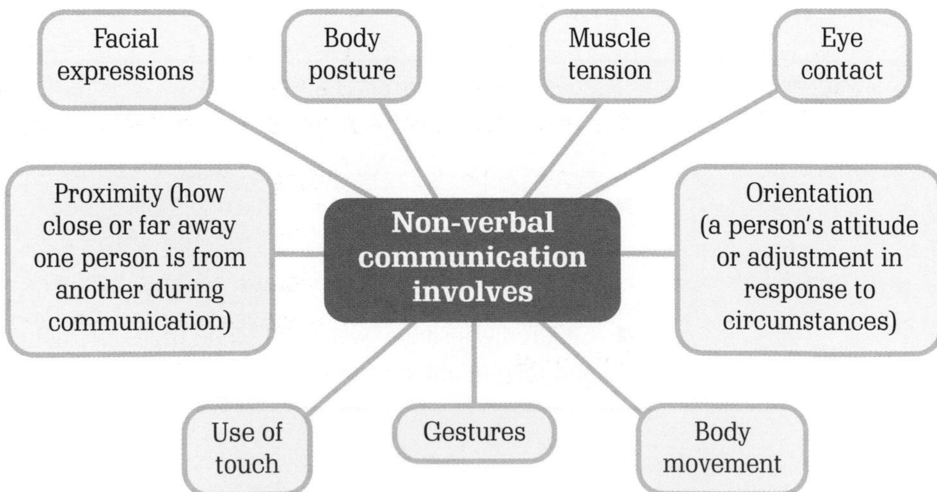

remember
A cultural 'norm' may not be followed by all families within that culture.

activity 3.2 INDIVIDUAL WORK

(a) Look at Figure 3.3 and think how important each of these aspects of communication is to you.

(b) Which give information about how you feel when conversing with another person? Is this information likely to be positive or negative?

keyword
Listening skills Different ways of really listening.

remember
Most people feel uncomfortable if someone, particularly someone they do not know very well, sits or stands too close to them during conversation. Being touched can be of comfort to one person but quite invasive and distressing to another.

Listening skills

Good communication skills can help you to support others. You will need to be able to listen well, to write clearly and concisely and to speak clearly and at an appropriate level. **Listening skills** are important. Listening involves taking in a range of different sorts of information. It is not the same as simply 'hearing' (as when listening to music); you need to *take in* the information and perhaps act upon it. In an early years setting, you will listen to:

- children telling you their news
- children asking for help
- children sharing their experiences of activities with you
- children explaining their problems
- parents giving you important information about feeds, diet, health, etc.
- parents confiding in you about family issues that may affect their child
- colleagues explaining things to you, for example a change to the routine
- colleagues passing on new thinking and ideas
- colleagues updating you through in-house training
- outside professionals, for example a Portage worker, giving you guidance on how to help a particular child.

Refer to Unit 8, page 371, to find out about the role of a Portage worker.

keyword
Active listening Ensuring that you are focusing on what you are listening to.

Active listening

Often referred to as paraphrasing, **active listening** involves summarising what has been said to you. It is an easy way of checking that you have heard correctly and understood fully. A response would start with statements such as:

- 'Would I be right in thinking …?'
- 'So what you are telling me is …?'

This checks that you have understood what has been said to you and also shows the speaker that you have been listening carefully and that you value what they are saying.

At times you may need to write down what has been said to you. This could be in the case of an accident or an accusation of injury or abuse. It is important that what you write is factual. It is inappropriate to add in what you 'think they meant'. This again emphasises why it is so important that you concentrate and use active listening skills. They will aid your ability to remember too.

Reflective listening

This form of communication is more about showing the other person that you understand what they are feeling, rather than the details of what they are actually saying. Your response might be something like:

- 'I can tell you are very cross about it.'
- 'That must have made you very sad.'

Reflective listening is linked to empathy and support for an individual's distress.

> *keyword*
> **Reflective listening**
> Where the listener echoes the last (or most significant) words spoken by the speaker.

Communication difficulties

Difficulties can arise when two people wishing or needing to communicate do not have the same level of communication skills, or do not use the same language. Communication can also be affected by distractions within the immediate environment. The following section provides information on different language systems that can be used to overcome some communication difficulties.

Signed language

> *keyword*
> **Signed language**
> Forms of language in which signs replace speech.

Signed language often involves facial, hand and body movements and is used by deaf people, those whose hearing is impaired, people with certain forms of disability and by many people communicating with them. There are a number of different forms of sign language, and each is a language in its own right. Each language has its own rules with regard to grammar and how words are put together. Examples include:

- sign language
- Makaton
- Bliss symbols
- cued speech
- Braille
- PECS (Pictorial Exchange Communication System).

Sign language

Figure 3.4
The standard manual alphabet: each of the letters is represented by different hand positions

Bliss symbols

These form 'a universal language of pictographic symbols, which is used by people with reading and writing disabilities' (Mukherji and O'Dea, 2000).

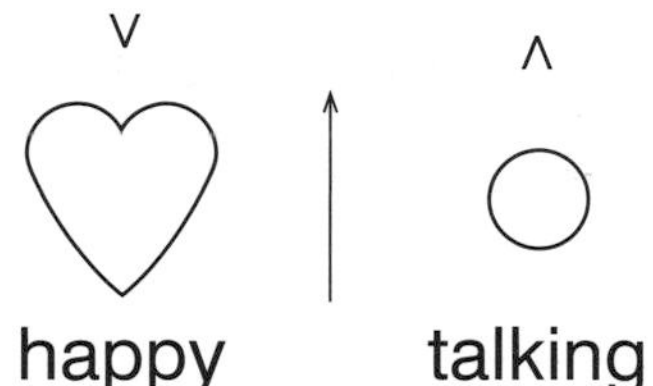

Figure 3.5
Bliss symbols: each child using this system has their own chart of the symbols that they wish to use

Makaton

This is 'a basic signing system using signs borrowed from British sign language; it is used by people who have severe learning difficulties' (Mukherji and O'Dea, 2000).

Figure 3.6
Makaton signs: a system used by many children and adults who have communication difficulties

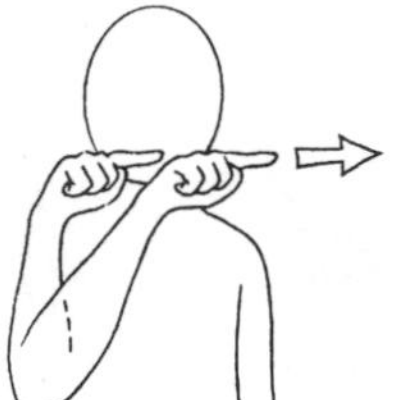

boy
Brush right index pointing left across chin

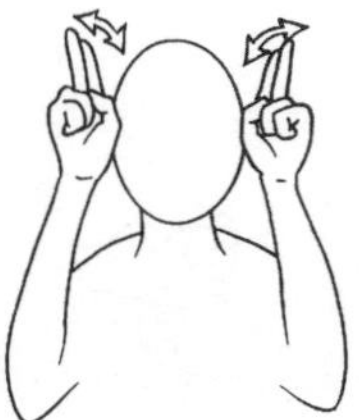

rabbit
Palm forward 'N' hands, held at either side of head, bend several times to indicate ears

fish
Right flat hand waggles forward like a fish swimming

bird
Index finger and thumb open and close in front of mouth like a beak

Braille

Braille is 'a touch-based reading and writing system used by people who are blind' (Mukherji and O'Dea, 2000).

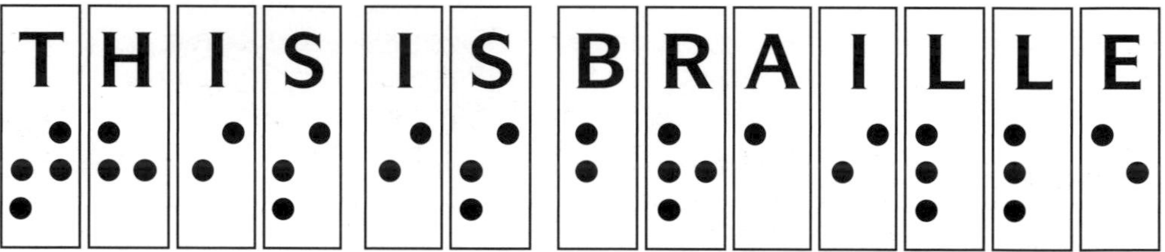

Figure 3.7
Braille is a system of letters made from raised dots

Cued speech

Cued speech is 'a system of eight hand shapes made in four locations near the face to assist children (or adults), who are deaf, in lip-reading' (Mukherji and O'Dea, 2000).

Picture Exchange Communication System (PECS)

Initially, this system uses pictures of items of specific interest to the child, for example preferred foods, toys and activities. The child is encouraged to select a picture and hand it to the adult to indicate their request. Each picture is backed with a Velcro fastening and can be placed on a picture exchange board.

As the child's ability to communicate using this system develops, the adult introduces pictures to assist in the building up of sentence structures, and the child selects pictures from a board, locates the adult and hands the pictures or requests to the adult.

case study 3.1 Declan

Declan is five years old and has just started to attend the reception class of Hollybank Primary School, having attended a pre-school for two mornings each week. He lives with his parents, who are both deaf, and can sign competently. Declan speaks very little, as his world has tended to be very quiet up until now.

activity
INDIVIDUAL WORK

(a) How might Declan benefit from being in school full time?

(b) How important will it be for staff to encourage Declan to continue his signing as he develops his speech?

(c) What creative activities do you consider will be of particular benefit to Declan?

keyword

Barrier to communication Any obstruction to understanding between individuals.

Overcoming barriers

Barriers to effective communication

At times, communication fails because something gets in the way. A **barrier to communication** is anything that causes an obstruction or prevents the progress of communication. This can include any of the items shown in Figure 3.8.

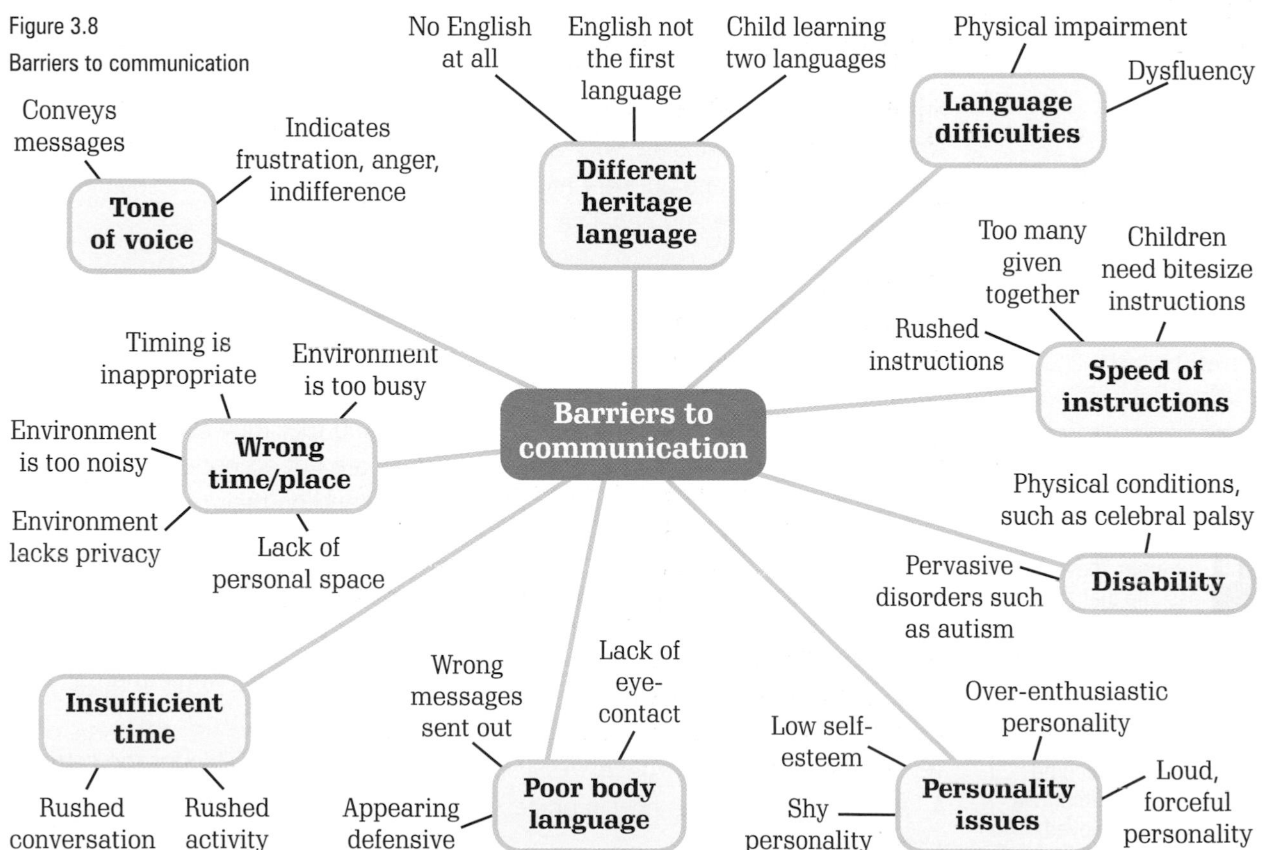

Figure 3.8
Barriers to communication

activity 3.3 GROUP WORK

(a) In a small group, discuss all the barriers to effective communication listed in the spidergram above.

(b) How could you help eliminate each barrier or alleviate its effects?

keyword

Self-esteem
Feeling good about oneself, feeling confident.

Promotion of self-esteem

As an early years worker, it is necessary for you to understand that how you respond to children will affect the development of their **self-esteem**. What we think and feel about someone can be expressed through our actions towards them, for example showing sympathy to someone who is crying suggests that we care about them. Conversely, we are affected by the actions of others towards us, for example we feel pride when our achievements are praised by another person. Responding positively to a child will enhance the development of their self-esteem.

Self-esteem and self-worth

Each of us is happiest when we are feeling good about ourselves. This involves having a good opinion of one's self as a person, feeling that we are admired, respected and valued by others, and being satisfied that we are achieving what we want to achieve. Simply put, self-esteem and self-worth are about liking who we are. This is equally important for children; liking who they are is important to their emotional security and therefore their subsequent development. They need to know that they are liked by other children, and they need the social approval of friends and playmates. As they move into primary school, the need for the approval of their same-sex peers is particularly strong, because this is the stage when such relationships are very important to them. Older children need to feel 'part of the group' and are very much influenced by their peers. These influences can be both positive and negative.

Belonging

Children need to feel that they belong. This applies both at home and in social situations outside the home. Children need the unquestioning love of their family; security comes from knowing that whatever happens they will still be loved. They need to know that they are accepted and that they fit in with their peers. If a child is not accepted, or feels that they are not accepted, it can have a negative impact on both their emotional security and on their behaviour. This can be seen in many ways. For example:

1. A child with low self-esteem will often give up on a task sooner than other children, as they assume that they cannot achieve it.
2. This 'lack of achievement' can lead to disruptive behaviour within the nursery or classroom.
3. The behaviour is declared unacceptable by the staff responsible for the setting.
4. A continuous cycle is now in process, and this will lower the child's self-esteem still further.

remember

If a child feels that they are not listened to or are not valued by the adults caring for them, they will assume that they are of less value than others and may well cease to try and build relationships or enter conversations. They can become isolated, withdrawn and feel unloved.

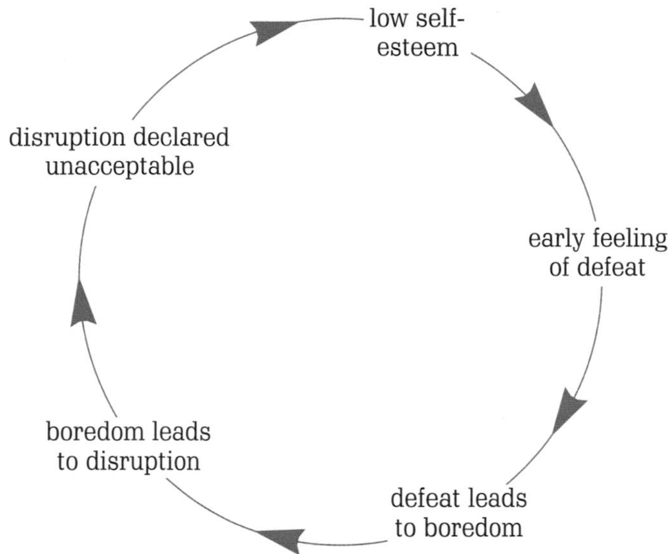

Figure 3.9
The self-esteem cycle

activity 3.4 INDIVIDUAL WORK

(a) Can you think of any examples from your work experience to fit the cycle above?

(b) Where did these happen?

(c) How were they dealt with?

To ensure that children feel valued and to maintain (or develop) a good sense of self-esteem, it is important to provide plenty of opportunities to learn through 'no fail' activities, such as sand and water play, and creativity. It can also be achieved by encouraging manageable tasks and challenges appropriate to the child's age and stage of development. Whenever possible, children should be encouraged, and enabled, to be independent, to make decisions, however small, and to take on appropriate responsibilities. This all helps them to feel competent and valued, thereby increasing their self-esteem.

Understanding how to interact and communicate with children

The age and stage of development of the child or children with whom you are working will help determine how you approach your interactions with them. When working with the under-threes, you will need to ensure that your speech is clear, vocabulary is simple, and that sentences or requests are short and include easily understood terms. Repetition will be needed as will praise for showing understanding.

As children move through the developmental stages, you can expect them to understand more. Therefore, the breadth of vocabulary that you use will increase, and the number and complexity of requests and instructions can be expanded. You will, of course, still need to clarify points, or ask questions when you do not fully understand something that the child has said. This should be done sensitively.

remember
Giving people your full attention when they are talking is good manners, as well as common sense.

Giving attention

Giving children your full attention is part of your role as a professional childcarer. It shows that you value them as individuals and respect them and their views, which will boost their self-esteem. When working with older age ranges, it is important to ensure that you do not treat children and young people as uninformed or talk down to them.

activity 3.5 GROUP WORK

(a) Refer back to the 'Barriers to communication' diagram on page 131. Make links between aspects of that illustration and the following age ranges:

0–3 years

3–7 years

7–12 years

12–16 years.

(b) Using the subheadings listed on the diagram to assist you, how differently would you communicate with each age range to:

(i) give an instruction?

(ii) raise a concern about their behaviour?

(iii) make a request of them?

(iv) help alleviate their distress?

You will find that both active and reflective listening skills will help you in the situations above. Refer back to pages 127–128 to remind yourself of these important skills.

Activities to encourage communication and language

With young children, communication and language can be encouraged through almost every activity offered, as describing, encouraging, explaining and giving praise are all part of daily life at home, in nurseries, pre-schools and primary schools. Activities that particularly encourage communication and language are likely to include:

Figure 3.10
Activities to encourage communication

activity 3.6 INDIVIDUAL WORK

(a) Using the following terms, identify which you would associate with the activities named in the spidergram:

(i) involves description
(ii) encourages sharing
(iii) prompts making requests
(iv) necessitates making decisions
(v) involves making choices
(vi) necessitates taking turns
(vii) encourages joint planning and interactions
(viii) involves taking the views of others into consideration
(ix) encourages the use of wider vocabulary
(x) involves pitch, volume and tone
(xi) involves gesture and body language
(xii) involves rhythm
(xiii) encourages listening skills.

(b) What else could you add?

When working with older children and young people, there will be a range of other activities to include, such as drama, reviews of television, plays, concerts, etc.

For more on play activities and how they relate to development, refer to Unit 6, page 203.

activity 3.7 INDIVIDUAL WORK

What other activities can you think of?

Communicating clearly

When you talk to a child or group of children, it is important that your language is appropriate for their age and stage of development. The tone of your voice should convey the same message as the words that you are using. Children can be confused if your words are saying yes, but the tone of your voice indicates no. Any stress or anxiety that you are feeling should not be passed on to the children with whom you are working. Clear communication is particularly important when working with children who have limited English and are perhaps learning English as a second or additional language. They will benefit from learning this new language within context, where words and phrases are emphasised at the appropriate time. For example:

- 'Here is your drink, Asif' – as you hand him a beaker at snack time.
- 'Let us put your coat on, Dipendra' – as you help him get ready for outside play.
- 'Shamilla, where is your shoe?' – as you help her dress to go home.

When working with a group of children who have different levels of understanding due to their age or ability, you should ensure that you are providing sufficient guidance and clarity for those with the less developed language skills, while offering appropriate stimulation and vocabulary extension to the older or more linguistically able children. This would often be referred to as working with a mixed-ability group. It is important that you constantly reflect on your own speech, paying attention to grammar and avoiding slang.

case study 3.2

Stephanie

Pre-school leader Heather asks her early years student, Stephanie, to organise the children for going out to play in the garden. Stephanie gets the children's attention and gives them the following instructions:

'It is time to go out and play now. You can each take a ball or a hoop or a beanbag out with you. It is very cold, so please put on your coats and do up the buttons. If you need help, please ask. If you have a hat or a scarf or mittens, you must put them on. Please check that your shoes are done up properly so that you do not trip. If you need the toilet, go now before you go outside.'

activity
INDIVIDUAL WORK

(a) How did Stephanie do?

(b) How many instructions were there?

(c) Do you think that the children will have responded to all the instructions? If no, why not?

(d) How could you have improved upon Stephanie's instructions?

remember

Don't issue too many instructions at once, as children won't remember, especially if they are excited.

Children will focus on the most obvious or most exciting thing that they hear. In this case, going outside to play or taking a resource with them. It is unlikely that they will have taken in many of Stephanie's instructions. She ought to have broken the instructions down into smaller 'groups' or, preferably, given them one instruction at a time. For example, 'Please get your coats on', then 'Who has got a hat or scarf?' and so on.

Enabling children to express themselves

Particularly when you are working with children in the older age ranges, whether as individuals or as a group, there are likely to be times when they wish to raise concerns, make suggestions or challenge authority. As in one-to-one and group situations with younger children, it is important that young people feel that their views are valued, and that they are listened to by the adults working with them. Having a forum through which they can be heard will be very important to them. It may at times be appropriate to have regular discussion sessions or meetings where views, concerns and grievances can be aired, and ideas can be put forward and considered.

The communication skills of many older children and young people will still need to develop and be refined, and your understanding of the difference between being assertive and being aggressive will help you to guide them, both by your own example and by what you say to them.

See Unit 5, page 177, for guidance on dealing with conflict and the difference between being assertive and being aggressive.

activity
3.8
INDIVIDUAL WORK

Think back to an occasion when you have been part of a group wanting to be heard by the adults responsible for you. This could have been at school or during time at a play scheme, youth group, etc.

(a) What happened?

(b) How well was your voice heard?

(c) How did you feel?

'Circle time' offers younger children the chance to speak and be listened to, as only one child speaks at a time, usually whilst holding a specific object, for example a teddy. This helps the shy child to feel more able to speak in front of others and helps the more outgoing child to learn how to wait, take turns and listen.

Understanding how to interact and communicate with adults

keyword
Partnership with parents
Active involvement of parents by the setting.

Appreciating that parents are partners in the care and education of their children has always been part of the ethos of a good early years setting. However, the Children Act 2004 made this the norm everywhere by including a directive for all settings to draw up a 'parents as partners' policy. Working in **partnership with parents** not only shows respect for the parents as the main carers of their children but also enables the most effective care of individual children to be put into place. If early years staff do not communicate with, ask questions of, and receive relevant information from children's parents, they will not be fully prepared to respond to children's individual needs, identify potential points of crisis for them, or have the awareness to help them to cope with new or worrying situations. Also, an understanding of cultural values and family needs is important, and should be respected within the boundaries of each setting's equal opportunities ethos.

remember
Parents are usually the people who know their child best. Early years settings play a supporting role in the child's care and development.

The *Special Educational Needs (SEN) Code of Practice* (DfEE, 2001) actively promotes working in partnership with parents. Involving parents in decisions about their child's education is seen as critical to achieving the most effective programme for any child, but it is particularly important if the child has an additional need. Again, good communication is crucial to fulfilling this need.

link
Refer to Unit 8, page 380, for more on the SEN Code of Practice.

Approaches

Understandably, parents new to an early years setting will worry about their child, particularly if it is the first time they have placed them into day care, and they need to know that they can trust the staff to care well for the child. Staff must take on the role of supporter, as well as carer, reassuring the parents that the child will receive a good standard of care and attention, offering opportunities for parents to check on their child's progress by telephone or other means when they feel that they need to, and keeping them fully informed of all relevant issues. This is part of building a positive relationship with parents.

Difficulties that can arise

Not all parents find it easy to interact with staff, and some may find it difficult to build up relationships with other parents linked to the setting. This can be for a variety of reasons. For example, parents may:

- be shy
- have low self-esteem and consider that others are not interested in what they do, or what they have to say
- not know what to say to people whom they do not know, naturally keeping to themselves
- have faced prejudice and discrimination in the past and therefore avoid new situations where they are unsure of how they will be regarded
- not have the language skills to interact easily with others
- feel socially excluded by others attending the setting
- lack the time to stop and chat, thereby missing out on opportunities to get to know people
- at times be embarrassed about the reason that their child attends the setting; perhaps they are attending on the direction of social services.

Parents' wishes

Caring for a child in a way that positively reflects parents' wishes can only be achieved if the care is based on good communication and interpersonal skills. The interpersonal skills that you will need involve an understanding of how your words, attitudes and actions are likely to be interpreted by the families with whom you work. This includes issues of discrimination, prejudice and stereotyping.

Refer to Unit 5, pages 179–185, and read about discrimination, prejudice, stereotyping and anti-discriminatory practice.

There will be times when you do not agree with a family's parenting methods, and you will be able to build a better relationship with some parents than you can with others. Not only is it important to remember that all parents have a right to the respect, time and interest of the staff who are caring for their child, but you should also remember that this applies to you as a student, too.

Communicating appropriately with parents

Appropriate communication involves:

- greeting parents warmly on arrival
- using appropriate forms of greeting
- using preferred names
- avoiding being too familiar
- key workers being available to parents on a regular basis (ideally daily)
- showing respect for all family members
- respecting issues of confidentiality and privacy
- respecting views and opinions
- giving equal time to all parents as needed

- giving your full attention
- using active and reflective listening, as appropriate
- using suitable methods of presenting information, i.e. verbal, written, visual
- ensuring that parents are informed of all procedures within the setting when they take up a place for their child
- keeping parents informed of their child's progress
- bringing to parents' attention specific areas of interest shown by their child
- sharing information with regard to a child's health.

The 'parents as partners' policy underpins all information exchanges. It should ensure that parents are kept informed about:

- admissions procedures
- administrative procedures
- health and safety procedures
- curriculum planning procedures
- assessment procedures
- complaints procedures.

remember Better relationships with parents will in turn help secure a safe and happy environment for the children.

Many settings also have regular parent surveys to help staff evaluate the quality of their provision for the children in their care.

Figure 3.11
Communicating with a parent

Professional Practice

- The importance of sharing information with parents that is accurate, relevant and presented in an appropriate manner cannot be over-emphasised. Information given should include personal contact, written material and visual material.
- Contact by telephone will also be necessary.

keyword
Communication cycle
A reciprocal form of passing and receiving information.

The communication cycle

The following diagram shows the **communication cycle**, in which we each in turn take the part of the 'encoder' (the person who sends the message) and the 'decoder' (the person who deciphers and therefore understands the message). During conversation, we continually swap roles from encoder to decoder, and, as the diagram demonstrates, the *common field of experience* is where the message is initially decoded. Without a common field, the message is likely to get lost or distorted, which would be like conversing with another person when there is no shared language between you.

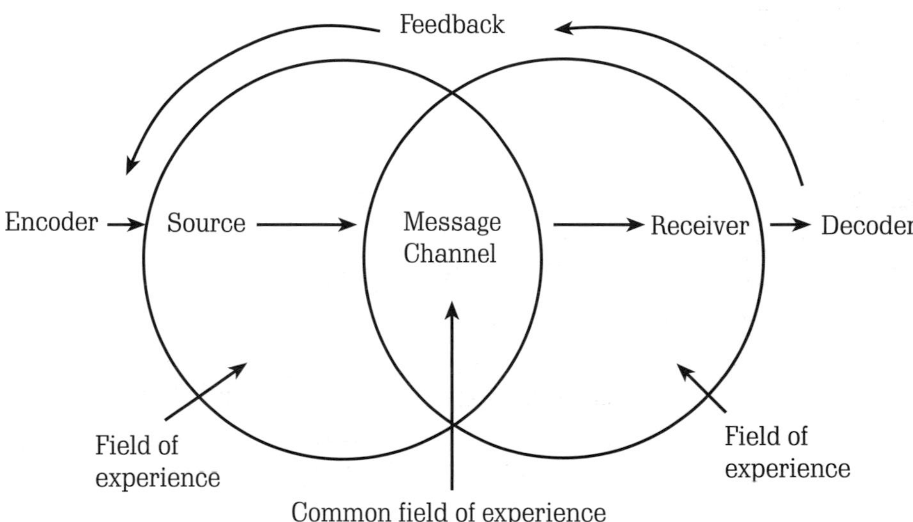

Figure 3.12
The communication cycle

For communication to work successfully, the message channel needs to be a common field of experience for both the encoder (the speaker) and the decoder (the listener).

Communication can fail because of:

- lack of vocabulary
- inability to speak, see or hear
- lack of listening skills
- inability to concentrate

- lack of knowledge
- lack of interest
- misinterpretation
- wrong (or confusing) body language/facial expression
- surrounding noises
- wrong timing/place/person.

Failing to communicate may make us feel:

- frustrated
- hurt
- angry
- misunderstood
- inadequate.

Coping with disagreements

From time to time, there will be differences of opinion between colleagues and between staff and parents.

See Unit 5, page 177, for an overview of how to deal with conflict.

activity 3.9 INDIVIDUAL WORK

Draw a blank 'communication cycle' and add text to show how a conversation in which you explain to a parent that their child has chickenpox could look.

Professional Practice

- You will need to find a suitable 'language' to enable you to communicate successfully with all the families with whom you work.
- Parents will have different levels of literacy skills, because of different heritage languages, limited education and, in some cases, learning difficulties. You should, therefore, find ways to provide parents with information in alternative formats appropriate to their needs.

Confidentiality

Within any organisation there will be a policy regarding confidentiality. The term used in connection with confidentiality is 'need to know'. This literally means that information on any individual child or adult should only be shared with those who *need* to know.

Confidentiality includes:

- respecting a family's privacy
- finding an appropriate place to speak to a parent when conversation is clearly of a sensitive nature
- working on a 'need-to-know' basis
- keeping parents informed of any concerns
- limiting access to children's records.

Professional Practice

- Confidentiality is an important aspect of being professional.
- You will be expected to be trustworthy and to keep to yourself any information that you are privy to.

When a child's welfare is of concern

If there is concern that a child is suffering abuse, or if their well-being is of general concern, information can be passed on to other professionals as is felt appropriate. This would be the role of the setting manager or the designated person for child protection. Parents would usually be informed that this has taken place.

At times, information may be given to you as an individual 'in secret' or 'in confidence' by a child or adult that you clearly should not keep to yourself: perhaps, for example, an abusive situation is disclosed to you. If you are ever in doubt about information you are given, or become aware of, talk to your placement supervisor or your course tutor.

Refer back to Unit 1, page 59 for more information on confidentiality.

Access to files

Each child will have a file within the setting, and parents have right of access to their child's file. This allows parents to see how and when their child has been observed and assessed, by whom, and any notes made about their development and progress. It is therefore important that staff back up any concerns they may have with evidence and talk to parents whenever they have a concern. It would be very inappropriate for a parent to find out about a staff member's unease about their child's development or behaviour by reading the child's file.

As part of a setting's commitment to confidentiality, access to files should be limited. Only staff needing access, the manager of the setting and the child's parents should be allowed to see a child's file.

Communication linked to the safety of children

At all times, the responsibility of every early years setting is to the safety of the children within its care. This includes acting upon any concerns relating to a child's safety and well-being when they leave the setting for home. A child protection policy, clarifying the procedures to be taken if there are any concerns, will help parents understand how the setting will act, when the setting will act, and why the setting will act, and should help maintain good communication.

When a referral has been made by the setting following concern about a child's safety or well-being, the relationship between staff and parents can come under strain. If a parent is the direct subject of the concern, there will most likely be embarrassment and awkwardness between staff and parent while any investigation takes place. If the parent had been unaware of the situation involving their child, or had felt powerless to stop the situation, again embarrassment is likely, together with deep distress.

Early years staff should remember that at times parents need help and support too. Staff can support parents by being a good role model in how they work with the children, demonstrating clearly the most appropriate ways of managing a child's behaviour, and by trying to maintain some form of communication with the child's parent, whatever the circumstances. A welcoming smile or a nod of acknowledgement will gradually encourage interaction to be resumed, as the parent feels more able to communicate directly again. If the referral came from the setting, the parents may well feel very hurt and angry with staff, especially if the concerns have been unfounded, and staff will need to absorb this anger as best they can. This highlights the importance of all parents being familiar with the setting's child protection policy and its implications if a concern is raised.

Once an unfounded concern has been cleared up, most parents will appreciate that staff were acting in the best interests of the child, and relationships will usually begin to heal.

To refresh your understanding of referral procedures in child protection, you may find it helpful to return to Unit 2, page 90; you may also wish to look at dealing with conflict in Unit 5, page 177.

remember

Children with unusual names can often be identified by their initials. For example, Zena Quigley (ZQ) would be more easily identified than Jasmine Smith, Jason Saunders or Jenny Sutton (all JS).

Confidentiality as a student

At times during your course of study, you will need to observe children and may make notes. You must have permission from your placement supervisor to do this. If these observations are then recorded into your portfolio or professional practice log, you must ensure that no child can be identified. Initials can be used if it helps you, but even these are often unnecessary.

case study 3.3 Denni

Denni is a student on placement at the Little Saplings pre-school. Another student in her group at college has told her that she saw a child from Little Saplings being smacked very hard by a man out in the street at the weekend. The little boy was cowering by the wall and sobbing.

activity
GROUP WORK

(a) Should Denni treat this just as gossip, or should she be concerned?

(b) If she is concerned, to whom should Denni talk about this?

Professional Practice

- Communication involves knowing when to speak, how to speak, what to say, and who to say it to.
- It is one of the most important aspects of being a professional working with people of all ages.

progress check

1. What are interpersonal skills?
2. Explain the difference between active listening and reflective listening.
3. What barriers to communication can you think of and how can they be overcome?
4. List at least three reasons why working in partnership with parents is important.
5. How could your interpersonal skills affect your relationships with parents?
6. Give as many examples as you can of how staff should communicate with parents.
7. What is the main benefit of good staff–parent relationships?
8. In what ways should settings present information to parents?
9. Give three examples of upholding confidentiality in an early years setting.
10. Why is it important for parents to be familiar with the setting's child protection policy?

References and suggested further reading

DfEE (2001) *Special Educational Needs (SEN) Code of Practice*. HMSO, London.

Green, S. (2007) *BTEC National Children's Care, Learning and Development*. Nelson Thornes, Cheltenham.

Hobart, C. and Frankel, J. (2003) *A Practical Guide to Childcare and Education Placements*. Nelson Thornes, Cheltenham.

Hobart, C. and Frankel, J. (2003) *A Practical Guide to Working with Parents*. Nelson Thornes, Cheltenham.

Mukherji, P. and O'Dea, T. (2000) *Understanding Children's Language and Literacy*. Nelson Thornes, Cheltenham.

Sadek, E. and Sadek, J. (1996) *Good Practice in Nursery Management*. Nelson Thornes, Cheltenham.

Whalley, M. (1994) *Learning to be Strong: Integrating Education and Care in Early Childhood*. Hodder & Stoughton, London.

Whalley, M. (1997) *Working with Parents as Partners in Education and Care*. Hodder & Stoughton, London.

Websites

www.capt.org.uk

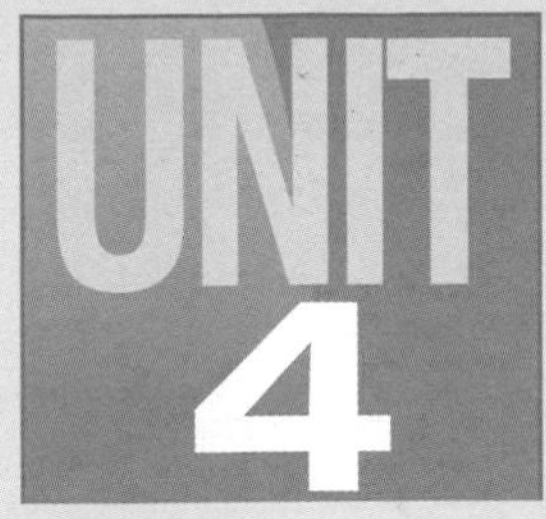

Preparing and Maintaining Environments for Childcare

This unit covers:

- knowing how to prepare and maintain the physical and play environment
- understanding how to prepare and maintain a stimulating environment
- understanding how to maintain an environment that builds children's confidence and resilience
- knowing how to support routines for children and integrate play.

The setting in which children are cared for should provide a warm, safe, secure environment where they are stimulated and stretched according to their age and stage of development, and where they are encouraged to explore, investigate, enjoy shared activities, and try new challenges and experiences.

This unit begins by looking at the preparation and maintenance of a suitable play environment, including relevant health and safety issues. It then examines the requirements for a stimulating environment containing features that will challenge children and help to build their self-confidence. Finally, the importance of providing a consistent and balanced routine and of integrating care routines and play is explained. The unit has links to several others.

grading criteria

To achieve a **Pass** grade the evidence must show that the learner is able to:	To achieve a **Merit** grade the evidence must show that the learner is able to:	To achieve a **Distinction** grade the evidence must show that the learner is able to:
P1 describe how all aspects of health and safety are ensured in children's environments	**M1** explain how all aspects of the physical and play environment should be prepared and maintained	**D1** justify the use of the senses in stimulating children's interest and involvement
P2 outline the steps needed in preparing and maintaining the physical and play environment;	**M2** explain how to ensure that the environment is stimulating for children	**D1** analyse the role of the environment and care routines in building children's confidence and resilience

grading criteria

To achieve a **Pass** grade the evidence must show that the learner is able to:	To achieve a **Merit** grade the evidence must show that the learner is able to:	To achieve a **Distinction** grade the evidence must show that the learner is able to:
P3 describe how to prepare and maintain a stimulating environment	**M3** explain the important elements of maintaining an environment that builds children's confidence and resilience	
P4 describe how to maintain an environment that builds children's confidence and resilience	**M4** explain how play can be integrated into all care routines	
P5 describe the basic nutritional needs of children and the provision of food and drink		
P6 outline how to support care routines and integrate play into routines		

Knowing how to prepare and maintain the physical and play environment

Health and safety

Risk assessment plays an important part in maintaining a healthy and safe environment; it enables potential risks and hazards to be identified. As no two environments will be the same, because their layout, fittings and resources will vary, there will be different risks in every environment. The level of risk will also be affected by the age range of the children being cared for in the setting.

activity
4.1 INDIVIDUAL THEN PAIR WORK

(a) Think of three examples of something that would be a potential risk to a baby or toddler but which would be less likely to be of risk in a setting where older children are cared for.

(b) Compare your examples with another student's.

Figure 4.1
Risk assessment document

A risk assessment

A risk assessment helps to minimise accidents and incidents through making checks in advance of children arriving, during a session where appropriate, and at the end of each session. Following any incident, the setting should re-evaluate the potential risks pertaining to its activities, resources and layout. Sometimes a potential risk can be removed simply by moving the object or activity to a different place.

Each setting needs to identify:

- who will be responsible for carrying out the inital risk assessment
- who will draw up the risk assessment document and where it will be kept
- who will have responsibility for safety in each specific area or situation, making the checks as directed by the risk assessment document.

Potential hazards that may be found within a setting include:

- doors, windows, gates
- furniture and flooring
- stairs
- safety of toys and resources
- hot water
- electric sockets and appliances.

No setting will be completely risk free. Children are often unpredictable and also like to climb, explore and investigate. Look around your current placement and try to identify as many potential hazards as you can:

(a) inside

(b) outside.

Hazards should always be considered in relation to the specific children being cared for; their age, stage of development and any special need that they might have must be taken into account. As new children join the setting, it is important that their individual needs are added into the risk consideration.

When conducting the risk assessment, it is important to be aware that there may be other users of the facility and that the nature of that other use could introduce additional risk. For example, it is possible that pins or needles might be left behind by a sewing group that uses the village hall where a pre-school group meets. Such items would be hazardous to the children in the pre-school group.

Use of space

When setting out a room for young children, there are a number of points to consider.

- The numbers of children being cared for in the room and the children's ages should be taken into account. Babies need a clear crawling space.
- The space requirements set out by the regulatory bodies should be adhered to at all times. These are set out as a minimum.
- Furniture should be positioned safely, providing appropriate space for each activity taking place, whilst still allowing room for moving around.
- Children with mobility problems should also be able to move around easily.
- Staff should be able to 'keep an eye' on the room as a whole, with no areas left totally secluded.
- Messy activities should ideally be positioned near to washing facilities.
- Fire exits should always be kept clear.
- Doorways should always be accessible.
- Activities should be positioned so that they do not have a negative impact on each other; for example, **small world play** is best positioned away from an area with constant through traffic. This avoids farm animals etc., being constantly knocked over.
- Cupboards should be kept secured unless being accessed by the children.
- Storage trolleys for resources should be stacked carefully and never overloaded. Children should be able to access the resources safely.
- In outdoor play areas, there should be sufficient space for activities such as ball games to take place successfully without trikes and cars getting in the way. At times when space is limited, activities should be restricted or alternated according to children's needs and current interests.

keyword

Small world play
Play with toys that are a scaled-down version of real life.

activity
4.3 INDIVIDUAL THEN PAIR WORK

(a) Draw a plan for a nursery room used for three year olds. Think about the activities you wish to include, space for floor play and storage.

(b) Compare your plan with another student's. What can you learn from each other?

Meeting children's needs

Not only should the environment be suitable but the resources provided for the children should also be appropriate.

Figure 4.2
Meeting children's needs

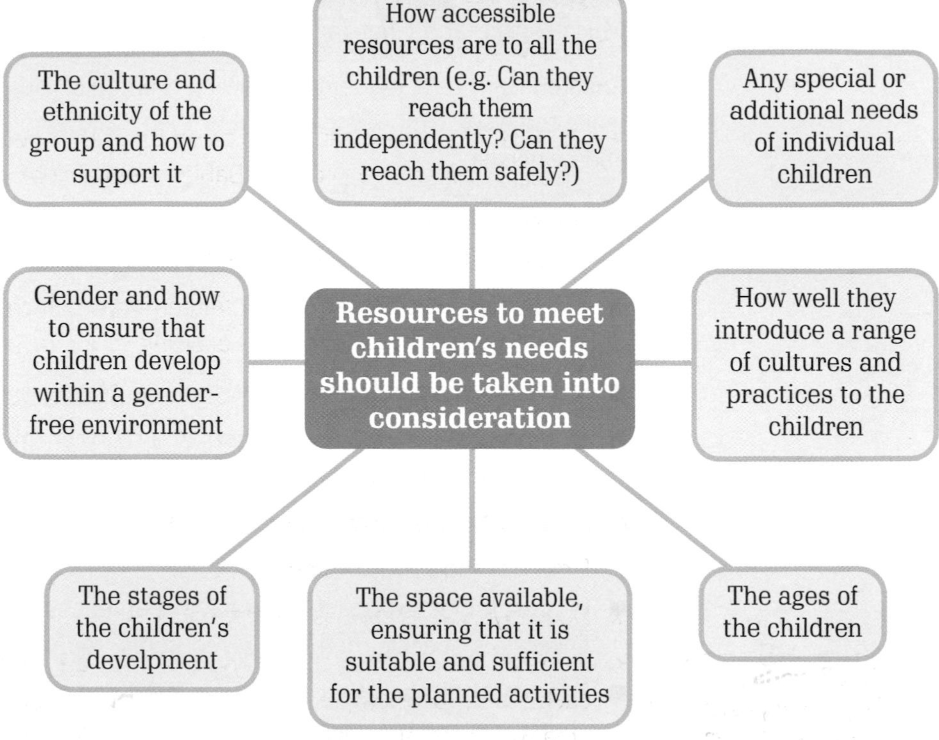

Age ranges

Activities will depend on the children's age; the age ranges are:

- birth to three years
- three to seven years
- seven to 12 years
- 12 to 16 years.

Unit 6, page 222, provides information on setting up activities covering the above age ranges, with the main focus on the younger age groups. You may find it helpful to read those sections now.

Understanding how to prepare and maintain a stimulating environment

Displays

Displaying children's work and creativity demonstrates that what they do is valued by you, the adult working with them. Displays enable parents and carers to see what their children have been doing and also provide a focus for discussion for each child. You can talk with their parent or carer and with other children about how a display was put together, who painted, drew or collaged which aspect, and what the overall focus of the display is, if there is one.

Children learn best by doing. Involving them in setting up a new display will make the display more meaningful to them, and give them a sense of both pride and ownership.

Types of display

Displays can take many forms, for example:

- wall displays of children's work, either individual pieces or a collection of linked items
- wall displays linked to a specific topic (e.g. spring, the seaside, transport)
- storyboards, where different parts of a story or rhyme are illustrated by the children and set out in the appropriate sequence
- window displays, often double-sided to look good from indoors and from outside
- interest tables, where children have been encouraged to contribute items linked to a specific theme (e.g. red items, round items, teddies)
- interactive displays that can be explored and added to by the children (e.g. stones and pebbles, autumn leaves and fruits, items linked to a specific festival or season).

Backgrounds

When setting up a wall display, consider using a linked background to help set off the items displayed. For example, blue makes a good background for a display on 'things that fly', and black makes a good contrasting background for a display on snow. Sometimes, a striped or chequered background works well.

remember

Always ensure that the children's work is not overshadowed by the background colour of a display or the use of a border.

Borders

Borders give a neat, professional finish to a wall display. The type of border that you use can also make a difference to the overall effect of a display. There are a number of ready-prepared borders available to purchase, but it is sometimes nice to use a border printed by the children, using their hands, cotton reels, potatoes, etc.

Professional Practice

- Encourage children to help you plan a display. Be ready to adjust your original ideas to incorporate their suggestions.
- It is important that the efforts of all children are included. It is inappropriate to use only the most recognisable or neatest drawing. Each child will be at a different stage creatively, and their efforts deserve to be treated equally.

Use of senses

Children learn from everything around them, absorbing information through the use of each of their senses. It is therefore important to provide an environment that stimulates them both visually and aurally and provides for tactile and olfactory experiences too.

activity 4.4 INDIVIDUAL WORK

Look at the examples of sensory experiences below. Can you think of any more ideas for each area?

Figure 4.3
Visual experiences

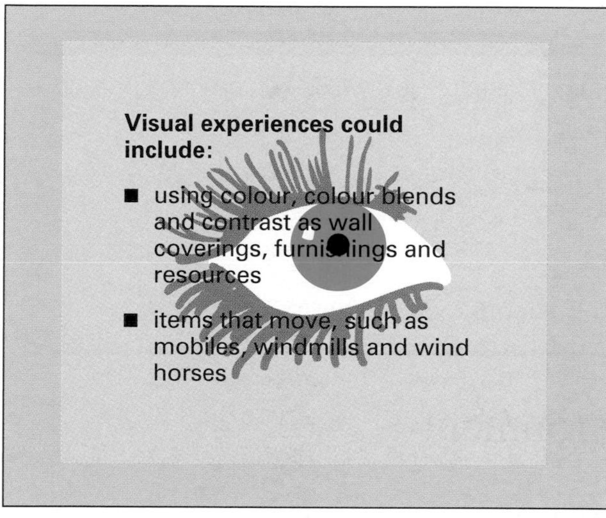

Figure 4.4
Aural experiences

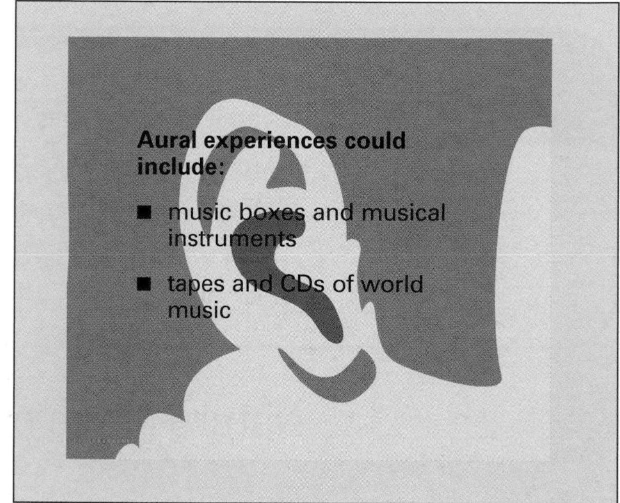

Figure 4.5
Tactile experiences

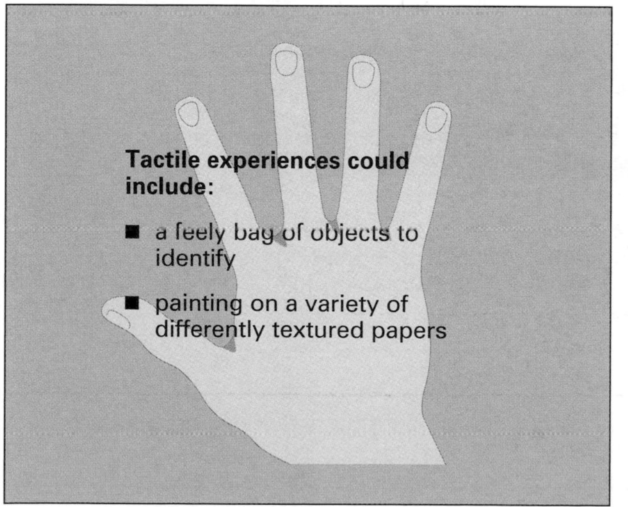

Figure 4.6
Olfactory experiences

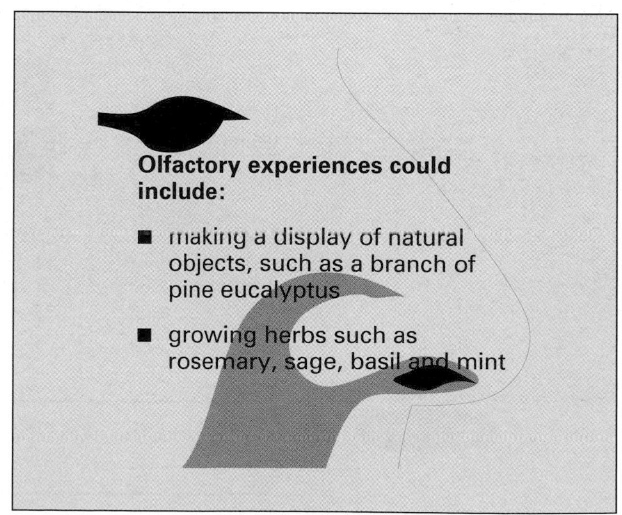

The provision of a variety of experiences for each of the senses encourages children to continue to use those senses to explore in greater detail the properties of any new objects that they come across.

As you play and work alongside children, it can be helpful to discuss how items, both familiar and new, feel, look, smell, etc. This will help children develop their vocabulary and use of description, for example by introducing words such as:

- fragrant
- pungent
- textured
- sour
- powdery
- glossy.

activity 4.5 INDIVIDUAL WORK

(a) Think of an object, for example a lemon. How would you describe it using each of your senses?
  (i) How does it feel?
  (ii) How does it smell?
  (iii) What does it look like?

(b) How many different descriptive terms did you think of?

Nature of the environment

Figure 4.7
Opportunities to play, work and gain experience

Refer to Unit 6, page 254, for discussion of suitable activities and places to visit.

Whenever practicable, children should be able to make choices within the setting about what they do and play, and with whom they play or do activities. When planning a day's activities and resources for children, there should be room for flexibility and negotiation. Younger children usually have shorter concentration spans than older children, and this will need to be reflected in how frequently the resources are changed throughout a session or day.

case study 4.1

Happy Learners Nursery

Happy Learners Nursery had provided a range of construction activities for children in the three to four-year-olds' room. These were put out once all the children had arrived. As the regular snack time approached, Lyn, the room supervisor, asked everyone to put the resources away.

Toby and Earl had been absorbed for a long time while building a model. They protested that they wanted to carry on building again later, but Lyn insisted that they broke up their model and helped pack away. Earl kicked the model hard causing pieces to fall off, which made Toby cry. Several other children protested that they had not yet had a turn at building and said they wanted to build after snack time. Again, Lyn ignored their requests.

Clearly, this was an activity popular with many of the children.

activity
INDIVIDUAL WORK

(a) How might Toby and Earl have been feeling?

(b) How might each of them have been affected by what happened?

(c) How might the other children have felt?

(d) What would you have done if you were Lyn?

(e) How could Lyn have shown some flexibility?

Flexibility

Sometimes, the plans that we have made do not meet the children's needs. We need to acknowledge this and recognise when we need to make adjustments and be more flexible. The needs of the children in Happy Learners Nursery were clearly not being met on this occasion.

Involving the children

Whenever possible involve children in planning the environment, particularly any permanent changes. Examples could include:

remember Being involved in decision making, and having their ideas listened to and welcomed not only helps children feel ownership of their environment, it also helps raise their self-esteem.

- selecting plants and bulbs for a new flower border
- choosing ground games to be painted on a paved area, such as hopscotch squares
- competitions to design a play area
- group discussions about a theme for the role-play area
- negotiating where a new bench is to be placed outside
- decisions on where plants are positioned
- selecting resources as a group.

activity 4.6 INDIVIDUAL WORK

What other potential examples can you add to the above list?

Understanding how to maintain an environment that builds children's confidence and resilience

Achievements

All children need praise. This should be readily given for effort and not saved only for achievement. It is in the process of trying to do something that much of the child's learning takes place and, in most cases, effort is therefore of greater importance. Achievements can vary from the almost imperceptible to the very obvious. Consider the difference between a three-year-old who discovers that they can now thread a bead onto a string without difficulty and a toddler who takes their first steps. Both are significant achievements and developmental milestones, but the toddler's walking will be the more obvious and probably the more celebrated. The achievement of threading could easily go unnoticed. Always make sure that you acknowledge and praise the small achievements too. There will be many of them.

Encouraging all children to participate in every activity will provide them with opportunities to try new things, make choices, make progress in the development of a range of skills and achieve at levels appropriate to their age and stage of development. An environment where there is plenty of scope to experiment and time to keep on trying, and where there is encouragement to reflect on the process and what went wrong, or how something has been successful, will be an environment that supports children best, giving them confidence, boosting their sense of self-esteem and helping them develop perseverance and resilience.

remember It is important to acknowledge and value effort and achievement in all its forms.

Change and consistency

Some children need the security of a consistent environment. They become anxious about change and can easily become insecure. It is particularly important that clear explanations are given in advance if there is likely to be a notable change to their routine, their familiar carers or their environment.

Parents and staff need to be prepared to offer greater levels of support during times of change. This could be the direct comfort of cuddles, verbal reassurance and hand holding, or simply a greater level of close contact during activities.

Foreseeable and unforeseeable changes

Some changes are easily predicted, for example a key worker leaving or a child changing to a new room or age-group setting. Other situations cannot be anticipated, for example key staff being taken ill, an emergency necessitating the evacuation of the building, or a parent being delayed and leaving the child at the setting for longer than usual.

It is important that you try to identify what will trigger anxiety in the children in your care and take steps to reassure them and help them maintain a feeling of security.

Socialising

For some children, making friends and developing relationships come naturally, but others need the help of the adults in their lives in order to develop the necessary skills. Situations and games that involve interacting, taking turns, sharing and making joint decisions help to build good social skills.

remember

Different cultures will have different social 'norms' and may place a different value on the importance of certain behaviours or interactions, such as making eye contact and showing respect for elders.

As your career develops, you will no doubt work with children who are harder to get to know. They may not readily interact with you, and you will need to find a way into their world. The quiet child who plays alone often needs help in building relationships, and you may have to take a different approach when working with them compared with how you work with others within the same group or classroom. It may initially mean working with the child one to one, or alongside them, offering comments on your play and modelling for them how to approach others by, for example, asking for and requesting resources.

Activities to encourage social skills

Figure 4.8
Activities to encourage social skills

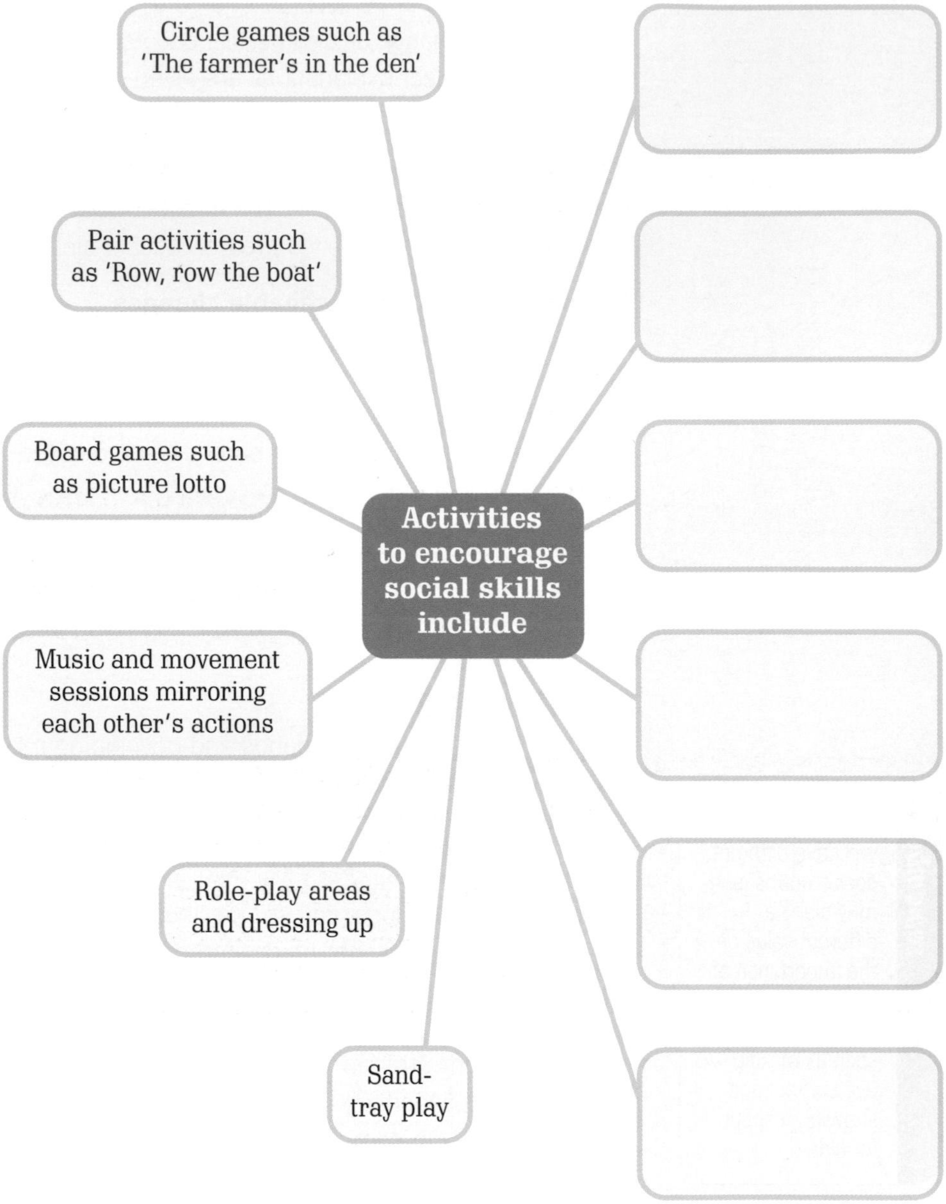

activity 4.7 INDIVIDUAL WORK

Look at the spidergram above and think of other activities that could help children to develop their social skills.

There are many activities that you could have added to the spidergram. For more ideas on play, refer to Unit 6, pages 243–254.

case study 4.2

Megan

Megan has been attending nursery for several weeks but rarely speaks to anyone and tends to play alone. Shelley, her key worker, has noticed that Megan unobtrusively watches other children as they play but never joins in. Shelley starts to sit alongside Megan whenever she can, talking to her and describing what she is doing. For example, at the sand tray Shelley asks Megan to pass objects to her and asks Megan's opinion about how best to make sand pies. When playing with cars on the road mat, Shelley encourages another child to join them in directing cars around the small world town.

activity
INDIVIDUAL WORK

(a) What do you think of the approach that Shelley has taken?

(b) Choose three activities commonly found in an early years setting. How might you involve a child such as Megan in those activities and, subsequently, in interacting with you or with another child?

Professional Practice

- Children learn by example and many of the social skills that we wish them to develop will be embraced more readily if introduced within context.
- For example, if a child is to follow social norms and say 'Thank you' and 'Please', they need to hear the terms said to them at appropriate times and be encouraged to use the terms themselves.

Cultural backgrounds

An environment that both acknowledges and values difference will help children to feel positive about their individual cultural backgrounds. The festivals and celebrations that form a central part of most religions and cultures can be enjoyed by children of all faiths and heritages. The festivals offer them fun and interesting experiences from which the children will further develop their understanding of the world in which they live and the beliefs and customs of their friends. As with all activities, occasions to develop physical, social and communication skills, and creativity will be found.

Consider the following example. By introducing children to the dragon dance performed annually at the Chinese New Year, you will give them an opportunity to:

- use social skills as they work jointly with others to plan the dance and move as one large dragon

- learn about 'give and take', as they follow and/or take the lead
- use gross motor skills and develop spatial awareness as they dance and weave around the room or garden area
- use fine motor skills as they join in arm movements and hold on to material or streamers as they dance
- learn about the customs of another country
- follow patterns within the music and move rhythmically
- learn new words and consolidate the meanings of others.

Refer to Unit 5, page 187, for more on activities to support cultural diversity.

Knowing how to support routines for children and integrate play

Provision of food and drinks

To understand the nutritional needs of children, it is necessary to know what makes up a healthy diet. The main food groups and information on the benefits of – and the effects of a lack of – various vitamins and minerals can be found in Unit 7.

You may find it helpful to refer to Unit 7, page 307, for information on the main food groups, and to page 308 for a chart setting out the estimated nutritional requirements of young children. Also, try referring to Green (2007, Book 2).

A table showing cultural food variations can be found in Unit 5, page 188.

Children need to understand hygiene and food handling, and you can help by setting them a good example.

For guidance on hygiene and safe food handling, refer to Unit 2, page 77.

remember

A drink of water should always be offered with meals.

Drinking water

Children need to drink regularly to avoid dehydration. Settings should provide water throughout the day, in covered jugs, bottles, water dispensers or fountains. If children are unable to decide themselves when to drink they should be reminded and encouraged. The amount that a child should drink will vary from child to child and according to the weather, the air temperature, the level of activity being undertaken and, for some children, the effects of any medication that they are taking.

Food preferences

Like adults, children have food likes and dislikes, which should be respected and accepted. However, children's tastes and preferences are likely to change as they get older, and it is therefore good to encourage children with many dislikes to try foods again from time to time, provided that you know that they do not have an allergic reaction to them.

Allergy and intolerance

If a child is allergic to a food, their body rejects the food completely. At times, this can become a medical emergency, called anaphylaxis. Symptoms of a food allergy include:

remember Any child who swells up or has difficulty breathing needs an urgent medical assessment.

- rashes
- vomiting
- diarrhoea
- breathing difficulties
- swelling of lips, face, etc.

Examples of allergies include:

- wheat allergy
- milk protein allergy
- peanut allergy.

When a child cannot tolerate a particular food, their body is unable to absorb the food or digest it.

For example, there is:

- lactose intolerance
- gluten intolerance (coeliac disease).

The number of children with food allergy or food intolerance is increasing. Every setting will have a policy regarding food and the management of food allergies and intolerances. A setting could, for example, have a board, showing names against relevant allergies, displayed clearly for all staff to see. Whatever the procedure, it is important that you always check before giving food or drink to a child.

Some settings have an outright ban on nut products even in lunchboxes brought from home. This is to prevent cross-contamination or inappropriate sharing of foods between children.

Consistency of routine

A consistent routine gives children security; they know what to expect and when to expect it. This can be especially important to younger children, those who have recently joined the setting, and any child who has social and emotional difficulties. For example, many of the children on the autistic spectrum need routine in their lives. It helps them cope with day-to-day experiences.

Routine can also be helpful to children with sensory impairment. A child with a visual impairment may be guided by the sound of certain activities and can gain greater independence within an environment where the layout is consistent and the routine regular. Similarly, a child with a hearing impairment will be guided by what they see around them.

It is important however, that children are able to deal with occasional change, as this helps to prepare them for life in general, and there should therefore be opportunities for them to experience spontaneity. Some children will require extra support to help them adjust at such times.

Balance

Children benefit when routines offer a balance between physical activities and those that are more restful. The opportunity to move around freely and use large motor movements is important to children's physical development and for the refinement of gross motor skills. For some children, especially those living in blocks of flats or in homes without regular access to outdoor play, the care setting or school may provide their only chance to play in a spacious environment. These children may need more guidance on the use of space and on how to avoid collisions or impacting accidentally on the play of others. Introducing games that involve adjusting movements around others, such as running round a zigzag pathway of cones or skittles, or riding round on bikes, will help children to develop these skills.

activity 4.8 INDIVIDUAL WORK

What other games and activities could you provide that will encourage spatial awareness?

Children use a lot of energy within their play and it is important that they have sufficient nutrients to provide for their level of activity. This will differ from child to child.

Refer to 'Provision of food and drinks' on page 160; and to Unit 7, page 307, for guidance on how to provide a healthy diet.

Planning the day so that there are periods of calm between periods of higher physical activity ensures that the children have time to re-boost their energy levels and encourages opportunities for relaxation and concentration, often lacking in children's lives at home.

Children's personal care

Supporting the personal care of children includes skin and hair care, using the toilet, safety in the sun and care of the teeth.

See pages 313–326 of Unit 7 for information on these aspects of care.

It is important to introduce the concept of personal care even before a child is able to take on the responsibility, by incorporating into play opportunities to learn aspects of self-care. This can be done in a variety of ways, for example:

- through stories and information books
- by placing appropriate posters where children can see them
- through action games, such as 'This is the way we brush our teeth' to the tune of 'Here we go round the mulberry bush'
- by providing real articles to use within role play (e.g. hair brushes, flannels and sponges)
- by setting up displays with the children (wall displays or interest tables) on personal health care practices
- by inviting health professionals to visit (e.g. dental nurse, health visitor, hairdresser, doctor)
- through having a specific theme for the role-play area (e.g. baby clinic, surgery, hairdresser, dentist, the beach)
- through group discussion
- through the use of puppets that sometimes get things wrong, with whom the children can identify and to whom they can give advice.

One of the most useful ways of promoting good personal care is by example.

activity 4.9 INDIVIDUAL WORK

(a) What instances can you think of when you have been a good example to children?

(b) Have you ever been a bad example? When was this, and why?

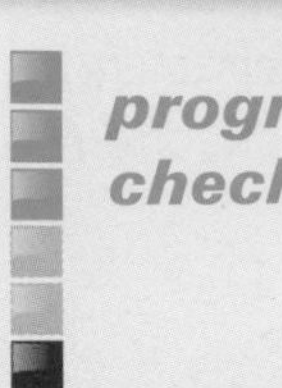

progress check

1. What is a risk assessment?
2. Who carries out risk assessments?
3. State four important considerations with regard to the use of space in a room for young children.
4. Explain what you need to consider when setting up a display.
5. Give three examples of how children can be involved in planning their environment.
6. How can children be helped to face change without losing their sense of security?
7. Give an example of how children can be encouraged to develop their social skills.
8. Name four factors that will affect how much water a child drinks in a day.
9. What is the difference between food allergy and food intolerance?
10. Give examples of activities that encourage the development of personal care.

References and suggested further reading

Dare, A. and O'Donovon, M. (2000) *Good Practice in Child Safety*. Nelson Thornes, Cheltenham.

Green, S. (2007) *BTEC National Children's Care, Learning and Development*, Book 2. Nelson Thornes, Cheltenham.

Mukherji, P. (2001) *Understanding Children's Challenging Behaviour*. Nelson Thornes, Cheltenham.

Olpin, J. (2005) *Displays and Interest Tables*. David Fulton Publishers, London.

Parker, L. (2006) *How to Avoid Illness and Infection*. David Fulton Publishers, London.

Parker, L. (2006) *How to Keep Young Children Safe*. David Fulton Publishers, London.

Parker, L. (2006) *How to do a Health and Safety Audit*. David Fulton Publishers, London.

Whalley, M. (1994) *Learning to be Strong: Integrating Education and Care in Early Childhood*. Hodder & Stoughton, London.

Professional Development, Roles and Responsibilities in Childcare

This unit covers:

- understanding relevant support systems and new knowledge and skills to develop own understanding of childcare practice
- understanding own roles and responsibilities within the team
- understanding values and ethics in childcare working practice.

This unit will help you to assess and make good use of your experience in a childcare setting.

As you work through the first section, you will be encouraged to reflect on your experience and identify your strengths and any areas requiring further work. How you use the available help, support and guidance to develop yourself as a person and as a professional childcarer is also considered.

You will then look at the benefits of teamwork and at how well you work within team situations.

Finally, you will learn about the values and ethics that underpin childcare work, including anti-discriminatory practice and the provision of culturally diverse resources.

grading criteria

To achieve a **Pass** grade the evidence must show that the learner is able to:	To achieve a **Merit** grade the evidence must show that the learner is able to:	To achieve a **Distinction** grade the evidence must show that the learner is able to:
P1 undertake a minimum of 240 hours of work experience in a childcare setting	**M1** explain how support systems have helped to develop own understanding of practice in childcare	**D1** evaluate the development of own understanding of practice in the childcare setting
P2 describe the use of support systems to develop own understanding of practice in a childcare setting	**M2** explain how new knowledge and skills have affected own understanding of practice	**D2** evaluate own contribution to the functioning of the team in the childcare setting

grading criteria

To achieve a **Pass** grade the evidence must show that the learner is able to:	To achieve a **Merit** grade the evidence must show that the learner is able to:	To achieve a **Distinction** grade the evidence must show that the learner is able to:
P3 identify the strengths and weaknesses in own understanding of practice	**M3** explain how they have supported the functioning of the team in own work setting	
P4 outline new knowledge and skills relevant to own understanding of practice in childcare work	**M4** explain how values and ethics are put into practice in childcare work	
P5 outline own roles and responsibilities as a member of the team in a childcare work setting		
P6 describe the values and ethics of childcare working practice		

Understanding relevant support systems and new knowledge and skills to develop own understanding of childcare practice

Support systems

Your training will provide a range of opportunities to help you develop your skills. These are likely to include:

- one-to-one tutorial guidance
- group tutorials
- time-bound assignments
- key skills development
- feedback from placement supervisors
- feedback from placement tutors
- reflective exercises as part of taught learning sessions
- guidance on and monitoring of planning
- guidance on and monitoring of observation skills.

One-to-one tutorial guidance

Most colleges provide opportunities for students to meet with their personal tutor on a regular basis. This provides a one-to-one situation where concerns can be raised by either student or tutor about placement, assignment work or attitude to learning and development. If you are falling behind, tutors will usually be happy to help you to manage your time better, by agreeing an individual time plan with you. This does not usually mean that you get extra time for your work, but it will help you learn how to spread out your workload more effectively.

Group tutorials

A regular group tutorial offers the chance for any course problems to be ironed out, information to be disseminated and questions to be asked. In most cases, if you have a question or query, it is likely that others also want the same information. It is important that you ask whatever you need to, in order to progress successfully and gain the most from your training.

Time-bound assignments

Assignments can be written or practical. Written assignments usually have a completion date that must be adhered to. Being unable to submit work when requested can mean that you lose grades. When work is submitted late, not only is feedback likely to be delayed, which may hold you back in your understanding of what you do next, but also, by not keeping on top of the work load, you will continue to get further behind.

Tutors are not unreasonable. They understand that from time to time everyone has a crisis, and procedures will be built into the programme to accommodate this. However, you will mostly be expected to plan sufficiently well ahead so that a minor hiccup in your intended work schedule should not make too much difference.

Using the guidelines for planning assignments that you are given at the start of your course will help you keep control of your work. It can be helpful to refer back to them regularly.

Key skills development

By working on and improving your key skills, you will be developing yourself as an individual; you will also be able to present your work to a higher standard. Gaining additional qualifications may well help you in the future too.

Feedback from placement supervisors

Your placement supervisor will be an experienced practitioner. Observing how they plan, work and conduct themselves with children, parents and colleagues should provide valuable guidance. Note how they approach and react to situations. Consider whether you would have done the same and reflect on how different the outcome may have been if your approach had been used. The placement supervisor will be your first point of reference for information about placement duties and will be the main person to give you critical feedback about your time in placement. From time to time, your placement supervisor will observe you as you carry out activities. They may want you to plan activities in

> **remember**
> 'Critical' does not mean 'criticise'. Critical means giving key information about your performance, offering a balance of praise for doing well and suggestions for moving forward.

advance and discuss your learning aims for the children. Your college tutors will give you guidance on this.

See also activity planning in Unit 6, page 222.

remember The more feedback you are given, the more accurately you can judge your level of competence.

Feedback from placement tutors

Often, your tutorials will be carried out by your placement tutor who will visit you in placement regularly during your course. They will have discussed your progress with your placement supervisor, gaining insight into how you are getting on. Use the feedback positively.

Evaluation Reflecting on and giving consideration to a past event, action or project.

Reflective exercises as part of taught learning sessions

Within class you may be asked to reflect on how you coped in certain situations, or to plan, implement and evaluate an activity, interaction or experience. You may be asked to complete simple checklists or charts. It can be good to return to these exercises from time to time to monitor how you are progressing. If you do not note any change in your outcomes, ask yourself why this might be. Are you using the feedback you are given to help you progress? Do you use your **evaluation** skills?

Refer back to Unit 1, page 52, to remind yourself about checklists.

Guidance on and monitoring of planning

As mentioned above, you will receive guidance on planning from your tutors. Evaluating the learning aims after an activity has been carried out offers a chance to see whether you had targeted your aims appropriately. It is through the regular process of planning, implementing and evaluating that you will learn to meet children's needs at the right level. This process will be helped by developing observational skills.

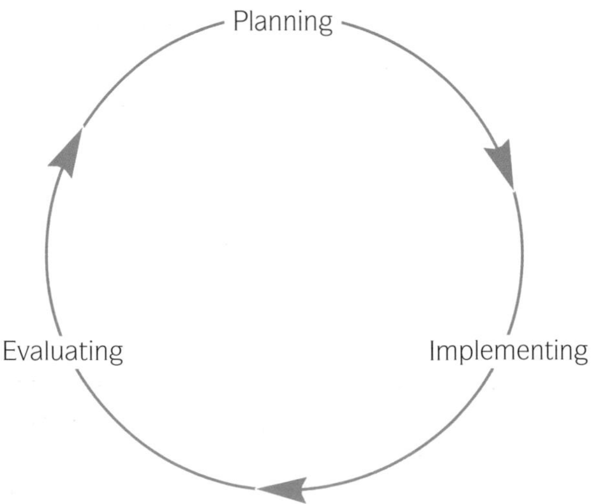

Figure 5.1
Planning circle

Guidance on and monitoring of observation skills

Again, tutors will guide you in how to plan and carry out observations. These are skills needed by all practitioners.

The importance of observation and how to carry out observations is covered in Unit 1, pages 42–60.

Use of feedback

You will have seen from the above that you will receive feedback from a variety of people during your course. Feedback helps you to:

- identify areas of practice that you need to develop further
- understand your strengths
- identify goals for the future
- plan targets, short term and longer term
- identify opportunities that will help you
- understand your role within teams.

Professional development

To be professional is to be competent, efficient and skilled, and to be qualified appropriately. Most individuals have certain expectations of professional people, such as doctors, solicitors or teachers, with regard to what they do and how they go about it. You should be aiming to achieve that same level of professionalism yourself.

Part of your professional practice will include being willing to undertake further development. This can be through:

- feedback from line managers
- training within your workplace
- local authority training sessions, for example through the Early Years Development and Childcare Partnership (EYDCP)
- obtaining further professional qualifications
- using relevant journals and magazines to keep you up to date with current ideas and thinking
- using internet access to keep abreast of the latest legislation and to answer questions.

Being professional involves a range of different skills and attributes, including presenting yourself appropriately and paying attention to the characteristics shown in Figure 5.2.

Figure 5.2 Characteristics of professionalism

Dressing appropriately

As with any job, it is important that what you wear is suitable. Some settings have a dress code with rules about the style of dress, the wearing of jewellery and suitable footwear. Some will have a staff 'uniform', usually a sweatshirt or polo shirt with plain trousers. As a student, you may be offered items that you can borrow to help you feel part of the team.

activity 5.1 GROUP WORK

(a) What clothing do you consider to be suitable for wearing when working with young children?

(b) What would you consider unsuitable?

(c) What are your views on jewellery, make-up and body piercing?

remember

Cotton clothing helps the body breathe more easily. It is absorbent and allows air to pass through its fibres, making it comfortable and reducing the likelihood of body odours.

Personal hygiene

When working in regular contact with other people, it is vital that personal hygiene is given a high priority. Your clothes should be changed and washed regularly, and you should ensure that you bathe and wash your hair frequently. Keep your nails short and your hair well groomed and tied back if long.

Children learn by example, and it is important that you are seen by the children in your care to wash your hands before food preparation, cooking activities and at mealtimes. It is not sufficient to explain that you have already done so.

activity 5.2 GROUP WORK

(a) What might be the impact if staff are not well presented and lack good personal hygiene? Consider this from the viewpoint of a child, a parent and as another member of the staff team.

(b) How would you explain the importance of hand washing to children?

Communication skills

Remember that you communicate both verbally and non-verbally. It is important that you are aware of the messages that you are giving out and also whether those messages are being received in the way that you intended.

Refer to Unit 3, pages 126–131, to develop your understanding of how to communicate successfully and the barriers that can occur.

Time management and reliability

Managing yourself is an important aspect of being professional. This applies equally to handing in assignments and to the commitment shown to your placement. Children need stability and routine in order for them to feel secure. A member of staff who takes time off work unnecessarily, or who is unreliable, can have an adverse affect on this.

activity
5.3
GROUP WORK

Think about how unreliable staff might affect the workplace.

(a) What impact might their unreliability have on the children?

(b) What impact might it have on the planning of the day?

(c) What impact might it have on the morale of the staff team?

(d) How might the long-term professionalism of the unreliable worker be affected?

Responsibilities of the individual early years carer

Everyone in the work setting has a degree of responsibility, and as a student you will too. This includes taking responsibility for your own safety by thinking ahead and identifying potential problems.

Staff in early years settings are responsible for the safety and well-being of all children within their care. They are entrusted by parents to provide a stimulating, safe and well-supervised environment. This involves staff:child ratios that meet or exceed legal minimums, and staff who are appropriately trained in care, education and in health and safety.

At this point, you may find it useful to refer back to Unit 2, pages 79–81, where these aspects of early years care are set out in more detail.

Being on placement

As a student, you will be under the supervision of an established member of staff at each placement setting. There is a minimum requirement of 240 hours' placement experience during the BTEC First Children's Care, Learning and Development programme, and, if finding a placement is your responsibility, it is advisable to arrange this as soon as you can. If you leave arranging this too late, you may miss out on the best placements and may have to accept types of placement that differ from the ones you had hoped for. In some colleges, a placement officer sets up the placements on behalf of students. You will be told which situation applies to your course.

When you join a placement setting, staff will have certain expectations of you. No one will expect you to know everything straight away, but they will expect you to make an effort to learn, to use your initiative and to show commitment to your training. Figures 5.3 and 5.4, respectively, give an overview of what is likely to be expected of you on your first day, and what is likely to be expected of you on a week-to-week basis once you have started attending regularly. It will be helpful to familiarise yourself with these expectations.

Figure 5.3
Professional expectations: the first day of a placement

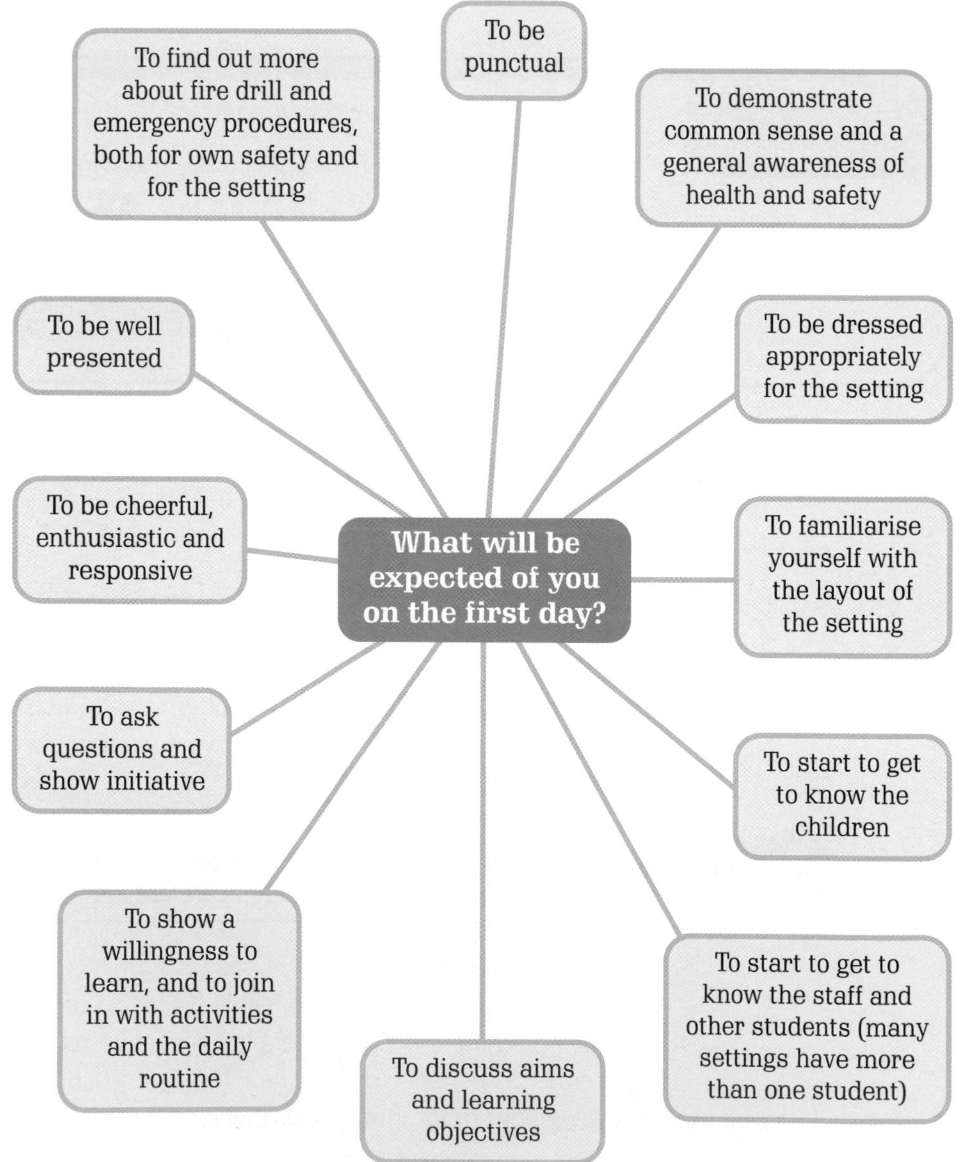

remember Your college will provide placement guidelines both for you and for your placement.

Figure 5.4
Professional expectations: week by week

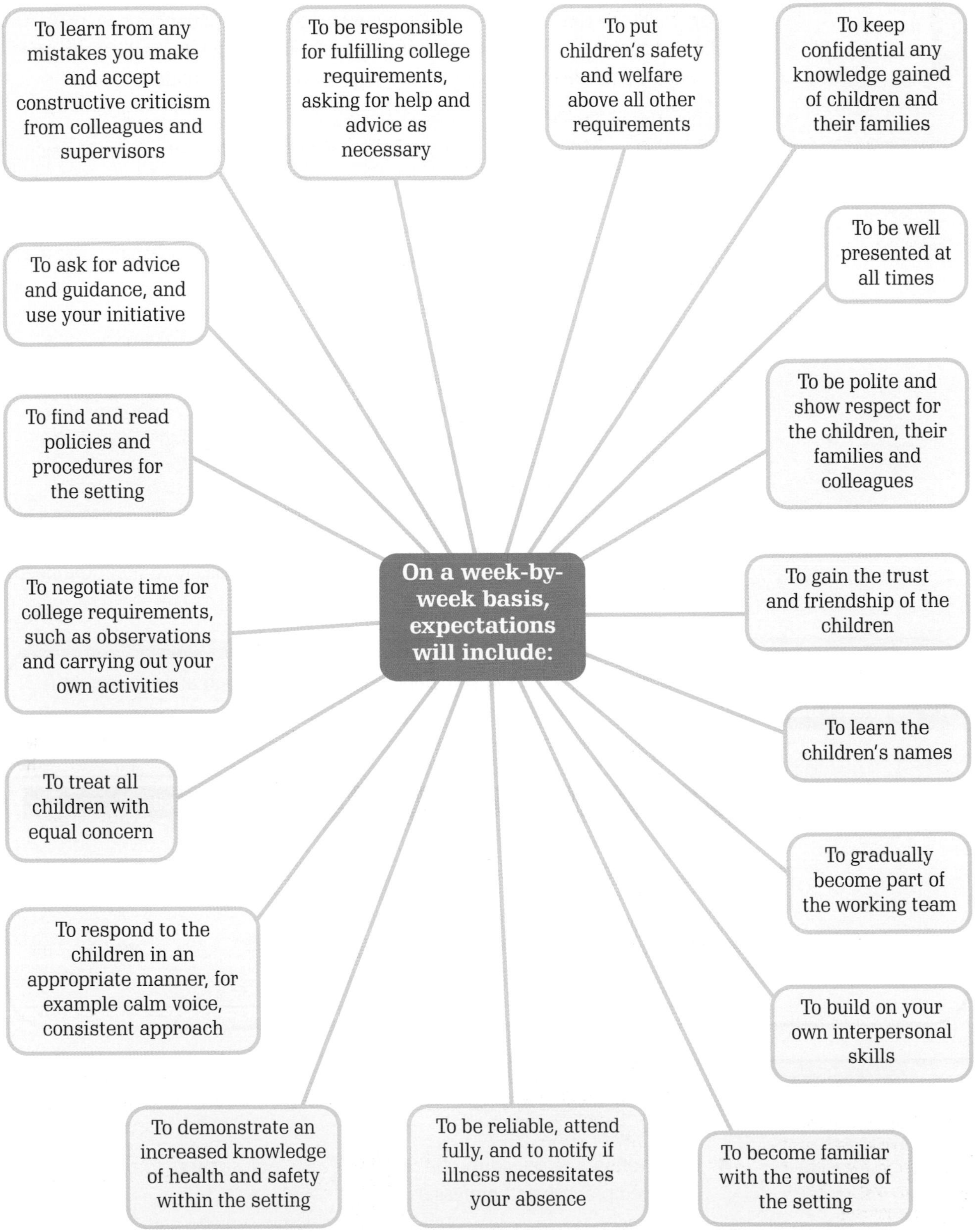

keyword

Reflection
The process of giving something thoughtful consideration.

Use of reflection

Reflection enables a practitioner to observe how their actions affect others (especially the children they are working with); doing so influences how they perceive the success or limitations of their actions and how they adjust practice to meet the needs of the children, the team or a specific situation.

Again, this is part of being professional. You are reviewing your own performance, noting where your strengths lie, which aspects of your professional practice you still need to develop, and understanding why, when, where and how to seek help when you need it.

As individuals, each of us will have our own preferred ways of learning. You may find that you learn best by:

- observing others
- discussion and verbal feedback
- reading further
- attending training updates
- just getting on with it and seeing what happens!

Most people will benefit from a combination of most of the above. However, just getting on with it and seeing what happens is not usually recommended as a strategy; it tends to lack planning and foresight and is unlikely to meet the needs of all the individuals you are working with.

activity
5.4
INDIVIDUAL WORK

Use the table below to help you identify what you are good at and what you could improve on for the future.

Table 5.1 Evaluation of current skills

Things I am good at	Things I could improve on
1.	1.
2.	2.
3.	3.
4.	4.
5.	5.

Professional Practice

- Identifying an area of your own practice that you need to work on is not a weakness. It is a strength.
- Observation + Thinking through (reflection) + Adjustments to practice = improved practice and professionalism.

Understanding own roles and responsibilities within the team

> *keyword*
> **Teamwork**
> Working co-operatively with a group of colleagues.

Teamwork, roles and responsibilities

Teamwork involves sharing, supporting and learning from each other. As everyone has different strengths and skills, good teams work in a complementary way that enables each member to contribute positively to the outcome. A setting's success is based on the successful teamwork of its staff. Each individual has a part to play, but no one person can carry the full weight of the organisation, although the owner or manager clearly has overall responsibility for the safety, standards and smooth running of their setting.

When working as part of a team you will need to share, to compromise and to accept that others may well, on some occasions, have better ideas than you.

In any team, it is necessary for individuals to:

- work together
- identify their own skills
- identify their own strengths
- share ideas
- be reliable
- be committed to a shared aim, objective or purpose
- co-operate with each other
- give and take
- be flexible
- find their 'best fit' within the team.

In a team, you will probably find that:

- some team members are good at planning
- some have good ideas
- some are very practical and 'hands on'
- some are good at keeping everyone motivated
- some are good at managing time and tasks
- some are good at finishing off small details
- some are natural team leaders
- some work best under regular guidance from others
- some will work better together than others; this needs to be accepted.

Flexibility with regard to the allocation of roles and responsibilities within the team will help to ensure that the greatest level of cohesive teamwork is achieved.

All teams need to observe certain rules and guidelines.

Figure 5.5
Teams need to observe …

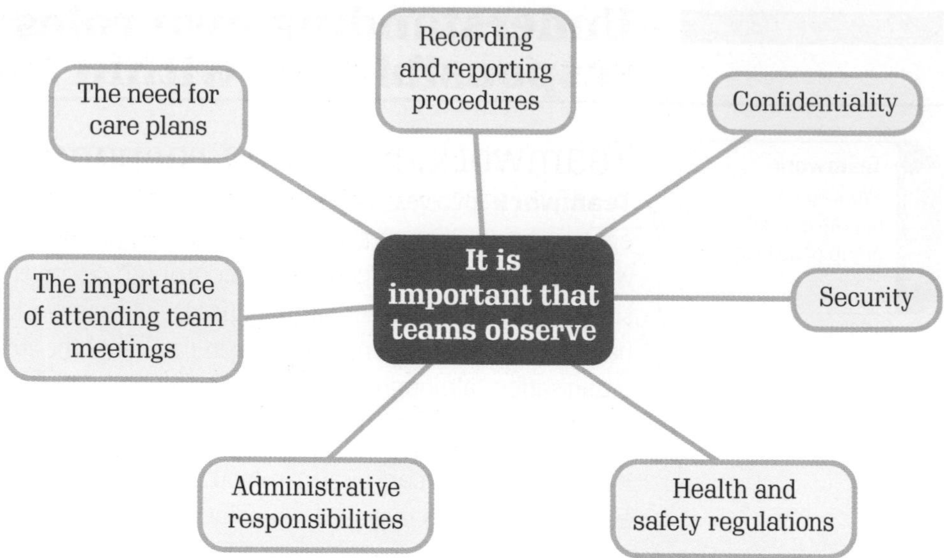

Interactions within the team

As a member of a team, you will need to ensure that others know your intentions. You should also keep them informed of your progress. Although you may sometimes do this through formal channels like team meetings, at other times it will be sufficient to pass on information in a brief conversation or exchange of greetings. For example, 'Hi, Dorian, I've arranged the delivery of …', or 'By the way, Melissa, the material arrived today, so you can start sewing as soon as you're able'.

remember Sensitivity is important within teamwork.

It is always important to be flexible. This helps to speed a project up, provides support for anyone who is struggling, and is in the true spirit of teamwork.

At times, you will notice that the approach being taken is not the most sensible or productive. Before jumping in and criticising, think how you would wish to be approached if the roles were reversed. Would you want it pointed out to you in front of a crowd, or would you rather have your errors discussed with you quietly?

keyword **Marginalised** Treated as insignificant or unimportant; placed at the edge (of importance).

The team should allocate priorities to tasks. There will always be some aspects of its work that are more essential or require a greater level of input than others. It is important that no member of the team feels **marginalised** by taking on a task of lesser urgency. The overall focus should be on the eventual outcome.

Commitments

Ideally, you should never commit yourself to something if you don't really have the time to carry it out or see it through to the end. The ability to prioritise is crucial.

activity
5.5
INDIVIDUAL WORK

Refer back to the list of 'types of people' in teams on page 175. Where do you fit into that list? Think about the following:

(a) If you are a person with lots of ideas, how much are you expecting from people? How reasonable are your expectations?

(b) If you are good at finishing off small details, how long do you take? Do you ever hold the task up through being too 'picky'?

(c) If you work best under the guidance of others, how much of their time do you take up? Should you be using your own initiative more?

(d) Have you ever held up an outcome? If yes, why was that? Was there an impact on anyone else? How did you feel?

Dealing with conflict

At some time, you will no doubt find yourself in a situation of conflict or will witness conflict between others. How you approach confrontation can make a big difference to the outcome. Think about the terms 'assertive' and 'aggressive'. They are often confused, but in reality they are very different.

Assertiveness

An assertive person is one who can remain calm during a confrontation or disagreement, clearly outlining what they wish to say and repeating their point if necessary without becoming over-excited or angry. They remain in control of themselves and stay within appropriate boundaries.

Aggression

An aggressive person is one who talks loudly and excitedly, during a confrontation, and displays agitated and angry body language. They may make personal comments unrelated to the subject of the conflict or disagreement. They are not fully in control of themselves or the situation.

(a) Do you recognise yourself in either of the above descriptions?

(b) Are you happy with how you respond to conflict?

(c) How do your usual reactions affect such a situation?

Being assertive can for example, help you to:

- justify a course of action that you have taken
- challenge a request made of you
- request additional support.

activity 5.7 INDIVIDUAL WORK

What impact might an aggressive approach have when you need to:

(a) justify a course of action that you have taken?

(b) challenge a request made of you?

(c) request additional support?

Understanding values and ethics in childcare working practice

keyword
Trustworthy Reliable, honest, dependable.

Values and ethics should underpin all aspects of working practice, including communication; it is essential that all members of staff are **trustworthy** and adhere to good anti-discriminatory practice.

Communication

In your communication and interactions with others you will need to respect their dignity, culture, background and values.

Some colleagues will be quieter than others and may lack confidence in pushing themselves forward. All should be listened to and treated equally, with extra time given to those that need it.

Sharing of information should always be in accordance with the policy of the setting, and confidentiality should be respected at all times.

Refer to the section on anti-discriminatory practice on page 185 for brief summaries of cultural practices.

Refer to Unit 1, page 59, for guidance on confidentiality and data protection.

Being trustworthy

remember
A trustworthy person is valued by all those they are in contact with. They can be depended upon. They can be turned to for help and support. They are respected.

Anyone working in a childcare setting must be reliable and trustworthy. Parents trust you with the care of their children. They expect honest feedback from you on their child's development, behaviour and well-being. The children trust you: they depend on seeing you when they arrive; they expect you to work and play with them, to care for them, and to help them cope with any difficulties they may face.

Your managers and colleagues will expect you to turn up when you should. The same applies within college. You will have been given a timetable for taught and practical sessions, and the expectation is that you will attend them. This is being reliable and trustworthy. It is part of being professional.

keyword

Prejudice
An opinion formed in advance, a pre-judgement.

Diversity
Being different or varying from the norm.

Anti-discriminatory practice

Equal opportunity issues

Working in any setting that cares for children requires a thorough understanding of what is meant by **prejudice** and discrimination and how to show your commitment to **diversity** within society and within each setting. This means valuing and meeting the needs of all children within your care.

The Children Act 1989 (superceded by the Children Act 2004) required local authorities to ensure that day care provision is staffed appropriately. It stated that:

keyword

Stereotyping
Categorising, taking away individuality.

> 'People working with young children should value and respect the different racial origins, religions, cultures and languages in a multi-racial society so that each child is valued as an individual without racial or gender **stereotyping**. Children from a very young age learn about different races and cultures including religion and languages and will be capable of assigning different values to them. The same applies to gender and making distinctions between male and female roles. It is important that people working with young children are aware of this, so that their practice enables the children to develop positive attitudes to differences of race, culture and language and differences of gender.'
>
> (*Source*: *Children Act 1989, Guidance and Regulations*, Volume 2, Section 6.10)

Working to the principles underpinning the Children Act 1989 and the Children Act 2004 ensures that practice in an early years setting is consistently good, rather than consistently adequate, and that the children cared for and educated within the setting benefit in all areas of their development.

keyword

Equality
The state of being equal, of having an equal opportunity.

Rights
Our entitlements as individuals.

Equality, diversity and rights

These terms can be broadly defined as follows:

- **equality** – the state of being equal
- diversity – the state or quality of being different or varied
- **rights** – in accordance with accepted standards of moral or legal behaviour, and justice. (Collins Dictionary, 1991)

Equality concerns fairness; everyone should be treated fairly. An individual's family or cultural background, the way they live, or their past or current state of health should not prevent them from receiving the same opportunities as anyone else in society.

Diversity refers to the differences found among the individuals, and groups, in society. Among the factors that contribute to diversity and to differences in individual experience are levels of ability, gender, culture, and religion.

Rights are the entitlements of each individual to receive the same opportunities as others. Many rights are linked to standards of service (such as the Patient's Charter regarding health care) and are protected by legislation (laws).

keyword

UN Convention on the Rights of the Child
This 'national constitution' was adopted by the United Nations assembly in 1989 to uphold agreed rights for children whenever possible.

remember

Under the Children Act 1989 (and 2004), children with disabilities are defined as 'children in need'.

Legislation

The most relevant charters and Acts of Parliament, which early years staff need to understand are:

- Children Act 2004 (previously the Children Act 1989)
- Human Rights Act 1998
- **UN Convention on the Rights of the Child 1989**
- Disability Discrimination Act 1995 and Carers and Disabled Children Act 2000.

Children Act 1989, 2004
The principles of the Act include the following:

- The welfare of the child is paramount (of ultimate importance), and it should be safeguarded and promoted at all times by those people in the position of providing services for a child.
- Children with disabilities are children first with the same rights as all children to services.
- The parents and families of a child are an important element of their lives. This should be recognised, and support given to them to help them fulfil their responsibilities.
- Parents should be valued as partners with local authorities and other agencies working to support their children.
- Children have a right to be consulted and listened to when decisions about them are being made. The views of both children and their parents must be taken into account at all times.
- There should be a co-ordinated approach when offering services to children with disabilities: for example, regarding health, education and social services.

Volume 2 of the Act specifically covers day care, and states that parents have a right to influence the quality of education that their child receives.

The Human Rights Act 1998
The Human Rights Act focuses on the individual's right to a life free from torture, loss of liberty, unfair punishment or discrimination. It also refers to respect for private and family life (Article 8), freedom of thought, conscience and religion (Article 9) and freedom of expression (Article 10). The Act is indirectly linked to the drawing up of no-smacking policies and is also relevant to the issue of female circumcision (which is illegal in the UK).

The UN Convention on Children's Rights 1989
This is an international agreement on human rights, which has been ratified (agreed formally) by 191 countries. It consists of 54 articles (statements), and its four main principles are:

- *Non-discrimination*. All children have the same rights and are entitled to the same treatment.

Figure 5.6
The Children Act 2004

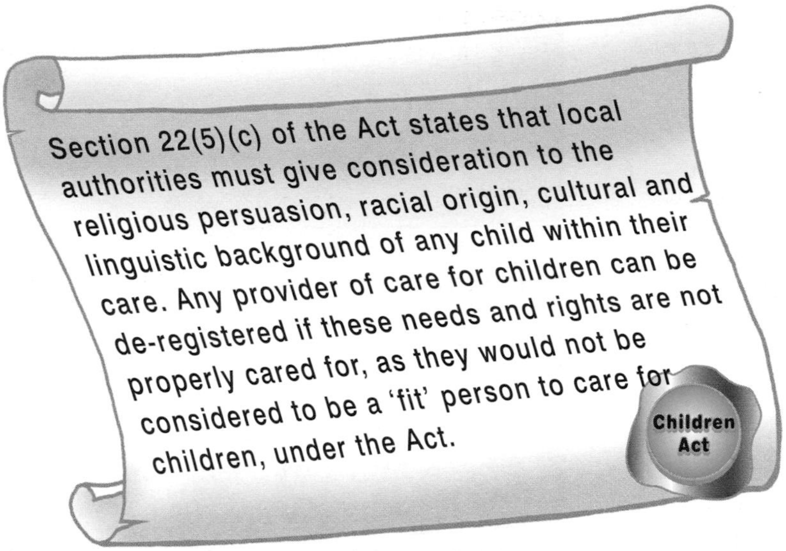

Section 22(5)(c) of the Act states that local authorities must give consideration to the religious persuasion, racial origin, cultural and linguistic background of any child within their care. Any provider of care for children can be de-registered if these needs and rights are not properly cared for, as they would not be considered to be a 'fit' person to care for children, under the Act.

Children Act

- *Children's best interests*. The best interest of the child should be placed as the highest priority when making decisions about their future.
- *Survival and development of children*. Children have the right to survive and the right to be able to develop to their full potential
- *Rights to participation*. The views of children should be taken seriously and they should be able to take part in what is going on around them.

The agreement is important because it brings together in one document all the rights of children and adults are asked to view children as individuals with all human rights being applied to children everywhere (based on a paper by Save the Children, 2000).

Examples of articles set out within the UN Convention have been unofficially summarised by authors Flekkøy and Kaufman (1997) as follows:

- *Article 2* – the principle that all rights apply to all children without exception, and the state's obligation to protect children from any form of discrimination: the state must not violate any right, and must take positive action to promote them all
- *Article 22* – special protection to be granted to children who are refugees or seeking refugee status, and the state's obligation to co-operate with competent organisations providing such protection and assistance
- *Article 23* – the right of handicapped children to special care, education and training designed to help them achieve greatest possible self-reliance and to lead a full and active life in society
- *Article 30* – the right of children of minority communities and indigenous populations to enjoy their own culture and to practise their own religion and language.

Figure 5.7
All children have the same rights and are entitled to the same treatment.

Disability Discrimination Act 1995 and Carers and Disabled Children Act 2000
This Act is directly relevant to early years in that it supports the ethos of the Education Act 1993, i.e. it recognises the necessity to provide all children who have a special need with an appropriate education at a suitable school.

All early years settings should have a special educational needs co-ordinator (**SENCO**) who takes overall responsibility for ensuring that the special needs of children are met. In schools, this would normally be a member of the teaching staff who liaises with parents and other staff and keeps records of the special educational needs within the school.

keyword
SENCO
Special education needs co-ordinator.

Refer to Unit 8, pages 380–383 for more on special educational needs policy.

Learning values from role models

From a very young age, children learn values and attitudes from their role models. They look to their role models for guidance, approval and encouragement, and they observe and take on their attitudes and actions. At first these role models are their families and immediate social group (**primary socialisation**); later their peers are role models, as are adults outside the family, including early years staff, teachers and health professionals (**secondary socialisation**). This includes you!

As an early years student, it is important that you understand what is meant by discrimination, stereotyping and prejudice, and that you are clear as to what is good practice. It can be helpful to explore how your own views were initially formed, and who or what influenced and shaped them.

keyword
Primary socialisation
The impact of immediate family and social groups on a child.

Secondary socialisation
The impact on a child of social contacts outside the child's immediate family and social group; these would include teachers, early years professionals, and so on.

activity 5.8 INDIVIDUAL WORK

Reflect back on your childhood and identify those who influenced you. Role models almost certainly included parents and teachers, and perhaps nursery or playgroup workers.

(a) Who else would you include?

(b) In what ways did each of the role models influence you?

(c) Were the influences positive, and what made them so?

(d) Were any of the influences negative, and what made them so?

Developing personal values is just the first step; putting them into practice is what counts. Upholding your views is not always easy, and it can sometimes be hard to challenge the practice of others and work in a way that does not compromise your own values. As you gain both confidence and experience in your role, you will develop your own strategy for dealing with challenge.

remember

Prejudice + Power = Discrimination.

Stereotyping

Stereotypes can be either positive or negative images of people that tend to be acquired from others and the media rather than from personal experience. When stereotyping someone, we see them not as an individual but simply as part of a group, thus taking away their personal identity. Clearly, this can be very unfair.

activity 5.9 GROUP WORK

What examples of stereotyping can you think of?

keyword

Direct discrimination Telling an individual that they cannot do something because of their race, sex, situation or disability.

Institutional discrimination The policies or practice of an organisation, which systematically discriminates against a minority group or groups.

Discrimination and prejudice

To discriminate means to give favourable or unfavourable treatment to someone or something because of a specific factor. There may be **direct discrimination**; or discrimination may be more subtle, for example when a single mother of five children is never asked to be involved in activities at her children's school because it is assumed that she will not have the time or means to do so.

Institutional discrimination occurs when the policies or practices of a workplace result in certain groups of people being treated differently. When there is individual discrimination, the prejudice (an opinion formed in advance) is the personal bias of one person.

activity 5.10 GROUP WORK

Focusing on early years settings, consider the following questions:

(a) What forms of gender stereotyping or discrimination might you find?

(b) What forms of racial or cultural stereotyping or discrimination might you find?

(c) What forms of disability stereotyping or discrimination might you find?

The points you raise in the above activity could most likely be avoided if there is a strong equal opportunities policy in place. Policies are important because they are drawn up and agreed by the staff of the setting. Copies are usually given to staff, parents, carers and students to read and understand; this helps everyone to work to the same ideas, values and procedures.

activity 5.11 GROUP WORK

(a) Discuss the following statement with others in your group.

'We do not have racism here. All the children are treated exactly the same.'

(b) What might this statement mean for the children?

(c) What might it mean for you as a practitioner?

(d) How could you make the statement more positive?

Discriminatory practice

Much discriminatory practice develops through ignorance and a lack of understanding. This is sometimes accidental, but it is often conscious. As a professional, you need to become better informed, to avoid discriminating accidentally, and to address any (conscious) personal prejudices that you may have. Changing your viewpoint is not easy, and you will only achieve this by exploring discrimination further and increasing your understanding of the effects that discrimination can have. This will, in turn, help you to develop and consolidate your value structure (moral code).

From time to time, you may come across discrimination between families registered with the setting where you work; this will need to be addressed. Think about the following case study.

case study 5.1

Helene

Helene does not want to sit by or play with Rajid. She says that her mummy told her not to. You are aware that the families of Helene and Rajid have different cultural and religious beliefs and that there are conflicts between them.

activity INDIVIDUAL WORK

How would you approach Helene's parent?

remember You cannot enforce your views on anyone, and similarly the views of others cannot be forced upon you.

Within a nursery, conflict of the nature described above is not acceptable. This would have to be explained to the child and to their parent. The setting's policy on equal opportunities would be helpful in such a case, as it gives a clear point of reference to back up the request for acceptance and tolerance on the part of the parents.

Sometimes acceptance and observation of a code of practice will be as much as you can achieve. Not everyone will fully agree with the underlying ethos.

remember The celebrations described here may well be important to some of your work colleagues as well as to the children and their families.

Different religions and cultures

Within different religions and cultures there are customs relating to diet, dress, worship, actions, gender, birth and death. Some of these are explored in more detail below. It will be helpful to familiarise yourself with them as this will increase your knowledge and understanding of what is important to many people in society, enabling you to provide a more inclusive environment for the children in your care, thereby demonstrating that their customs and beliefs are valued by you.

Festivals

There are many different festivals, and these can provide a wonderful range of learning opportunities for children across all aspects of the educational curriculum. Here are some examples.

Figure 5.8 Hanukkah candles

Jewish festivals

- Tu B'Shevat (February) – celebration of the new year for trees; new trees are planted and, if possible, fruit from Israel is eaten.
- Pesach (Passover) – commemorates the Jewish exodus from slavery in Egypt; matzah (unleavened bread) is eaten. Houses are cleaned to ensure that no food containing 'leaven' remains.
- Sukkot (October) – a harvest festival commemorating the 40 years that Jews spent in the wilderness; a sukkah is a temporary hut used for meals and socialising during this time.
- Hanukkah (December) – candles are placed in a Hanukkah candle holder each evening; foods, such as latkes (potato cakes) and doughnuts, are cooked in oil.

Figure 5.9 Ganesh, the elephant-headed deity

Hindu festivals

- Raksha Bandhan (August) – sisters tie coloured bracelets around their brothers' wrists to symbolise 'protection from evil'.
- Ganesh-chaturthi (August) – a celebration of the birthday of Ganesh; Hindus worship the elephant-headed deity at the beginning of new projects such as exams, moving house, etc.
- Navaratri (October) – Navaratri means 'nine nights' (the length of the festival); food and presents are often given to young girls
- Diwali (October or November) – lasts for one to five days; the story of Rama and Sita is a popular part of this festival.

Sikh festivals

- Vaisakhi (the first day of the Sikh year) – the Sikh new year, during which the five signs of Sikhism (uncut hair, a comb fixed in the hair, a steel bracelet, a short sword and a pair of shorts – known as the five Ks) and the turban are obligatory.
- Diwali (October or November) – this commemorates the release from prison of Guru Hargobind, the last human Guru of Sikhs; it includes wearing new clothes, giving gifts and sweets.

Christian festivals

- Lent – for 40 days prior to Easter something is given up to mark the 40 days that Jesus spent in the wilderness.
- Easter – the celebration of the resurrection of Jesus; Easter eggs are given as a symbol of new life
- Advent (December) – the first day of the Christian year, four Sundays before Christmas; four candles are lit in an Advent crown, one on each Sunday.

Muslim festivals

- Eid-ul-Fitr (December) – the end of fasting for Ramadan (lasts three days); it involves family gatherings, new clothes, nice food and gifts.

Chinese festivals

- Yuan Tan (Chinese New Year) – the most important event in the traditional Chinese calendar, which begins on the first day of the lunar calendar each year. Gifts are given, and fireworks and dances such as the lion dance take place at this time.

Figure 5.10
A Chinese lion dance

Japanese festivals

- Ganjitsu (Japanese New Year) (January) – lasts up to three days; families get together, decorations are put up, businesses close, and people pay their first visit to local shrines.
- Hanamatsuri (April) – Japanese celebration of the birthday of Buddha Shakyamuni; floral shrines are made, in which images of the infant Buddha are set and bathed.

activity 5.12 INDIVIDUAL WORK

(a) With which cultures would you associate the following items of clothing (if you do not know, do some research to find the answers):

- sari?
- kimono?
- shalwah and kameez?
- yamulka?
- hijaab?
- turban?

There are many more religions and cultures than those referred to in this section.

(b) Note down the names of others that you already know about.

(c) Which other festivals have been explored in your placement?

Diet

Diet is an important aspect of providing appropriately for children's needs. It is essential that the customs of a child's family are upheld within each early years setting, and there are a number of dietary requirements linked to culture and religion. If staff have any concerns or doubts with regard to any particular child's diet, the parents should always be asked for guidance. The table below sets out a useful 'at-a-glance' guide to what is acceptable and what is forbidden for many of the most commonly found groups of people.

Providing culturally diverse resources

Tokenism

keyword

Tokenism
Making only a small effort, or providing no more than the minimum, in order to comply with criteria or guidelines.

Be aware of **tokenism**. This is a pretence at being committed to diversity and equality. Settings with a tokenist approach may have a few items depicting positive messages on show in prominent places, but when you explore the resources further, the picture of equality that emerges overall is less satisfactory. For example, it may be that the books on the shelf show positive images, whereas many of those in the book box are less positive. Similarly, there may be one or two dressing up clothes relevant to non-Western cultures, but no cooking equipment or tableware that would be familiar to children of cultures other than Western.

Table 5.2 Food-related customs

	Jewish	Hindu[1]	Sikh[1]	Muslim	Buddhist	Rastafarian[2]
Eggs	No blood spots	Some	Yes	Yes	Some	Some
Milk/yoghurt	Not with meat	Yes	Yes	Yes	Yes	Some
Cheese	Not with meat	Some	Some	Possibly	Yes	Some
Chicken	Kosher	Some	Some	Halal	No	Some
Mutton/lamb	Kosher	Some	Yes	Halal	No	Some
Beef and beef products	Kosher	No	No	Halal	No	Some
Pork and pork products	No	No	Rarely	No	No	No
Fish	With fins and scales	With fins and scales	Some	Some	Some	Yes
Shellfish	No	Some	Some	Some	No	No
Butter/ghee	Kosher	Some	Some	Some	No	Some
Lard	No	No	No	No	No	No
Cereal foods	Yes	Yes	Yes	Yes	Yes	Yes
Nuts/pulses	Yes	Yes	Yes	Yes	Yes	Yes
Fruits/vegetables	Yes	Yes[3]	Yes	Yes	Yes	Yes
Fasting[4]	Yes	Yes	Yes	Yes	Yes	Yes

Source: from Walker (1998), page 68

'Some' means that some people within a religious group would find these foods acceptable.

1 Strict Hindi and Sikhs will not eat eggs, meat, fish and some fats.
2 Some Rastafarians are vegan.
3 Jains have restrictions on some vegetable foods. Check with the individual.
4 Fasting is unlikely to apply to young children.

case study 5.2 Sylvia

Sylvia has recently started to work in a nursery class. While reading stories to the children, she has already noticed that there are almost no books with images of people other than white people, and the only book portraying a person with a disability always depicts them on their own, rather than in the pictures that show other children. There are two black dolls in the role-play corner, both undressed and in a cupboard, whereas the white dolls are dressed and in the prams, ready for play. There is a wok on the shelf, but it doesn't seem to be in use; the children don't ask for it, and Sylvia has never seen the staff add it to the kitchen equipment used for play. A poster on the wall gives a welcome message in a variety of languages, but Sylvia is not convinced that there is real commitment to promoting equality and cultural diversity within the nursery.

activity
INDIVIDUAL WORK

(a) What sort of resources would you expect to see, even in a setting with limited finances?

(b) With whom should Sylvia raise her concerns?

(c) How would you introduce more cultural diversity into the nursery if you were Sylvia?

(d) Why are Sylvia's concerns important?

Although having the right resources is important, this does not in itself ensure that equality and diversity is being promoted. It is necessary to use positive language and adopt the correct approach to utilising the resources and activities provided so that it is evident to children and their families that the valuing of diversity goes beyond the welcome message.

Books, stories and visual displays

Every setting should provide books that offer positive images of gender, race and disability and avoid stereotyping. Images should be varied, incorporating both men and women, and boys and girls, all enjoying similar leisure activities and seen to be involved in tasks at home as well as at work, school, nursery, and so on. A range of cultures should be represented, and no one culture or gender should always be depicted in more 'powerful' positions than any other. For example, doctors should not all be portrayed as white, and mostly male, while all nurses are portrayed as women, and often black. Men should not always be the ones digging the garden, nor should women always be the ones washing the dishes or ironing.

Figure 5.11
Books and stories

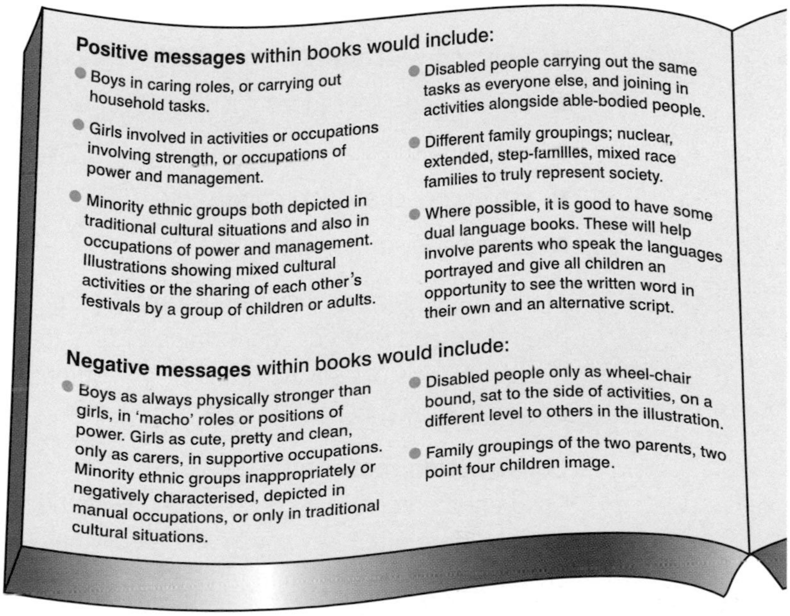

Positive messages within books would include:

- Boys in caring roles, or carrying out household tasks.
- Girls involved in activities or occupations involving strength, or occupations of power and management.
- Minority ethnic groups both depicted in traditional cultural situations and also in occupations of power and management. Illustrations showing mixed cultural activities or the sharing of each other's festivals by a group of children or adults.
- Disabled people carrying out the same tasks as everyone else, and joining in activities alongside able-bodied people.
- Different family groupings; nuclear, extended, step-families, mixed race families to truly represent society.
- Where possible, it is good to have some dual language books. These will help involve parents who speak the languages portrayed and give all children an opportunity to see the written word in their own and an alternative script.

Negative messages within books would include:

- Boys as always physically stronger than girls, in 'macho' roles or positions of power. Girls as cute, pretty and clean, only as carers, in supportive occupations. Minority ethnic groups inappropriately or negatively characterised, depicted in manual occupations, or only in traditional cultural situations.
- Disabled people only as wheel-chair bound, sat to the side of activities, on a different level to others in the illustration.
- Family groupings of the two parents, two point four children image.

The examples of positive and negative images given for books and stories apply to all resources and activities that involve illustrations.

Professional Practice

- It is acceptable for there to be a range of images, some neutral and some positive, as long as the overall emphasis is on the positive.
- It is never acceptable for a setting to continue to include negative images within its resources.

Role play

In the role-play corner, issues of gender are mostly found in the use of the resources rather than the resources themselves. Most important for combating gender stereotyping here is to encourage all the children to enjoy all the resources and take different roles within their play. An array of artefacts, clothes and foods from a range of cultures will enhance the learning of all children and positively promote the self-image of children from those cultures.

activity 5.13 INDIVIDUAL WORK

Have a look in the role-play area of your current placement setting. What cultures are portrayed by the dolls in your placement?

If all the dolls in the role-play corner are pink skinned, blonde haired and stereotypically 'English', they are likely to support a racist message of who is important and needs caring for.

Resources that depict a good range of cultures include:

- fruit and vegetables from around the world
- breads and other foods such as pizza
- cooking utensils
- tableware, chopsticks, bowls, etc.
- clothing for dressing up.

Many dressing-up clothes can be made quite cheaply using materials that have been dyed and printed, and a range of play foods can be made from salt dough. Cheap versions of cooking utensils can sometimes be found in markets or may be donated by parents.

Construction materials

Children often consider construction kits to be boys' toys. This can be because parents more often buy construction activities for sons than for daughters. Encouraging both boys and girls to use construction materials will help erase stereotypical views, but it is important to be aware of who dominates the construction area. It is sometimes appropriate to encourage girls to use construction materials without the 'help' of the boys. This will ensure that girls have opportunities to plan, predict, experiment and achieve on their own. As construction kits often come in boxes illustrated with pictures of boys playing, it is a good idea to remove the kit from its original box and place it in an alternative container.

Figure 5.12
Encouraging both boys and girls to use all toys will help erase stereotypical views

Creativity

Creative activities are non-competitive, as you cannot paint your own picture 'wrong'. A broad range of media and utensils can be utilised to provide opportunities for creative expression. It important to ensure that tools are tailored to children's specific needs; for example, a child with limited manipulative skills will benefit from using brushes with chunky handles (lightweight wallpaper brushes can be useful). All children will enjoy the experience of painting with (thoroughly cleaned) roll-on deodorant containers or large sponge rollers.

> **remember**
> Strict supervision is needed when using materials such as cling film.

If children have skin problems such as eczema, direct contact with paint and other 'messy' media can cause further irritation. However, it is possible to devise activities that can keep them involved without risking infection or further discomfort, for example finger painting under a length of cling film. Using large bubble-wrap as an alternative can add to the sensory experience.

Enormous scope for creative activity is offered by the range of festivals celebrated by people of different religions and cultures throughout the year (e.g. those described on pages 185–187). Take, for example, the Hindu Diwali festival of light; children could be introduced to:

- Diwali cards – a popular design is to use a hand shape and decorate it with the traditional mehndi patterns
- Rangoli patterns – a decoration laid at the entrance to the home to welcome the goddess of fortune, Lakshi.

Figure 5.13
Examples of Rangoli patterns

Or you could explore Chinese New Year, the first day of the lunar calendar each year:

- Teng Chieh – the lantern festival denotes the end of the New Year celebrations; decorated sheets of paper are cut up and made into lanterns.
- Money envelopes (lai see) – it is traditional for children to receive money in red envelopes decorated with gold writing.
- Dragons, one of the 12 animals in the Chinese animal years – making a huge dragon can be an exciting whole-group activity, culminating in the 'dance of the dragon'.

Such activities allow every child to contribute and encourage them to work together towards a joint goal.

Professional Practice

- Parents of children from different cultures will usually be pleased to help with improving the setting's resources. It is always worth asking them for advice. This will show that the setting values their culture.
- Providing a range of skin-tone colours in both paints and crayons will enable all children to represent themselves and their families accurately in their pictures.

Figure 5.14
Lanterns used in the celebration of the Chinese New Year

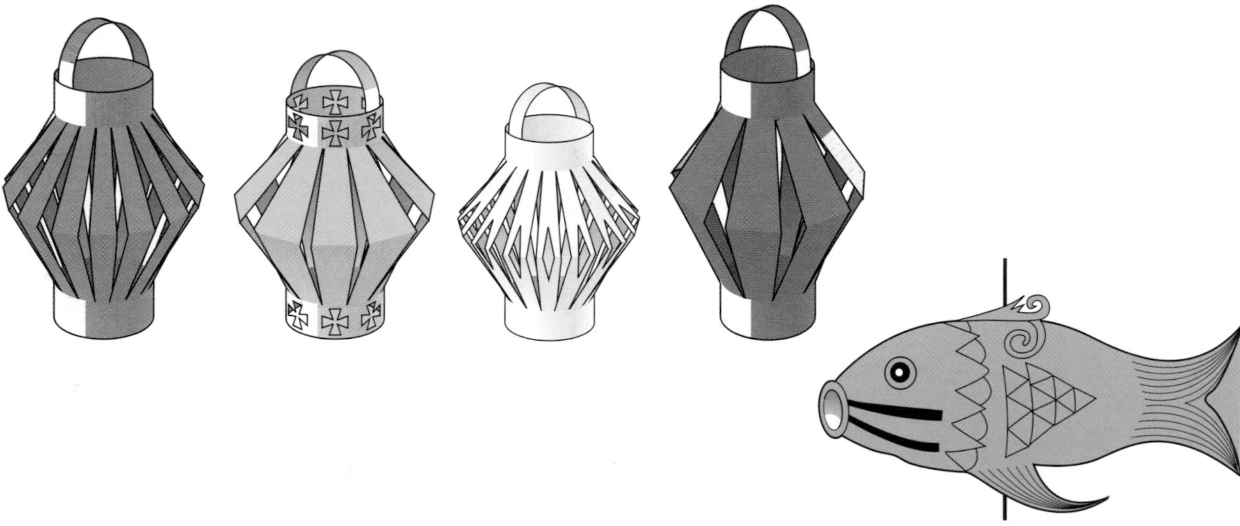

Puzzles

Puzzles can be for table or floor use, and can have both large and small pieces. Again, it is important to consider different levels of manipulative skill. Large pieces will be helpful to the less able or less dexterous child, as will puzzles in which pieces have sturdy knobs for lifting and positioning. However, just because a child needs large pieces to meet their physical needs, it does not necessarily mean that they cannot enjoy a puzzle with a challenging picture.

The issue of positive images applies in the same way as with books and stories.

> **remember** Physical and intellectual needs are not always parallel with each other. Children increase different aspects of their development at different rates.

Music, movement and singing

It is so easy to include diversity in this area of the curriculum by choosing musical instruments from a range of cultures and putting together a selection of instruments that will accommodate most physical needs. A musical instrument box should not simply hold tambourines, drums and cymbals, as this is so limiting for expression and restricts opportunities.

Dance is an important part of many cultures, and including dance on a regular basis encourages children to explore and communicate through a range of expressions and movements. Although the emphasis may be on rhythm and dance, the children will also learn to appreciate what other cultures have to offer.

Combining dance with the use of musical instruments will encourage children to accompany each other, building on their ability to co-operate with others, and to appreciate each other as equal partners in a joint activity.

> **remember** Electronic musical activities, and those involving vibration, are particularly useful for children with severe hearing loss, as they offer multiple sensory experiences.

Libraries

Public libraries loan out tapes and CDs, which are good sources of world music, enabling children to enjoy a range of songs from around the globe and learn to sing in different languages.

Cooking activities

There are medical, practical and cultural issues to be taken into account when planning activities with food. Consideration must be given to the needs of:

- children who have medical conditions such as:
  - diabetes
  - coeliac disease
  - cystic fibrosis
  - food allergies, particularly when children are anaphylactic (suffer a potentially life-threatening reaction, which needs immediate medical attention).
- children who are vegetarian or vegan
- children from cultures where certain foods, or combinations of foods, are not allowed (look again at the table on page 188).

Examples of foods linked to religious and cultural festivals that can be made with children include:

- vegetarian foods, such as dahl and chapattis, which can be made to celebrate the start of Guru Nanak's travels, as part of the Sikh festival of Baisakhi
- pancakes, which are traditionally made on Shrove Tuesday, the day before the start of Lent, the Christian period of 40 days leading up to Easter, which Jesus spent in the wilderness
- coconut barfi (similar to coconut ice), which is traditionally offered between siblings and close friends at the Hindu Raksha Bandhan festival of protection and care.

activity 5.14 INDIVIDUAL WORK

Try making gluten-free playdough suitable for use with children who have coeliac disease.

The recipe for gluten-free playdough can be found in Unit 6, page 247.

Persona dolls

keyword

Persona dolls
Dolls designed to represent children from various cultures and/or with a range of disabilities.

A type of doll has been developed to represent children with a range of disabilities, and children from a variety of cultures. They are called **persona dolls**, and they are introduced to children by an adult who describes the persona doll's background, or their 'special story' that covers their disability, and the situation that brings them to the nursery or classroom, for example as part of a family that is seeking asylum. This offers opportunities for children to discuss and explore the difficulties that are sometimes faced by others, and to consider the bias that can be experienced and the hurt that can be felt.

A persona doll can be provided for any individual need and is an ideal way of encouraging children to accept diversity and of paving the way for a new child to settle and integrate easily into the group or class.

case study 5.3 Raisa

Raisa is Turkish and is new to your school. She is learning English as a second language; at home and with her friends outside of school she speaks mainly Turkish.

Raisa tries hard in school and copes very well, but she gets upset when children laugh at the way that she pronounces some of her words.

activity INDIVIDUAL WORK

How could the use of a persona doll have helped pave the way for the other children to accept Raisa and her heritage more easily?

Professional Practice

- Children need to learn how to value and include others. It is important that you give guidance, rather than criticism, and offer suggestions to help their understanding.
- The responses and thinking that they learn from home may at times be unacceptable within the setting, and tact is needed in helping parents understand the importance of good (inclusive) practice.
- Having an understanding of a range of religious and cultural practices is important, but anti-discriminatory practice can only be maintained if all staff within a setting are committed to promoting anti-discriminatory practice, challenging discrimination, and reflecting on their own practice and attitudes.

1. What is meant by the term 'professional'?
2. How can poor time management and being unreliable have an impact on the children in your care?
3. What does each member of a team need to do and/or consider?
4. What different sorts of people make up a good team?
5. Give at least three examples of the rules and guidelines that early years teams need to observe.

6. Which groups of people within society are often marginalised in some way?
7. Why is confidentiality important in early years settings?
8. What examples can you give of diversity within society?
9. Give an example of how gender may affect equality in early years.
10. What legislation can you think of that is linked to the rights of individuals?
11. What is the difference between institutional and individual discrimination?
12. Give one example of how discrimination can be direct and one example of how it can be indirect.
13. Give an example of a food-related custom.
14. Explain tokenism and how it can be avoided.
15. What is a persona doll?

References and suggested further reading

Brown, B. (2001) *Persona Dolls in Action: Combating Discrimination*. Trentham Books.

Burnard, P. (1992) *Communicate! A Communication Skills Guide for Health Care Workers*. Edward Arnold Publishers.

Collins Dictionary (1991), Harper Collins, Glasgow.

Dare, A. and O'Donovan, M. (1997) *Good Practice in Caring for Young Children with Special Needs*. Nelson Thornes, Cheltenham.

Flekkøy, M. G. and Kaufman, N. H. (1997) *Rights and Responsibilities in Family and Society*. Jessica Kingsley Publishers, London.

Green, S. (2007) *BTEC National Children's Care, Learning and Development*. Nelson Thornes, Cheltenham.

Malik, H. (2002) *A Practical Guide to Equal Opportunities*, 2nd edn. Nelson Thornes, Cheltenham.

Petrie, P. (1991) *Communicating with Children and Adults*. Edward Arnold Publishers, London.

Walker, C. (1998) *Eating Well for the Under-5s in Childcare*. The Caroline Walker Trust, St Austell.

Websites

www.cre.org.uk
www.eoc.org.uk
www.homeoffice.gov.uk

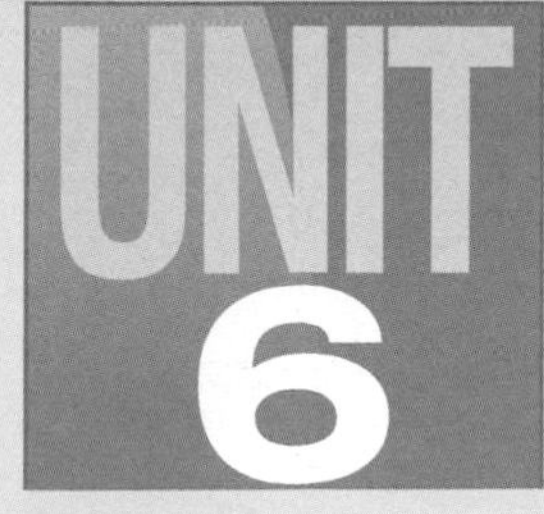

Supporting Children's Play and Learning

This unit covers:

- understanding how to support children's play
- understanding how to help to provide opportunities for children's imaginative and creative play
- understanding how to help to support physical play
- understanding how to encourage children to explore and investigate.

Think about the last time that you used a new music system or mobile phone, the fun you had finding out what it could do and the sense of achievement when you made it work. Much of children's play is concerned with exploring and investigating, and they too get enjoyment from their achievements.

Play is important to many aspects of a child's development. This unit introduces you to different types of play and shows how you can support children's learning, the resources that you will need, the levels of supervision required, how to encourage involvement and exploration, and how play fits into the relevant curriculum frameworks.

Although some reference is made to the full age range (birth to 16 years), the emphasis is on the under-eights, as this is the age range mostly being cared for by students on this course.

grading criteria

To achieve a **Pass** grade the evidence must show that the learner is able to:	To achieve a **Merit** grade the evidence must show that the learner is able to:	To achieve a **Distinction** grade the evidence must show that the learner is able to:
P1 describe different types of play	**M1** explain how children should be encouraged and supervised in their play	**D1** evaluate the potential role of physical play in the development of children
P2 describe the role of the adult in the provision, encouragement and supervision of children's play	**M2** explain why it is sometimes important for adults to be involved and to intervene in children's imaginative and creative play	**D2** evaluate the role of the adult in all aspects of children's play

grading criteria

To achieve a **Pass** grade the evidence must show that the learner is able to:	To achieve a **Merit** grade the evidence must show that the learner is able to:	To achieve a **Distinction** grade the evidence must show that the learner is able to:
P3 outline the involvement and intervention of the adult in children's play	**M3** explain how physical play can be encouraged for children's benefit.	
P4 describe the role of the adult in providing for imaginative and creative play		
P5 outline the benefits of physical play for children and how this can be supported		
P6 describe how children can be encouraged to explore and investigate		

Understanding how to support children's play

Figure 6.1
Play allows children to …

Play assists children to develop holistically (as a whole person). This means that it helps them develop:

- socially – building relationships with others
- intellectually – learning more about the world they live in
- morally – understanding right and wrong, fair and unfair, good and bad
- physically – building on their physical skills, to achieve new ones and enhance those they already have
- linguistically – through opportunities to talk, question and discuss
- emotionally – helping them feel independent and secure
- spiritually – encouraging a sense of wonder and enquiry, and also an understanding of cultural beliefs.

From the above list, you can see that play forms the basis of learning for young children. You need therefore to understand both how to plan a range of activities and why those activities are of value. This unit will help you.

Understanding play

Different types of play

Play takes many forms. It can be:

keyword
Exploratory play
Play in which a child is able to find out by experimentation and discovery.

- physical
- manipulative
- imaginative
- **exploratory**
- creative.

Examples of activities can be found on pages 204–221, 243–254 and 263–270. You may find it helpful to refer to them from time to time as you read through the unit.

The stages of play

keyword
Stages of play
The changes in how children's play develops, usually linked to age.

There are several **stages of play**. To understand the role of play in development you first need to understand the sequence in which the play stages develop. Children learn initially through observing what others are doing, gradually moving towards imitating and then co-operating with them. The stages of play are usually identified as:

- solitary
- parallel
- associative (looking on)
- simple co-operative
- complex co-operative.

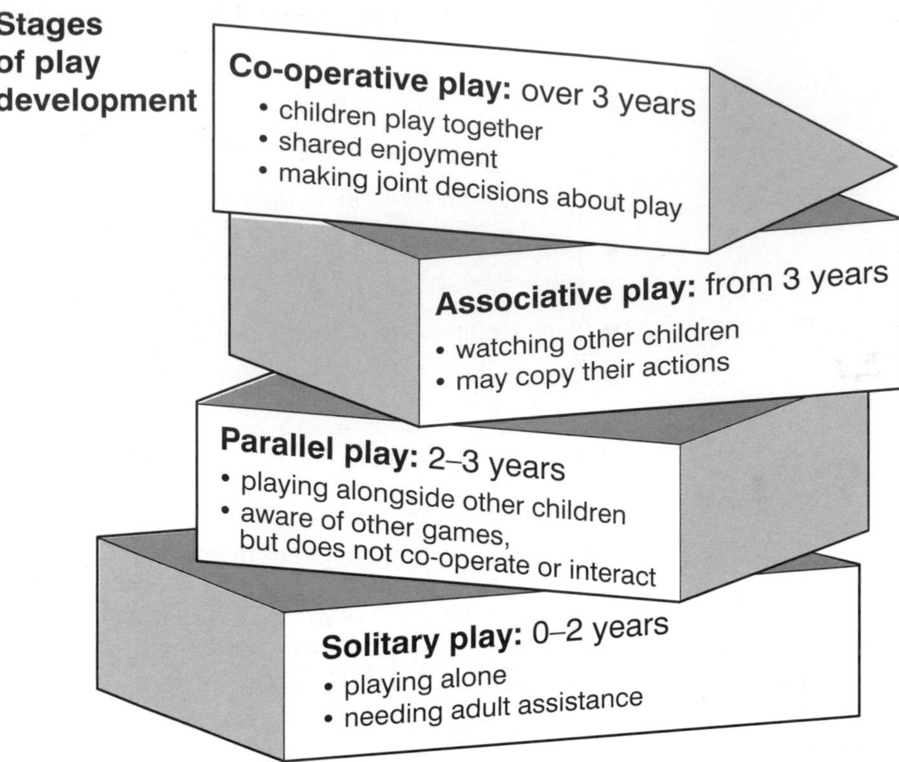

Figure 6.2
Stages of play development

As you can see from Figure 6.2, play develops stage by stage, gradually becoming more social as the child moves from the solitary actions of the toddler absorbed in their own world through to the complex games involving rules that are seen in the infant school playground. The ability to co-operate with others also develops in stages, which are dependent both on the age and stage of development of the individual child and on the opportunities and experiences that have been made available to them.

Solitary play

The first stage of play is referred to as solitary play. The child plays contentedly alone, still needing the reassurance of the adult. This play is typical up to the age of two years. It is frequently imitative, demonstrating that the child has a basic understanding of the actions of others within their social world. An example of solitary imitative play would be the child pretending, even briefly, to brush the hair of a doll or teddy.

Figure 6.3
Solitary play

Parallel play

Parallel play usually begins to emerge between two and three years of age; now the child finds enjoyment playing alongside, but not with, another child. The children do not necessarily even acknowledge that each other exists, and they make no reference to what the other is doing.

Figure 6.4
Parallel play

Figure 6.5
Associative play

Associative play (looking-on play)

At this stage, the child begins to watch the actions of others engaged in the same activity and enjoys observing their play from a distance. **Associative play** is typically seen between three and four years of age; the children are not yet ready to play with others, but will learn a great deal from their observations.

> *keyword*
> **Associative play**
> Children play with the same activity, watching what others are doing, but are not yet playing co-operatively.

Joining-in play (simple co-operative play)

By four years, most children will be ready to play co-operatively with others. This simple co-operative play involves the shared enjoyment of a similar activity. A good example would be a group of children all dressing dolls together: there are no rules and no restrictions; it is just a pleasurable play experience, with others.

Co-operative play (complex co-operative play)

During this, the last and most developed stage of children's play, children interact as a group. This can entail physical co-operation to complete a joint task or play that includes complex rules, involving the taking on of agreed (although 'evolving as they go') rules.

Figure 6.6
Simple co-operative play

Figure 6.7
Complex co-operative play

Social influences on play

It is important to remember that social development and play are affected by various experiences, including the effects of stereotyping.

See Unit 5, page 179 to remind yourself about stereotyping.

remember

Negative as well as positive messages can be portrayed by actions, words and non-verbal behaviour.

Children learn about social behaviour from watching and imitating other people. They are particularly influenced by the adults whom they admire and look up to. As an adult working with young children, you are a role model, and should therefore be aware of how your actions, attitudes and words can affect the children in your care.

You may find it useful to refer to pages 384–387 for examples of inclusive play and to the section on social learning theory in Unit 1, page 21.

Adult involvement

Not only does play develop in accordance with the child's age and stage of development, play will also be influenced by how much or how little adult involvement there is, and by how much freedom children are given to make decisions for themselves. Depending on the amount and nature of adult involvement, play can be:

- structured
- adult-led
- child-initiated
- free-flow
- spontaneous
- therapeutic.

Structured/adult-led play

Structured play tends to be led by the adult, with the adult often working alongside the child. Most people agree that children benefit from an element of structure and that it is necessary to structure the day within a routine that meets everyone's needs. It is important that the structure set by the adult does not impact on the free flow of play that enables children to explore activities, investigate ideas and manipulate resources in the ways they choose.

Child-initiated/free-flow play

Free-flow play tends to be child initiated. The children use their imaginations and learn through discovery.

Tina Bruce (1991) described free-flow play as the only true concept of play. With a partner, find out more about the thinking of Tina Bruce.

(a) Do you agree with her description of free-flow play?

(b) Can you think of an example to support it?

Spontaneous play

As children play spontaneously, they develop their play for themselves. They explore ideas and are enabled to seize the moment. Here, the role of the adult is to enjoy the 'moment' with them, either directly, or through observation, offering suitable resources to develop the experience, introducing related stories or information books, and encouraging discussion, without dictating what is used and what should be done.

Therapeutic play (often known as play therapy)

Therapeutic play can be of help to children who are troubled in some way, aiding them to explore and work through their troubles. It can also help children to understand medical care procedures that they have experienced, or are likely to experience shortly.

The right to play

All children deserve the right to play. Play supports all aspects of their development; you can see examples of how various activities support the main areas of development in the next section.

You may also like to refer to Unit 1, page 13, for further information on the links between play and development.

Importance of play in development

Sometimes, it is easy to see the learning value of activities and toys, for example, a push-along dog clearly helps the development of balance and walking in toddlers. Sometimes, however, the learning value is less obvious. The following pages outline a range of popular activities, noting the support that these give to the following aspects of children's development:

- social development
- emotional development
- physical development
- intellectual development
- language development.

Construction play

Figure 6.8
Construction play encourages social development

Social development
Construction play supports social development by providing opportunities for:

- developing confidence in selecting resources
- sharing resources with others
- negotiating exchanges of resources
- asking and responding to requests
- when building, using ideas from observations of their own environment.

Emotional development
Construction play supports emotional development by providing opportunities for:

- showing satisfaction with own achievements
- showing frustration and disappointment if they do not succeed in their intentions.

Figure 6.9
Construction play encourages emotional development

Figure 6.10
Construction play and physical development

Physical development
Construction play supports physical development by providing opportunities for:

- handling resources with increasing confidence and skill
- using manipulative skills with smaller construction pieces
- developing precision and the increased ability to place pieces carefully
- developing large motor skills when using large boxes, tables, chairs, etc.
- using the senses to explore shape and texture (e.g. Stickle bricks, Duplo, Popoids).

Intellectual development
Construction play supports intellectual development by providing opportunities for:

- increasing understanding of how pieces fit together
- developing planning and intention
- increasing understanding of stability and strength

Figure 6.11
Construction play encourages language and intellectual development

- increasing understanding of weight and height
- increasing understanding of the differences between resources
- increasing ability to select and group pieces together by size, shape, colour, etc.
- sustaining concentration.

Language development
Language development is helped by:

- using new words and terminology (e.g. build, construct, stability, planning)
- describing plans and intentions
- discussing ideas and what the child is doing.

Sand play

Figure 6.12
Sand play

Social development
Sand play supports social development by providing opportunities for:

- playing alongside or with others
- developing the ability to interact
- imitating the actions of others
- passing and exchanging tools and resources
- sharing tools and resources.

Emotional development
Emotional development is helped because sand play:

- can be a soothing experience
- can be a very satisfying experience
- is a safe, non-fail activity; you cannot play 'wrong' with sand
- provides the opportunity to develop confidence in interactions with others.

Physical development
Sand play supports physical development by providing opportunit

- handle the sand, experiencing the feel and textures of both the and the various tools that may be provided (sensory experience
- develop manipulative skills, i.e. those needed to use both dry and wet sand
- increase control over body movements.

Intellectual development
Sand play supports intellectual development by providing opportunities to:

- understand about the properties of sand, for example that dry sand pours and wet sand can be moulded
- learn that adding water can alter the sand and the type of play
- increase understanding of absorbency
- increase understanding of the effects that various sand 'tools' can have
- sustain concentration.

Language development
Sand play helps language development by:

- encouraging the use of new words and terminology (e.g. sift, sieve, pour, trickle, mould, pat, shape)
- offering opportunities for expressing ideas and plans.

Water play

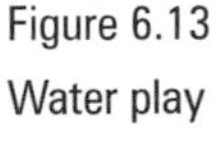

Figure 6.13
Water play

Social development
Water play supports social development by providing opportunities for:

- playing alongside and then with others
- selecting tools and resources
- sharing and passing tools to others
- swapping and negotiating for tools
- asking for tools and resources and responding to requests.

Emotional development
Emotional development is encouraged because water play:

- can be a soothing experience
- allows a sense of achievement
- is a non-fail activity; you cannot play 'wrong' with water
- allows child to display expressions of pleasure and excitement at new and favourite activities.

Physical development
Water play supports physical development by providing opportunities to:

- increase manipulative skills
- increase control over body movements
- handle the water, noting the feel, texture, etc.
- explore physically, such as tipping, pouring from one container to another.

Intellectual development
Water play supports intellectual development by providing opportunities to:

- increase understanding of what water can do
- investigate and try out ideas
- increase understanding of 'full up' and 'empty'
- increase understanding of volume and capacity
- increase understanding of floating and sinking
- develop sustained concentration.

Language development
Water play supports language development by providing opportunities for:

- acquiring new words and terminology (e.g. float, sink, pour, swish, splash, empty, full, more, less, greater than, less than, heavier, lighter).

Dough play

Figure 6.14
Playing with dough

Social development
Dough play supports social development by providing opportunities for:

- playing alongside or with others
- developing confidence in own ability to interact with others
- sharing
- asking for resources or tools and responding to requests
- passing tools to others.

Emotional development
Dough play supports emotional development because:

- Dough is a very satisfying medium to use.
- Dough play is a non-fail activity; you cannot play 'wrong' with dough.
- Actions can be repeated and developed; you can make, squash and remake.

Physical development
Dough play supports physical development by providing opportunities for:

- handling the dough and experiencing the feel and texture
- developing manipulative skills by rolling, prodding, poking, pulling, pushing, moulding
- increasing control over body movements
- increasing control of tools (e.g. knives, cutters, forks, rolling pins, graters).

Intellectual development

Dough play supports intellectual development by providing opportunities to:

- increase understanding of which tools are appropriate for specific actions
- select tools for intended actions
- develop planning skills to achieve intended 'end results'
- develop sustained concentration.

Language development

Dough play supports language development by providing opportunities for:

- acquiring new words and terminology to describe the various actions (e.g. rolling, pressing down, forming a ball)
- describing texture and how each action feels
- explaining ideas and making suggestions.

Role play, including dressing up

Figure 6.15
Dressing up

Social development

Role play and dressing up support social development by providing opportunities for:

- imitating others (e.g. when 'being mummy', making dinner, brushing a doll's hair, going shopping)
- trying out different people's roles
- linking up with the games of others
- co-operative play, planning who will be who and what each will do
- demonstrating understanding of social greeting and politeness (e.g. hello, please, thank you).

Emotional development

Role play and dressing up support emotional development by providing opportunities for:

- increasing confidence in interacting
- experiencing a sense of release and understanding through acting out situations that may concern, confuse or worry the child (e.g. a new baby at home, mummy crying, going into hospital)
- developing understanding of how other people might feel
- in role play, moving in and out of reality, as the child's needs arise.

Physical development

Role play and dressing up support physical development by providing opportunities to:

- use large motor skills as they dress and undress
- develop manipulative skills as they manoeuvre buttons, zips, etc. with increased control and dexterity
- show precision and dexterity as children lay the table, set out the items for a shop, etc.

Intellectual development

Role play and dressing up support intellectual development by providing opportunities for:

- demonstrating understanding of different people's roles
- demonstrating understanding of cooking processes (e.g. cakes go in the oven; pans go on the hob)
- demonstrating understanding of shopping processes (e.g. asking for items, paying for them, taking them home)
- selecting appropriate resources for different roles
- pretending that one object is something else (symbolic play)
- matching, grouping and pairing (e.g. cups to saucers, knives to forks)
- demonstrating knowledge of various situations (e.g. hospitals, cafes)
- responding to ideas and situations.

Language development

Role play and dressing up support language development by providing opportunities for:

- conversation
- expressing ideas from their own imagination
- using language to organise and make suggestions
- interacting with others

- developing new vocabulary as new 'game situations' arise
- developing writing skills as the child makes shopping lists, menus for the café, etc.

Activities involving paint

Figure 6.16
Children painting

Social development
Painting supports social development by providing opportunities for:

- making choices (e.g. choosing colours, paper sizes)
- sharing ideas with others
- using observations as a basis for pictures.

Emotional development
Painting supports emotional development because:

- Paint is satisfying and non-competitive; you can't paint your own picture 'wrong'.
- There are opportunities to show pleasure and excitement at new and favourite activities.
- Joining in the 'messiest' activities helps the child to develop confidence.

Physical development
Painting supports physical development by providing opportunities for:

- developing manipulative skills when using pens, brushes, rollers, etc.
- increasing control of body movements
- handling paint textures (e.g. runny paint, thick paint)

- handling and using the various alternative 'tools' (e.g. sponges, print blocks, straws, rollers)
- learning how to fold paper and card for printing and making cards, etc.

Intellectual development

Painting supports intellectual development by providing opportunities for:

- increasing the ability and confidence to make choices
- mixing colours to make additional colours
- choosing colours (showing understanding of how to illustrate specific things, e.g. blue for the sky, green for the grass)
- experimenting with new ideas and activities (e.g. printing)
- developing and identifying patterns in colours, shapes, etc.
- using paint to demonstrate what the child has observed.

Language development

Painting supports language development by providing opportunities for:

- using language to describe colours, textures, etc.
- using language to describe ideas and intentions
- discussing what the children have painted or created.

Junk modelling

Social development

Junk modelling supports social development by providing opportunities for:

- developing confidence in selecting materials
- observing others and learning from them
- sharing resources, using negotiating skills.

Emotional development

Junk modelling supports emotional development because the child:

- experiences satisfaction when model is complete
- feels pride when showing models or having them admired
- learns to deal with frustration if model falls apart
- learns to deal with disappointment if there is not enough of, for example, a certain sized box.

Physical development

Junk modelling supports physical development by providing opportunities for:

- developing manipulative skills
- increasing control of body movements
- increasing ability to hold items in place while constructing

- developing ability to use staplers, fasteners, tape, etc.
- handling a range of materials – texture, feel, etc. (e.g. glue is sticky; Sellotape is tacky)
- increasing understanding of safety issues, such as the safe use of scissors.

Intellectual development

Junk modelling supports intellectual development by providing opportunities for:

- increasing understanding of how things hold together
- making choices as to which junk items to use
- planning from their own imaginations (e.g. making rockets, space ships)
- planning from observations of their environment (e.g. making a vacuum cleaner)
- increasing their understanding of stability and instability
- increasing their understanding of strength
- developing understanding of the need to negotiate to acquire the space to build and the items required to build a specific object
- sustaining concentration.

Language development

Junk modelling supports language development by providing opportunities to:

- acquire new words and terminology in relation to shape, size and materials
- ask for items and resources
- use language to describe their model
- use language to describe their plans and intentions
- discuss the size, shape, colour and use of their models.

Books and stories

Figure 6.17
Enjoying a story

Social development
Books and stories support social development because:

- the experience is often shared
- the experience can be one to one or in a group
- the experience helps children learn about their social world (e.g. families, holidays, everyday situations)
- the experience helps extend understanding of situations that may cause concern (e.g. new baby, moving house, having a tantrum, illness)
- the experience helps develop observation skills
- there are often opportunities to join in with actions – to be part of a group.

Emotional development
Books and stories support emotional development because:

- a range of emotions can be explored (e.g. those connected with having tantrums, worries about moving house, going into hospital, mother having a new baby)
- the repetition of familiar stories and the repeated sequences in many books are comforting to most children
- books and stories offer opportunities to express emotions (e.g. laughter, mock 'fear').

Physical development
Books and stories support physical development by providing opportunities for:

- developing manipulation skills through handling books appropriately (e.g. turning pages, holding books the right way up, holding books still while looking at them)
- improving hand–eye co-ordination – following the text even before they can read
- performing actions as the story is told.

Intellectual development
Books and stories support intellectual development by providing opportunities for:

- developing an understanding of how books 'work' – from top to bottom and left to right (in English)
- understanding that books can be both for pleasure and a source of information.

Also:

- children learn a great deal about their own environment through the stories they hear and the books they look at
- a child's understanding is consolidated by the repetition of familiar stories.

Language development

Books and stories support language development by providing opportunities for:

- acquiring new words and terminology
- learning about new objects, new situations, other cultures
- joining in with repetition
- describing what will happen next
- suggesting what might happen next.

Musical instruments

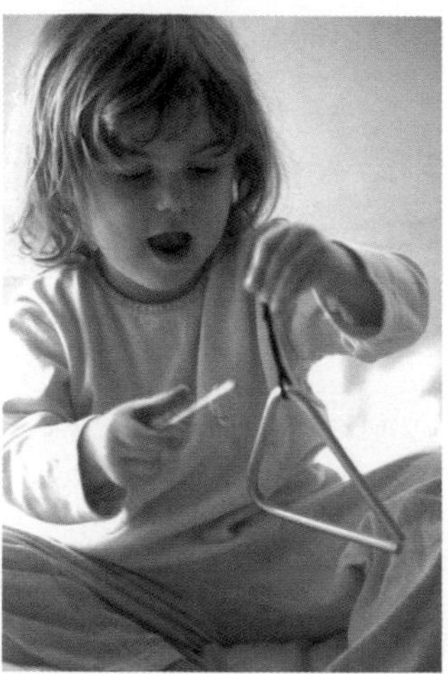

Figure 6.18
Playing musical instruments

Social development

Playing musical instruments supports social development because:

- this is often a joint activity with others
- children learn to play co-operatively
- children learn to respond to instructions and guidance (e.g. when to start and when to stop)
- turn taking is required.

Emotional development

When playing a musical instrument:

- there can be an emotional release through music
- gentle sounds can soothe a distressed child
- bold sounds can liven up a sad or unusually quiet child
- children learn to enjoy and value the sounds and instruments of their own culture
- children learn to enjoy and value the sounds and instruments of other cultures
- taking turns to listen to each other play encourages consideration of other people's needs.

Physical development

Playing musical instruments supports:

- development of fine motor skills
- development of large motor skills through opportunities to balance, dance and march to music (locomotion)
- development of the ability to move rhythmically
- the linking of music to dance and movement
- learning about the different feel of various instruments (e.g. cymbals – metal; drums – skins; maracas – wooden; shakers – gourds, a hollowed-out fruit).

Intellectual development

Playing musical instruments supports:

- increased knowledge of the origins of instruments and music
- increased knowledge of the different types of sounds that can be made
- sequencing and patterning within music
- linking music to dance and movement
- understanding changes in pitch, tempo, etc.
- sustained concentration.

Language development

Language development is supported by:

- increased vocabulary (e.g. sound names; instrument names; rhythmic words – slow, slow, fast, fast, slow)
- development of voice pitch and learning how it can be changed to match different instruments
- improved listening skills.

Puzzles

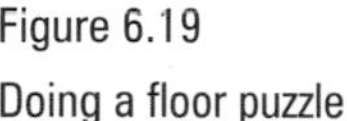

Figure 6.19
Doing a floor puzzle

Social development
Puzzles support social development because:

- younger children often share the activity with an adult
- floor puzzles are usually enjoyed in pairs or small groups
- pictures often depict objects or situations from children's own environment and experience.

Emotional development
Puzzles support emotional development because:

- confidence increases alongside skill development
- satisfaction is experienced when puzzles are completed
- the child learns to deal with frustration if a puzzle is difficult to complete.

Physical development
Puzzles support physical development by providing opportunities for:

- developing fine motor skills
- increasing ability to handle small pieces
- improving hand–eye co-ordination.

Intellectual development
Puzzles support intellectual development by providing opportunities for:

- developing understanding of how to match pieces to gaps, identifying shape, size, etc.
- learning through trial and error in the earliest stages
- demonstrating understanding by matching pieces to accompanying pictures
- sustaining concentration
- developing memory by remembering the completed picture, helping the child visualise what they are trying to achieve.

Language development
Puzzles support language development by providing opportunities for:

- using language to talk about the picture
- using language to talk about shapes, size and how to position pieces
- acquiring new words (e.g. place, hold, edges, twist, turn, flat, turn over).

Figure 6.20
Building with blocks

Stacking toys and posting boxes

Social development

Stacking toys and posting boxes support social development because:

- the activity would initially be shared with an adult or older sibling who helps the child (perhaps hand over hand), guiding them to success when posting a shape in a post box or shape sorter
- children learn to build jointly with another person
- knocking down the tower could be a joint fun action
- there are opportunities for the child to select which piece to post, or which piece to stack next.

Emotional development

Stacking toys and posting boxes support emotional development because:

- satisfaction and pleasure is experienced when successful
- pleasure and excitement is experienced when knocking down the tower
- confidence increases in line with improved physical (manipulation) skills.

Physical development

Stacking toys and posting boxes support physical development by providing opportunities for:

- developing fine motor skills, i.e. handling with increasing control
- practising precision and positioning skills
- improving hand–eye co-ordination
- exploring shapes with hands and mouths.

Intellectual development
Stacking toys and posting boxes support intellectual development by providing opportunities for:

- learning to stack by size (e.g. beakers and rings)
- learning to enclose by size (e.g. beakers, 'Russian doll'-style objects)
- matching shapes to correct shape holes
- learning by trial and error
- counting when stacking and sorting objects
- learning about colours as each colour is stated for them by the adult.

Language development
Stacking toys and posting boxes support language development by providing opportunities for:

- the adult to introduce vocabulary (e.g. shape names, colour names, biggest, smallest, bigger than)
- counting.

Threading reels and buttons

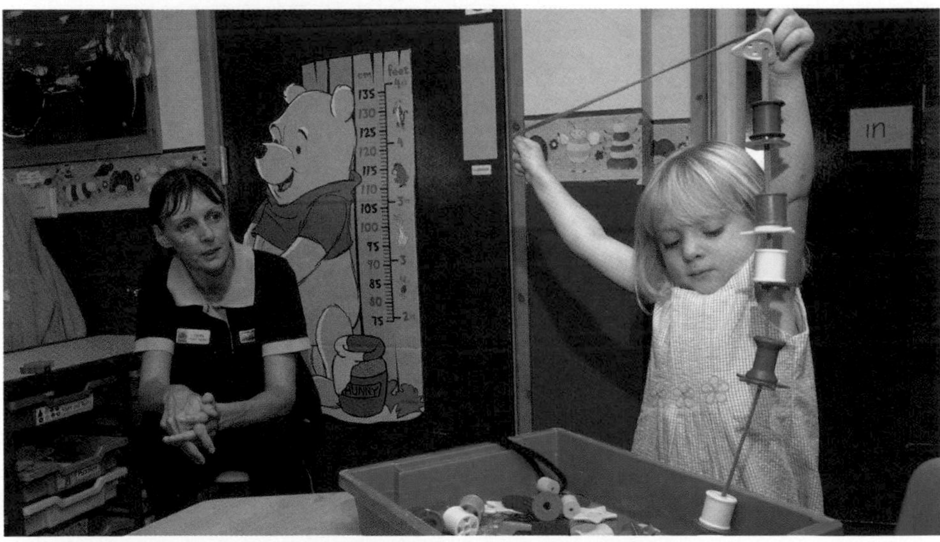

Figure 6.21
Threading cotton reels

Social development
Threading reels and buttons support social development by providing opportunities for:

- playing alongside or with others
- making decisions and selecting resources
- asking for resources and responding to requests
- sharing and swapping resources.

Emotional development
Threading reels and buttons support emotional development because:

- the activity is calm and satisfying
- a sense of pleasure is experienced when the task is achieved
- children enjoy being able to make their own choices.

Physical development
Threading reels and buttons support physical development by providing opportunities for:

- developing manipulative skills
- improving hand–eye co-ordination
- increasing control over body movements
- handling the threading of objects with increased ability and precision.

Intellectual development
Threading reels and buttons support intellectual development by providing opportunities for:

- developing the ability to sequence by shape, size and colour
- developing the ability to group by shape, size, colours, etc.
- learning to plan and have intentions
- learning to add on and count
- learning to take one away
- sustaining concentration

Language development
Threading reels and buttons support language development by providing opportunities for:

- acquiring words and terminology (e.g. colour names, shape names and counting)
- using language to ask for and negotiate
- using language to talk about length, purpose, etc.

Development of play as children grow older

It is important that play opportunities take into account new and developing skills, changes of interest, and levels of trust, common sense and awareness of hazards and danger.

Junior and middle school children are often adventurous and eager to explore their environment without supervision. The ability to make judgements about safety will vary enormously within the age group, and supervising adults will need to reflect on each activity or play experience, to build a picture of each individual child's awareness of safe practice.

Children need to be given opportunities to explore and take risks so that they can learn to make judgements about their own safety and the impact of their actions upon others. It is, however, important that this learning occurs within a controlled environment.

Adolescents

Activities for older children and young people are likely to be more successful if they have been involved in the planning. This will help to ensure that supervising adults are in touch with current interests and demonstrate that they value the group's input. A good relationship between adults and young people is important, but a balance is needed to ensure that friendliness is not given priority over fulfilling the supervisory role and all the responsibilities that it carries. This balance can be quite hard to achieve, particularly when the adults are themselves young.

Peer pressure

Peer pressure plays an important part in adolescence. This can pose problems with regard to safety and risk taking. The influences of the more outgoing or forthright individuals within a group should be assessed and observed carefully.

Resources

The suitability of the materials and equipment provided can make all the difference to the fun and enjoyment derived from an activity and to the value of the learning experience. Many resources can be found around the home, and children do not need to be provided with manufactured products for every activity. As long as items are clean and safe, they are likely to be used as effectively as many purpose-made products.

activity 6.2 INDIVIDUAL WORK

As you start to plan and implement activities, keep a record of the resources and materials that you use. This will form an 'at a glance' record for you for future reference. You may wish to use the following ideas on pages 000–000 to get you started.

remember

This is not a comprehensive list. There will be many more ideas that you could add.

Suggestions for construction play

A carpeted area helps to keep down the noise of construction play, and a thick table cloth or blanket protects surfaces and also absorbs noise.

Chairs, tables, clothes driers, etc. can form dens and houses indoors. Planks, crates, boards, etc. can be used to form dens outside.

Materials could include:

- building bricks of different sizes and materials (e.g. wood, plastic, foam – there are many commercial types available)
- off-cuts from carpenters etc., smoothed down and splinter free
- geometric shapes

Figure 6.22
Construction materials

- hollow shapes
- cardboard boxes of different sizes and shapes, including extra-large boxes (e.g. from washing machines)
- cardboard tubes
- commercial construction kits of varying sizes and types (e.g. straws, tubes, bricks, and shapes)
- tyres, cones, hoops, planks and blankets, etc. for constructing an obstacle course outside
- real tools (but child sized) for woodworking activities
- glues, staplers, string, screws, etc., suitable for the materials being used.

Suggestions for sand play

Remember to let children explore sand with their hands first of all. This helps them understand its natural properties. They do not always need tools and other objects.

Materials could include:

- a blanket with raised patterns (old candlewick bedspreads are ideal) to catch sand and stop it spreading too far away from the sand box
- dustpan and brushes close to hand, to help clear up spills quickly
- bowls, buckets, storage boxes
- spoons, spades, scoops
- sieves, rakes
- sand wheels
- shapes for making sand structures (e.g. small boxes, jelly moulds, ramekins)

- pastry cutters, three-dimensional stencil shapes
- small world items (e.g. animals, people, vehicles)
- flags, twigs, shells, pebbles.

Suggestions for water play

A non-slip floor covering helps prevent accidents. Newspaper can help absorb the worst of the spillage. Have towels nearby, to avoid children walking across the room with dripping hands. Waterproof aprons with sleeves are the most useful design to help keep children dry.

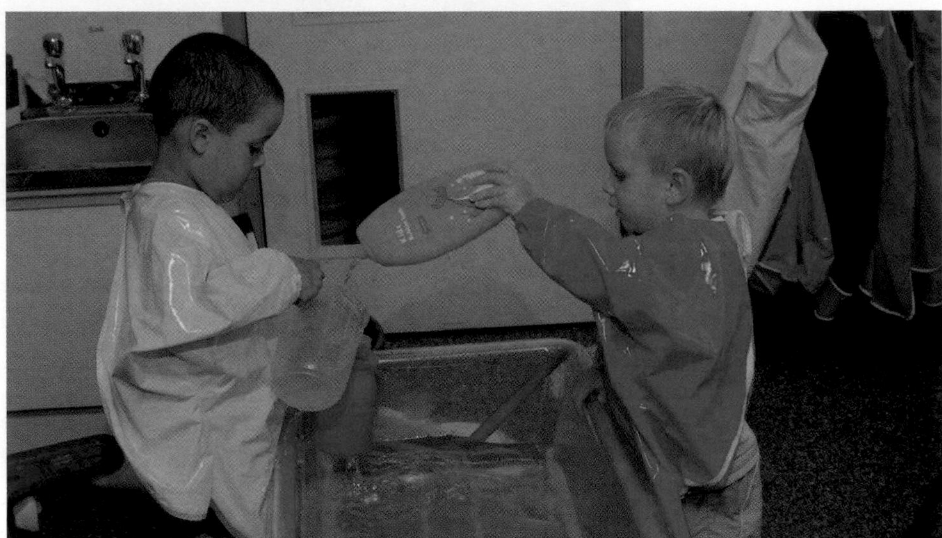

Figure 6.23
Playing with water

Materials include:

- items that float (e.g. sponges, sticks, rubber balls, pencils)
- items that sink (e.g. stones, soap, a cloth)
- jugs, bowls, buckets, cups
- spoons, scoops, ladles
- sieves and whisks
- tubes, funnels, water wheel
- food dyes to colour the water
- soap suds or washing-up liquid to produce bubbles
- ice cubes (containing food dye to help them show up) to observe as they melt.

Suggestions for dough, clay and other malleable play

As with sand, encourage children to experience the material with their hands initially.

A wipe-clean covering for the table is useful.

Materials could include:

- individual boards
- rolling pins, pie wheels, pizza cutters
- garlic presses, pasta makers, slotted spoons
- blunt knives, palette knives, forks and spoons
- pastry cutters, three-dimensional stencil shapes.

Suggestions for role play

Room dividers give privacy and shape to the play, and old curtains or drapes can transform a table into a den or a cave to create an enclosed space. Adding stars to the underside of a 'roof' can give a night-time outdoors feel (e.g. for camping or 'on safari' play). Role play can be linked to house play, or to themed play (e.g. post office, pet shop, garden centre).

Materials could include:

- household items (e.g. cutlery, china, cooking pans, woks, griddles, baking tins, telephone, TV, radio, newspapers, magazines, broom, dusters)
- gardening items (e.g. broom, rake, wheelbarrow, plant pots)
- for themed play such as vet play: soft toy animals, stethoscopes, record cards, chairs for waiting room, examination table, overalls for vet and nurses, cages, blankets, leads and collars, empty pet food containers, till and money
- for themed play such as post office play: table for counter, till and money, pens, paper, pamphlets, stamps, ink pad and ink stamp, savings-type books, parcels, weighing scales, a post box
- for themed play such as air travel: chairs in rows, suitcases and bags, uniforms for the flight attendants, a globe or large map of the world, tickets, headphones, lap trays, trolleys, luggage labels.

Other themed play ideas could include a hospital, baby clinic, pet shop, book shop, supermarket, café, place of worship, a ship, i.e. almost any setting you wish.

Try painting a 'scene from a window' linked to the current theme to put on the wall (e.g. a view of the sea if the role-play area is a ship; the sky and clouds if the children will be 'travelling by air'; a garden for outside the café play area).

Suggestions for dressing up

As with role play, dressing up can be linked to house play, with the child taking on the role of mummy, daddy, baby, granny, etc. It can also be linked to superhero play (e.g. Superman, Spiderman) or to a theme (e.g. a nurse in a hospital setting, the lollipop person at a school crossing, a police officer).

Materials could include:

- an old plain cotton sheet, which can easily be transformed into simple costumes

- cast-offs from friends and family, cut down to size
- lengths of sari material, which can be cut to more manageable lengths for the children to use safely
- an array of hats, scarves and helmets (always popular)
- bags and costume jewellery; beautiful jewellery can be made from pasta shapes, string, card, etc.

Professional Practice

- Dressing-up clothes are better if they are big, rather than small, as this offers more opportunities for independence.
- An old plain pillow case makes a good costume for a Roman, a soldier, a shepherd, etc. Just vary the trimmings.

Figure 6.24
Dressing up

Suggestions for paint activities

Painting with hands or fingers allows children to experience how the paint actually feels. Provide a good range of experiences (e.g. finger-painting; printing with hands, feet, vegetables, etc.; bubble painting; string painting; blow painting) and ensure that paint is the right thickness for the activity.

A wipe-clean surface is needed; a wipe-clean floor covering, or lots of newspaper, will help deal with spillages. There should be hand-washing facilities nearby to prevent unnecessary dripping of paint across the room, and somewhere will be needed for the children's artwork to dry – clothes dryers can be helpful for paper creations.

Materials include:

- brushes – these can be long or short handled, fat or thin to hold (e.g. tooth brushes, stencil brushes, shaving brushes, decorators' brushes); a good rule of thumb is that the younger the child, the chunkier the brush needs to be
- flour shakers, which give a good effect
- cleaned roll-on deodorant containers, which are brilliant for children with less-refined dexterity
- printers – these can be bought commercially but try using cotton reels, combs, yoghurt pots, biscuit cutters, large corks, leaves
- paper – make sure that the paper you provide is suitable for the activity. (Is it sufficiently large, absorbent and strong?)

Try adding extra ingredients to paint for a new experience (e.g. soap flakes, glitter, sand, cornflour).

Professional Practice

- All materials must be non-toxic.
- Be aware of skin allergies; some children may benefit from wearing disposable gloves.

Suggestions for junk modelling

A wipe clean surface will be needed. A wipe clean floor covering, or lots of newspaper, will help deal with spillages. There should be hand-washing facilities nearby and somewhere will be needed for the children's models to dry.

All materials and glues must be non-toxic.

Careful supervision will be needed when scissors and staplers are in use.

Ask families to send in boxes well in advance, or ideally keep a constant supply for regular use. Check that all boxes are clean and suitable (medicine boxes should not be used as these should not be handled by children). You should also check local policy regarding the use of egg cartons.

Junk modelling can be linked to a current theme (e.g. transport).

Suggestions for books and stories

Books should be easily accessible so that the children can look at them as and when they wish; book boxes, low shelving and open racks are all useful.

Include story books, poems and rhymes, information books, factual books, funny books, and books that support the exploration of emotions.

Ensure that the books show equality of gender, culture and ability, and include books in dual languages, books that pass on heritage, and books that depict other cultures.

Encourage children to enjoy group story times, one-to-one story times and using books as a source of reference.

Link drama to familiar stories.

Use props (e.g. puppets, linked items or storyboards) for greater visual impact.

Ensure that you have always read a book before you read it to children, so that you know what is coming and you can give appropriate emphasis where it is needed.

Always read with enthusiasm: when a bored adult reads a story, it is likely that the children will be bored with listening.

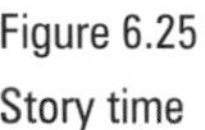

Figure 6.25
Story time

Suggestions for music and singing

Make collections of instruments (e.g. those that you shake, those that you hit with something, those that you blow).

Try making instruments with the children, using plastic bottles of different sizes and different fillings, but ensure that you maintain good health and safety practice at all times.

Provide music on tape or CD from around the world for the children to listen to. Whenever possible, provide a range of instruments from around the world,

Use music to calm children when they are hyped up, and also to enliven everyone on a despondent day.

Try to invite real instrumentalists to visit (e.g. a violist, trombonist, sitar player).

Make a recording that features instruments that the children are familiar with and play it to them to see which they can identify.

Suggestions for outdoor play

Play surfaces should be suitable for the activity, for example anything involving climbing should only be set out on a safety surface.

Trikes, bikes, ride-on animals, etc. are always popular and help balance, spatial awareness and co-ordination.

Use barrels, tyres, cones, hoops, ropes, etc. to make obstacle courses.

Use playground chalk to set out games such as hopscotch, or to draw boundaries for other play.

Encourage spatial development through action games using large motor movements and locomotion.

Encourage the children's enjoyment of ring games and parachute play.

Paint on a large scale (e.g. painting walls and bushes, using water and largish paintbrushes).

Use the outdoor environment as a resource for observation of mini-beasts and plant life.

If possible, plant vegetables, flowers and herbs and care for and monitor their growth and progress.

Care for birds by feeding regularly.

Encouragement

It can be very easy to plan, set out and organise children to take part in activities of your choosing. However, this is not necessarily the way they learn best. Sometimes, of course, we as adults need children to take part in certain situations and activities, but there are often opportunities for children to make their own choices, and it is important that these opportunities are clear to them and genuinely given.

A child who chooses freely to take part in an activity is likely to have done so because the activity interests them in some way, perhaps because it offers a new experience or exciting materials, or they wish to work alongside particular friends. Sometimes, the repetition of familiar favourites provides stability and security. Whatever the reason, learning situations initiated by children themselves are usually of greatest value and should always be encouraged.

Activities for children with specific needs

All children within a setting, whatever their specific needs, must be considered when planning activities. Part of the planning process includes identifying how different levels of need can be incorporated. At times, this will simply mean providing a greater level of support and encouragement through increased adult involvement. At other times, it will involve exploring the resources you are planning to use more thoroughly and providing more appropriate resources where necessary. Examples might include:

- providing paint brushes with chunkier handles for a child whose fine motor skills are less well developed
- providing puzzles with larger knobs on the pieces to aid lifting and replacing of pieces, again to aid manipulation
- ensuring that balls and hoops are in a bright colour to help children with visual impairment follow them more easily
- ensuring that there is sufficient space at a table to accommodate a child in a wheelchair or using a standing frame
- ensuring that there are opportunities for a child who may be overwhelmed by group activities to play near to the main group, by providing a mini sand tray, small bowl of water, etc.

keyword
Transmission model
An approach in which the adult controls the learning process, often suppressing the child's own initiative.

keyword
Laissez-faire model
An approach involving unrestricted freedom or indifference; e.g. the adult lets the child play without restriction and with little or no guidance.

keyword
Social constructivist model
An approach to learning that emphasises the importance of exploring a range of experiences and objects from everyday life.

Encouragement for parents

As an early years worker, you will need to demonstrate a calm, reassuring manner in order to ensure that parents feel confident leaving their child in your care. They will expect you to use common sense, to be aware of health and safety issues, and to show interest in their child. Figure 6.26 summarises aspects of your work where the support and encouragement that is intrinsic to your role can contribute to the building of good relationships and to providing safe, stimulating care for the children in the setting.

Supervision

Every adult has certain expectations of children. This will vary from person to person and can be influenced by generation, experience and culture. Our expectations can also affect the level of autonomy and supervision that we feel is needed in any given situation.

Theoretical models of adult involvement and supervision

The three main theoretical models with regard to adult involvement and how it can affect children's learning are:

- the **transmission** model
- the **laissez-faire** model
- the **social constructivist** model.

Transmission model

- Adults control the learning process for the child.
- The adult decides what learning will take place by being directly involved with the child's activity.

Figure 6.26

Role of the early years worker

The role of an early years worker involves:

Involving parents wherever possible
– parents should be made to feel welcome within the setting and encouraged to be as involved with the setting as they are able to be. This will include discussions with their child's key worker or the setting's supervisor, as well as being involved with fundraising and social events. The amount of involvement will vary according to circumstances and each parent should be valued for whatever level of involvement they are able to contribute

A calm, reassuring manner
– to help parents feel confident that you can care for their child appropriately

Being a good listener
– at times parents may have concerns about their child and need to talk them over with another person who knows their child well

Being able to give praise and encouragement
– it is important that effort is acknowledged as well as achievement

Use of observation skills
– to identify any potential problems regarding a child, or any specific aspect of their care that needs to be altered in any way

Being a good teamworker
– to be aware of the need to work with others and not in isolation, to ensure that your actions complement the actions of others in the team, rather than hinder or contradict

Upholding confidentiality
– the importance of working within a 'need-to-know' basis regarding confidentiality is vital in maintaining the privacy of children and families with whom you work

Providing appropriate care plans
– the individual needs of children must be taken into account when planning for their daily and longer-term care

Upholding health and safety
– all general health and safety rules should be adhered to at all times with all staff ensuring that they understand the procedures for the setting and the rationale (thinking) behind them

Being aware of security needs
– issues such as who is allowed to collect a child from the setting and what to do about strangers arriving at the setting need to be fully understood

Promoting equal opportunities
– issues of equality regarding gender, culture and disability need to be fully understood, together with an understanding of how personality can also be an important consideration (the opportunities for a shy child as well as those of the more outgoing child)

Meeting individual needs
– identifying and providing for the specific needs of each child to enable them to be fully involved in the setting and what it provides

Consulting and communicating with parents
– parents should be included in any decisions made regarding a child, and their advice and opinion should be both sought and valued

- The child has fewer opportunities to put forward their own ideas.
- The adult's dominance means that children's ideas often go unheeded.
- Children cease to be actively involved.

As a result, children may be less willing to try out new experiences.

Laissez-faire model

- Adults 'leave the children to get on with it'.
- The adult does not get actively involved with the children's activities, as they do not want to 'interfere' with the children's learning.
- There are many opportunities for children to make choices and explore their own ideas.
- The lack of adult involvement can mean that children are unable to extend their learning as far as they could have done.

As a result, children may not be able to reach their full potential.

Social constructivist model

- Children are encouraged to learn by being involved with the environment around them.
- Children are encouraged to interact with all they see.
- The emphasis is on learning through practical experience.

The usual result is that children learn at a pace suited to their stage of development.

The theorist Lev Vygotsky suggested that a child can be helped to a higher level of understanding by an adult who is able to support their learning sensitively. This does not mean forcing new skills upon a child, but observing when a child

Figure 6.27
Play can move understanding forward to new levels

seems ready to move forward in their thinking, so that they can be encouraged to try something different or more complex, and helping them to understand it. This often results in children achieving a new level of understanding. For example, a child who was unable to get a construction model to stand was helped by an adult to try adding a larger block to the base, thereby improving the model's stability. At a later date, the same child was being observed once again, and she was seen constructing a stable model in the same way as before, demonstrating that her understanding had moved forward to the new level.

case study 6.1

Dawn

Dawn has set up a creative activity in which she is supervising four children.

You notice that Dawn is directing the children as to where they should stick the various pieces of material and has an example for them to copy. She is correcting them if they position the pieces in the 'wrong' place.

activity
INDIVIDUAL WORK

(a) What model of adult involvement is Dawn following?

(b) How might Dawn's approach affect the children's response to the activity?

(c) What approach would you have taken if you were Dawn?

When supervising children's play, you should be aiming to support rather than to direct. It is your role to ensure that the children's play is contained within safe boundaries whilst still enabling them to explore and to develop skills. You should strive to enable all children within your care to participate; therefore, you must look at their individual needs and consider whether additional support, resources or specialised equipment is required to achieve their participation.

remember Children learn through observation of adults and of their peers.

Whatever you plan, you should be aiming for the activity to stimulate interest, knowledge, skills and understanding.

remember Many hazardous or unacceptable situations can be avoided if the activities, equipment and resource materials are suitable for the ages, needs and ability levels of the children for whom they are provided.

Setting ground rules for play

All situations, out of necessity, have boundaries. These help to ensure that children play and work within a safe environment and that fair distribution of input, experience and resource materials is assured. Understanding the need to share and take turns does not come naturally to many children, particularly at the earliest ages, and they will need guidance.

Whenever possible, clear explanations with regard to boundaries and restrictions should be given in advance of activities. When the need arises, explain why a child's action or approach is unacceptable and the impact that it is having on others or on the environment.

Involvement

An important part of your development as a practitioner will be identifying when to take part in children's play and when to remain as an observer. When you do involve yourself, you should consider not only how your involvement will be of benefit to the children but also any potentially adverse effect that it may have.

You may find it helpful at this point to refer back to Unit 1, page 35, for an outline of the theories of Lev Vygotsky (see 'the zone of proximal development') and Jerome Bruner (see 'scaffolding').

Curriculum

The curriculum guidance for under-fives is currently under review. The planned update will incorporate both the Birth to Three strategy guidance and the Foundation Stage curriculum guidance described below.

See Curriculum update on page 260.

Birth to Three Matters

Birth to Three Matters provides a framework to support children in their earliest years. The purpose of the framework is to provide support, information, guidance and challenge for all those with responsibility for the care and education of babies and children from birth to three years. The framework:

- values and celebrates babies and children
- recognises their individuality, efforts and achievements
- recognises that all children have from birth a need to develop, learning through interaction with people and exploration of the world around them (For some children, this development may be at risk because of difficulties with communication and interaction, cognition and learning, behavioural, emotional and social development or sensory and physical development.)
- recognises the 'holistic' nature of development and learning
- acknowledges, values and supports the adults that work with babies and young children
- provides opportunities for reflection on practice
- informs and develops practice whilst acknowledging that working with babies and children is a complex, challenging and demanding task and that often there are no easy answers.

Principles which underpin the framework

The principles which underpin the framework come from a number of sources, including representative organisations, leading childcare writers, experts and practitioners. They are as follows:

- Parents and families are central to the well-being of the child.
- Relationships with other people (both adults and children) are of crucial importance in a child's life.
- A relationship with a key person at home and in the setting is essential to young children's well-being.
- Babies and young children are social beings; they are competent learners from birth.
- Learning is a shared process and children learn most effectively when, with the support of a knowledgeable and trusted adult, they are actively involved and interested.
- Caring adults count more than resources and equipment.
- Children learn when they are given appropriate responsibility, allowed to make errors, decisions and choices, and are respected as autonomous and competent learners.
- Children learn by doing rather than by being told.
- Young children are vulnerable. They learn to be independent by having someone they can depend upon.

How the framework is organised

The framework takes as its focus the child and steers away from subjects, specific areas of experience and distinct curriculum headings. It identifies four 'Aspects', which celebrate the skill and competence of babies and young children and highlights the interrelationship between growth, learning, development and the environment in which they are cared for and educated.

These four 'Aspects' are:

- A Strong Child
- Skilful Communicator
- Competent Learner
- Healthy Child.

Each Aspect is divided into four 'Components'.

Table 6.1 Aspects and statements

A Strong Child	Me, Myself and I	Being Acknowledged and Affirmed	Developing Self-assurance	A Sense of Belonging
A Skilful Communicator	Being Together	Finding a Voice	Listening and Responding	Making Meaning
A Competent Learner	Making Connections	Being Imaginative	Being Creative	Representing
A Healthy Child	Emotional Well-being	Growing and Developing	Keeping Safe	Healthy Choices

Source: DfES (2002)

Refer to Unit 7, page 327, for a section on stimulating play for babies and children under three.

keyword **Foundation Stage curriculum** A Government-led curriculum for children from the age of three years.

keyword **National Curriculum** The curriculum followed by children in all state schools.

The Foundation Stage curriculum

The **Foundation Stage curriculum** is used as a guideline for learning for children from three years until they begin to follow the **National Curriculum** key stage 1, which is normally introduced during Year 1 or 2 of primary school. The principles of the Foundation Stage are supporting, fostering, promoting and developing children's:

- personal, social and emotional well-being, in particular by supporting the transition to and between settings, promoting an inclusive ethos and providing opportunities for each child to become a valued member of that group and community so that a strong self-image and self-esteem are promoted
- positive attitudes and dispositions towards their learning, in particular an enthusiasm for knowledge and learning and a confidence in their ability to be successful learners
- social skills, in particular by providing opportunities that enable them to learn how to co-operate and work harmoniously alongside and with each other and to listen to each other
- attention skills and persistence, in particular the capacity to concentrate on their own play or on group tasks
- language and communication, with opportunities for all children to talk and communicate in a widening range of situations, to respond to adults and to each other, to practise and extend the range of vocabulary and communication skills they use and to listen carefully
- reading and writing, with opportunities for all children to explore, enjoy, learn about and use words and text in a broad range of contexts and to experience a rich variety of books
- mathematics, with opportunities for all children to develop their understanding of number, measurement, pattern, shape and space by providing a broad range of contexts in which they can explore, enjoy, learn, practise and talk about them

- knowledge and understanding of the world, with opportunities for all children to solve problems, make decisions, experiment, predict, plan and question in a variety of contexts, and to explore and find out about their environment and people and places that have significance in their lives
- physical development, with opportunities for all children to develop and practise their fine and gross motor skills and to increase their understanding of how the body works and what they need to do to be healthy and safe
- creative development, with opportunities for all children to explore and share thoughts, ideas and feelings through a variety of art, design and technology, music, movement, dance and imaginative and role-play activities. (Adapted from DfEE, 2000, pages 8–9.)

activity 6.3 INDIVIDUAL WORK

As you read through the following section, consider the links between the range of activities set out on pages 204–221 and the aims of the curriculum guidance framework. Reflect on your thinking whenever you plan learning opportunities for children.

Providing learning opportunities across the Foundation Stage
The following material has been taken from the publication *Curriculum Guidance for the Foundation Stage* (DfEE, 2000).

keyword

Early Learning Goals
The aims of the six areas of learning that make up the Foundation Stage curriculum. Most children achieve these goals before they enter key stage 1 of the National Curriculum.

The **Early Learning Goals** for each of the six areas are listed below. You will also find it useful to read through the full document, as this provides examples of how to support learning across each area, in addition to showing the stepping stones that build towards each Early Learning Goal. College libraries or resource centres usually stock copies.

Early Learning Goals for personal, social and emotional development

By the end of the Foundation Stage, most children will:

- continue to be interested, excited and motivated to learn
- be confident to try new activities, initiate ideas and speak in a familiar group
- maintain attention, concentrate and sit quietly when appropriate
- have a developing awareness of their own needs, views and feelings and be sensitive to the needs, views and feelings of others
- have a developing respect for their own cultures and beliefs and those of other people
- respond to significant experiences, showing a range of feelings when appropriate
- form good relationships with adults and peers
- work as part of a group or class, taking turns and sharing fairly, understanding that there need to be agreed values and codes of behaviour for groups of people, including adults and children, to work together harmoniously

- understand what is right, what is wrong, and why
- dress and undress independently and manage their own personal hygiene
- select and use activities and resources independently
- consider the consequences of their words and actions for themselves and others
- understand that people have different needs, views, cultures and beliefs, which should be treated with respect
- understand that they can expect others to treat their needs, views, cultures and beliefs with respect.

In order to foster these goals, children need opportunities to work both alone and in groups of different sizes. They need to develop independence and be able to both lead and follow.

Early Learning Goals for communication, language and literacy

The objectives set out in the *National Literacy Strategy: Framework for Teaching for the Reception Year* (DfEE, 1998) are in line with these goals. By the end of the Foundation Stage, most children will be able to:

- enjoy listening to and using spoken and written language, and readily turn to it in their play and learning
- explore and experiment with sounds, words and texts
- listen with enjoyment and respond to stories, songs and other music, rhymes and poems and make up their own stories, songs, rhymes and poems
- use language to organise, sequence and clarify thinking, ideas, feelings and events
- sustain attentive listening, responding to what they have heard by relevant comments, questions or actions
- interact with others, negotiating plans and activities and taking turns in conversation
- extend vocabulary, exploring the meanings and sounds of new words
- retell narratives in the correct sequence, drawing on the language patterns of stories
- speak clearly and audibly with confidence and control, and show awareness of the listener, for example by their use of conventions such as greetings, 'please' and 'thank you'
- hear and say initial and final sounds in words, and short vowel sounds within words
- link sounds to letters, naming and sounding the letters of the alphabet
- read a range of familiar and common words and simple sentences independently
- know that print carries meaning and, in English, is read from left to right and top to bottom

- show an understanding of the elements of stories, such as main character, sequence of events, and openings, and how information can be found in non-fiction texts to answer questions about where, who, why and how
- attempt writing for various purposes, using features of different forms such as lists, stories and instructions
- write their own names and other things such as labels and captions and begin to form simple sentences, sometimes using punctuation
- use their phonic knowledge to write simple regular words and make phonetically plausible attempts at more complex words
- use a pencil and hold it effectively to form recognisable letters, most of which are correctly formed.

Early Learning Goals for mathematical development
By the end of the Foundation Stage, most children will be able to:

- say and use number names in order in familiar contexts
- count reliably up to 10 everyday objects
- recognise numerals one to nine
- use language such as 'more' or 'less', 'greater' or 'smaller', 'heavier' or 'lighter', to compare two numbers or quantities
- in practical activities and discussion begin to use the vocabulary involved in adding and subtracting
- find one more or one less than a number from one to 10
- begin to relate addition to combining two groups of objects, and subtraction to 'taking away'
- talk about, recognise and recreate simple patterns
- use language such as 'circle' or 'bigger' to describe the shape and size of solids and flat shapes
- use everyday words to describe position
- use developing mathematical ideas and methods to solve practical problems.

Early Learning Goals for knowledge and understanding of the world
By the end of the Foundation Stage, most children will be able to:

- investigate objects and materials by using all of their senses as appropriate
- find out about, and identify some features of, living things, objects and events they observe
- look closely at similarities, differences, patterns and change
- ask questions about why things happen and how things work
- build and construct with a wide range of objects, selecting appropriate resources, and adapting their work where necessary
- select the tools and techniques they need to shape, assemble and join the materials they are using;

- find out about and identify the uses of everyday technology and use information and communication technology and programmable toys to support their learning
- find out about past and present events in their own lives, and in those of their families and other people they know
- observe, find out about and identify features in the place they live and the natural world
- begin to know about their own cultures and beliefs and those of other people
- find out about their environment, and talk about those features they like and dislike.

Early Learning Goals for physical development

By the end of the Foundation Stage, most children will be able to:

- move with confidence, imagination and in safety
- move with control and co-ordination
- show awareness of space, of themselves and of others
- recognise the importance of keeping healthy and those things that contribute to this
- use a range of small and large equipment
- travel around, under, over and through balancing and climbing equipment
- handle tools, objects, construction and malleable materials safely and with increasing control.

Early Learning Goals for creative development

By the end of the Foundation Stage, most children will be able to:

- explore colour, texture, shape, form and space in two and three dimensions
- recognise and explore how sounds can be changed, sing simple songs from memory, recognise repeated sounds and sound patterns, and match movements to music
- respond in a variety of ways to what they see, hear, smell, touch and feel
- use their imagination in art and design, music, dance, imaginative and role play and stories
- express and communicate their ideas, thoughts and feelings by using a widening range of materials, suitable tools, imaginative and role play, movement, designing and making, and a variety of songs and musical instruments.

Linking activities to the Early Learning Goals

To ensure that you understand the relevance of the Early Learning Goals, you may find it helpful to read through them again and then carry out the activity linked to the following case study.

case study 6.2

Jumping Jack nursery

A staff development session at the Jumping Jack nursery is focusing on planning. The staff have been asked by their manager to use the Early Learning Goals for each of the six areas of learning and identify how each of the activities set out on pages 204–221 supports each Early Learning Goal. An example is set out in Table 6.2.

activity
INDIVIDUAL WORK

(a) Carry out the task yourself using a copy of Table 6.3.

(b) Compare your answers with those of others in your group.

Table 6.2 Musical instruments

Personal, social and emotional development ■ Select and use activities and resources independently	*Knowledge and understanding of the world* ■ begin to know about their own culture and beliefs and those of other people
Community, language and literacy ■ explore and experiment with sounds, words and textures	*Physical development* ■ move with control and confidence
Mathematical development ■ talk about, recognise and recreate simple patterns	*Creative development* ■ recognise and explore how sounds can be changed, sing simple songs from memory, recognise repeated sounds and sound patterns and match movements to music

Table 6.3

Personal, social and emotional development	*Knowledge and understanding of the world*
Community, language and literacy	*Physical development*
Mathematical development	*Creative development*

Planning activities to promote development

As you prepare activities for children there are a number of specific points that need to be taken into consideration. You must remember that each child is at their own stage of development. They have different concentration spans, and individual preferences. Therefore, working with a group means that you need to consider the stages of development of all the children, not just the majority, and plan the activity to support each of their needs. Having decided upon the main aim of your planned activity, you will have to consider how to cater for children who need help and guidance to join in, and decide how you will extend the scope of the activity for children who are more able and require more complex tasks. This is known as meeting differentiation of need.

remember Planning often needs to support one or more specific areas of the curriculum.

Refer back to pages 237–240 to remind you of specific curriculum guidelines.

Preparation

When planning an activity you will need to think about:

- the people who have to be consulted (for example, the class teacher or room supervisor)
- the design of play activities
- the outcomes to be achieved (will you need to try to meet an Early Learning Goal or stepping stone, etc.?)
- how the activity fits into the planned curriculum
- cultural differences and how you can ensure that these are taken into account
- equal opportunities and whether your activity will offer them
- how much time you have for planning
- how much time the activity will take
- how much space you will need, taking into account the numbers of children and the environment in which the activity will take place (e.g. room, hall, garden)
- what equipment and resources you will need;
- your role as either an adult helper or as leader, and what difference this makes;
- what level of supervision will be required
- any safety precautions that you will need to take
- any practical problems likely to arise and how to avoid them or put them right
- how to provide opportunities for children to learn new skills and ideas
- how to adapt the ideas for younger children, or those with particular needs.

You will also need to produce:

- a written plan to show how the activity will be carried out
- a checklist showing the sequence of actions and proposed timings
- confirmation of how you intend to record achievement of the planned outcome
- a way of evaluating the activity.

remember The best early years provisions are built on forward planning and teamwork.

From the lists above, you can see that planning play activities for an early years setting does not simply mean getting out the toys or materials. It can be quite time consuming and takes a great deal of advance thinking and preparation.

An exploration of practical activities

This section of the unit is about what might be included in the activities that you provide. It notes many of the options that are possible through the use of each activity, and a range of activities are set out below with a list of ideas under each activity heading. It should be understood that the lists are not exhaustive. There are many more activities that could be included. You will be able to build up a list of ideas as your career develops.

The practical aspects of health and safety are discussed in Unit 2. You may find it helpful to refer to this unit as you plan your activities. Other useful information can be found in Unit 1, where development stages are outlined; Unit 7, where the focus is on babies and children under three years, and Unit 8, where ideas to support children with disabilities or special educational needs are discussed.

remember With the younger age groups, small parts need to be removed or used under strict supervision.

Creative activities

Creativity includes:

- adult-led activities
- encouraging children to use free expression
- the skill of using scissors

Figure 6.28 Creative activities

- using mark-making implements (for drawing, colouring, etc.)
- a range of creative resources.

Music and language

Music and language activities incorporate:

- conversation, description and the general use of language
- musical instruments from around the world
- songs and rhymes
- rhythm and dance
- music and movement
- listening to music
- making music
- background music.

remember Babies enjoy music too, but be careful of instruments with edges that may hurt them.

All these activities should involve the use of world music.

Books and stories

Figure 6.29 Books and stories

Included under this heading would be:

- group story times
- one to one story times
- the use of big books
- drama and stories involving participation by the children
- using props, such as puppets
- reading with children
- children having daily access to books by being able to choose a book freely
- children enjoying books on their own, preferably in a cosy corner or quiet area
- both adults and children using books as a source of information, as well as pleasure

Construction activities

Construction can be either on a large scale or small scale. It can involve household equipment and furniture, or a bought commercial product can be used. A combination of these is best. Examples include:

- large scale – chairs, tables, the clothes horse
- small scale – construction kits such as Duplo, Lego, Mobilo, Stickle bricks, wooden blocks of different shapes and sizes.

Professional Practice

- Babies can choke on small parts and should not have access to construction kits with small pieces.
- Guidelines for suitable ages are usually given on packages and in advertising catalogues.

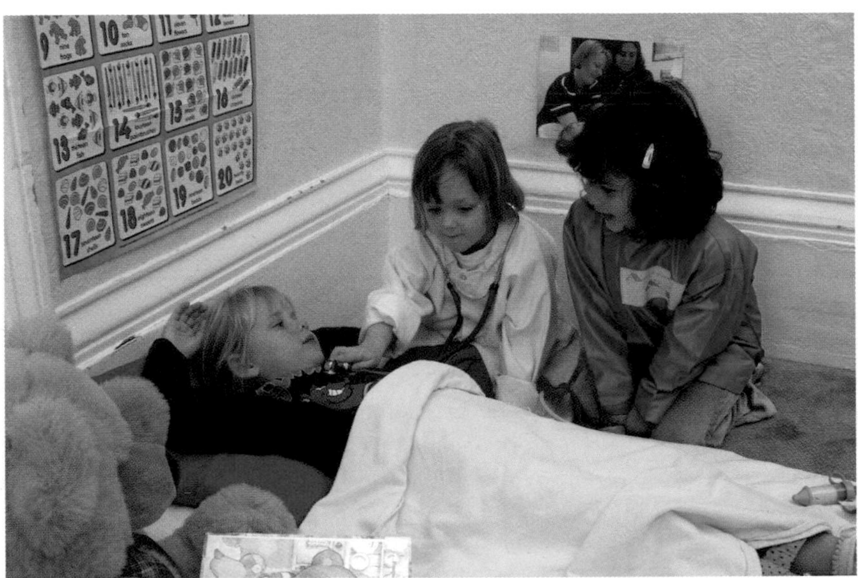

Figure 6.30
A role-play setting

Role play

Role play offers opportunities to learn about many aspects of everyday life. Children can 'become' familiar people who have a link to them already, for example a doctor or a postal worker, or 'types' of people whom they have seen in real life and books or on television, such as lorry drivers, pilots and train drivers. Role-play areas can be made into different types of settings, for example shop, post office, railway station, or hospital.

Opportunities to develop understanding through role play are almost endless. For example, children have opportunities to develop their language and literacy skills when writing letters, making train tickets, producing signs and price tags, setting out menus and bills, taking lunch orders, writing cheques, and so on. Each activity would reinforce their acquisition of the skills and develop their understanding of the world in which they live and the role of language and literacy within it.

Similarly, understanding of early mathematics is developed as children match cups to saucers, group similar items together and count how many of any item is needed.

Resources for role play include:

- dressing-up clothes that reflect a range of cultures and enable both boys and girls to 'be' men and women in a variety of domestic and employed roles
- domestic (household) equipment to support learning about a range of cultures and to show that the cultures of all children attending the setting are valued
- a range of dolls and teddies, with prams, cots, baby baths and baby equipment, to help children identify with and act out domestic and care routines familiar to them.

Professional Practice

- Dressing-up clothes need to be washed regularly.
- Hats should be regularly cleaned especially if there have been any cases of head lice in the setting.

remember

The six areas of learning are personal, social and emotional development; communication, language and literacy; mathematics; knowledge and understanding of the world; physical development; and creative development.

Cooking

Cooking is an excellent activity for young children, as it is both fun and a good learning opportunity. It is important that any dietary or cultural need is taken into account, and any doubts should be checked with parents or carers. Suggestions for cooking with children include:

- suitable healthy snacks
- making reference to different cooking methods (e.g. baking, mixing, rolling, pan cooking)
- foods for different ages, understanding their suitability for toddlers and older children
- foods popular with specific cultural groups
- links to festivals and special occasions
- personal preferences of the children.

Ideal foods to prepare and cook include:

- bread, chapattis, pitta bread and pizza bases
- cakes, buns and biscuits
- sweets
- pancakes
- simple vegetable soups
- fruit salads
- sandwiches.

activity 6.4 INDIVIDUAL WORK

Plan a cooking activity for a group of young children. Start by making a recipe card for the activity. The following example may be helpful.

Figure 6.31
Setting out a recipe card

How to make a recipe card

1. Title of the recipe e.g. Butterfly cakes, vegetable soup.
2. Whenever possible, add a picture. This helps to make the activity more realistic for the children as they can see what they are aiming to achieve.
3. State what equipment will be needed.
4. State what ingredients will be needed.
5. Set the process and measurements out clearly, stage by stage. Although the children are unlikely to be able to read these, adding an illustration of kitchen scales etc. will help them understand.
6. Explain how long it needs to cook (if at all).
7. Give suggestions for decorations, icing and so on.
8. If the recipe links to a particular festival or celebration, make sure that it is clearly stated, showing how it links and why it is relevant to the festival or celebration.

Figure 6.32
Recipe card for gluten-free playdough

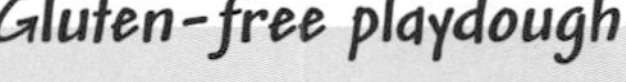

Gluten-free playdough

What you will need:

1 cup of rice flour
1 cup of corn flour
1 cup of salt
4 teaspoons of Cream of Tartar
2 cups of water
2 tablespoons of vegetable oil
Food colouring

What to do:

1. Place all the ingredients in a saucepan.
2. Stir well whilst cooking over a gentle heat.
3. Continue to stir as the mixture changes from runny to firm.
4. Remove from the cooker and turn out onto a board.
5. Knead well to ensure a smooth texture throughout.
6. When cool, place in a plastic container.
7. This dough should keep well if stored in a refrigerator when not in use.

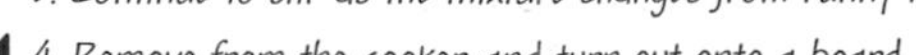

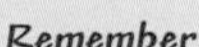

Remember:

It is not appropriate to add textures such as oats to gluten-free playdough.

An alternative idea could be to make a bird cake. Not only is this a nice weighing and mixing activity but it teaches children that other creatures also need care and a nutritious diet.

Professional Practice

- Cross-infection can be prevented by teaching children the importance of hand washing and not putting hands to their faces while cooking or preparing food.
- Only the adult should use ovens and cooker hobs; children are safest if kept out of the kitchen completely.

Outdoors play

The physical fitness levels of young children are of increasing concern to health professionals. The outdoors provides scope for additional opportunities for physical activity that can contribute to helping children develop a healthy attitude to being outside and in the fresh air.

Many of the activities that take place indoors could be taken out into the garden too, and the outdoor environment should ideally be seen as an extension of the indoor play area. However, this section includes activities that are mostly planned for outside.

Table 6.4 Outdoors play

Equipment for locomotor skills, running, climbing, cycling and so on, such as: ■ climbing frames ■ a slide ■ trampet ■ bikes ■ trikes ■ ride-ons ■ see-saws Equipment for non-locomotor skills, throwing, catching and so on, such as: ■ balls ■ beanbags ■ quoits ■ skittles	Action games such as: ■ Simon says ■ Farmer's in the den ■ There was a princess long ago 'Ground' games using chalk, such as: ■ hopscotch
Equipment for fine motor skills, hand and finger manipulation, such as: ■ water tray ■ sand tray or sand-pit ■ gardening	Spontaneous games using: ■ tents ■ dens ■ table ends

Professional Practice

- Sandpits should be covered when not in use.
- Water should be replenished daily.
- Hands should be washed thoroughly after gardening.

Natural (and malleable) play

Today, so many children's toys and pieces of equipment are made of plastic and other manufactured materials that it is very important for children to have the opportunity whenever possible to experience natural materials, such as sand, water, clay and wood.

Sand can be:

- wet and dry, with and without other textures (e.g. shells)
- played with on its own or with tools (e.g. rakes, diggers, buckets, sieves and sand wheels).

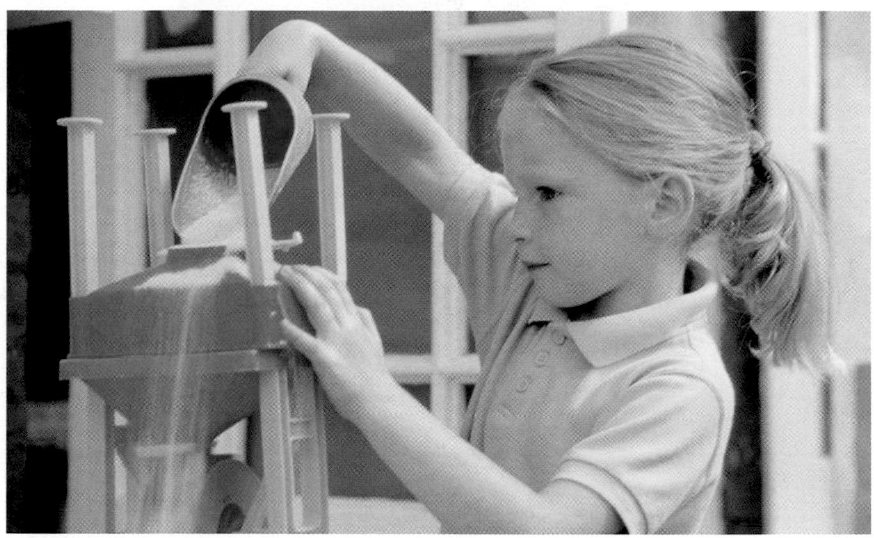

Figure 6.33
Sand is a valuable, natural asset to play

Water can be:

- plain, coloured, bubbly, warm, cold
- played with on its own or with objects to help children develop various scientific and mathematical concepts, such as floating and sinking, absorbency and measurement of quantity.

remember

Dough is also malleable but it is not a natural material.

Clay can be:

- played with on its own
- or with tools for cutting, rolling, prodding and shaping.

Woodwork should be done:

- under careful supervision
- using 'proper' child-sized tools.

It is important that real tools are used rather than toy ones, as this helps to develop children's understanding of and respect for real tools and their use.

Figure 6.34
It is important that real rather than toy tools are used

Gardening activities can include:

- digging, planting, watering and weeding
- rearing flowers and plants from seedlings or bulbs (fast-growing plants include sunflowers, bean sprouts and cress)
- growing vegetables and salad items to pick and enjoy for lunch or snack time
- growing plants in soil beds, pots or jars.

Professional Practice

- Although when working with wood real tools are always the preferred option, continuous supervision will be necessary to teach children how to use tools safely and respect what each tool can do.
- When gardening, ensure that all plants are safe for children to handle and avoid sharp thorns, poisonous berries, etc.

Small world play

Any toys that are a scaled-down version of real life are referred to as small world play. This includes:

- dolls' houses
- farms and farm animals

- zoos and zoo animals
- a car mat, vehicles and garage
- train sets.

As children develop, they will often combine small world activities and play quite complex games for extended lengths of time.

Information and communication technology (ICT)

Figure 6.35
Information and communication technology

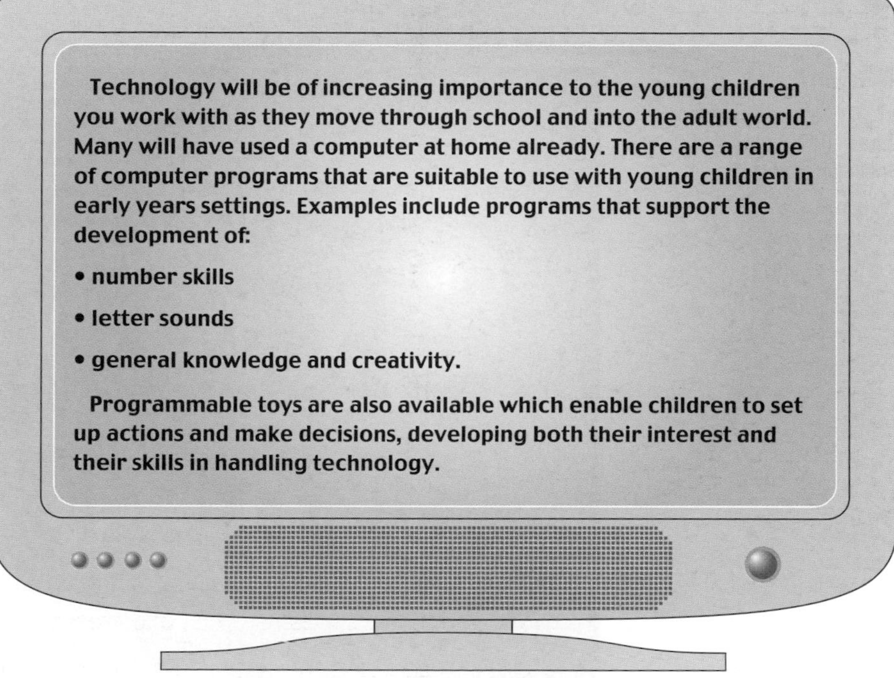

Structured activities

Many resources have a specific structure, which means that, in order for the objects to be used as intended, a particular action is required. Examples include:

- tray puzzles (with knobs to lift each piece out)
- jigsaw puzzles
- floor and table puzzles
- threading activities (e.g. using cotton reels or large buttons)
- sewing cards, Binca (woven cloth rattan for learning to sew) and other easy-to-puncture materials such as felt
- shape sorters and posting boxes
- peg boards
- bead frames
- pattern boards, using nails and elastic bands.

remember
Small objects such as pegs and beads are not suitable for younger age groups.

remember

Some of these activities are also available in floor and outdoor versions. This adds another dimension to the play, as the boards and pieces are usually much larger.

Paired and small group play

Activities that involve co-operation help children learn to share, to take turns, to have patience and to lose graciously. Examples of such activities are:

- picture lotto
- dominoes
- memory pairs
- noughts and crosses
- boxed games such as snakes and ladders.

Figure 6.36
Outdoor versions of indoor games add another dimension to play

Interest tables

An interest table that focuses specifically on one topic or on a general area of learning provides a lovely way to support learning. Interest tables extend both learning and imagination. In general, they are linked into the current theme or topic that is being covered within the setting. It is usual to encourage children to bring items for the interest table, providing an excellent potential link with their home and family. Having a variety of objects 'on loan' from the children's homes is important as a way to encourage respect for the belongings of others. Good examples of topics for an interest table are:

- seasons
- ourselves
- transport
- seaside.

Each interest table should include:

- a variety of objects to raise interest, curiosity and the desire to explore and investigate
- objects to stimulate the senses of sight, touch and smell (on occasion, auditory (hearing) stimulation may also be possible)
- reference books and stories (familiar and new).

remember

Make sure that there are no items that could be hazardous for a child to explore unsupervised.

Although taste would not usually be included, it could be introduced through an activity related to the interest table, such as making mince pies if the theme is Christmas, or coconut barfi if the theme is the Hindu festival of care and protection (Raksha Bandhan).

Professional Practice

- Labelling items on the interest table is a useful way to help children start to link the written word to the names of objects.
- When the interest table is for older age groups, simple questions would add to the children's development by encouraging discussion and further thinking.

case study 6.3

Planning an interest table

Helen and Jess have been asked to choose and plan an interest table for the pre-school room at their placement. They opted to focus on 'Water'.

activity
INDIVIDUAL WORK

(a) What might they be aiming for the children to learn?

(b) What items do you think they would include?

(c) What books could they add to the table, linked to 'Water'?

(d) How might the interest table be linked to other activities within the setting?

Improvised games

Although it is important to plan ahead and for the children's day to follow a basic structure, it can at times be just as valuable to encourage children simply to play with each other. Some children do this spontaneously, but others may need suggestions to help them get started. Examples of improvised play include:

- playing chase
- hide-and-seek
- hopscotch
- What's the time Mr Wolf?
- May I cross the river please?
- hand-clapping games.

Each of these games helps to give children a sense of belonging, of being part of something. This helps to boost self-esteem and develops social interaction skills.

activity 6.5 INDIVIDUAL WORK

What other examples of improvised play have you seen? Make a list and add to it if you observe new ones when on placement.

Outings with children

An outing is an exciting experience for most children; for many, it will be the first time that they have been somewhere special without their parent or main carer. Outings with children need careful planning.

Refer to Unit 2, page 94 for more on planning outings.

Suitable outings for children of a variety of ages could include:

- the zoo
- a country farm or a city farm
- a country park
- a listening walk (specifically getting everyone to focus on what can be heard)
- a walk to look at the local environment (e.g. buildings such as houses, churches or shops; aspects of nature such as trees, wild flowers, wildlife and mini-beasts)
- a hands-on science or technology centre where many new ideas can be tried out
- an interactive museum, specially designed for young children.

Professional Practice

- Although an outing can be exciting, some children may feel apprehensive, particularly if it is an unknown experience for them. They may need a great deal of reassurance initially.
- Strict supervision is needed when taking children outside the setting.

Carrying out planned activities

When preparing activities for young children it is necessary to take into account a number of factors. The overall aim of the activity needs to be clear, but you must also consider:

- the environment in which the activity will take place
- what facilities the activity will require, for example, floor space, a table surface, access to hand-washing facilities
- the number of children who will be enjoying the activity at any one time
- the amount of supervision that will be necessary
- whether you have sufficient resources for the activity (enough for everyone to have a turn)
- how long the activity will last
- health and safety issues relevant to the activity
- how much help individual children will be likely to need
- the impact the activity could have on the rest of the setting. Will it create a great deal of noise, excessive mess or a high level of excitement?

case study 6.4 BMI indicators

Monica is a student preparing an activity that will be assessed as part of her course assignment. Monica has decided to prepare an outdoor activity involving the planting of bulbs. She intends the children to dig an area of soil, clear away any snails etc. that they see, and then plant and water the bulbs.

activity
GROUP WORK

(a) Ideally, where and when should the activity take place?

(b) What facilities and resources will the planting activity require?

(c) How many children will be able to join in the activity at any one time?

(d) How much supervision will be necessary?

(e) What health and safety issues would be relevant to this activity?

(f) How much help would individual children be likely to need?

Setting up and using play equipment – general points to remember

Point 1. The equipment or play materials provided must be appropriate for the ages of the children who are going to be using them. Guidance is usually given by manufacturers, and should be referred to if in any doubt. For example, small parts are not suitable for toddlers and babies.

Point 2. Safety surfaces are necessary underneath any equipment from which a child may fall a distance of 60 cm (2 ft) or more. This applies to all large equipment, for example a climbing frame or a slide.

See Unit 2 page 75 for details of the types of surfaces that can be used.

Point 3. Equipment should be placed on surfaces that are suitable for the way they will be mostly used. For example, play tunnels are best placed on grass or smooth concrete rather than gravel or stones, as children will be crawling on their knees as they play; drawing and colouring materials are best placed on a table, as this allows children to hold the paper securely and gives them a smooth surface to rest on.

Point 4. The layout of the setting should allow sufficient space for children to move about the room freely and safely.

Point 5. Staff should be able to supervise the children easily, without unnecessary barriers to their vision. Consideration should be given to the position of cupboards, bookshelves, and so on.

Point 6. Furniture and fixtures must be securely in place, locked if appropriate, kept in good condition, and any storage facilities should be safely stacked and never be overloaded.

Point 7. When providing construction materials, it is important that there is either sufficient of the material for each child to have a worthwhile experience while playing, or to limit the number of children using the activity at any one time. If children find that they are unable to build what they wish to build with a resource, because there are insufficient pieces, they are likely to lose interest in the activity altogether and therefore lose out on a potential learning opportunity. This may have implications in the long term.

Point 8. When children are model making, building or playing with small world toys, such as farms and car mats, it is important that their play will not be interrupted by other children walking across their activity, or by a draught, caused by an opening door, knocking over their models or animals. This type of disturbance will interfere with the child's enjoyment and may possibly lead them to feel frustrated and dissatisfied with the activity itself.

Point 9. Many activities can be provided both indoors and outdoors. It can be nice for the children to 'ring the changes' with regard to where certain activities are placed, and it is good to encourage children to go out into the fresh air.

However, it is important to provide shade for children on sunny days, and they should not be exposed to the sun when it is at its highest in the sky. It is also unsuitable for children to play out on very foggy, damp days.

Point 10. All equipment should be kept in good condition and cleaned regularly and appropriately with an anti-bacterial cleaning product.

Point 11. Equipment should be safety marked whenever possible.

Point 12. Plants and animals offer an important learning experience for young children and can be a useful way to help children learn about caring for the needs of others. They can find out about the similarities and difference between humans, animals and plants in their needs for food, water and sunlight. However, before incorporating plants and animals within the setting, the pros and cons should be carefully considered. For example, animals should be avoided if there is a child with a severe allergy; and staff must be prepared to carry out pet-care routines, keeping the pets scrupulously clean.

remember Plants should be non-poisonous, without thorns or berries.

In Unit 2, pages 69–73, you will find more on setting out a room, accommodating children with a specific need, and safety and health issues. You might wish to refer back to that section now.

Avoiding stereotyping and discrimination

It is important to ensure that the setting and its resources do not, even unwittingly, promote stereotyping and discrimination. Therefore you should:

- Check that books, posters, puzzles, etc. show positive images of men, women, boys, girls, people with varying disabilities and people from varying cultures.
- Read books yourself before you read them to a child or group of children to ensure that no negative messages are given.
- Provide a range of resources in the role-play area to reflect positively a range of cultures and to enable children of either gender to 'be' whoever they wish to be. This applies to clothing, utensils and any pretend foods.
- Ensure that all children are encouraged to use all equipment and resources in the setting.
- Introduce a range of festivals and celebrations to children, widening their knowledge of the world around them.
- Answer children's questions honestly and sensitively. There is nothing wrong with their being inquisitive about the differences that they notice. It only becomes a problem if they begin to place different values on those differences.
- Challenge prejudice or racism if you come across it.

case study 6.5

Jermaine

Jermaine is building a wall with the 'life-size' plastic bricks. Carmen wants to join in the activity too. She picks up some bricks and starts to add them to the wall. You hear Jermaine tell her, 'No, Carmen, you're a girl. You can't do building. Girls can't be builders.'

activity
INDIVIDUAL WORK

(a) What will you say to Jermaine?

(b) What will you say to Carmen?

(c) What else should you do?

Giving children appropriate support

How you can best give children appropriate support in their learning will depend on:

- their age
- their stage of development
- the activity they are involved in
- the aims of the activity.

Depending on the age of the children you are working with and their levels of ability, you will need to provide some or all of the following:

- clear explanations
- initial guidance as a prompt to get them started
- gradually decreasing levels of guidance
- continuous guidance, prompting them throughout the activity
- physical support, perhaps help with cutting or in how to hold a pencil
- language support, offering explanations and naming objects for them
- close supervision, particularly of younger children
- gradually decreasing levels of supervision, as children become more competent
- generalised supervision, particularly when children are carrying out activities that are familiar to them.

Evaluating activities

Evaluating activities is important as it enables you to reflect on how well you have targeted, planned and carried out the activity and on how well the children have achieved your intended aim for them. You can think about how successful your judgements were with regard to resources, supervision, and health and safety issues. It also gives you the opportunity to reflect on what changes you would make to improve the activity for the next time.

activity
6.6
INDIVIDUAL WORK

Using the headings in the table below, evaluate an activity for physical play that you have planned and carried out by yourself.

Table 6.5

Activity ______________________________
Did you target the activity appropriately?
What worked best?
What problems (if any) occurred?
Did the activity meet the intended aims?
Were resources sufficient?
Was supervision appropriate?
Were there any health and safety issues?
What would you change another time?

Curriculum update

From September 2008, early years providers will be working within a mandatory new framework known as the Early Years Foundation Stage (EYFS). This framework is designed to help practitioners support the well-being of babies and children from birth to five years of age, helping them to reach their potential in a safe and stimulating environment. It builds on the strengths of the Birth to Three Matters framework, the current Foundation Stage curriculum, and *National Standards for Under Eights Day Care and Childminding* (DfES, 2003). It is embedded in the aims of the Government document *Every Child Matters: Change for Children* (DfES, 2004) in which the aim is for every child from birth through to age 19, whatever their background or circumstances, to be supported to:

- be healthy
- stay safe
- enjoy and achieve
- make a positive contribution
- achieve economic well-being.

The National Curriculum

The National Curriculum is a mandatory (compulsory) curriculum for children in all state schools. Privately funded schools are not obliged to follow the same guidelines but, in practice, many of them do. The National Curriculum is divided into key stages.

Table 6.6 The Key Stages

Key Stage	Pupil ages	Year groups
Key Stage 1 (KS1)	5–7 years	1–2
Key Stage 2 (KS2)	7–11 years	3–6
Key Stage 3 (KS3)	11–14 years	7–9
Key Stage 4 (KS4)	14–16 years	10–11

keyword
Standard attainment tasks (SATs)
Tests carried out at regular intervals during formal schooling.

At the end of each key stage, there are a number of tests that all children must complete. These are the National Curriculum **standard attainment tasks (SATs)**, which are used to monitor each individual child's performance as they progress through school.

Key stage 1

Key stage 1 includes:

- English
- Mathematics
- Science

- Technology (design and technology, and information technology)
- History
- Geography
- Art
- Music
- Physical Education.

The attainment targets at the end of key stage 1 are based around the following areas of learning:

- English
  - speaking and listening
  - reading
  - writing
- Mathematics
  - using and applying mathematics
  - number and algebra
  - shape, space and measure
  - handling data
- Science
  - experimental and investigative
  - life processes and living things
  - materials and their properties
  - physical processes
- Design and Technology
  - designing
  - making
- Art
  - investigating and making
  - knowledge and understanding
- Music
  - performing and composing
  - listening and appraising.

For other subjects, teachers make a decision about the level attained based on the range of descriptions set out for each key stage level. Details of these can be found in *Key Stages 1 and 2 of the National Curriculum* (DfEE, 1995). Your college library probably stocks a copy.

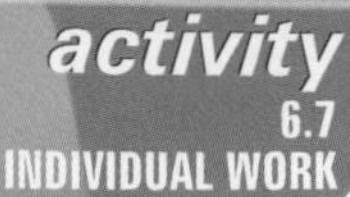
activity 6.7 INDIVIDUAL WORK

Using the internet or your college resource centre, access a copy of the complete National Curriculum. Read through it to familiarise yourself with the main aspects of each subject.

Understanding how to help to provide opportunities for children's imaginative and creative play

Resources

The provision of resources is an important aspect of planning and setting up any activity. At times, the resources that you provide will direct play in a certain way. As adults, we should be aware of this and try not to influence children, but simply provide materials that they can use in whatever way their imagination and needs take them.

link

Refer back to pages 243–254 for suggestions of resources suitable to support imaginative play and creativity: role play, dressing up, making music and using musical instruments, junk modelling, play with malleable materials such as dough and clay, and paint activities.

Intervention

A knowledgeable and sensitive adult is able to identify when children need help or guidance to move on in their play. This could perhaps be in relation to reaching a solution or a conclusion, solving a problem, fine-tuning a skill or exploring something further than before. As you become more knowledgeable and gain confidence as a practitioner, you will gradually become more skilled at identifying such occasions and at intervening sensitively.

activity 6.8 INDIVIDUAL WORK

During your various placement experiences, take time to observe the approaches of the staff already working at the setting.

(a) How do they approach children?

(b) When do they approach children?

(c) Why do they approach children?

Look at what happens following the adult input.

(d) Did the children's play change and, if so, in what ways?

(e) Were the children more focused, or did they lose interest?

(f) Was the input by the adult direct and obvious, or was it subtle and unobtrusive?

(g) How would you sum up the effect of the adult intervention? Do you think that it was successful? Or do you think that the children's play was impaired in any way by it?

Reflect on your observations regularly and act according to what you have learned.

Encouragement

Avoiding stereotyping in imaginative play

Many adults still have stereotyped images of how children play and what they like to play with. Clearly, some children will seem to fit the gender stereotype, with girls pushing prams and boys playing football, but this is often due to the experiences and resources that they have been provided with up to that point. Within an early years setting, it is important that all children have an equal chance to play with all equipment and that parents are made aware of the equality practice within the setting with regard to gender, disability, culture and religion.

activity 6.9 INDIVIDUAL WORK

Think about the resources at your current placement. What messages do they give to the children and their families?

Refer back to Unit 5, pages 187–195, for ideas for activities linked to culture and for how to avoid tokenism.

Exploring the feelings of others

During imaginative play, children take on many different roles. They may be mummy or daddy one day and spend their time caring for babies and walking the dog, cooking and ironing and generally imitating what they know from home, and then be Superman the next day, saving the world, flying round imaginary planets and entering a place of total fiction. All role play fulfils a need of some kind whether it is the need to have fun or the need to 'sort something out'. Children learn to experience how others act and feel, and this can help them develop understanding, responsibility and empathy. Sometimes, they will use role play to escape from reality; at other times, they will return from their role play to reality to regain familiarity and security if they are beginning to struggle with how their play is developing.

Professional Practice

- Provided that the safety of the child and everyone else around them is maintained, and play is not causing distress to anyone, a child's imaginative play should be allowed to flow freely.
- But, if at any time you are concerned about the actions or talk taking place within a role-play situation, for example if a child is acting out or describing sexual experiences, speak immediately to your placement supervisor who will know what action to take.

Refer to Unit 2, page 83, for more information on child protection.

Mark making

Creative play includes many opportunities for mark making, including drawing, writing and pattern making, using:

- crayons and pencils
- felt pens
- charcoal
- stamps and printers
- easel painting
- table painting.

Children usually enjoy creative activities and with encouragement soon develop the fine motor skills needed to control a pencil etc. To create opportunities for mark making during imaginative and role play, provide easy 'within context' situations which help children see how beneficial and important mark making is within the world around them. Opportunities within this area of play include:

- writing letters and invitations
- writing menus, taking dinner orders and setting out bills and receipts
- making lists of passengers on bus, train, or airplane
- making luggage labels and passports
- writing prescriptions
- making name-bands for patients in hospital and noting temperatures on a chart
- preparing shopping lists
- pricing shop items
- making signs for the door or wall announcing the theme, such as 'Post office', 'Hospital'.

Understanding how to help to support physical play

The benefits of physical play

Physical benefits

Physical play involves the whole body in a variety of ways. It helps with the development of both large and fine motor skills and has a significant impact on a child's health in general. As children move about in both controlled and free-play situations, they learn to interact safely without impacting on others; their sense of balance is enhanced, leading them to try more advanced actions, and improvements in manual dexterity enable greater control of mark-making tools and other small apparatus. A child who enjoys playing out of doors and is encouraged to do so will benefit from fresh air and the freedom of running, skipping and generally exercising with less restraint.

Refer back to Unit 1, page 5, for an outline of locomotor skills, non-locomotor skills and manipulation.

Physical play can take place both indoors and outside. Children use their bodies in one way or another all of the time. Some actions are instinctive, and children perform them automatically. However, others need to be practised in order for children to develop them as fully as they are able, and it is the adult's role to plan a range of activities to stimulate children in a variety of ways across all aspects of physical movement.

activity 6.10 GROUP WORK

Physical play helps develop strength, stamina, agility and balance. Select three active play opportunities, one each to support the development of locomotion skills, non-locomotion skills and manipulation.

(a) When and where would your chosen activities ideally take place?

(b) What resources (if any) would you need to provide?

(c) Which aspects of strength, stamina, agility and balance are likely to be enhanced by the activities?

(d) What impact would each activity be likely to have, for example on bones and muscle use?

Social and emotional benefits of physical play

Physical play usually involves interacting with other children. Interactions and co-operative situations help with social development and enable the child to feel part of a group. Taking turns, sharing resources and taking other people into consideration are social skills each child needs to learn. Being asked to join in a game helps children feel good about themselves, as does having others respond positively to their requests to join in. These situations help them develop a sense of worth, boost their self-esteem and therefore benefit emotional development too.

remember

In a world where more and more people lead sedentary lives and physical activity is decreasing, any form of physical play will benefit children by helping them to develop the interest and inclination to be active.

Encouragement

As children work and play alongside each other, they learn by observing others. Younger children can benefit from time spent with those older and at a more advanced developmental stage than themselves. Sometimes as adults, we model actions for children to indicate what they need to do or something they may wish to try. This helps them to build on their skills in a more independent way.

Children with impaired movement

Many conditions and disabilities adversely affect a child's physical development; in such cases, a child may need additional help to enable them to use their body as fully as possible. When planning activities for a mixed-ability group, you will need to identify alternative ways to achieve the outcome. For example, it may be necessary to have an extra adult on hand to ensure that there is sufficient adult help to support all the children taking part.

Refer to Unit 8, pages 350–368, for examples of how various specific needs can be supported within a mainstream environment.

See pages 204–221 for a range of activities for young children set out under the main developmental headings. You may find it helpful to refer back to the physical development sections at this point, and you may also like to re-read the suggestions for outdoor play on page 229.

Supervision

Effective use of space

When planning how to set up a room, playground or activity area, the positioning of static fixtures and equipment such as cupboards and tables must be considered carefully. If large areas are required for such activities as movement, dance or drama, fixtures must be kept to the outer edges of the area, or to one end. If, however, the need is for an integrated free-play space where children are to be encouraged to move from activity to activity as they wish, the requirement will be for sufficient space to be left for children to move between activities and for adults to have good vision of where children are playing or working.

Professional Practice

It is important to make sure that the requirements and actions relating to one activity do not encroach on the success of another. For example, ensure that:

- children with dripping hands from playing at the water tray do not repeatedly pass the writing area and drip water on the paper
- wooden building blocks, which will produce quite noisy play, are not positioned next to the book area where children may go for some quiet time.

On page 150 of Unit 4, there is an activity on room planning. You may like to refer to that now.

Suitability for children's age, needs and ability levels

The level of supervision required to ensure that play takes place safely will differ according to what the play involves, where the play is taking place and the children's ages, developmental levels and ability to understand and respond to instructions.

As babies learn to crawl, they find amusement in moving as fast as possible away from the adult calling them. They do not understand danger and are not therefore likely to stop when approaching a hazard. They spot miniscule items and will investigate them by putting them in their mouths. As adults, we need to step in to guide infants and keep them safe. We must also keep floors clear of small items.

Toddlers and young children also do not identify danger. Their instinctive curiosity and sense of adventure can easily lead them to hurt themselves as they climb to greater heights or reach for objects with little or no regard as to what else might fall. Again, it is up to us as adults to be on hand to save them if their investigations become unsafe.

Refer to Unit 2, page 69, for more information on issues that impact on safety, such as safety surfaces, space and suitability of lighting and heating.

As children grow older they gain a better understanding of hazards, but they are often willing to take chances and test the boundaries set by the adults responsible for them. They also test their own abilities and can be influenced by their peers to try actions that they know they should not really attempt.

Supervision of older children has to be planned carefully and sensitively. With children of all ages, it is better to have a few clear, non-negotiable rules and boundaries than a greater number, some of which you sometimes give in on. This approach will ensure a higher level of safety and more effective adult influence.

Understanding how to encourage children to explore and investigate

Resources

remember Children need to want to know, to find out and to explore, in order to gain knowledge and develop understanding.

Children learn best through investigation and exploration. At the earliest stages, babies are learning through experience by using their senses, to smell, touch, etc. As they hold a soft toy or rattle, they will feel its shape, hear the sounds as it moves, have some awareness of its weight and of how easy it is to manipulate. Each of these experiences will help the child to evaluate and make decisions as to how to use and handle other objects at a later stage. If children lack opportunities for stimulating exploration when they are young babies, they may not develop the curiosity and investigative urge that is usually seen in the toddler stage and beyond.

Community resources

The community surrounding each school, early years setting or play centre offers many opportunities for stimulating children's learning and furthering their understanding. Human resources include people who live in the locality and represent its cultural and social mix, and people who work within the local area and have an impact on the lives of many within that community (e.g. health visitors, nurses, dentists, religious leaders, lollipop persons, the vet, builders, the park warden or an animal sanctuary worker).

Much can be learned from walking through the local environment and observing the architecture, shopping precincts and housing. Also consider visiting theatres, art galleries, community sculptures, recycling depots, and the fire station.

activity 6.11 GROUP WORK

(a) Think about your local community and list a range of people who could be asked to visit a setting caring for children.

(b) Why might you invite them and what you would expect from them?

(c) When would be the best time of year to introduce them? For example, would it make sense to invite a religious or cultural representative to visit near to an approaching religious or cultural festival, or the dentist or health visitor to come in during a week when the setting is focusing on a specific topic such as tooth care?

Refer to page 272 for details of a useful DVD called *People Who Help Us*.

Indoor resources

In the indoor environment, children will explore and investigate most resources and activities that they are provided with. However, some activities will require greater levels of investigation than others. For example, a set of stacking beakers of differing sizes offers more opportunities for exploration (e.g. size, shape, balance and stability) than building blocks of uniform shape and size.

Outdoor resources

The natural world is clearly an ideal resource for children to explore. Opportunities for gardening – planting, tending and enjoying plants, flowers and vegetables – will help children learn about life cycles, where food comes from, the needs of living and growing items, and will of course give pleasure too.

Depending on where a childcare setting is situated geographically, there may be opportunities to explore woodland and nature reserves.

activity 6.12 GROUP WORK

(a) What resources can you identify within your local community?

(b) Choose one from (a) and plan how you would use it as an opportunity for exploration and investigation for groups of children in the following age ranges:

(i) pre-school

(ii) key stage 1

(iii) key stage 2.

(c) What differences would you need to take into account with regard to their needs, knowledge and ability?

Information technology

Information technology (IT) plays a huge part in communication and learning in society today. Most early years settings now have access to computers and other technology resources, enabling all children to gain some familiarity with them. Many useful programs are available to support all aspects of learning; some directly teach certain skills, whereas others encourage children to explore, predict, make choices and take decisions.

As children get older, their investigations will become much more advanced. They are likely to be particularly interested in how technology works and will wish to experiment with computers, testing both capacity and limitations. Whenever possible, it is good to have an adult who is proficient in IT on hand to answer queries and help direct investigations if problems arise.

At your current placement and any subsequent ones, ask to spend time using the IT resources that they have for that particular age range of children. Compare programmes for different ages/ability levels, looking for the similarities and differences.

Encouragement

Engaging children's curiosity

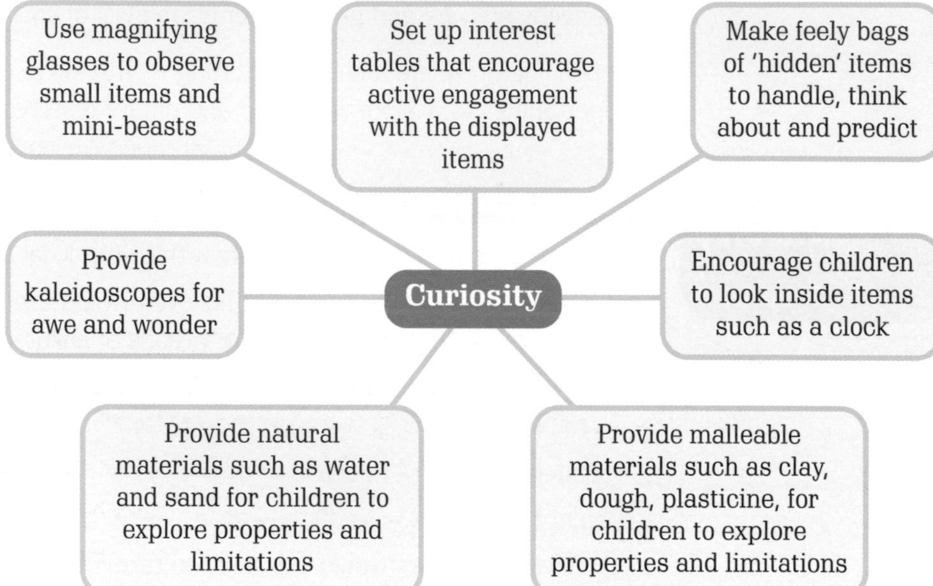

Figure 6.37 Curiosity

activity 6.14 INDIVIDUAL WORK

The spidergram above provides a few suggestions for activities that encourage children to be curious. What else can you add to the spidergram?

Showing your own interest in exploring and investigating

Children will often take their example from us. It is therefore important that we demonstrate to them that we too are interested in learning more, that we explore the properties of items and resources that we use, and that we utilise books, the internet and other people as sources of information for our investigations.

case study 6.6

Esther

Esther worked with children in a Year 2 class. Danny, aged six, brought a very large conch shell into class to show her. His grandparents had brought it back from a holiday abroad. Esther discussed with the children where the conch shell might have come from and what might have lived inside it, using a globe to show areas of the world where the shells are typically found. She supported the class in writing about the shell, helping them to develop new vocabulary to describe it. Using the internet they explored sites about shells and scanned the classroom's bookshelves for books on the sea, the shoreline and oceans in general.

activity
INDIVIDUAL WORK

Clearly, Esther made good use of the opportunity initiated by Danny. Can you think of anything else she could have included?

Professional Practice

- Planning for learning is important, but it should never be so rigid that spontaneous opportunities cannot be taken up.
- Children need to be able to take risk at times in order to learn. Risks should however be managed carefully, and be appropriate to a child's ability level.

Refer back to Unit 2, page 69, for a brief overview of what is meant by the term 'risk assessment'.

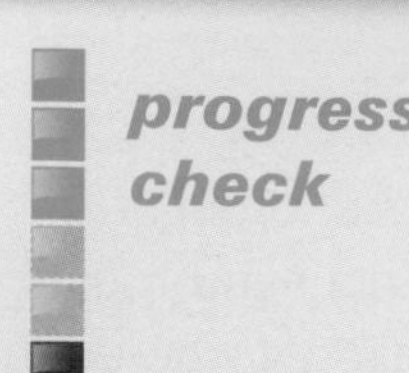

1. In what ways does play help a child develop?
2. What does the term 'holistic' mean?
3. What are the main stages of play development?
4. In what ways can the role-play corner provide opportunities for mathematics development?
5. How can you ensure equal opportunities within role play?
6. Give at least five examples of how music can be introduced to children.
7. Give at least three examples of equipment to support locomotor development and three to support non-locomotor development.
8. Thinking about the Foundation Stage curriculum, list at least 10 activities that can support personal, social and emotional development.
9. Thinking about the Foundation Stage curriculum, list at least 10 activities that can support communication, language and literacy.
10. Thinking about the Foundation Stage curriculum, list at least 10 activities that can support mathematical development.
11. Thinking about the Foundation Stage curriculum, list at least 10 activities that can support knowledge and understanding of the world.
12. Thinking about the Foundation Stage curriculum, list at least 10 activities that can support physical development.
13. Thinking about the Foundation Stage curriculum, list at least 10 activities that can support creative development.
14. Shape sorters and puzzles are both structured activities. How do they help physical development? What other examples of structured activities can you think of?
15. In what ways do plants and animals offer valuable learning opportunities for young children?

References and suggested further reading

Boyd, L. (2004) *Construction*. David Fulton Publishers, London.

Bruce, T. and Meggitt, C. (1996) *Childcare and Education*. Hodder & Stoughton, London.

Child's Eye Media (2006) *People Who Help Us* (DVD).

Dare, A. and O'Donovan, M. (1997) *Good Practice in Caring for Children with Special Needs*. Nelson Thornes, Cheltenham.

DfEE (1995) *Key Stages 1 and 2 of the National Curriculum*. HMSO, London.

DfEE (1998) *National Literacy Strategy: Framework for Teaching for the Reception Year*. HMSO, London.

DfEE (2000) *Curriculum Guidance for the Foundation Stage*. HMSO, London.

DfES (2002) *An Introduction to the Framework*. HMSO, London.

DfES (2003) *National Standards for Under Eights Day Care and Childminding*. DfES/DWP, Nottingham.

DfES (2004) *Every Child Matters: Change for Children in Schools*. HMSO, London.

Dumo, J. (2006) *Music and Singing*. David Fulton Publishers, London.

Green, S. (2004) *Baby and Toddler Development Made Real*. David Fulton Publishers, London.

Green, S. (2004) *Creativity*. David Fulton Publishers, London.

Green, S. (2005) *Role Play*. David Fulton Publishers, London.

Green, S. (2006) *Books, Stories and Puppets*. David Fulton Publishers, London.

Green, S. (2007) BTEC *National Children's Care, Learning and Development*. Nelson Thornes, Cheltenham.

Harper, S. (2005) *Nature, Living and Growing*. David Fulton Publishers, London.

Harpley, A. and Roberts, A. (2006) *Helping Children to be Skilful Communicators, from Birth to 3 Series* (ed. S. Green). David Fulton Publishers, London.

Harpley, A. and Roberts, A. (2006) *Helping Children to Stay Healthy, from Birth to 3 Series* (ed. S. Green). David Fulton Publishers, London.

Harpley, A. and Roberts, A. (2007) *Helping Children to be Competent Learners, from Birth to 3 Series* (ed. S. Green). David Fulton Publishers, London.

Harpley, A. and Roberts, A. (2007) *Helping Children to be Strong, from Birth to 3 Series* (ed. S. Green). David Fulton Publishers, London.

Hewitson, C. (2004) *Festivals*. David Fulton Publishers, London.

Hobart, C. and Frankel, J. (1999) *A Practical Guide to Activities for Young Children*, 2nd edn. Nelson Thornes, Cheltenham.

Howe, A. (2005) *Play Using Natural Materials*. David Fulton Publishers, London.

Mukherji, P. and O'Dea, T. (2000) *Understanding Children's Language and Literacy*, Nelson Thornes, Cheltenham.

Qualification and Curriculum Authority (QCA) (2000) *Early Learning Goals*, DfES, London.

Sheridan, M. (1997) *From Birth to Five Years: Children's Developmental Progress*, revised edn. Routledge, London.

Tassoni, P. and Hucker, K. (2000) *Planning Play and the Early Years*. Heinemann, Oxford.

Series

'Ready, Steady, Play!' series published by David Fulton Publishers.

Titles include:

Books, Stories and Puppets
Creativity
Festivals
Play using Natural Materials
Role Play

'Exploring Play' series published by David Fulton Publishers.

Titles include:
Bears
Flight
Water
Woodland Creatures and their Homes.

'Stepping Stones' series published by Nelson Thornes.

Titles include:
At Home and Far Away
Creatures Great and Small
Food
Gardens
Ourselves
Toys

Journals and magazines
Child Education
Creative Steps
Early Years Educator (EYE)
Nursery Education
Nursery Projects
Nursery World
Practical Pre-school
Practical Professional Child-Care

The Development and Care of Babies and Children Under Three Years

This unit covers:

- understanding and observing the expected sequence and development of babies and children in the first three years of life
- knowing how to help provide physical care requirements for babies and children under three
- understanding how to provide play activities to encourage learning and development
- understanding how to communicate with babies and children under three, interpret their needs and respond to them.

During the first three years of life, development proceeds at an incredible rate, from the helplessness of the newborn baby through to the active, investigative stage of the three-year-old. This unit starts by showing you the sequence of that development; the relevance of observation to understanding child development is also explained.

You will then learn how to carry out care routines such as feeding and bathing and about the clothing needs of babies and young children.

The unit will also help you to appreciate the importance of play in development and show you how to communicate with babies and young children so that you can interpret and respond to their needs.

grading criteria

To achieve a **Pass** grade the evidence must show that the learner is able to:	To achieve a **Merit** grade the evidence must show that the learner is able to:	To achieve a **Distinction** grade the evidence must show that the learner is able to:
P1 describe the development, including communication, of babies and young children in the first three years of life	**M1** explain how to undertake observations of babies and young children under three years	**D1** justify the use of observation of babies and young children in the first three years of life

grading criteria

To achieve a **Pass** grade the evidence must show that the learner is able to:	To achieve a **Merit** grade the evidence must show that the learner is able to:	To achieve a **Distinction** grade the evidence must show that the learner is able to:
P2 outline what needs to be considered when observing babies and children in the first three years of life	**M2** explain how babies and young children under three years should be fed and cared for safely	**D2** evaluate the range of methods used in communication with babies and children under three to ensure that understanding is taking place
P3 identify what can be learned through observation about babies and children in the first three years of life	**M3** explain what is meant by challenge in play activities	
P4 describe the feeding and routine care of babies and young children under three years	**M4** explain how to interpret needs and respond to babies and young children	
P5 identify five different play activities that help to support different aspects of learning and development		
P6 describe the different methods used to communicate with babies and children under three years		

Understanding and observing the expected sequence and development of babies and children in the first three years of life

When supporting the all-round development of young children, you will need to understand not only what each of the different areas of development is and its associated maturational pattern, but you also need to be able to see how developmental areas link together. Although at times you will offer a child individual activities and opportunities to help a particular skill develop, you will most often be supporting the development of the child as a whole.

Main areas of development

Figure 7.1 shows the types of development that are usually studied.

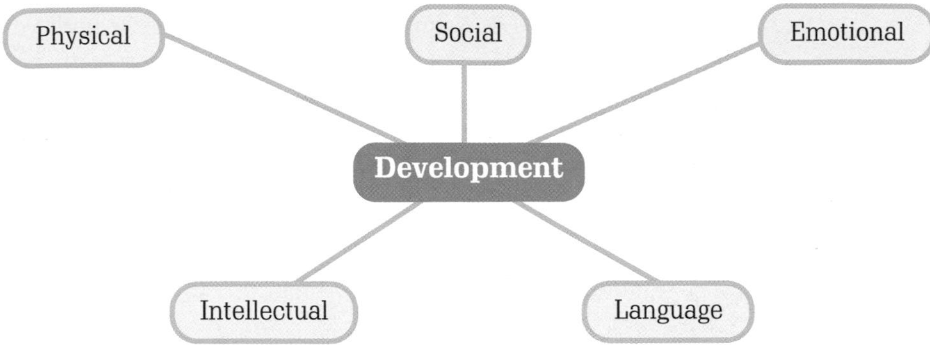

Figure 7.1 Development

keyword

Neonate
An infant under one month old.

As you read through this unit, you will find that the development of the **neonate** is covered first. This is followed by discussion of the types of development shown in Figure 7.1; physical development is divided into gross and fine skills; social and emotional development are considered together, as are intellectual and language development.

The expected pattern of physical development

Physical development includes the primitive reflexes seen in newborn infants, as set out on page 284. It also involves motor development and manipulation. Motor development includes the acquisition of locomotor skills and non-locomotor skills.

- Locomotor skills involve the body moving forward in some way (e.g. walking, running, hopping).
- Non-locomotor skills describe the physical movements that take place while stationary (e.g. bending, pulling and pushing).
- Manipulation involves actions using dexterity (e.g. throwing and catching a ball, threading cotton reels, and placing one brick on top of another).

Physical skills, which can be gross (large) or fine, include movement and balance. Movements can be either precise or casual and can involve the whole body or just one part of it.

Development becomes increasingly more complex, and children acquire more difficult physical skills as it progresses. The maturational changes can be described as moving:

- *From the simple to the complex*. A child learns simple actions, such as learning to stand, before learning the more complex actions of being able to walk.
- *From cephalo (head) to caudal (tail)*. Physical control starts at the head and gradually progresses down through the body. For example, head control is attained before the spine is strong enough for an infant to sit unsupported, and sitting unsupported is achieved before the child is able to stand.
- *From proximal (near to the body) to distal (the outer reaches of the body)*. A child develops actions near to the body before they develop control of the

outer reaches of the body. For example, a child can hug and carry a large teddy bear (arm control) before they can fasten their clothing (finger control).

- *From general to specific*. Generalised responses give way gradually to specific ones. For example, when recognising a favourite carer, an infant shows the generalised physical responses associated with excitement, but in the same situation an older child would make the specific facial response of smiling.

The normal neonate

The first month of life is known as the neonatal stage, and the infant is referred to as a neonate. Most infants are born at full term and thrive well, settling quickly into a routine with their mother and other carers.

> **keyword**
> **Lactation**
> The production of milk by the breasts.

This settling-in period involves many new experiences and the beginning of body processes not previously experienced. In the neonate, these include breathing, circulation, and digestion of new forms of nutrition (milk). In the mother, these include the onset of **lactation**, healing from the trauma of birth, and the resettling of the uterus. Each of these is a normal process, but each can also present problems.

Birth

> **keyword**
> **Apgar score**
> Score denoting the health of a baby at birth.

Birth is a traumatic experience for both mother and child. The length of labour and the type of delivery can affect the level of distress experienced by the infant, and therefore how well the infant is at birth. All infants are assessed immediately after delivery using a benchmark known as the **Apgar score**. This is a process of assessment that was devised by Dr Virginia Apgar in 1953; it sets out the vital signs of initial health, indicating whether an infant requires resuscitation or any other form of medical treatment. The five features of the assessment are as follows:

- *Heart rate*. How fast is the infant's heart beating?
- *Respiration*. How well is the infant breathing?
- *Muscle tone*. Does the infant appear limp and floppy?
- *Response to stimulus*. Does the infant respond when stimulated?
- *Colour*. Does the infant's skin colour indicate good circulation?

Each feature is scored after one minute, and then again at five minutes, continuing at five-minute intervals as necessary until the infant is responding satisfactorily and the medical team is happy.

> **keyword**
> **Pre-term**
> Born before 37 weeks of pregnancy.

The higher the infant's scores, the less likely it is that they will need any treatment. Most healthy infants score 9 at one minute. They often lose a point due to discoloration of their hands and feet; this is common and occurs because the circulation is not yet working fully. An infant who is **pre-term**, of a low birth weight or who has experienced a difficult delivery is more likely to have a lower Apgar score. A score below 5 would indicate a very poorly baby. The infants who fall into this category make up a large percentage of those who do not survive or who will have ongoing problems.

Table 7.1 The Apgar score chart

Sign	0	1	2
Heart rate	Absent	Fewer than 100 beats per minute	More than 100 beats per minute
Respiration	Absent	Slow, irregular	Good, regular
Muscle tone	Limp	Some flexion of extremities	Active
Response to stimulus (stimulation of foot or nose)	No response	Grimace	Cry, cough
Colour	Blue, pale	Body oxygenated Bluish extremities	Well-oxygenated Completely pink

A premature, difficult or traumatic birth, particularly if either mother or baby is ill and in need of special care, can also have an effect on the bonding process, owing to separation and lack of physical contact, for example if the baby is placed in a neonatal care unit, often known as a special care baby unit (SCBU). Health professionals work hard to encourage and maintain links between mothers and their babies in these circumstances.

Bonding is discussed in Unit 1, page 21; it is a vital aspect of emotional development. You may find it useful to refer back to that section now.

What to expect to see in a neonate

At delivery, babies are wet and covered to some degree in mucus, maternal blood and body fluids. Their skin colour will vary due to both their ethnic origin and their state of health, with black babies appearing pale at birth, as the skin pigmentation melanin does not reach its full levels until later on. The extremities

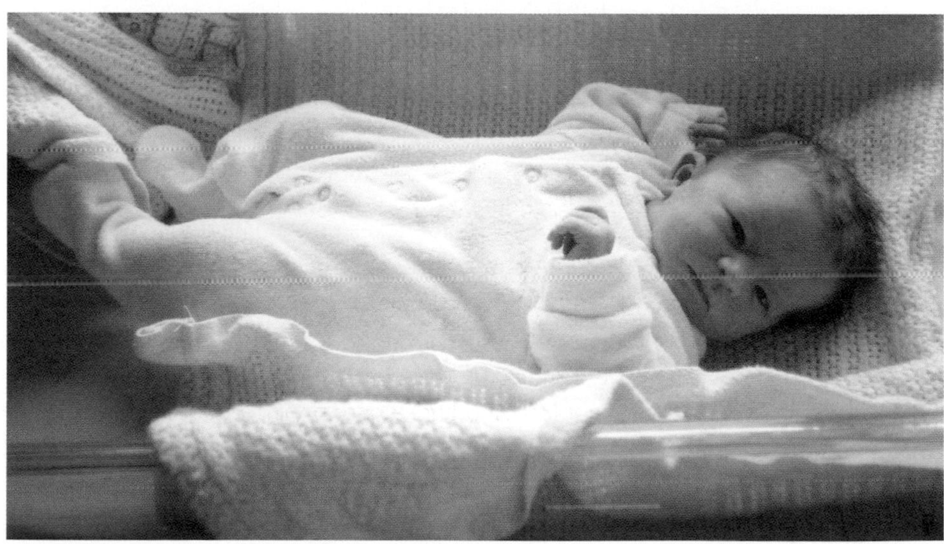

Figure 7.2
The neonate

(feet and hands) are often bluish in colour due to poor circulation. Most infants are delivered on to their mother's abdomen, and the umbilical cord is clamped and cut shortly after birth. Depending on the type and duration of the delivery, infants vary from being alert and wide awake to drowsy and unresponsive. Medication given to the mother during labour can have an effect on the neonate's state of alertness.

Sleep
At birth the infant will sleep most of the time, mostly waking for feeds and nappy changes. They often fall asleep while these routines are being carried out. Sleep patterns change as the infant develops; gradually, they remain awake for longer periods.

Figure 7.3
An infant in a flexed pose

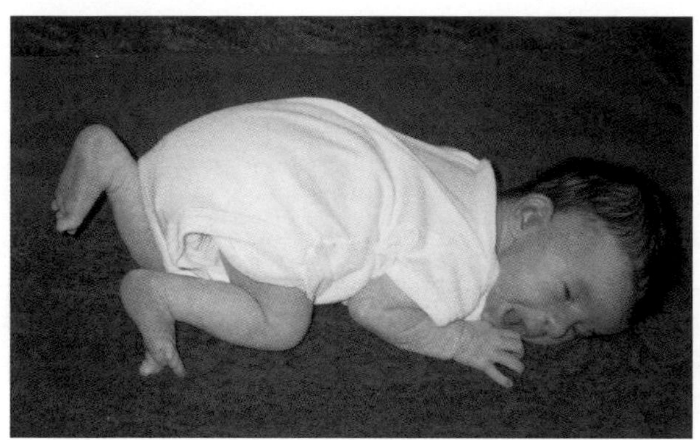

Posture and motor skills
Immediately after birth, many infants naturally curl into the foetal position with their head to one side. Limbs are kept partly flexed and are hypertonic (have tension) and tend to display jerking movements.

Head lag
The head and neck are hypotonic (weak) and there is no head control. This is often referred to as head lag. Full support of the head and neck area is essential whenever the infant is handled to ensure that no damage is caused or undue strain placed on the neck muscles.

Vernix caseosa
Vernix caseosa may be present. This is a creamy-white protective substance, which covers the body of an infant during the latter stages of pregnancy. It is usually seen in pre-term infants and is often present in full-term infants too. It lubricates the skin and should be left to come off on its own, rather than be washed or rubbed.

Lanugo
Lanugo is a soft, downy hair that covers the infant while in the uterus. Traces of lanugo are often found on the back, shoulders and ears at birth.

Fontanelles
There are two fontanelles on the infant's skull. Fontanelles are areas of the skull where the bony plates of the skull meet. They enable some movement of the skull during the birth process. The posterior fontanelle is a small triangular area near to the crown, which closes within a few weeks of birth. The anterior fontanelle is near the front of the head and is diamond shaped. It usually closes over by 18 months of age and pulsates at the same rate as the infant's heartbeat. If fontanelles appear sunken, it may indicate that the infant is not getting sufficient fluids. A bulging fontanelle may be a sign that there is a high level of pressure around the brain, or an infection, and should always be investigated.

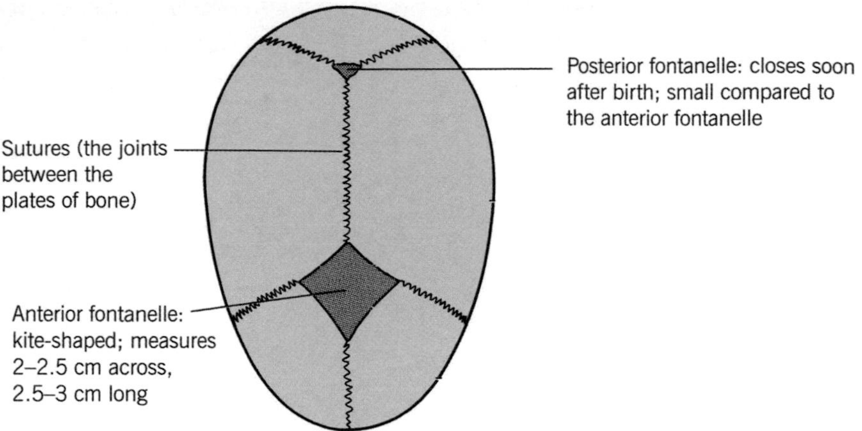

Figure 7.4
The fontanelles

Misshapen skulls

The head of a newborn infant may be flattened or misshapen because of pressure experienced when passing down the birth canal or as a result of delivery by forceps or ventouse suction. In a multiple birth, the head may become misshapen owing to lack of space. It can take some weeks for the skull to realign itself and resume its natural shape.

Umbilicus

The most well-known sign of the neonate is the umbilical 'stump'. The umbilical cord is clamped and cut at birth; the small stump of cord that remains is left to drop off on its own, usually seven to 10 days after birth. The stump must be kept dry and clean, although actual cleaning of it is not usually recommended.

Swelling and bruising

Some infants show signs of swelling or bruising; this is normally the result of a difficult birth and tends to ease within a few days.

Eyes

Sticky eyes are common in the first few days and uncoordinated eyes are usual. All babies are born with dark eyes; their permanent eye colour is not established until much later on.

Genitals

Genitalia appear to be swollen in both boys and girls, and blood loss from the vaginal area in girls is quite common. Both are caused by the mother's hormones crossing the placenta.

Breasts

The neonate's breasts may be swollen and leak a little milk. This is commonly seen in boys as well as girls and is caused by the mother's hormones crossing the placenta.

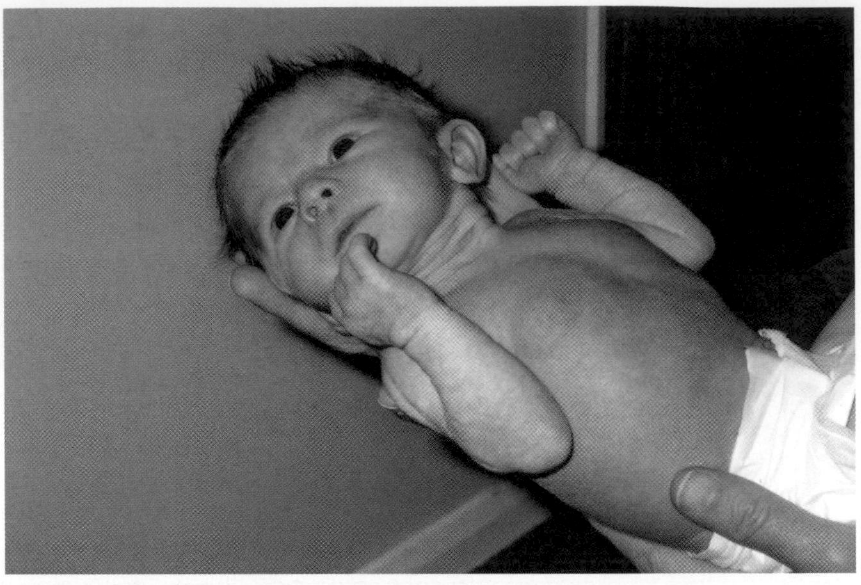

Figure 7.5

Breasts may be swollen and leak a little milk

Stools

The stools (faeces) of the neonate are a dark, greenish black because they contain a tarry substance called meconium. Meconium is very sticky. The colour and consistency of the stools change within a few days, as the mother's milk comes in or formula feeding is established.

Spots and rashes

Spots and rashes are very common in the first few days, but the infant's skin soon settles down. Milia are particularly common; these are tiny white spots often known as 'milk spots'.

Peeling skin

Peeling skin is quite common on the hands and feet but usually only lasts two or three days and soon settles down.

Neonatal jaundice and raised bilirubin levels

Some infants suffer from neonatal jaundice in which the skin and eyes become yellowish due to the infant's immature liver function and a subsequent rise in levels of bilirubin. Bilirubin is formed when red blood cells break down and the liver is unable to cope with its workload. Jaundice usually occurs (if it is going to) on about day three after birth. Jaundice occurring before the neonate is three days old needs particular investigation as liver disease or sepsis may be present and the infant's life could be in danger. Some jaundice in breastfed babies is normal. However, on occasions, jaundice can be a sign of the condition galactosaemia (a metabolic disorder), rubella virus (German measles) or cytomegalovirus (herpes). Some infants with raised bilirubin levels require phototherapy. Liver function problems are monitored by nurses who check the colour of each infant's stools and urine.

Birth marks

There are various types of birth marks, including the following.

- *Port wine marks*. These are permanent, dark-red marks, often on the face or neck. In the past, they were often a permanent disfigurement, but many of these marks can now be successfully removed or depleted by laser treatment.
- *Strawberry naevi*. These raised marks full of blood vessels are quite common. They are not actually present at birth but develop in the first few days or weeks. They have usually disappeared by eight years of age. The full name for this type of naevus is haemangioma.
- *Stork bites*. These are tiny red marks found on the eye lids, the top of the nose and on the back of the neck. They are quite common and gradually disappear; they are not usually a problem.
- *Mongolian blue spot*. These are dark marks found at the base of the spine on non-Caucasian (non-white) infants. On occasions, these marks have been wrongly attributed to physical abuse. They are usually 'mapped' by health professionals in the early weeks to prevent unfounded concerns being raised. Early years workers need to be aware of these marks.
- *Moles*. Most people have moles, but some moles can be large and unsightly, for example congenital melanocytic naevus (CMN), which gets progressively darker as the infant grows. Unsightly moles can sometimes be successfully removed or depleted with laser treatment or plastic surgery.

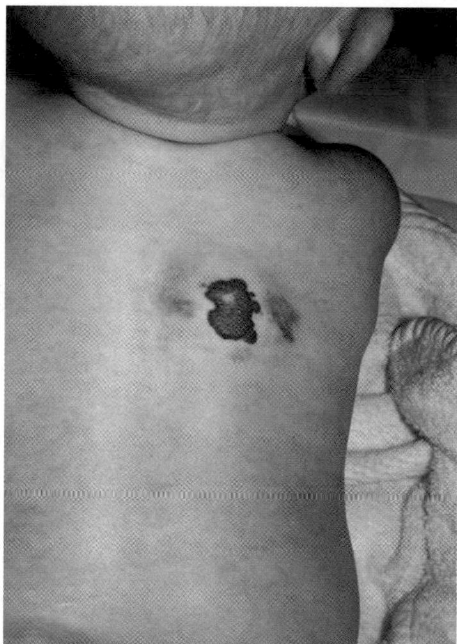

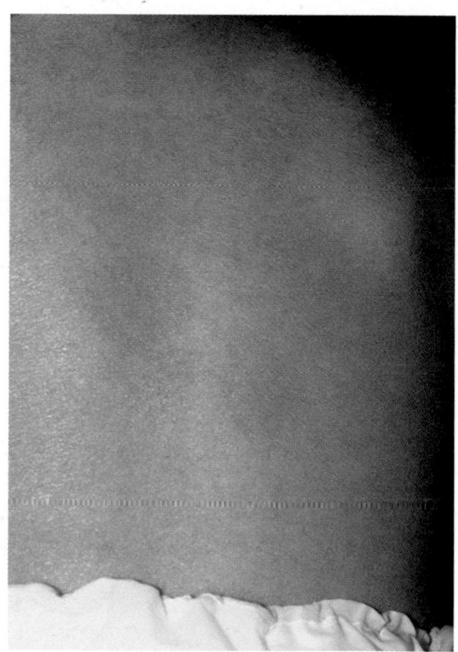

Figure 7.6
Various birth marks
a) Stawberry naevus,
b) Mongolian Blue Spot

Primitive reflexes

Bee (1992, page 105) defines reflexes as 'automatic body reactions to specific stimulation'.

A neonate's reflexes include the following.

- *Blinking*. The neonate reacts to sudden lights, noises or movements in front of the eyes.
- *Rooting*. The neonate turns their face towards their mother to locate the breast.
- *The sucking reflex*. Infants will usually suck a (clean) finger, placed gently in their mouth.

Figure 7.7
Rooting reflex

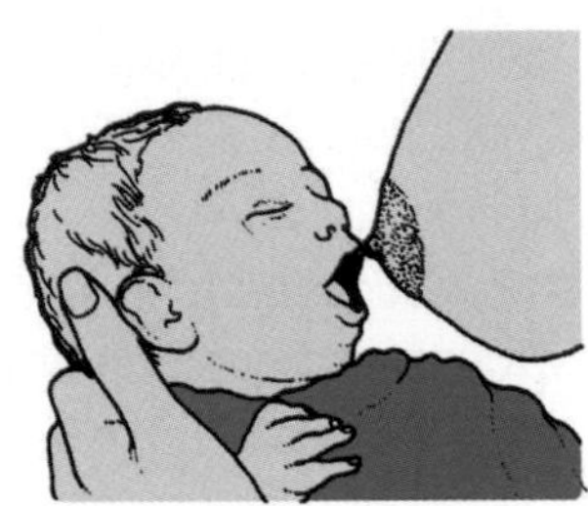

- *The palmar grasp*. The infant holds firmly to whatever touches the palm of their hand (gently stroking the back of the infant's hand will usually release the grasp).
- *The plantar reflex*. Touching the sole of the infant's foot with a finger will result in the flexing of their toes towards your finger.

Figure 7.8
Sucking reflex

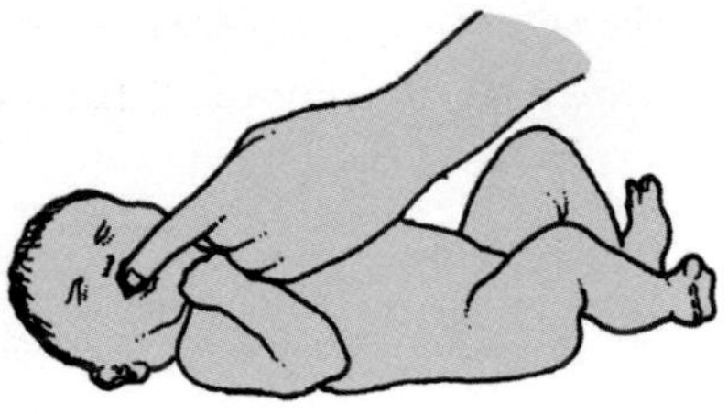

Figure 7.9
The palmar grasp

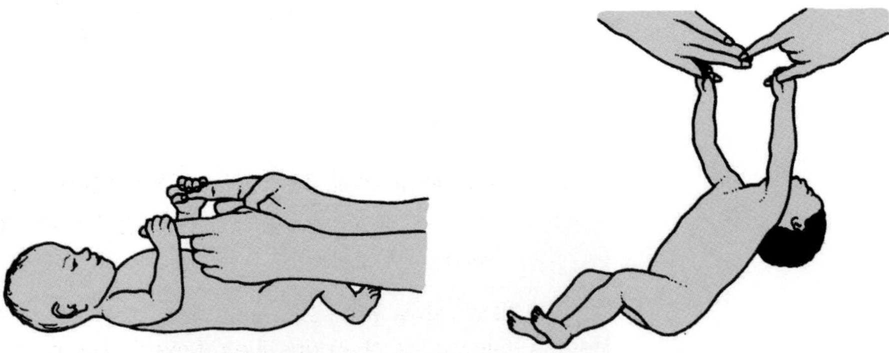

- *The stepping reflex*. The neonate's foot responds to contact with a firm surface, resulting in a small 'step' being taken.

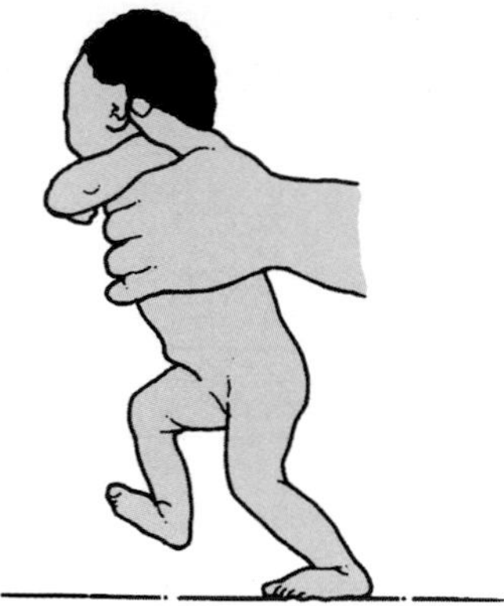
Figure 7.10
The stepping reflex

- *The moro reflex*. A sudden movement of the neck is interpreted by the infant as falling, and they will throw out their arms with open hands and re-clasp them over their chest.

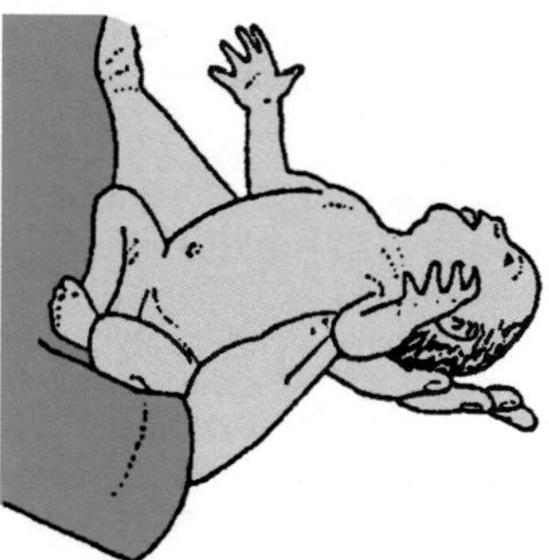
Figure 7.11
The moro reflex

- *The startle reflex*. The infant throws out their arms at a sudden noise or movement, but the fists remain clenched.

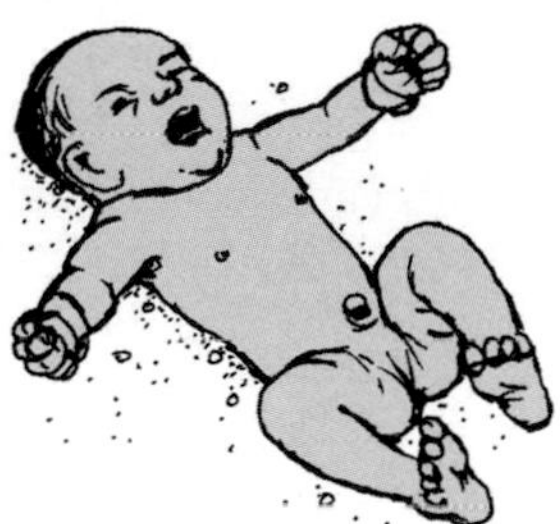
Figure 7.12
The startle reflex

- *The asymmetric tonic neck reflex*. When the infant's head is turned to one side, they will respond by straightening the arm and leg on the same side, while flexing the limbs opposite.

Some reflexes stay with us for life, for example blinking, but some are lost after the first few weeks (the primitive reflexes). The presence of the primitive reflexes is an indicator of how well an infant's nervous system is functioning (their neurological well-being). As the brain gradually takes over the body's responses, the primitive reflexes disappear. If the primitive reflexes are present for longer than is considered usual (they start to diminish at six weeks, to be replaced by more deliberate actions), it can indicate that there is a developmental problem, which may need to be investigated. The infant's progress will then be monitored in addition to the usual planned screening procedures.

All infants are usually assessed by a doctor at six weeks of age.

See Unit 1, page 3, for details of the planned screening programme.

The senses

Table 7.2 The senses

Hearing ■ The hearing of infants is acute (sharp) ■ They blink in response to sound ■ The neonate can identify the voice of their main carer almost immediately ■ Noisy objects can only roughly be located ■ Sudden noises distress the infant ■ Infants respond to soothing rhythmic sounds
Vision ■ Newborn infants are sensitive to both light and sound ■ Vision is diffused and limited initially to objects within about a 30 cm (12 inch) radius ■ Eyes do not initially work together and they will often 'cross' or 'wander' ■ Eye-to-eye contact with the main carer (usually the mother) is an important means of establishing a bonding relationship ■ Infants show a preference for human faces ■ Infants will turn towards a light
Touch ■ Skin-to-skin contact is important to the bonding process, and for breast-feeding ■ Most infants are delivered on to their mother's abdomen ■ Contact and handling usually soothe a distressed infant but may be less welcomed by a premature baby ■ The temperature control of infants is ineffective
Smell ■ Infants can identify their mothers by smell ■ Research has shown that infants can distinguish their mother's milk on a breast pad

An infant's development can be influenced by the health and life style of the mother. Refer back to Unit 1, pages 36–42, for information on factors affecting growth and development.

Normal growth and development

Throughout childhood, growth is rapid, particularly during the first year, with a steadier rate of development from the toddler stage onwards. Slight differences in the growth of girl infants and boy infants are expected, with boys, on average, being slightly heavier than girls at birth.

Centile charts

Infants and young children are measured using centile charts (see illustrations below). These charts enable health visitors and paediatricians to monitor development, and to identify any causes for concern in babies' growth rates. The 50th centile line is the central line on the charts. It indicates the average at each age. The upper and lower lines represent the boundary within which 80 per cent of children will fall. A child who falls outside these boundaries will be monitored more closely and may at some stage need further investigation into their development.

The pattern (or line) formed as a child's measurements are plotted on the centile chart is known as a 'growth curve'.

In the following centile charts you can see that there are slight differences between the expectations for girls compared with the expectations for boys.

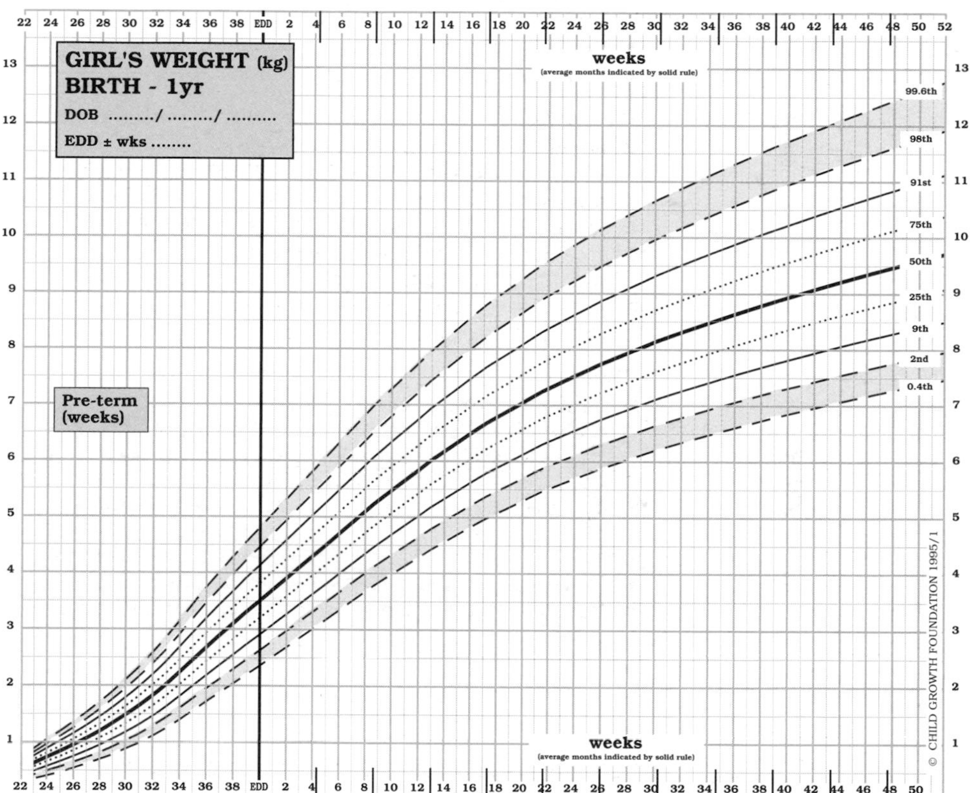

Figure 7.13
Centile chart for the weight of a baby girl

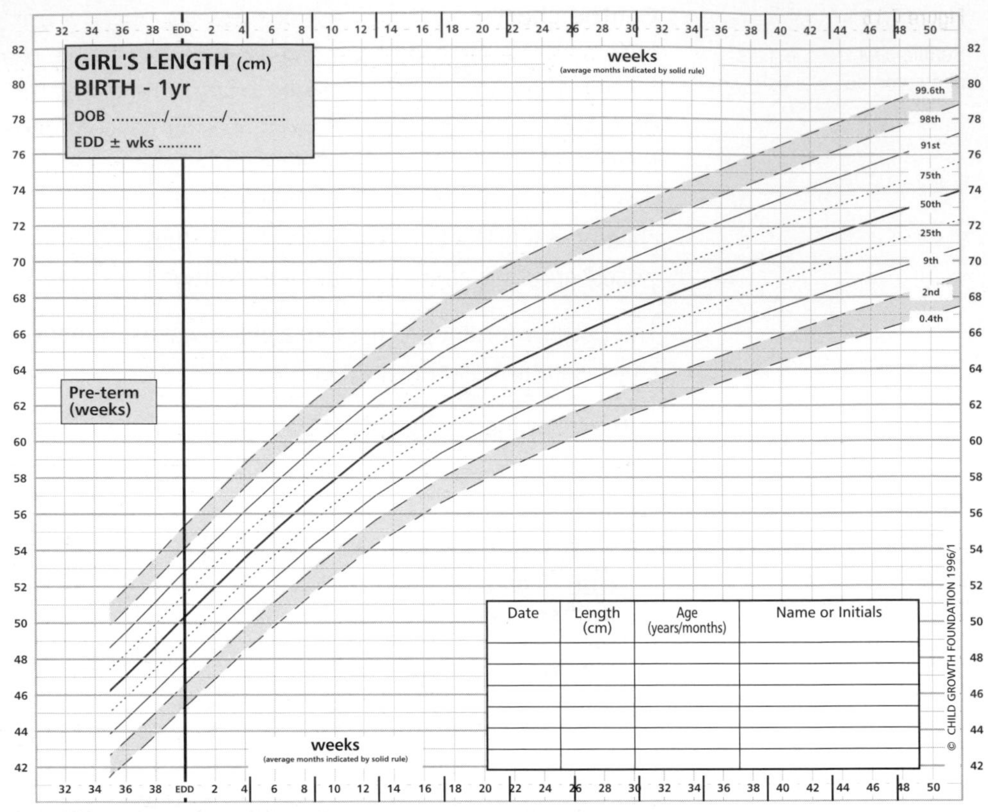

Figure 7.14
Centile chart for the length of a baby girl

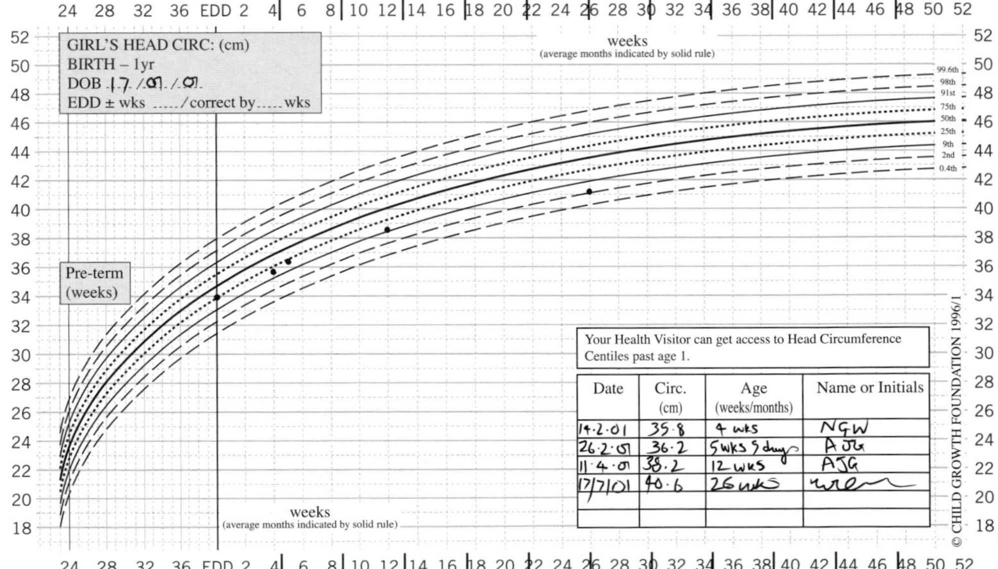

Figure 7.15
Centile chart for the head circumference of a baby girl

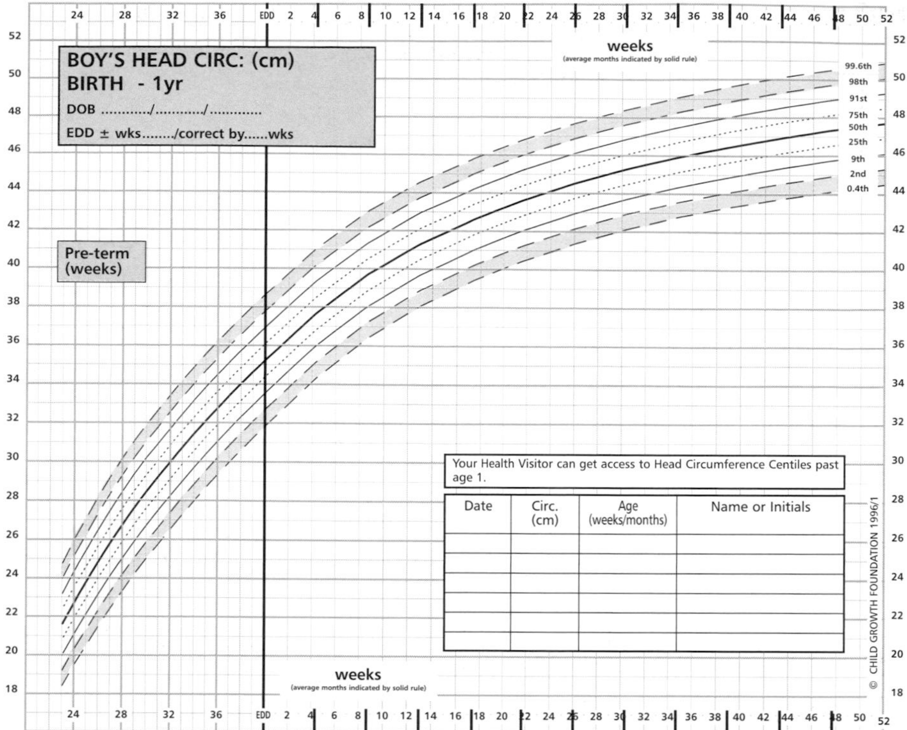

Figure 7.16
Centile chart for the head circumference of a baby boy

Milestones of physical development: infant (one month to one year)

Summary of the development of gross motor skills

- Movements remain jerky and uncontrolled.
- Head lag gradually decreases and head control is usually achieved by five months.
- Rolling over is first seen between four and six months (from back to side), and then from front to back by about eight months.
- Reaching for objects begins at about four months with the ability to pass toys from hand to hand seen from about seven months; the infant discovers their feet.
- At four months the infant manages to sit with support.
- Sitting alone commences at about seven to eight months, with greater balance developing gradually.
- Crawling can start from six months (commando crawling) and traditional crawling is seen from about eight months. Some infants bear-walk or bottom-shuffle.
- Some infants miss out the crawling stage, and move straight to pulling themselves up on furniture at around eight to 10 months.
- Standing alone can occur any time from 10 months but is more usual at around a year, when balance is generally more established.
- Walking is normally achieved by 12–16 months.

Summary of the development of fine motor skills

- Hand and finger movements gradually increase, from the grasping of adults' fingers in the earliest months, through to playing with own fingers and toes, handling and then holding toys and objects from three to four months.
- Everything is explored through the mouth.
- At about seven months, the infant will try to transfer objects from one hand to the other with some success. Pincer grasp (index finger and thumb) is emerging; it is developed by about 10 months.
- The infant will pick up small objects.
- Toys are pulled towards the infant.
- Pointing and clapping are deliberate actions for most infants by 10–12 months.
- Controlled efforts to feed themselves meet with some success.

Milestones of physical development: toddler (one to two years)

Summary of physical development

- Standing alone is achieved but children of this age are unable at first to sit (without help) from being in a standing position. They begin to let themselves down in a controlled manner from about 15 months.
- When walking, hands are held up for balance and the infant's steps are uneven; they have difficulty in stopping once they have started.
- They can creep upstairs on hands and knees quite safely (not advisable without an adult supervising).
- They begin to kneel.
- By 18 months, walking is usually well established, and the arms are no longer needed for balance. The toddler can now back into a small chair and climb forwards into an adult chair.
- Squatting when playing is now common.
- They can usually walk upstairs holding an adult hand.
- Manipulation skills (the ability to use their hands and fingers in a controlled manner) are developing. Pages of books can usually now be turned quite well, and pencils can be held in a clumsy (primitive) grasp.
- By two years, the child can usually run safely, starting and stopping at will.
- They are able to pull wheeled toys, with some understanding of direction.
- They are usually able to control a ball to throw forwards.
- They can walk up and (usually) down stairs, holding on and two feet to a stair.
- They cannot yet kick a football without falling into it, losing their balance as they kick their foot forward.
- They cannot usually pedal a tricycle.

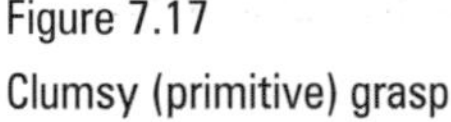
Figure 7.17
Clumsy (primitive) grasp

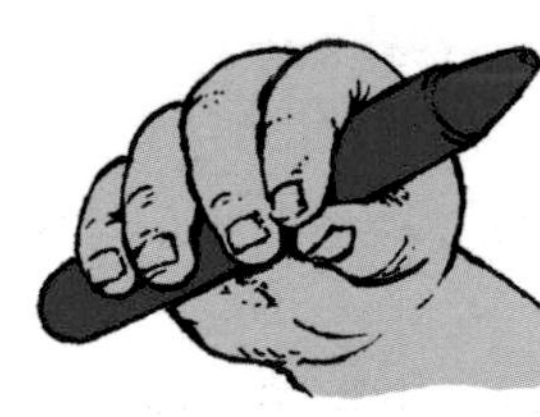

Milestones of physical development: two to five years

Summary of physical development

- Pushing and pulling of large toys is achieved by two and a half.
- Walking up stairs with alternating feet is usually achieved by three years. Going securely up and down on alternate feet is seen by three and a half.
- At two and a half, children can kick a football gently; by three years they can kick with force.
- Locomotor skills (movement forwards, backwards, and so on) improve rapidly during this stage of development.
- Use of pedals is often achieved by three years, and a child can steer around corners.
- Balance gradually improves, and by four years a child can usually stand, walk and run on tip-toes, and navigate skilfully when active.
- From three years, ball skills increase (catching, throwing, bouncing and kicking).
- Manipulation skills improve.
- Scissor control is developing and greater pencil control is achieved by three years.
- By four years, threading small beads and early sewing is achieved.
- Adult pencil control is usually present by four years.

Milestones of social and emotional development: infant (one month to one year)

Summary of social and emotional development

- The first social smile is usually seen by six weeks.
- Smiling is first confined to main carers and is then in response to most contacts.
- The infant concentrates on carers' faces.
- Pleasure during handling and caring routines is shown by eight weeks, through smiles, cooing and general contentment.
- From about 12 weeks, expressions of pleasure are clear when the infant gains attention and in response to the main carers' voices.
- Social games, involving handling and cuddles, elicit chuckles from four to five months onwards.
- The infant enjoys watching other infants.
- Sleep patterns begin to emerge from about four months onwards, although these will continue to change.
- From about nine or 10 months, the infant may become distressed when the main carer leaves them, temporarily losing their sense of security and becoming wary of strangers. This is a normal stage in development.
- Playing contentedly alone increases by one year, but the reassuring presence of an adult is still needed.

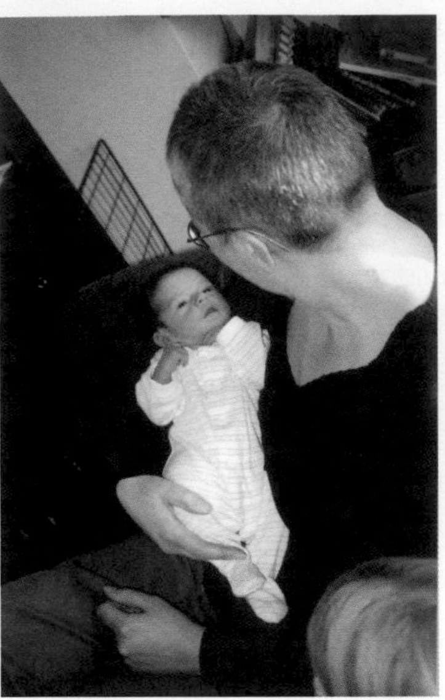

Figure 7.18
Making eye contact

Milestones of social and emotional development: toddler (one to two years)

Summary of social and emotional development

- By about 15 months, the child will usually indicate a wet or soiled nappy.
- The child co-operates (helps) with dressing, for example, holding up arms for a jumper.
- The child is dependent on an adult's presence for reassurance.
- They experience frustration at not being able to achieve their aim (e.g. putting two bricks together), which leads them to discard toys in anger.
- By 18 months, the child is usually very successful at feeding self with a spoon.
- The child handles a cup confidently but does not put it back down (gives it to adult).
- The child removes hats, shoes, etc. but can rarely replace them.
- The child makes urgent vocalisations when making a demand.
- Bowel control is sometimes attained by 18 months and is usually attained by two years.
- By two years, the child will play parallel alongside others without actually interacting.
- Children can be rebellious and resistive and get frustrated when trying to make themselves understood, but they can easily be distracted from their tantrums at this age.
- It is both common and normal for there to be no idea of sharing and no understanding of the need to defer their wishes.
- The child follows adult around and needs reassurance when tired or fearful.
- By two years, the child can usually put on hat and shoes, and can reposition a cup on a surface.

Milestones of social and emotional development: two to five years

Summary of social and emotional development

- At two and a half, tantrums are common when needs are thwarted. The child is less easily distracted from them now.
- The child is very resistive of restraint, for example when having a hand held in a busy shop.
- The child mostly still watches others or plays in parallel; occasionally, the child joins in briefly.
- By four years, the child can eat skilfully and can dress, wash and clean their teeth (with supervision).
- This is generally a more independent age; children tend to want to try things on their own.
- Children co-operate with others but can also be uncooperative if their wishes are refused.
- Children can be very strong-willed.
- At five years, behaviour is noticeably more sensible and controlled.
- Children understand sharing and turn-taking and the need for fair play.
- Co-operative play is constant at five years.
- Children choose their own friends and play well; they are very protective towards younger children, pets and distressed playmates.

Refer to Unit 6, page 202, for details of types of play.

Intellectual and communication skills

As well as physical growth and development, which can be observed and measured quite easily, children develop their knowledge and understanding too. This is often referred to as intellectual (or cognitive) development. The development of knowledge and understanding is closely linked with the development of language and communication skills, and it involves the senses too.

At birth, the infant's nervous system is incomplete and understanding their level of sensory awareness is not easy. It has been established by researchers that an infant's system for vision is not initially strong, but that it develops considerably in the first few months, whereas an infant's hearing is quite well developed right from birth. Vision and hearing are important for language and cognition (understanding) and are both assessed at regular intervals during infancy and early childhood.

Sensory development: vision

From birth, infants turn to look at sources of light. Within a few days of birth, babies can demonstrate both spontaneous and imitative facial expressions, and the eyes of the newborn infant can at times be seen to move in the direction of sounds. These early visual interactions (eye contacts) between the infant and their carer strengthen the process of bonding and therefore enhance their emotional security.

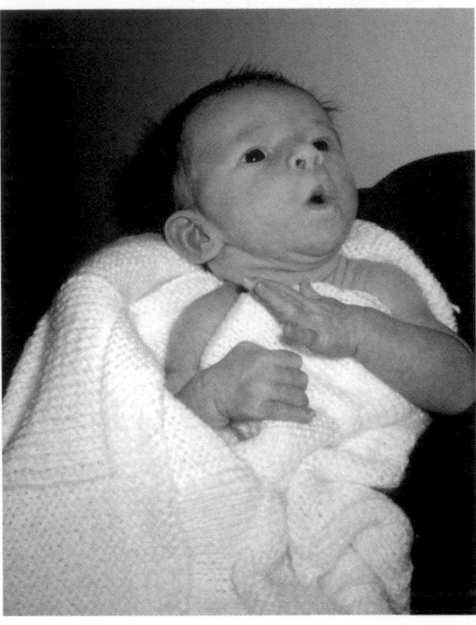

Figure 7.19
A newborn infant making eye contact

Table 7.3 Stages of visual development

Birth ■ Infant turns to the source of light ■ Imitative facial expressions are seen, for example, poking out the tongue ■ The human face gains the greatest level of an infant's attention ■ An infant's eyes do not at first move co-operatively
1 month ■ Infant turns to light source ■ Staring at face of an adult carer is usual ■ The eyes are now usually working in co-operation ■ Vision is held by a bright mobile or similar object ■ The infant can visually track their mother's face briefly
3 months ■ The eyes move in co-operation ■ A defensive blink has been present for some time ■ The infant follows the movement of main carer ■ There is more sustained visual tracking of face or similar ■ Infant may now be demonstrating visual awareness of their own hands
6 months ■ Infant is visually very alert ■ Infants appear visually insatiable (their eyes fix on anything and everything) ■ Their eyes and head move to track objects of interest
12 months ■ Hand–eye co-ordination is seen as small objects are picked up using pincer grasp (index finger and thumb) ■ The infant's eyes follow the correct direction of fallen or dropped objects

(Based on Sheridan, 1991)

Concerns relating to vision

The following would cause concern:

- lack of eye contact with main carer
- no social smile by six weeks
- lack of visual tracking of carer's face or bright mobile by two months
- lack of visual response to breast or bottle feed
- lack of co-operative eye movement after three months
- lack of signs that infant reaches out for toys in response to visual stimulus
- lack of mobility or directed attention by 12 months.

Sensory development: hearing

At birth, the hearing of infants is acute (sharp). They can often be seen responding to sound by blinking and by showing startled movements (the startle reflex). Newborn infants respond to the sound of their mother or main carer. They also show signs of auditory awareness by turning towards other sounds. Many infants are settled by calming or familiar music, often first heard within the safety of the womb.

Table 7.4 Stages of auditory development

Birth ■ Startle reactions to sound is normal ■ Blinking is common in response to ongoing gentle sounds ■ The infant turns to sounds, including their mother's voice
1 month ■ Infant is still startled by sudden noises ■ They stiffen in alarm, extending their limbs ■ They usually turn to sound of a familiar voice ■ They are usually calmed by the sound of a familiar voice
3 months ■ The infant turns head or eyes towards the source of sounds ■ They often appear to search for location of sounds ■ They listen to musical mobiles and similar sounds
6 months ■ They now show considerable interest in familiar sounds ■ Infant turns to locate even very gentle sounds ■ Now vocalises deliberately, listening to self ■ Infant vocalises to get attention, listens and then vocalises again ■ Infant can usually imitate sounds in response to carers
12 months ■ Now responds to own name ■ Infant's behaviour indicates hearing, by appropriate response to carers

(Based on Sheridan, 1991)

Concerns relating to hearing

The following would cause concern:

- lack of response to sudden or loud noises in first few months
- lack of response to familiar sounds, either by listening or by becoming calm
- no tracking of gentle sounds by nine months
- no indication of turning to the sound of familiar voice
- limited changes in vocalising from about six months
- no obvious response to carers' simple instructions at 12 months.

From one year onwards, the development of speech is the greatest indication of how well a child hears, although health problems such as 'glue ear' or repeated ear infections can have an effect on hearing.

Infant perception

Perception is the organisation and interpretation of information received from the sensory organs; it helps us to understand all that is happening both to us and around us. Even very young babies can perceive some features of their environment, such as familiar smells and textures, for example their mother's skin. Visual perception and auditory perception are two early indicators that development is progressing as expected.

Even very young infants show an interest in the human face, and researchers (particularly Robert Fantz in the 1950s) have repeatedly shown that the human face receives a greater response than other similar options, for example a 'head' with the facial features muddled up.

Figure 7.20
The faces used in Fantz's experiments

Milestones of intellectual development: birth to one year

- Throughout most of the first year, the infant learns mainly by exploring orally (with their mouth). Jean Piaget, a developmental psychologist, called this the sensorimotor stage.
- By about four months, recognition of an approaching feed is demonstrated by excited actions and squeals.
- By nine to 10 months, the infant achieves what Piaget called 'object permanence'. They know that an object exists even if it has been covered up. For example, they will pull a cover off a teddy that they have seen being hidden, in order to 'find' it again.

- The understanding of simple instructions or statements begins from about nine months and is clearly evident by one year; for example, the child can respond appropriately when told to 'Wave bye-bye to Daddy'.

Figure 7.21
The infant's main source of learning is to explore orally

Milestones of intellectual development: one to two years

- Toddlers of this age are very curious, and they investigate everything they can.
- They are interested in all that happens around them.
- A precise pincer grasp (index finger and thumb) is now seen.
- They enjoy putting objects into containers.
- They take toys to their mouth less often now.
- They enjoy activities that need fitting together, for example a simple construction or a 'build up' clown.
- They will place an object on another to create a two-object tower.

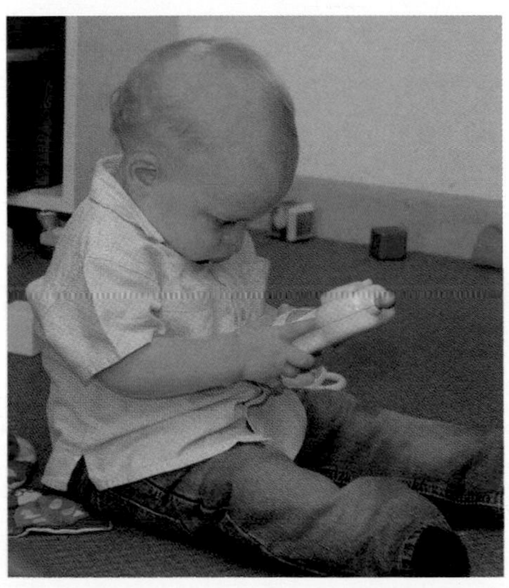

Figure 7.22
A busy toddler

Milestones of intellectual development: two to three years

- From two years children rarely take toys to mouth.
- They are able briefly to imitate everyday activities, for example the feeding of a doll.
- They are usually content to play alone.
- Simple role play is demonstrated.
- They can build six to eight objects into a tower.
- They can follow simple instructions, for example 'Fetch your shoes, please'.
- They can complete simple jigsaw puzzles.
- They can draw vertical and horizontal lines.

Milestones of intellectual development: three to five years

- Children of this age can usually draw a person with the main details.
- Role play is frequent and detailed by five years of age.
- Floor play is very complex, with cars, train sets, farms, and so on.
- Understanding of time, linked to routine, is emerging; for example they begin to understand that they will be picked up from pre-school after the singing has finished.

Nature–nurture theory

Over the years, there has been a fierce debate as to whether development is influenced by nature or through nurturing:

- *Nature*. Those who adopt the 'nature' position believe that children are born with the necessary abilities to achieve whatever they achieve and that a child's genetic make-up influences both behaviour and learning.
- *Nurture*. Those who adopt the 'nurture' position believe that the environment into which a child is born, including the way that they are raised and guided by parents and carers, is the sole influence.

Today, however, most people agree that a combination of both nature and nurture influences the overall development of a child. Biological factors such as chromosomal make-up and dominant and recessive genes determine the physical characteristics of each individual, and these factors in turn influence the achievements and choices that the individual makes.

activity 7.1 INDIVIDUAL WORK

Think about the factors that have influenced your own development. Which were due to nature, and which were due to nurture?

Frameworks for effective practice

Birth to Three Matters

Birth to Three Matters is a framework for practitioners working with children under three to inform, guide and challenge them. It is not intended to be prescriptive, nor should it be seen as a curriculum. The framework focuses on the child and has links with both the guidance given in the *National Standards for Under Eights Day Care and Childminding* (DfES, 2003) and the curriculum guidance given for the Foundation Stage.

The principles which underpin the framework are as follows:

- Parents and families are central to the well-being of the child.
- Relationships with other people (both adults and children) are of crucial importance in a child's life.
- A relationship with a key person at home and in the setting is essential to young children's well-being.
- Babies and young children are social beings; they are competent learners from birth.
- Learning is a shared process and children learn most effectively when, with the support of a knowledgeable and trusted adult, they are actively involved and interested.
- Caring adults count more than resources and equipment.
- Schedules and routines must flow with the child's needs.
- Children learn when they are given appropriate responsibility, allowed to make errors, decisions and choices, and respected as autonomous and competent learners.
- Children learn by doing rather than by being told.
- Young children are vulnerable. They learn to be independent by having someone they can depend on.

The framework is made up of four main aspects, each divided into four components, as shown in Figure 7.23.

(a) Take one of the components in Figure 7.23 and think about what it means to you.

(b) What aspects of the everyday care of a young child support that component?

(c) What activities can you think of to enhance the component further?

Observation

When working with babies and children under three, you will need to carry out a range of observations. These will be both formal and informal. Observations are

Figure 7.23
The framework of effective practice

A Strong Child
- Me, myself and I
- Being acknowledged and affirmed
- Developing self-assurance
- A sense of belonging

A Healthy Child
- Emotional well-being
- Growing and developing
- Keeping safe
- Healthy choices

The framework of effective practice

A Competent Learner
- Making connections
- Growing and developing
- Keeping safe
- Healthy choices

A Skilful Communicator
- Being together
- Finding a voice
- Listening and responding
- Making meaning

used to note progress, assess needs and to enable accurate feedback to be given to parents and, in some cases, health care professionals. They also help day care staff to ensure that safe practice is carried out at all times.

To refresh your understanding of observing babies and young children, refer back to Unit 1, page 42, where the role of observation is discussed.

Reporting concerns, data protection and use of personal information
Any concern about a child in your care must always be reported. Your placement supervisor would normally be the person to speak to, but if this is difficult for you for any reason, you should raise your concern with your course tutor. There are guidelines and legislation regarding reporting, storing and sharing information on children.

Refer back to Unit 1, pages 58 and 60 for more on this topic.

Knowing how to help provide physical care requirements for babies and children under three

Feeding young babies

Everyone working with young babies needs to be able to make up a formula feed accurately. They should also know how to store breast milk, previously expressed by the mother, to give to the infant during the time in their care.

Supporting a mother's choice of feeding is important.

Breastfeeding

The mother's own breast milk contains protective substances that help to keep her newborn infant free from infection. The mother's milk has a high protein content, which is particularly beneficial to the well-being of a pre-term infant (one under 37 weeks of pregnancy). Breast milk is often referred to as 'Nature's designer food', a nutritious option that develops with the infant and adjusts to their needs as they grow. Although modern-day formula feed is an excellent alternative to breast milk, there is no product so ideally suited to each individual baby. It provides for their total nutritional needs for the first months of life.

Throughout the first year, a high intake of milk is necessary to ensure that the infant receives sufficient calcium. This supports the development of healthy bones and teeth.

Lactation (milk production)

Lactation occurs following a hormone 'trigger' from the brain following birth. This sends signals to the mother's breasts to start the lactation process.

remember A mother has the right to choose the feeding method that suits her needs. At times you may be asked for information on feeding options, but you should not try to influence a woman's decision.

Fore milk and hind milk

Lactation produces two stages of milk production. The fore milk is the milk that the infant receives initially, which satisfies the initial thirst and hunger, whereas the hind milk, which is richer due to its higher fat content, offers longer-term satisfaction for the infant. Breastfeeding provides sufficient nutrition for infants until they are aged four to six months. By this stage, the iron stores within the mother's milk, which were built up during pregnancy, have been used up and the process of weaning needs to begin. Weaning helps the infant to develop a healthy attitude to food for the future, as well as replenishing the iron supplies that have now been reduced, and nourishing the body in general.

Formula feeding

Formula milk is an extremely good alternative, but no artificial milk can ever be as ideal for a baby's stomach as breast milk. As the baby's nutritional needs change, linked to growth rate and levels of hunger, parents should make changes to the formula that they use. In early years settings, babies' feeds will usually be supplied ready prepared by the parents and stored in a refrigerator until needed.

remember Wash your hands thoroughly before you handle any feeding equipment.

Preparing a formula feed

You will need:

- formula feed
- bottle
- teats
- knife
- kettle (pre-boiled).

Table 7.5 Breastfeeding or formula feeding?

Advantages of breastfeeding	Advantages of bottle feeding
■ The balance of breast milk nutrients is perfect for the infant ■ The milk 'matures' with the baby, constantly meeting their needs ■ Breast milk offers a degree of immunity against infection in the early weeks ■ Breast milk protects against eczema, asthma and jaundice ■ Breastfeeding helps the mother to regain her figure more quickly ■ Breastfed babies have less gastro-enteritis and fewer chest infections ■ The baby's nappies are less smelly ■ There is a lower risk of diabetes later on ■ Breast milk is always 'on hand' ■ Breast milk is cheaper – the milk is free!	■ Feeding routines can be shared ■ Siblings can be more directly involved ■ It may be less tiring for the mother ■ Mother can leave her baby for a while, knowing that their feeding needs will be met ■ Formula milk can now be bought ready made up ■ It is easy to see how much milk the baby has had
Disadvantages of breastfeeding	**Disadvantages of bottle feeding**
■ Only the mother can feed, so there are fewer opportunities to involve siblings and others ■ Mother can become over-tired as she has to cover all the night feeds too ■ There is no record of how much milk the infant has had; you judge by contentment ■ There is always a possibility of feeding problems such as mastitis, sore nipples etc. ■ Mother needs a good, healthy diet ■ Mother needs support/feeding bras ■ Breast pads may need to be bought	■ Formula milk lacks the immunological qualities of breast milk ■ There is always a risk of bacterial infection from teats, bottles, etc. ■ Making up feeds correctly is vital to ensure that a correct balance is achieved: over-diluting a feed = hungry baby; over-concentrated feeds can harm baby ■ Formula feeds need to be bought ■ A range of equipment is needed for both feeding and sterilising

remember Prepare feeds on a cleaned surface. Have spare teats handy in case you drop one!

Method

1. Boil the kettle in advance.
2. Remove a bottle from the steriliser unit and rinse with boiled water.
3. Pour sufficient cooled boiled water into the bottle for the feed required (1 fl. oz. boiled water for each scoop of formula).
4. Check that the level is accurate.
5. Open the tin of formula.
6. Using the scoop enclosed in the tin, add the correct number of scoops to the bottle. Remember to level each scoop off with a flat knife.
7. If using straight away, put on the teat, ring and lid, and shake gently to dissolve the formula.
8. The feed is ready for use after checking that the temperature is OK.
9. If storing the feed for later, put a disc and ring on the bottle and shake the bottle gently to mix.
10. Remove disc and replace with upside-down teat (do not allow formula to touch the teat, as bacteria could begin to form).
11. Refrigerate until needed.

> **remember** Making up feeds in advance is particularly useful for families with twins or other multiples.

Checklist

1. It is important that the scoops of formula are level.
2. Heaped scoops or 'packed-down' scoops lead to over-feeding, and over-feeding can lead to weight gain, high levels of salt intake and possible kidney strain.
3. Insufficient scoops of formula to the number of fluid ounces of water leads to under-feeding, and under-feeding can lead to poor weight gain and a hungry baby.
4. A baby needs 75 ml of formula per 500 g of body weight ($2^1/_2$ fl. oz. per lb) in each 24-hour period.
5. If suitable refrigeration is available, it is easier to make up enough feeds for the day in one go.

> **activity 7.3 INDIVIDUAL WORK**
>
> Calculate the amount of formula needed in each bottle for the following babies.
>
> (a) Clyde who weighs 6 kg and is having seven feeds in each 24-hour period.
>
> (b) Josh who weighs 9 kg and is having six feeds in each 24-hour period.

> **remember** Always refer to the guidelines given by the manufacturer when an infant's needs change and a new strength of formula is given.

> **remember** Wash your hands thoroughly before feeding a baby or handling feeding equipment.

Giving a formula feed

It is important to have all that you might need to hand. You should be seated comfortably and be able to give the baby your full attention. Often, a baby will be more comfortable if their nappy is changed prior to feeding, but individual routines will vary.

Method

1. Have all equipment together and suitably covered.
2. The bottle can be kept warm in a jug of hot water while you settle with the baby.
3. Hold the baby close to you, offering a sense of security and pleasure.
4. Test the temperature of the formula against the inside of your wrist. It should feel warm, not hot.
5. Check that the milk is flowing at the appropriate rate for the particular baby that you are feeding. The usual is several drops per second, but rates do vary from baby to baby.
6. Encourage the onset of feeding by touching the teat against the baby's lips before placing the teat into the mouth.
7. Milk should always cover the whole teat to stop the baby taking in excess air and becoming frustrated at not receiving enough milk at a time.
8. If the baby is reluctant to suck, pull the teat gently; the tension created will often give them the impetus to suck harder.
9. About halfway through the feed, stop and wind the baby (see below).

remember
Always throw away left over milk and never use the same bottle twice without sterilising.

10. Wind again when the feed is over and settle the baby down to sleep. They may need another nappy change.
11. When a baby has finished feeding, any remaining formula should be discarded and the bottle washed thoroughly before being placed in a steriliser.

Winding

Winding a baby helps them to release any trapped air taken in during the feeding process. The baby is best held in an upright position to allow the air to 'rise'.

Useful positions for winding include the following:

- sitting the baby forward resting against your hand – this allows you to rub or gently pat their back with your other hand
- placing the baby on your shoulder and, again, rubbing or gently patting them
- resting baby along your forearm (very young babies only) and rubbing their back.

In some cases, laying the baby prone across your lap and rubbing their back works well.

Professional Practice

- Have a cloth handy, as many babies posset (regurgitate) some milk during the winding process.
- The head and neck of young babies should always be well supported.

keyword
Sterilising techniques Methods of ensuring that utensils (bottles, teats, etc.) used for babies are free from bacteria.

Sterilising methods

Bottles and all other feeding utensils need sterilising to prevent the growth of bacteria. There are various **sterilising techniques** to choose from:

- cold-water sterilisers
- steam sterilisers
- microwave sterilisers
- sterilising by boiling.

remember
Fully submerge items such as bottles, ensuring that all air bubbles are released, as any air bubble leaves an unsterilised area that is a potential source for bacteria growth.

Cold-water sterilisers

This method uses chemicals either in solution or tablet form. The steriliser should be filled to the required capacity and the solution added (or sterilising tablet allowed to dissolve), before adding bottles and other feeding equipment. Each washed bottle, teat, etc. must be fully submerged and held under water by a 'float'. Sterilising takes 30 minutes from the time the last piece of equipment has been added. The solution must be replaced every 24 hours. Most tanks hold a large amount of feeding equipment.

Steam sterilisers

Steam sterilising is quick and efficient, but it is expensive. Once the steriliser is opened, the bottles need to be prepared within a short period of time, because of the potential for bacteria growth. There is the risk of scalding from the release of steam if the unit is opened while still very hot, so care must be taken. Steam sterilisers usually hold six or eight bottles at a time. Items are ready for use within approximately 12 to 15 minutes from switching the unit on.

Microwave sterilisers

This method works on the same principle as the steam steriliser. Usually, the units only hold four bottles, but the method is quick. Metal objects cannot be placed in the microwave steriliser.

Boiling method

Boiling feeding equipment is a cheap, but no longer popular, choice. There is considerable potential for accidents owing to the use of large quantities of boiling water. However, if another form of sterilising is not possible, the method can offer reassurance that equipment is sterile. It is quick; only 10 minutes of boiling time is required. All equipment must be fully submerged, as with the cold-water method.

Storage of formula and breast milk

Many mothers choose to express breast milk, to be given in a bottle or cup; doing so allows the mother to continue to breastfeed after returning to work, should she so wish. Breast pumps, which can be either manual or mechanical, produce a vacuum that draws out the milk in much the same way as the baby's sucking. Hand-, battery- or mains-operated pumps are far quicker to use than expressing by hand and are suitable for expressing significant quantities.

Expressing milk enables other family members to enjoy feeding the baby, giving the mother some time for herself. It is also useful if, for personal or cultural reasons, the mother is embarrassed to breastfeed in front of other people.

Leaving sufficient bottles of expressed milk with day care staff ensures that the baby gets the type of nutrition that the parents have chosen. Expressed milk must be kept in sterile containers and refrigerated until needed. Breast milk can be frozen (ice-cube trays are useful for this) and used in preparing solid food when the baby reaches the onset of mixed feeding. Usual sterilising procedures must be followed, as set out above.

Professional Practice

- Each baby must have their feeds labelled clearly.
- The feeds must be stored separately to avoid confusion or cross-infection.

activity 7.4 PAIR WORK

In pairs, choose one of the following topics and prepare a short presentation for the rest of your group. Select from:

(a) the advantages and disadvantages of breastfeeding and formula feeding
(b) different methods of sterilising feeding equipment
(c) the preparation and storage of formula feeds.

Weaning

Babies grow fastest during their first year and it is important that they are given a healthy and varied diet. This means a good balance of calcium, protein, carbohydrates and fats, together with a range of vitamins and minerals.

Ideally, infants should remain on a full milk diet until around six months. Research has suggested that this could help lower their chances of developing an allergy or intolerance to some foods. However, no baby should be allowed to go hungry and, when it is clear that they are beginning to be less satisfied with a purely milk diet, whether breast or formula, an introduction to solid food becomes appropriate.

keyword
Weaning
The introduction of solid food to an infant's diet.

This transition into mixed feeding is called **weaning**. Breast and formula milks do not have sufficient iron for continued healthy development, and prolonged (exclusive) milk feeding will not provide enough of this important mineral. At first, the baby has sufficient stocks of iron taken from their mother during pregnancy, and during the earliest months the baby's digestive system is not usually mature enough to cope with the components of solid food. It is unusual for an infant to begin taking solid food before the age of four months.

Weaning should be a pleasurable experience for both carer and child, and the infant should be encouraged to explore new tastes over a period of time. Weaning should not be stressful. At times, it can be difficult to get a baby interested in taking solids from a spoon, but it is important to keep on offering, without worrying about regular refusals. The baby will get there in time, and in the early stages of weaning the baby will still be having all of their milk feeds and so will not be losing out nutritionally.

Weaning is an important part of development, both socially and physically. Research from Bristol University has shown that babies who are not introduced to mashed (rather than puréed) food by 10 months of age are likely to be fussier eaters later on in their lives. It is not usually beneficial to an infant to hold back the start of weaning for any length of time, even if they still seem content with their milk feeds.

The aim of weaning is to introduce babies to a variety of textures, tastes and experiences to integrate them fully into family mealtimes. As the level of solid food intake increases, the milk feeds will decrease until the baby is having sufficient solid food at a mealtime to be satisfied with an accompanying drink of water.

Professional Practice

- Do not introduce weaning (or a new food) when the baby is unwell or tired.
- Offering half of the milk feed before the solids and half afterwards works well for most babies, but each baby is different and they will soon indicate their preference!

Nutritional requirements of babies and children under three years

As with children and adults of all ages, babies and toddlers need a balanced diet which includes foods from the four main food groups.

A well-balanced diet is one that provides all the nutritional requirements for growth, maintenance and development of the body. What we eat helps us to repair and maintain our body tissues, supports the functioning of muscles and organs and helps to prevent infection. It also supplies us with the energy that we need in order to function from day to day.

The four main food groups are:

- proteins, which help growth, development and tissue repair
- carbohydrates, which provide energy
- vitamins, minerals and fibre, for general good health and the prevention of illness
- dairy products, which are high in calcium, enhancing and maintaining bones and teeth.

A fifth food group – fats and oils – comprises higher-energy-giving foods, which are essential to children, but should be consumed sparingly by adults.

Figure 7.24 The food groups

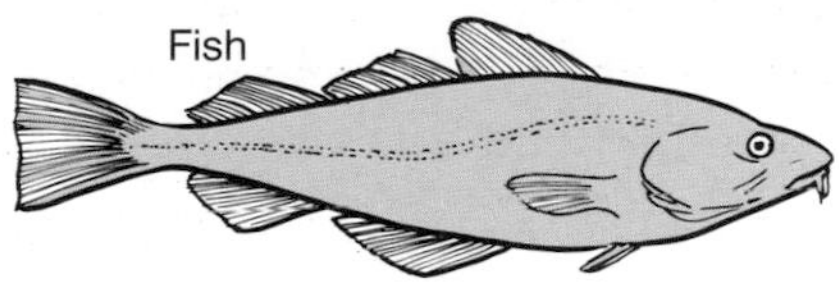

Proteins: meat, fish, poultry, offal, eggs, pulses, nuts (avoid giving to young children), textured vegetable protein (TVP, mostly made from soya)

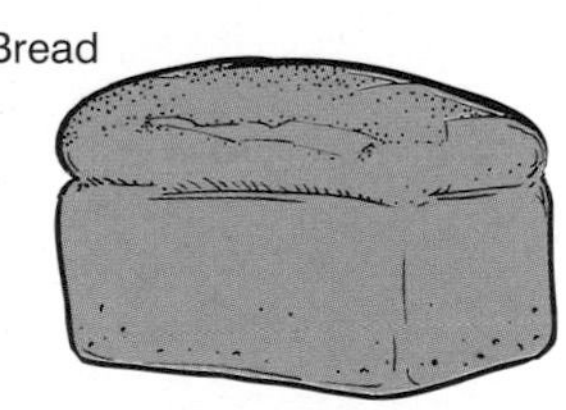

Carbohydrates: cereals, breads, pasta, rice, starchy vegetables (e.g potato, yam, plantain)

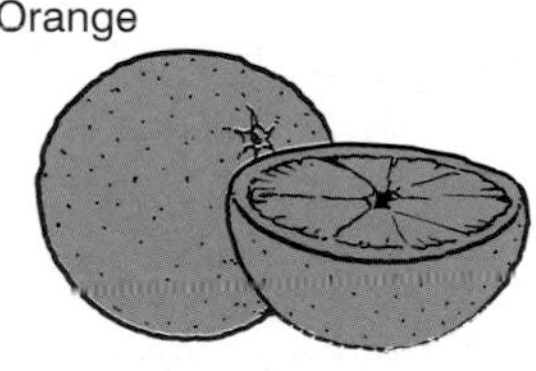

Vitamins, minerals and fibre: all vegetables, all fruits, fresh and dried

Dairy products: milk, cheese, yoghurt, fromage frais

Fats and oils: butter, margarine, vegetable spreads, oils (cooking and dressing)

Many foods contribute to more than one food group; for example, meat is a good source of iron, and pulses are a good source of fibre. Look at the illustrations in Figure 7.24, which indicate where the main benefits of each food lie.

Estimated average requirements (EARs)

The following table shows the estimated average requirements (EARs) for energy in the UK (per day). As the infant becomes more active, their energy levels increase, and again this indicates the need for solid foods to complement the nourishment provided by milk feeds.

Table 7.6 Average requirements for energy in the UK (per day)

Age range	Males		Females	
	mJ[1]	kcal[2]	mJ[1]	kcal[2]
0–3 months (formula fed)	2.28	545	2.16	515
4–6 months	2.89	690	2.69	645
7–9 months	3.44	825	3.20	765
10–12 months	3.85	920	3.61	865
1–3 years	5.15	1230	4.86	1165
4–6 years	7.16	1715	6.46	1545
7–10 years	8.24	1970	7.28	1740

[1] megajoules
[2] kilocalories

Vitamins and minerals

The tables that follow set out the benefits of a range of vitamins and minerals, showing how they help the body, and the problems that may occur if there is a deficiency.

It is important to encourage children to eat a variety of foods, including:

- foods with different textures
- foods with different sorts of tastes
- foods from a range of cultures
- seasonal foods.

This will help them develop a healthy and diverse approach to diet throughout their lives.

Mealtimes should be pleasurable, and encouraging children to take pleasure in the social aspects of sharing a meal and conversation with others will help them to continue to enjoy these as they grow.

Children need a diet that is high in protein and carbohydrates in order to meet their high energy needs. Ideally, the carbohydrates should be provided in the form of starchy foods, such as potatoes, bread and cereals.

Table 7.7 The main vitamins

Vitamin	Food source	Function	Notes
A	Butter, cheese, eggs, carrots, tomatoes	Promotes healthy skin, good vision	Fat-soluble, can be stored in the liver; deficiency causes skin infections, problems with vision
B group	Liver, meat, fish, green vegetables, beans, eggs	Healthy working of muscles and nerves; supply forming haemoglobin	Water-soluble, not stored in the body, so needed regularly; deficiency results in muscle wasting, anaemia
C	Fruits and fruit juices especially orange, blackcurrant, pineapple; green vegetables	For healthy tissue, promotes healing	Water-soluble, daily supply needed; deficiency means less resistance to infection; extreme deficiency results in scurvy
D	Oily fish, cod liver oil, egg yolk; added to margarine, milk	Growth and maintenance of bones and teeth	Fat-soluble, can be stored by the body; can be produced by the body as a result of sunlight on the skin; deficiency results in bones failing to harden and dental decay
E	Vegetable oils, cereals, egg yolk	Protects cells from damage	Fat-soluble, can be stored by the body
K	Green vegetables, liver	Needed for normal blood clotting	Fat-soluble, can be stored in the body

(Adapted from Beaver *et al.*, 2001, page 99)

Table 7.8 The main minerals

Vitamin	Food source	Function	Notes
Calcium	Cheese, eggs, fish, milk, yoghurt	Essential for growth of bones and teeth	Works with vitamin D and phosphorus; deficiency means risk of bones failing to harden (rickets) and dental caries
Fluoride	Occurs naturally in water, or may be added to the water supply	Combines with calcium to make tooth enamel more resistant to decay	There are different points of view about adding fluoride artificially to water supply
Iodine	Water, sea foods, added to salt, vegetables	Needed for proper working of the thyroid gland	Deficiency results in enlarged thyroid gland in adults, cretinism in babies
Iron	Meat, green vegetables, eggs, liver, red meat	Needed for formation of haemoglobin in red blood cells	Deficiency means there is anaemia causing lack of energy, breathlessness; vitamin C helps the absorption of iron
Sodium chloride	Table salt, bread, meat, fish	Needed for formation of cell fluids, blood plasma, sweat, tears	Salt should not be added to any food prepared for babies: their kidneys cannot eliminate excess salt as adult kidneys do; excess salt is harmful in an infant's diet
Other essential trace minerals: potassium, phosphorus, magnesium, sulphur, manganese and zinc			

(Adapted from Beaver *et al.*, 2001, page 99)

Variation in colour and texture will make meals more appealing. This will be particularly important if you are catering for a 'fussy' or reluctant eater.

Children can sometimes be resistant when being introduced new foods. It is important to introduce one new food at a time, ideally alongside a portion of something they like, and encourage them to eat a little of both.

A large portion of food can be off-putting. It is far better for a child to eat all of a small meal, rather than just half of a larger meal. This encourages the good habit of 'finishing' a meal and reduces the possibility of conflict. The portion size can gradually be increased as the child's appetite grows.

Having a drink of water with their meals is another good habit to encourage. Many children will automatically ask for juice or squash, without really considering water. If they have been offered water regularly when very young, they are more likely to continue to drink it later on, which is good for their health.

Professional Practice

- Children have preferences, just like adults, and preferences should be taken into account up to a point.
- It is, however, important to provide a balance between allowing children to select what they do and do not eat, and encouraging them to try a range of different foods.
- A dislike of one food or drink does not automatically mean that the child is being 'fussy'.

remember Processed foods contain many hidden ingredients, such as sugar and salt.

Cultural and other dietary needs

Many children have specific dietary needs. These must be clearly understood by all staff in the early years setting. Examples include a child who is vegetarian or vegan by parental or personal choice, one whose culture includes specific dietary requirements, or a child who has an allergic reaction to certain foods, or a medical condition that is affected by certain foods.

activity 7.5 INDIVIDUAL WORK

(a) Ask to see the menus for the children in your placement. How are dietary needs incorporated?

(b) How many cultures are represented within the menus?

remember Milk remains an important part of the baby's diet until they are at least a year old.

Diet and the unwell child

Children who are unwell are likely to be more selective in what they want to eat, and it is often more appropriate to allow them to eat what they feel like eating, rather than insist that they try something they do not want with little food being consumed as a result. Again, portion size is important. A child who is unwell will generally require far less food at each meal than usual.

activity 7.6 GROUP WORK

(a) Plan a main meal for a toddler, ensuring that you include foods from as many food groups as you can.

(b) How will the meal differ in texture?

(c) How will the meal differ in colour?

(d) If you have not included foods from all the food groups, what will be missing? Why might this be a problem?

Professional Practice

- Whenever possible, offer children fresh foods and use fresh ingredients in your cooking.
- Do not provide salt or sugar at the table for children to add to their meals as this can become an expectation and set up bad habits for the future.

activity 7.7 INDIVIDUAL THEN PAIR WORK

(a) Use the following blank table to set out a sample programme for weaning a baby.

(b) Compare your programme with that of another student and discuss any differences.

Table 7.9

Age	5–6 months	6–7 months	7–8 months	9–12 months
On waking				
Breakfast				
Lunch				
Tea				
Late evening				

Overcoming feeding difficulties and food allergies

At times, babies repeatedly refuse solid foods. It is important during these periods to consider the following questions.

- Is the child unwell?
- Is the child teething?
- Are you giving them too many new foods too quickly?
- Are you offering food at the right consistency?
- Are you feeling anxious about the weaning process, possibly passing your anxiety on to the child?

It is important to make sure that you:

- make mealtimes a pleasure, not a battle
- make gradual changes to the consistency of foods
- only offer one new food or new consistency at a time
- only offer new foods when the infant is well and content
- offer a new food alongside a familiar food, to ensure that at least part of the meal is eaten.

remember Babies need to try to feed themselves in order to learn.

Babies experimenting with feeding themselves

Babies enjoy trying to feed themselves. They can usually cope with finger foods from eight months onwards; suitable foods would include rusks, fingers of soft bread, pieces of pear and slices of banana. When the infant shows an interest in trying to handle the spoon, give them a spare one. You will then remain in control of the feeding process, while satisfying their curiosity and skill development.

Professional Practice

- Feeding can be messy, so feed babies in a suitable environment.
- Happy mealtimes will encourage a positive attitude to food.

Complying with parental wishes relating to feeding babies

When working in care settings you will need to be aware of a variety of dietary needs. These can be for:

- medical reasons, for example chronic conditions such as lactose intolerance, gluten intolerance or food allergy
- cultural reasons, for example forbidden or restricted foods and food combinations
- social reasons/family choice, for example vegetarian or vegan diets.

Parental wishes concerning their child's diet should be valued, and it is perfectly acceptable to seek their advice with regard to meeting their child's needs. Most parents will be pleased that you have shown an interest and taken the time to ensure that you are providing appropriately for their child.

You may find it helpful to refer back to the chart of food-related customs in Unit 5, page 188.

Routine care: washing, nappy changing and dressing

Hygiene must always be a top priority when dealing with body fluids. In day care, it is now the norm to use disposable gloves during nappy changes; however, good personal hygiene practice should be sufficient in a home setting.

Topping and tailing

Babies are usually topped and tailed in the mornings and bathed in the evening before being put to bed. Topping and tailing involves washing the face and refreshing the top half of the body; the nappy is usually changed.

Preparation

Get everything ready in advance. You will need:

- towel
- changing mat
- bowl of cooled boiled water
- bowl of warm water
- cotton wool
- barrier cream (if using)
- a clean nappy
- a fresh set of clothes
- access to a nappy bucket (for towelling nappies) or
- a nappy sack (if using disposables)
- access to the laundry basket for clothes.

Method

1. Place baby on changing mat and undress to their vest and nappy.
2. With the cooled boiled water, wipe each eye from the nose corner outwards, using each piece of cotton wool only once.
3. Repeat two or three times for each eye.
4. Dry gently with the corner of a clean towel.
5. Gently clean ears and around the face using moistened cotton wool, ensuring that you reach all the creases, particularly under the chin and behind the ears. Dry gently.
6. With a larger piece of moistened cotton wool, freshen up the baby's armpits and hands, removing all fibres collected between the fingers. Dry gently.

7. For newborn babies, check that the umbilical stump is clean, but do not clean it unnecessarily; whenever possible, it should be left alone. (The stump tends to shrivel up and drop off seven to 10 days after birth.)
8. Remove soiled nappy and place in bucket or nappy sack.
9. Clean the nappy area thoroughly, with warm water (or baby wipes if used), ensuring that you clean all creases, wiping from the front to the back.
10. Put on clean nappy (applying barrier cream if used), dress baby and have a cuddle!

Professional Practice

- Cleansing of a girl's nappy area should always be by wiping from the front to the back to avoid any infection from the bowels passing into the vaginal area.
- Cleansing of a boy's nappy area does not necessitate the pulling back of the foreskin. Excessive cleaning can actually cause irritation and infection, rather than preventing it.

Changing nappies

Parents and carers today have a vast array of choices with regard to types of nappies. Disposable nappies are extremely absorbent and can be easy to use, but they are expensive and are a significant environmental concern. Towelling nappies are cheaper to use but have to be washed and dried. In many areas, there are nappy-laundering services. These are expensive but sometimes appeal to the environmentally conscious parent who does not want to do the extra washing. Towelling nappies have been revolutionised. They can be bought ready 'shaped', often with a waterproof wrap. These nappies are usually secured with a Velcro-type fastening (aplix), poppers or a nappy nipper (a three-pronged rubber grip). If the infant in your care wears nappies made from folded towelling squares, you will need to know how to fold them. There are a number of ways to do this, as shown below.

remember

A baby or child should never be left alone on a raised changing surface. All necessary resources should be gathered in advance.

Every care setting should have separate nappy-changing facilities. The surfaces used should be safe, clean and offer privacy. Each baby or child should have their own changing items, which should be labelled and stored separately. Creams and lotions should not be shared between children. Staff should follow hygiene protection practices as directed by the policy of the setting.

Bathing

Bathing young babies is usually pleasurable; it can be done by either the 'traditional' or the 'modern' method. Early years professionals need to be able to carry out both methods, to meet with parental preferences.

Traditional method

Prepare everything in advance, ensuring that the temperature of the room is suitable (at least 20°C/68°F) with no draughts, and that all windows and doors

Figure 7.25
Changing nappies

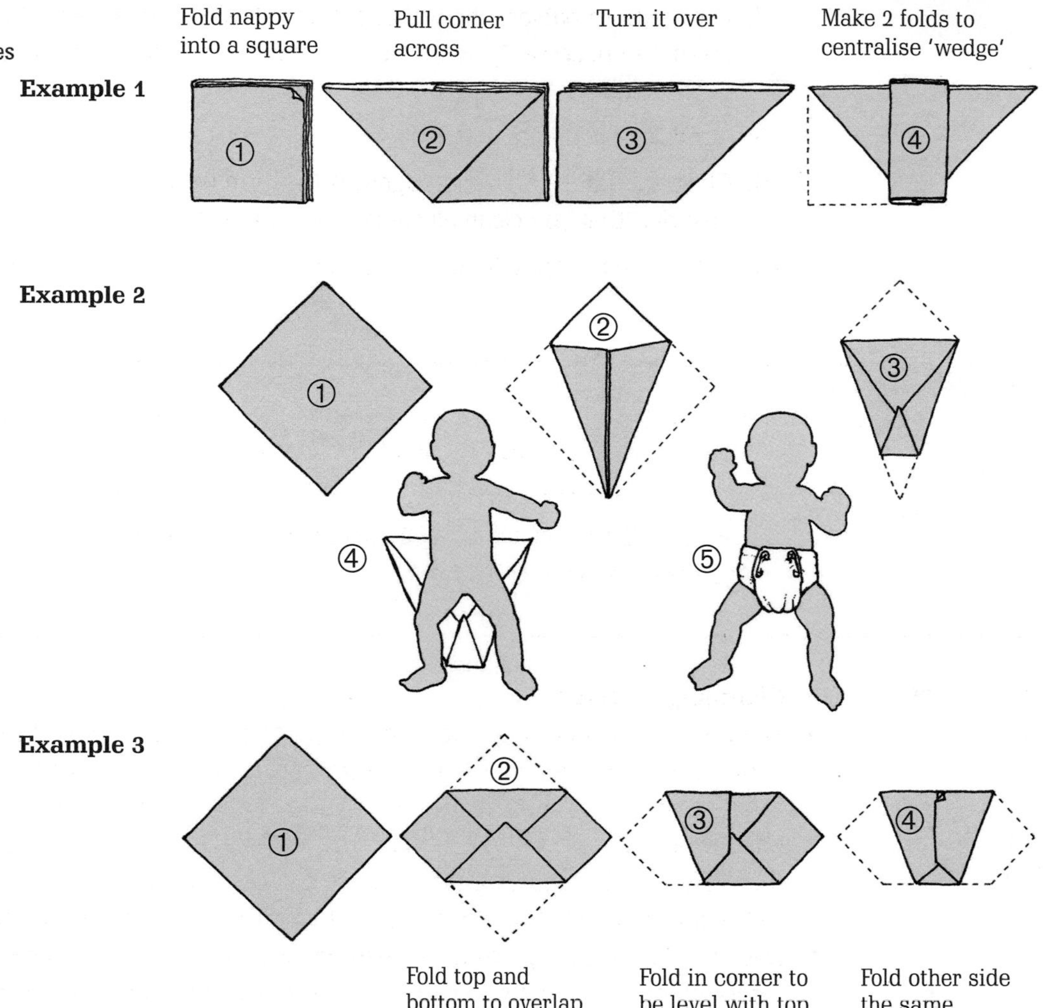

are closed. All that you will need must be to hand, and the bath should be in a safe and secure place. A special bath stand or a firm surface is ideal, but many people choose to place the baby bath in the family bath or on the floor. Any of these options is acceptable.

You will need:

- bath, with water at 37°C – always check this before putting the baby in (use your elbow or preferably a bath thermometer)
- changing mat
- towels
- cotton wool
- bowl of cooled boiled water (for the eyes)
- shampoo (if using)
- soap

- barrier cream (if using)
- a clean nappy
- a fresh set of clothes
- access to a nappy bucket (for towelling nappies) or
- a nappy sack (if using disposables)
- access to a laundry basket for clothing.

How to do it

1. Undress the baby to just their nappy and wrap them in the towel with the top corner folded away from you.
2. Wash eyes and face as in topping and tailing guidelines on page 313.
3. Hold the baby over the bath (still wrapped in towel) under your arm, resting on your hip.
4. Gently wet their hair all over.
5. Add shampoo or soap and rub in gently but firmly.
6. Rinse the hair by leaning the baby backwards over the bath, towel-drying the hair with the folded-over corner of the towel.
7. Lay the baby across your lap and remove nappy, cleansing away excess faeces.
8. With your spare hand, gently wet and soap the baby all over, turning them by pulling them over towards you (holding shoulder and thigh) and on to their tummy. When their back and bottom are also soaped, turn again in the same way (always towards you).
9. Supporting the baby's head and neck with one hand and their bottom with the other, lower them into the bath.

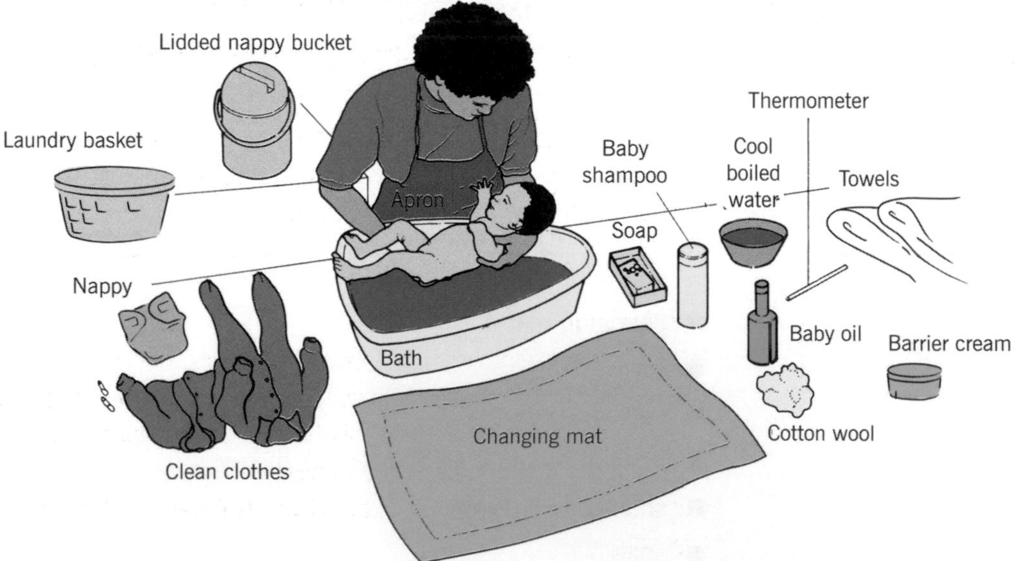

Figure 7.26
The traditional method of bathing a baby

> **remember**
> Always keep hold of the baby, by firmly holding the arm and shoulder furthest away from you. Even very young babies can move suddenly.

10. Gently rinse the baby all over, continually supporting the head and neck with your wrist, and holding their shoulder and arm.
11. When the baby is ready to be dried, lift on to your lap, wrap in the towel and cuddle dry!
12. Put on nappy and clothing.
13. Brush or groom hair as appropriate.
14. Trim nails as necessary using blunt baby scissors (with parents' permission).

Other points to remember

- Babies usually have a feed after a bath and are then put down to sleep.
- Only use talcum powder if parents insist. It has been suggested that its use may be linked to the development of asthma in early childhood.
- Cultural practice with regard to hair care, use of oils and creams should be adhered to.
- Never poke cotton buds into ears, noses, and so on.
- Babies need total supervision by a responsible adult at all times when being bathed.

Modern method

How to do it

1. Bath water, clothing and so on should be prepared in the same way as with the traditional method.
2. A bathing preparation is added to the water.
3. The baby is lowered into the water after the eyes and face have been washed.
4. Baby is soaped using the 'bubble bath'.
5. The process then continues as for the traditional method.

> **Professional Practice**
>
> - Bathing preparations can make the water (and baby) quite slippery, so take particular care to hold the baby securely.
> - If a bathing preparation causes irritation of the baby's skin do not continue its use. Some preparations irritate a baby's skin in the early weeks but can be used without problems later on.

Bathing older babies

From seven or eight months onwards, babies can be bathed in the family bath, although some will prefer the security of the baby bath for far longer. Babies are usually much more active by this time and appreciate the additional room for splashing. They are often able to sit alone quite well, but remember that the water will make them buoyant and you will need to be ready to support them if they slip.

Other points to remember

- The same precautions are needed regarding temperature, preparation and supervision as with younger babies.
- Ensure that the baby cannot touch the hot tap, which remains hot for some time after use.
- Do not have the water too deep, or the baby will float.
- Sitting on a rubber mat can help them feel more secure.
- A range of containers and bath toys will be enjoyed.
- Many babies enjoy bathing with a parent.

Fearful babies

At times a baby may become fearful of water. This may be due to:

- slipping in the bath
- disliking water getting in their eyes
- stinging eyes from soaps or shampoos.

remember Although most parents and carers like to freshen their babies at the end of each day with a bath, it is not absolutely essential. A thorough wash using the top and tail method can also maintain good health care.

You should ensure that you:

- always hold babies securely when in the bath
- never allow babies to try and stand in the bath
- always use non-stinging products, especially designed for babies' delicate skin
- use a hair-ring to keep water out of their eyes if they dislike the sensation
- do not make a big issue of bathing if it becomes a battle; often if you omit the bath or the hair wash for a couple of days, the issue will go away, as the baby 'forgets' that it was a problem.

Clothing for babies and children

Adults need to take responsibility for what children wear, as young children are unable to make informed choices for themselves, often stating their preferences with no regard to temperature, weather or planned activity.

remember It is better for babies to wear several layers that can be removed or replaced according to temperature than one warmer layer that offers no opportunity for adjustment, as babies are unable to control their body temperature and could become overheated.

Babies

Clothing for babies should:

- be easy to put on and take off
- have room for them to grow
- allow unrestricted movement
- be suitable for the time of year and temperature of the environment
- avoid cramping of toes (for example in all-in-one suits)
- be free from long ties or ribbons (to avoid choking)
- be free from loose buttons or poppers (another choking hazard)
- be free from looped edgings on seams (may catch fingers)
- avoid lacy designs that may also catch small fingers

- be easy to wash and dry
- be made of natural materials such as cotton to allow skin to breathe; avoid fluffy materials or wools such as mohair as this can irritate noses and get in hands and mouths
- be of a suitable length so that it does not get caught when child is toddling or crawling
- be washed in non-biological powders to avoid reactions to harsh detergents.

Figure 7.27
A baby's clothing

remember

When a baby is ready to have their first pair of proper shoes, it is important to have their feet measured and shoes fitted by a foot-care specialist.

Care of babies' feet

Babies' feet are very delicate and their bones are still forming; babies should not therefore be given shoes before they are walking. Wearing shoes too early can hinder the natural growth and development of their feet, leading to deformity. Socks, all-in-one suits and bootees should have sufficient room for natural movement and growth.

Children

Clothing for children should:

- be easy to put on and take off, to encourage independence
- allow for growth, as children's growth rate is so rapid
- allow unrestricted movement, particularly for outdoor play
- be suitable for the time of year and the temperature of the environment
- be free from long or loose ties or ribbons that could get caught during play
- be kept in good repair and washed regularly, setting a good example with regard to cleanliness
- be easy to wash and dry
- be made of natural materials to allow skin to breathe
- be of a suitable length to avoid the possibility of tripping
- be suitable for the activities being undertaken, enabling the child to play without worrying that they might spoil a special outfit
- allow for temperature adjustment; several layers are better than one thicker garment.

Figure 7.28
Children's clothing should be suitable for the activities being undertaken

It is unhealthy for a child to wear trainers for long periods of time.

Care of children's feet

Children's feet develop quickly; it is not uncommon for a child to need four new pairs of shoes during the course of one year. Foot-care specialists recommend that children should have their feet measured every 12 weeks and sooner if there is any concern about cramping of toes or if soreness occurs. It is important that sock sizes are monitored, because socks that are too small can cause damage to the structure of a child's feet.

Hygiene and protection practices

It is important that all care staff understand the health and safe practice procedures for the setting. This helps prevent the spread of illness and infection.

Refer back to Unit 2, page 75, for more on this important aspect of caring for children.

Safe disposal of waste

Soiled nappies and clothing must be safely and hygienically dealt with. Every care setting should have a policy regarding:

- the safe disposal of nappies, baby wipes, etc.
- the safe disposal of cleaning materials
- the sending home of soiled clothing.

If the setting washes soiled items on site, the items should be sluiced in a sink kept for that purpose and washed on the appropriate heat setting of an industrial-strength washing machine. Blood-stained garments are likely to benefit from an initial rinsing on a cold-water cycle.

Any soiled garments sent home with the child should be sluiced to remove body fluids, double bagged and tied securely to prevent leakages.

Disposable nappies and any items used during care routines should be securely bagged and disposed of in a waste bin set aside for that purpose.

Routine care of skin, hair and teeth

Skin care

Care of the skin is important because it is the front-line area of defence for the body as it comes into contact with the environment. It is necessary to protect the skin from short-term problems:

- discomfort
- irritation
- infection.

It is also necessary to protect the skin from long-term problems:

- sunburn
- sun damage (that can lead to skin cancers)
- scarring from repeated irritation or infections.

remember

Any oil used on babies and young children should be free of nut traces, as there is concern about links with the increase in nut allergies in young children. Almond oil used to be popular but is no longer used. Many specialists now recommend the use of organic sunflower oil.

Babies have sensitive skin, and many of our everyday products are far too harsh for them. It is therefore important to use specially prepared baby products suitable for sensitive skins during all care routines.

Skin types

Skin types vary, as do family practices, and it is important that in any early years setting the preferences of parents are taken into account. Most day care settings ask parents to provide their own products; these should be clearly labelled and kept solely for the use of their baby.

Example

Jerome is West Indian and his skin tends to be very dry. His parents rub cocoa butter into his skin after his bath. They also massage his skin with oil, particularly his arms and legs, at each nappy change. They have supplied Jerome's nursery with a bottle of oil, and asked them to continue this practice during the day.

Eczema

keyword

Eczema
A dry, scaly, itchy skin condition.

Eczema is a common skin complaint in young children. Children with this condition need particular support during bad phases. Some need to have prescribed ointments applied during the day, and staff taking on this role should wear disposable gloves to reduce the risk of passing any infection on to the child, and also to prevent themselves from absorbing the ointments or creams (which often incorporate corticosteroids) into their own skin.

Professional Practice

- Older children with eczema may need to be encouraged to wear gloves during activities such as sand play to avoid exacerbating their condition.
- They should be taught to wash and dry their skin carefully and thoroughly.

Skin infestations and conditions

From time to time, skin infestations and infectious conditions occur in early years settings and can spread very quickly. However, preventative measures for cross-infection should be standard practice and should help to contain them. There is usually a policy regarding the admittance of children and babies with an infectious condition. Ask your current placement setting if you can see what is included in their policy. Skin infestations and infectious conditions include:

- scabies
- impetigo
- hand, foot and mouth disease.

Scabies

- *What is scabies?* Scabies are tiny parasites that burrow into the skin. They are sometimes known as 'itch mites' because they cause intense itching, particularly at night. It is an extremely infectious condition, passed on by physical contact, either from person to person, or via towels, flannels and bedding.
- *Identifying scabies*. The scabies mites burrow into the skin, leaving thin track marks under the skin where they have passed through. The itching causes redness and sore patches, which may at times be mistaken for eczema.
- *Treatment*. Scabies will not disappear without treatment. A special lotion prescribed by the GP is needed, and each individual who has been in contact with the infected child should be treated. This usually includes the whole family and the staff in their care setting who have worked closely with them.

Impetigo

- *What is impetigo?* Impetigo is an extremely infectious skin condition, which often affects the mouth and nose. It also affects the nappy area. It is caused by bacteria, which enter the body through a break in the skin. As with scabies, it is passed on by physical contact, either from person to person, or via towels, flannels and bedding.
- *Identifying impetigo*. Red skin with tiny blisters is the most noticeable sign. The blisters weep and gradually crust over with yellowish scabs.
- *Treatment*. Antibiotic creams will be needed from the child's GP. It is important to try to avoid cross-infection, and to discourage children from scratching. Babies and toddlers may benefit from wearing cotton gloves at night. Scarring can occur if scratching is intense. Complications are a possibility, causing a general infection of the body, which can affect the child's kidneys.

Hand, foot and mouth disease

This is a mild, but highly infectious condition.

Hand, foot and mouth disease is discussed in Unit 2, page 115. You may find it useful to refer back to that section now.

Sun care

Research has shown how seriously our skin can be damaged by the sun's rays, and children and babies should not be exposed to the sun for more than a very short period of time. Babies should be kept in shade whenever possible (watch out for the sun moving round if they are in prams or pushchairs) and outdoor play in sunny areas should be restricted, particularly around midday when the sun is at its highest point.

Hats should be worn, and each setting should have a policy regarding the application of sun creams. Sunscreen creams and lotions for children and babies should be of the highest factor, or be a total sun block. Written parental permission should be obtained before staff apply cream to any child.

Hair care

Hair care is needed to prevent infestation from head lice and to encourage good grooming for the future. Again, cultural practices differ. Muslim babies will have their heads shaved within 40 days of birth as part of cultural tradition, and many Caribbean parents traditionally weave and plait their babies' hair at a very early age.

Washing the hair of babies can at times be traumatic, as not all babies are happy to have water in their eyes. Hair-rings can be purchased, which prevent water from reaching the eyes and can make for a happier bath time. Hair-washing products should always be 'non-stinging' to the eyes.

Dental care

The brushing of teeth should commence as soon as the first ones arrive and definitely when a baby has corresponding teeth, top and bottom. Soft toothbrushes are specially designed for the delicate gums and first teeth, and their regular use will encourage the baby into a habit of good oral health care. In day care, each baby and child should have their own toothbrush, which should be labelled and kept separately.

It is important to teach children the correct amount of toothpaste to use, and to remember that toothpaste should not be swallowed. Cleaning of teeth should be encouraged after eating and before bed.

Routine care: toilet training

Bowel and bladder control cannot be achieved until a child is both physically and emotionally ready. The nervous system must be mature enough for there to be physical control, and a child has to be both interested in using a potty and

Figure 7.29
The usual order in which milk teeth appear

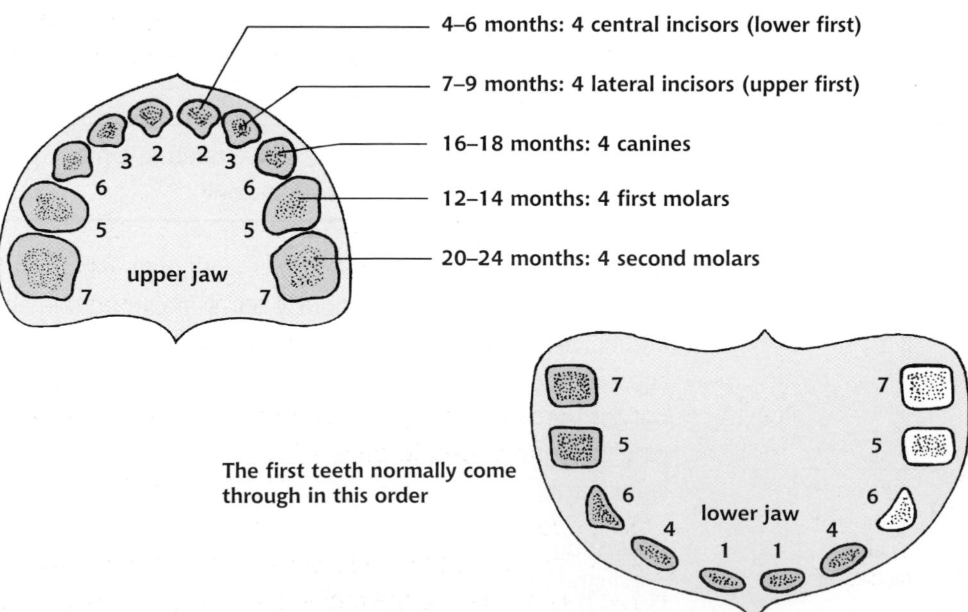

willing to sit on it. The age at which control is achieved varies enormously, and the process needs to be child led, not thrust upon them by an adult.

Gastric upsets such as diarrhoea and constipation (see below) may temporarily interfere with toilet training.

Professional Practice

- It is useful to have a potty around so that the child becomes familiar with it; make positive comments when the child shows interest in the potty.
- Once the process has started it is important that accidents are dealt with in a matter-of-fact manner and that the child is not made to feel anxious.

Physical signs of illness

Most babies are born with a degree of immunity passed to them from their mother via the placenta. Those who are breastfed continue to benefit from their mother's protection during the early months. Although the common childhood illnesses are mostly seen from the toddler stage onwards, it is possible for young babies also to be affected, if they come into contact with older siblings with an infectious condition or when an infection enters their care setting.

Signs, symptoms and care needs for a range of common childhood illnesses are set out in Unit 2, pages 111–121. You may find it helpful to refer back to refresh your knowledge and understanding.

Minor bowel problems

All children suffer from diarrhoea and constipation at some point. These are usually due to gastro-enteritis, a viral infection (diarrhoea) or changes in the diet (constipation). Diarrhoea and constipation are unpleasant conditions, but rarely serious.

Diarrhoea

Food should be avoided for 24 hours; drinking plenty of clear fluids usually helps a child remain hydrated until the virus has passed. If, however, a child suffers from vomiting and diarrhoea for a considerable length of time, they may begin to dehydrate, particularly babies and toddlers, and medical attention will be important to ensure that the body is re-hydrated.

More information on gastro-enteritis and other illnesses common in children can be found in Unit 2, page 117.

remember

Laxatives should never be given to a child without medical advice.

Constipation

Usually, increasing the child's consumption of roughage (fruits and vegetables in particular) will reduce the problem and improve their general health too. If constipation persists, advice from a health professional may be needed.

More serious bowel problems

Children with certain chronic conditions suffer from either intermittent or constant bowel problems. This includes children with cystic fibrosis (CF) and coeliac disease. Both of these conditions are regularly diagnosed by the toddler stage.

Cystic fibrosis

This condition is mostly associated with respiratory problems, due to the sticky secretions that build up in the lungs, but is a serious digestive condition too. The obstruction in the bowel associated with CF is often found shortly after birth.

An outline of the main symptoms associated with CF can be found in Unit 8, page 362.

Coeliac disease

This condition affects the lining of the small intestine; it is caused by intolerance of the protein gluten, which is found in wheat, barley, rye and oats.

Symptoms indicating coeliac disease begin to show once foods containing gluten are introduced to the infant's diet. Sufferers of this condition fail to thrive in the usual way; they do not put on weight and remain low on the centile growth charts. Children are lethargic and pass pale, unpleasant stools.

The condition can be confirmed through blood tests or a biopsy of the jejunum (part of the small intestine).

The only way to control the symptoms of coeliac disease is for a gluten-free diet to be adopted. This will be necessary for life. Advice will be given to the family from a dietician, as gluten is found in many everyday foods, and establishing what is suitable and what must be avoided can take time.

If coeliac disease remains untreated it can lead to iron deficiency anaemia. In the long term, bone density may be affected; calcium supplements are often given throughout life.

Understanding how to provide play activities to encourage learning and development

Play and learning go hand in hand. Babies and young children learn through exploration, i.e. their play. From the moment that infants find their toes, or wave their fingers in front of their face, they are starting to play. The turn-taking exchanges of vocalising and visual focusing are early forms of play. The infant explores through all of their senses.

As an early years practitioner, you will need to provide a range of stimulating experiences for the babies and toddlers within your care. This does not necessitate using expensive toys and resources; many stimulating opportunities are found within the home or care environment. The responses of the adult carer are a source of stimulation, and it is important to remember that the adults in a child's life are a vital resource; each offers knowledge, skills and experience drawn from their own upbringing, education and general life experiences.

This section of the unit sets out a range of ideas for stimulating the under-threes; there are of course many, many more. As your practical experience grows, you will become familiar with an assortment of resource ideas and activities, some needing forward planning, but many offering opportunities for spontaneous entertainment and stimulation. An early years worker should always be open to new ideas; practitioners with many years' experience continue to discover fresh ideas or new ways of doing things.

Professional Practice

- All activities and resources should meet safety standards and be checked, cared for and replaced according to the practice of the setting.
- Risk assessment procedures help to identify any potential problems in advance, providing time to withdraw items or adjust the age group to which they are offered.

To remind yourself of safety marks and symbols, refer back to Unit 2, page 74.

Play activities

Activities should be carefully thought through for the baby or child being cared for. As a general guide, the selection of activities and/or resources offered should:

- be appropriate for the age and stage of the child's development
- be stimulating
- hold attention
- provide challenge, but with achievable outcomes
- provide opportunities for making choices.

As a carer you should:

- plan for each child and provide suitable resources and activities to meet their needs
- supervise and observe the individual child's responses to help inform planning for the future
- encourage the child to explore new items, and at times present resources in different ways to help them explore from a different perspective
- give praise and show delight in their discoveries
- support their development by, at times, modelling the use of unfamiliar resources.

Children respond well to praise and encouragement, and this applies to babies too. When interacting with babies you can make them feel wanted and valued as a person by remembering to:

- give them your full attention
- imitate their actions, showing pleasure
- make eye contact with them
- offer objects to them and accept objects when they offer them to you.

Planning a suitable environment

Babies and toddlers need sensory experiences, so it is important to ensure that each sensory area is considered in turn and resourced accordingly.

Suggestions for sensory play

To encourage visual experiences (sight), try providing:

- three-dimensional mobiles
- safety mirrors
- bubble tubes
- bubbles for blowing
- balloons and streamers.

To encourage tactile experiences (touch), try providing:

- textured mats and 'surprise' bags
- natural wooden items
- messy play such as finger-painting
- silk scarves and hankies
- malleable play such as sand and dough
- blocks and cotton reels.

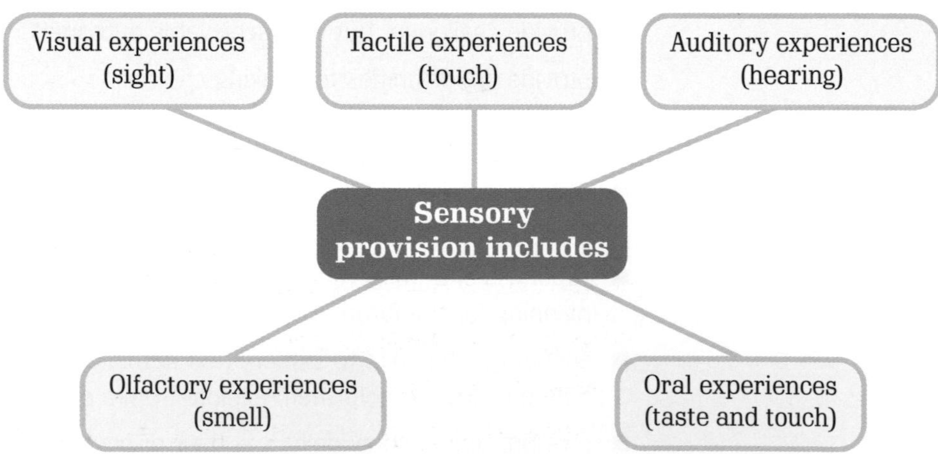

Figure 7.30 Sensory provision

To encourage auditory experiences (hearing), try providing:

- wind chimes
- music boxes
- rattles, shakers and bells
- objects to bang (box and spoon)
- music to listen to and bounce, jiggle, clap and wave to.

To encourage olfactory experiences (smell), try providing:

- wooden items permeated with smells such as lavender or lemon
- bags of herbs, lavender or flowers
- scented tissues inside a box or cloth bag
- citrus fruit (changed regularly).

Young babies explore objects by using their mouths; to encourage these experiences, try providing:

- hard objects in different shapes
- squashy objects made from various materials
- spoons and cups
- feely books
- textured mats.

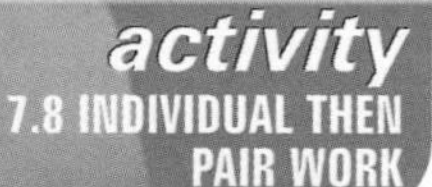

(a) Select 10 play items from a baby setting with which you are familiar.

(b) Make a note of which senses each item will stimulate.

(c) Compare your ideas with those of another student. Did you both agree?

The visually interesting environment

When planning play for babies and toddlers, an important consideration is the positioning of visual stimuli around the room. Try lying down on the floor to see the room from the viewpoint of the baby. How good or how limited is your vision?

The different stages in the physical development of babies and toddlers should be taken into account, and visual stimulation should be available when they are:

- lying on their backs (supine)
- lying on their tummies (prone)
- sitting, either propped up with cushions or in a chair
- moving around.

Figure 7.31
Baby who is supine

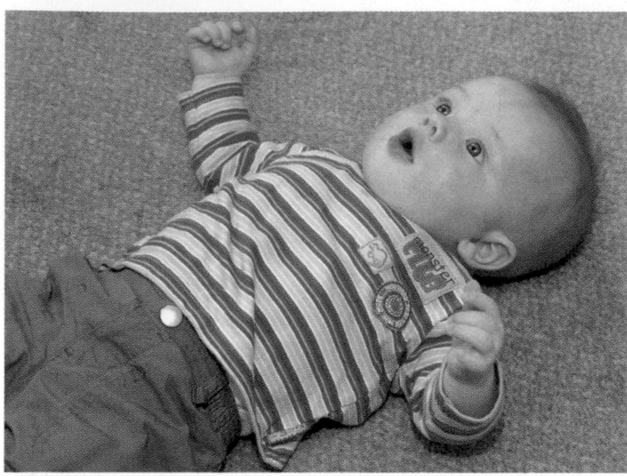

Figure 7.32
Baby who is prone

Figure 7.33
Baby sitting

Figure 7.34
Toddler standing

Figure 7.35
Crawling and bear-walking

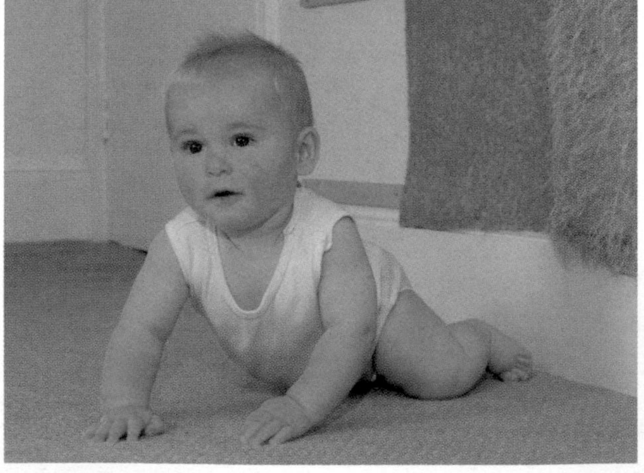

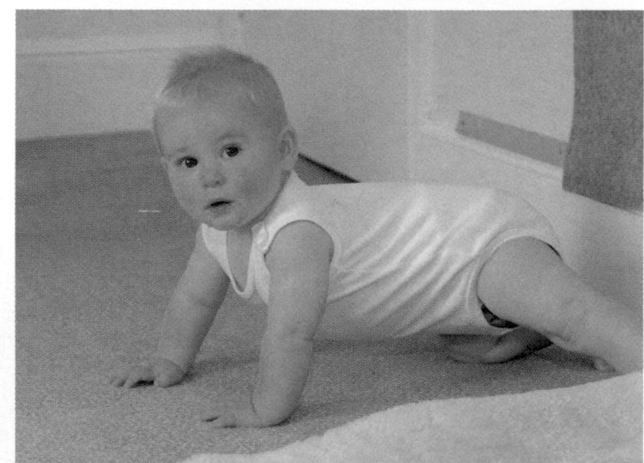

Items of interest could be positioned:

- at skirting board levels (e.g. safety mirrors)
- on windows and on walls (e.g. pictures, designs, areas of colour)
- on the wall behind and immediately above a sofa (a good place for a safety mirror)
- as objects hanging from ceilings (mobiles, balloons and wind chimes are favourites)
- as attachments to prams, cots, highchairs, etc. (e.g. music boxes, soft toys and wobbly objects).

From around six weeks, babies benefit from an activity frame or something similar that can be placed above them. Not only will this encourage them to focus visually and aurally on the items hanging in front of them but they will also enjoy tactile experiences, as they come into contact with the items during their natural body movements. Eventually, these movements become more intentional, and repeated actions will be observed, often in response to the 'reward' of a noise or visual 'experience' (movement, reflection or fluttering of material). Bath time and nappy changing provide opportunities to play free from the restriction of clothes and with full leg mobility; such play should be encouraged whenever possible.

Outside

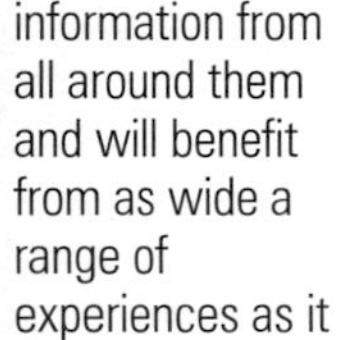

Babies absorb information from all around them and will benefit from as wide a range of experiences as it is possible to give them.

Babies enjoy being outside, watching the leaves on trees fluttering and taking in the sounds and smells of the garden. Fresh air is good for them, but they should never be left unsupervised. Care should be taken to ensure that prams are not positioned in the sun, as a baby's delicate skin burns extremely easily. Whenever possible allow a baby to lie out of doors in warm weather without a nappy on, as exposure of the nappy area to fresh air is healthy and stimulating for the skin too. Although most professionals agree that taking a baby out each day is a good idea, this does not apply if the weather is particularly cold, or it is foggy.

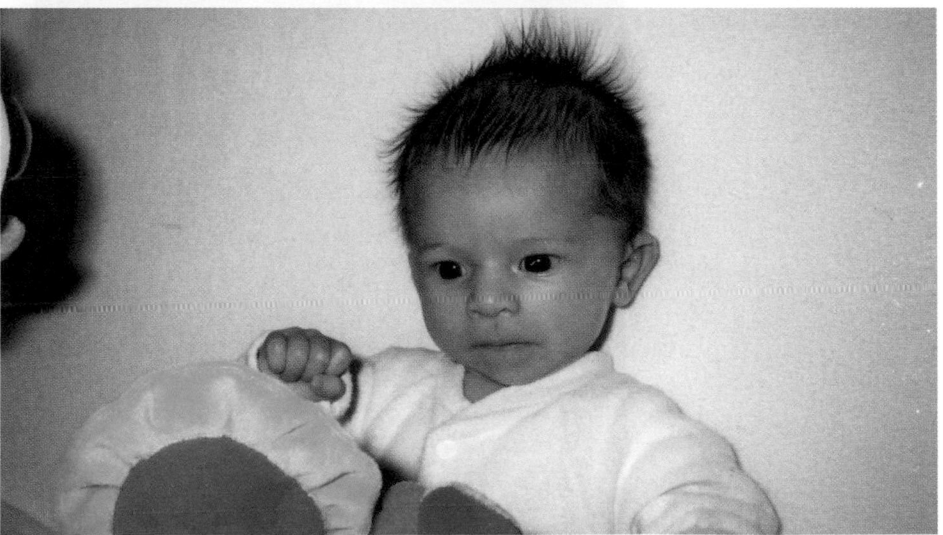

Figure 7.36
Stimulating play is an essential part of a child's experience

Figure 7.37
An activity frame encourages babies to focus visually and aurally

Stimulating play for older babies

As they develop, older babies will be interested in a range of household articles. Sturdy boxes can be handled easily, passed from hand to hand from about six months onwards and knocked together as there is more control of manipulation. Older babies will also enjoy banging things in order to make a noise; a useful item is a wooden spoon to bang on a saucepan lid or on the tray of their highchair. Babies enjoy activities that enable them to explore by themselves through all of their senses. An excellent resource for this is a treasure basket.

Treasure baskets

Infants from about six months of age will enjoy exploring a treasure basket. Ideally, they need to be able to sit up securely in order to benefit from the

Figure 7.38
From about the age of six months, a baby will enjoy exploring a treasure basket

freedom to explore the basket's contents. A treasure basket contains various objects that are made of natural materials and can easily be handled by the infant. Objects should be selected carefully to stimulate all the senses and should be completely safe. The infant should be allowed to focus on the objects they are handling without distraction from the adult or older children. Nothing in a treasure basket should be made of plastic or any other manufactured material.

The treasure basket principle can be extended, with baskets containing only items of a particular type (e.g. shiny objects, furry objects, sparkly objects, or metal objects).

Some older children with additional needs may also benefit from exploring a resource prepared along the lines of a treasure basket.

activity
7.9
GROUP WORK

You have been asked to prepare a treasure basket for the babies in the baby room where you are on placement; the babies' ages range from eight to 10 months.

(a) What will you include in your basket?

(b) What senses will each item stimulate?

(c) What health and safety issues will you need to take into consideration?

Professional Practice

- The objects included in a treasure basket must be kept very clean. They should not have sharp or rough edges or be likely to come apart, and none should be small enough to be swallowed, or put up noses.
- The infant will need supervision while exploring their treasure basket, but not direct adult intervention. The adult's role is to provide, to oversee and to allow freedom of exploration.

Stimulating play for toddlers and young children

Toddlers enjoy a wide range of play activities: not only do they like developing new ideas for games using 'baby' toys but they also get pleasure from exploring activities enjoyed by the over-threes. Their first encounters with such activities as sand play, painting, model making, clay, and construction materials will often highlight the limitations of their manual dexterity, their creativeness and, at times, their confidence when trying new experiences, compared with the over-threes. The adult's role here is to provide opportunities, encouraging children to participate in their own time at a level at which they feel secure; when appropriate, the adult should model actions and help the child in their attempts to voice their intentions. As with all aspects of development, children progress at different rates.

Popular activities/resources for toddlers and children up to three years old include:

- push-along toys (e.g. brick trolley, dog on wheels)
- pull-along toys (e.g. caterpillar, train)
- climbing frames, tunnels, trikes, etc.
- resources to support mimicry of real life (e.g. telephones, tea sets, shopping bags)
- dolls, dolls clothes and bedding
- books needing greater concentration and 'staying power'
- dressing-up clothes.

In many ways, two- and three-year-olds enjoy the same range of activities as the over-threes; they just use resources differently according to their stage of development.

See Unit 6, pages 204–221, for a range of play activities and their role in a child's development. Refer back to that section to support your understanding of this unit.

Procedural practice

It is important that you always follow the procedures of the setting in which you are working. These will vary from place to place but will always be based on safe practice. All activity planning should fit in with the overall plans of the setting, and whenever relevant a risk assessment should be made.

Refer back to Unit 2, page 69, and Unit 4, pages 148–149, to remind yourself about risk assessments.

Linking play to development

With experience comes an understanding of which areas of development are supported by which activities. Sometimes, it is obvious. For example, providing creative play with crayons and pencils clearly helps to improve fine motor skills; encouraging play on climbing frames, through tunnels and generally running around clearly helps large motor skills to develop. However, it is usually more complex, as most activities offer stimulation and support for more than one area of development. The following case study shows that many areas of development are involved in just one play experience.

A range of play activity ideas is set out in Unit 6, pages 243–254. It would be useful to refer back to these to remind you or to enhance your understanding.

case study 7.1

Henry aged 2 years and 9 months

Henry is engaging with a play-tray type puzzle. During this type of play experience, Henry is using fine motor skills (manipulation) to move and adjust the puzzle pieces into place. He is using cognitive (intellectual) skills as he considers shape, order or the picture involved. Henry's satisfaction on completion of the puzzle will produce feelings of self-esteem and pride and contribute to his emotional development.

Henry talks to his key worker about the puzzle, and shares his pleasure with them. Through these actions Henry is using communication skills and is also socialising.

activity
INDIVIDUAL THEN PAIR WORK

(a) Think about a range of everyday play experiences with which you are familiar. Make a list of 10. Which areas of development does each support?

(b) Share your ideas with a friend. Do you both agree?

Understanding how to communicate with babies and children under three, interpret their needs and respond to them

As explained in Unit 1, human communication involves:

- facial expressions
- tone of voice
- body posture
- expression of meaning through the use of words and symbols.

See page 22 in Unit 1.

Language development is affected by the other aspects of our development. For example, some understanding of the benefits of social interaction and communication is required, and the child has to have a sufficient level of physical ability in terms of vision, hearing and speech. Without these, it can be difficult for language to develop normally.

Communication with babies

Communication with babies can be both verbal and non-verbal. Pre-verbal communication plays a vital part in supporting an infant's future language skills.

It is seen as the adult encourages the baby to take a share in the conversation, as they ask the baby questions and supply them with answers or make reaffirming comments following a pause in which the infant adds their own vocalisations. Welcoming the vocal sounds of babies encourages them to vocalise further.

activity 7.10 INDIVIDUAL WORK

Take time to observe an adult with a young baby. It will give you an example of how you can 'converse' with a baby in their earliest weeks.

remember

Adults communicate with babies in many ways.

When you spend time with a young baby, talk to them and watch them respond to you, then talk to them again. Taking turns with a baby encourages their efforts to communicate and enhances their communication skills. This 'turn taking' between carer and infant was identified by Stern in the 1970s; Stern suggested that infants learn the basis of their social interactions in this way.

Ways in which adults communicate with babies include:

- making eye contact during breast- or formula feeding
- turn taking vocally or visually
- initiating 'conversations' with babies as you play
- observing the needs of babies through their body language or facial expression
- responding to their cries
- encouraging them to vocalise
- showing appreciation of their vocalising
- giving praise
- calling to them when out of their visual range
- stimulating them aurally
- stimulating them visually.

case study 7.2

Mary

Mary works in the baby room. She is preparing a formula feed for William who is six months old. William is in his chair, and Mary is currently out of his line of vision as she gets his bottle ready. She calls to him in a sing-song voice, pausing to hear him make a noise in response, before calling him again. When she brings William his feed, Mary takes him out of his chair and cuddles him on her lap while he is fed. He watches her face, and she smiles at him, talking quietly to him all the time.

activity
INDIVIDUAL WORK

(a) Which forms of communication listed above do you consider that Mary used?

(b) Do you think there were opportunities for any other form of communication to have taken place?

(c) What might be the outcome for a baby who does not have opportunities for communication?

Motherese

The term 'motherese' refers to what we often call 'baby talk'. Motherese speech:

- has a higher pitch than that used with other people
- is slower, with simplified words and phrases usually being employed
- includes frequent pauses, to facilitate the turn taking
- consists mostly of key words linked to the current situation, for example naming words if playing jointly with a toy (nouns), or action words (verbs) when moving the infant or referring to a specific action. Examples could include 'Here is teddy' or 'Up you come for a cuddle'.

Language development in young babies

- By about four months, recognition of an approaching feed is demonstrated by excited actions and squeals. This is communication.
- Language develops through cooing, gurgling, excited squealing and changes to tone of voice.
- By five months, the infant's enjoyment of their own voice is obvious. Chuckles and laughs are evident.
- By about eight months, the infant babbles continuously and tunefully, for example 'mamamama', 'babababa'.
- First 'words' may be apparent by a year, usually 'dada', 'mama', 'baba'.
- Understanding of simple instructions or statements begins from about nine months and is clearly evident by a year.

Communicating distress

Babies become distressed for many reasons; they may be tired, wet, hungry, uncomfortable, unwell, teething or simply bored. Working out the cause of the distress is not always easy. If a young baby is distressed at the same time of day, every day, their distress can often be attributed to a condition known as colic. Sometimes, babies will simply want a drink; small amounts of cooled boiled water can be introduced to even very young babies, especially in hot weather.

Figure 7.39
Babies become distressed for many reasons

remember

Babies are best dressed in layers of lightweight clothing that can be taken off or added to as necessary.

Professional Practice

- Every baby is different. Each baby has their own individual personality. Some babies cry much more than others. Offer support to parents of a constantly crying baby as it can be very draining.
- It is possible to overstimulate a baby, tiring them and causing irritability.
- Illness must never be ruled out but will usually be considered when other causes have been eliminated unless additional symptoms are present.

activity 7.11 GROUP WORK

(a) Research the support group Cry-sis.

(b) Prepare a leaflet about Cry-sis that could be given to parents or carers of a regularly distressed infant.

Stages of language development

As with every aspect of development, children develop language at differing rates within what is considered to be the normal range. This process of language development can be divided into 10 basic stages. These are as follows:

1. non-verbal communication/expression
2. speech-like noises
3. controlling sounds, using mouth and tongue
4. imitating sounds
5. first words
6. development of vocabulary (50 words is usual at two years)

7. putting words together to form simple phrases and sentences
8. using grammar
9. using meaning
10. using language to develop other skills, for example early literacy.

Refer back to Table 1.4 on page 24, which outlines the sequence of language development.

An example of one infant's language development is shown below:

Table 7.10 An example of one infant's language development

Age	Understanding	No of words	Type of words or sounds	Average length of sentence
3 months	Calmed by Mummy's voice and by music (Pachelbel's Canon and Sinead O'Connor)	0	Chuckles, coos and gurgles conversationally, turn taking with adults	0
6 months	Responds to familiar voices	0	Babbles almost incessantly, mainly using the sounds 'ummm' and 'yi yi yi'	0
1 year	Knows own name and a few others	2	'In air?' (Who's in there? or What's that?), 'dor' (dog), 'hooray'	1 word
18 months	Repeats her own new word – 'gollygollygolly' and understands 'car' and 'duck'	8	Nouns plus gobbledegook	1 word
2 years	Understands much of what is said to her. Enjoys simple and familiar stories	Approx. 120, some clear, others less so	Verbs and pronouns, e.g. 'Mummy fine it' (Mummy find it), 'Daddy a gate' (Daddy's opening/shutting the gate'), 'boon in sky' (the hot air balloon is in the sky')	2–3 word phrases, e.g. 'bean a sausee' (beans and sausages), 'Cackers a chee' (Crackers and cheese), 'Socks a pink' (the socks are pink)

(*Source*: Green, (2004).

activity
7.12
INDIVIDUAL WORK

During placement experience, make a note of the differences in speech, questioning and grammar of children at different ages and stages. You will probably notice that some children will be quite advanced in their speech, but are perhaps less skilled physically, or a very physically active child may communicate less well. Very few children are 'advanced' in all developmental areas.

Speech sounds

Speech sounds in the English language are made up of consonants and vowels. The approximate sequential development of consonants in the English language is as follows:

Table 7.11 The development of speech sounds in English

At age 2 years	m, n, p, b, t, d, w
At age 2½ years	k, g, ng (as in sing), h
2½–3 years	f, s, l, y
3½–4 years	v, z, ch, j, sh
4½ years onwards	th (as in thin), th (as in the), r
Double consonants such as sp, tr and fl and also the sounds r and th, can develop as late as 6½ years in some children	

Double consonants, such as sp, tr and fl and also the sounds r and th, can develop as late as six and a half years in some children.

Developing communication through bonding

Forming a bond is essential to a child's secure two-way relationship with a parent or regular carer. One very pleasurable way of developing a bond with a baby is through baby massage.

See Unit 1, page 21, for more on bonding.

Baby massage

Baby massage enhances the adult's understanding of the baby's needs. It involves eye contact, touch, smiling and other pleasurable facial expressions. Such close contact heightens the intensity of interaction between parent and baby, or carer and baby. Baby massage is also used by therapists to help mothers who are suffering from post-natal depression; the mothers are taught how to massage their babies because it strengthens their contact with their baby and encourages the bonding process.

Baby signing

Baby signing is another form of communication. The thinking is that, during the pre-verbal stage, the infant can use simple signs to indicate, for example, that they need a drink, or wish to go to sleep. This may help avoid some of the frustration felt by infants who are unable to make their needs understood. Some early years settings are adopting signing with babies as a new strategy for supporting care, but always with the agreement of the babies' parents. There are training programmes for staff and parents.

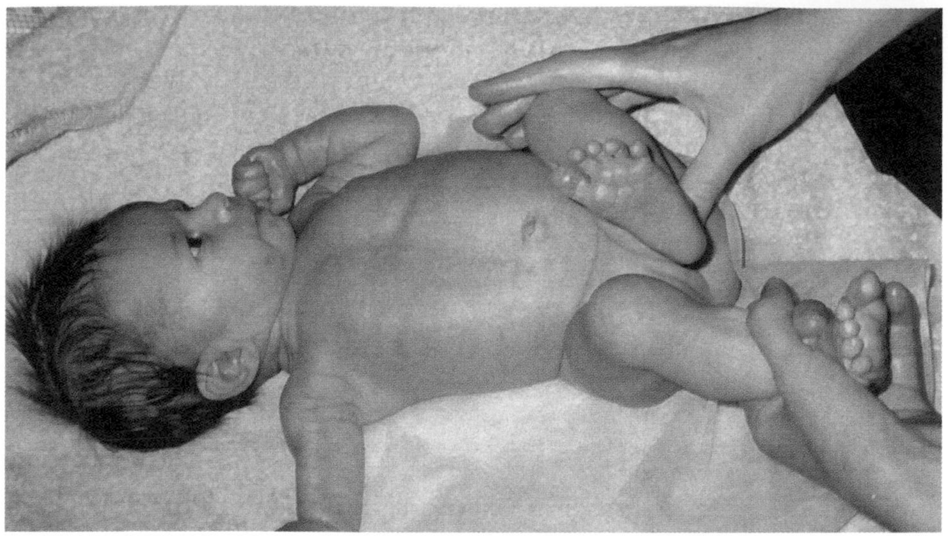
Figure 7.40
Baby massage

remember

Within a care setting, it is not usual for staff to carry out massage with the babies. Permission is always needed from parents.

Responding to children

Relationships with babies and young children are built on familiarity, stability and continuity of care. How you respond to a baby or young child will impact on the communication channel between you, affecting how well you 'tune in' to each other, the child's self-esteem (their feeling of being worthy and valued by their carers), and how well they settle into your care.

As a carer, you need to be an interested enabler of children, enhancing their confidence in their ability to undertake and persevere at tasks by acknowledging what they do and offering encouragement as they attempt new activities, whether they may be constructing a tower of bricks or recounting an experience to a group of their peers.

remember

The special object could be a particular teddy, large shell, puppet, etc.

It is important to remember that all children are different. You will therefore need to develop a range of strategies for encouraging communication. Opportunities for one-to-one time will be extremely important for those who have not yet developed sufficient confidence to speak in a larger group. Not all children feel able to contribute at circle time: the rule that only the child holding the 'special object' may speak makes it easier for quieter children to participate and helps over-enthusiastic children to develop their listening skills.

Communication barriers

Barriers to communication can be social, emotional or cultural.

Refer back to Unit 3, page 131, for information on these barriers.

When communication breaks down, a child may only be able to express this through their actions. For example, the tantrums often seen in two-to-three-year-olds reflect their frustration at not being able to communicate fully and are a feature of that stage of emotional development.

Enhancing communication

Ways of enhancing communication include:

- greeting everyone as they arrive, and giving a verbal farewell
- reading stories and sharing poems as a group, enjoying excitement and outcomes together
- singing rhymes such as 'Head and shoulders, knees and toes'
- playing circle games such as 'Farmer's in the den'
- playing rocking games such as 'Row, row your boat'
- using descriptive terms when eating (yummy), bathing (splish, splash), waking through leaves (crunch, crunch), etc.
- playing music and encouraging children to move to it
- making eye contact especially during one-to-one activities
- talking and smiling during care routines
- whispering during one-to-one times, at the start of story reading or perhaps when putting to bed
- joining in with games and laughter
- giving a message to be passed on to someone else
- encouraging children to describe what they are doing
- describing for babies what they are seeing, hearing or feeling
- providing instruments and encouraging children to make differentiated sounds, such as loud and soft, high and low, short and long
- using pictures of facial expressions to talk about emotions
- showing pictures of regular routines and discussing the order in which they happen, their importance to each individual and individual preferences
- making a tape of familiar sounds to see which can be identified
- playing memory games, such as 'I had in my basket ...'
- providing opportunities for co-operative play such as role play, drama (stories such as 'The Three Bears' and 'The Three Little Pigs' can be great fun)
- photographing children at play and discussing with them what they were doing
- providing software packages to develop skills in using information and communication technology (ICT).

Think about the above ideas for enhancing communication.

(a) Which have you experienced already?

(b) Which encourage one-to-one communication and which encourage communication with a range of others?

(c) Which encourage communicating, and which encourage listening?

Whenever you are with children, take as many opportunities as you can to communicate with them. You will find out more of what they think, enjoy and hope to achieve. The children will feel valued and wanted, knowing that adults enjoy being with and talking with them. At home, many children lack the opportunity simply to chat. Early years settings can help fill that gap for them, enabling them to become more confident communicators.

Talking to parents

Every parent wants to know how well their child is settling into their early years setting. They want to hear how they are developing, what they enjoy doing, who they enjoy being with and also about anything that becomes a problem. Developmental milestones need to be dealt with sensitively. For example, a parent does not wish to hear that they have missed their child's first steps (they will no doubt see this 'miracle' for themselves within a day or so), but they will appreciate hearing how helpful the child has been, how they have mastered control of scissors or pencils, or about the child's acts of kindness to others.

The child's key worker will be the main person to keep parents informed and updated. It is important that any communication with the parent is as positive as possible. Unacceptable behaviour is a difficult issue to discuss; should such discussion be necessary, give praise first for what the child has done well before moving on to talk about the problem.

It is the setting's responsibility to arrange regular feedback to parents about their child. This takes place on a daily basis in some settings, usually at collection time. In other settings, a home-link book enables written comments to be added each day and provides a format for two-way communication with parents, helping them to notify carers of any potential problems (e.g. a family occasion or crisis resulting in lack of sleep), or concerns they may have (e.g. if the child is suddenly reluctant to go to nursery).

See Figure 8.6 on page 370, for an example of entries in a home-link book.

Communication with parents can be blocked for a number of reasons. To develop your understanding of communication barriers and how to overcome them, refer to Unit 3, page 131.

1. What does the Apgar score measure?
2. Why are black infants usually pale at birth?
3. Which fontanelle closes by 18 months of age?
4. What is the usual cause of neonatal jaundice?
5. Which birth mark is only found on dark-skinned infants?
6. Explain what is meant by the term 'primitive reflexes'. Give three examples.
7. What does infant perception involve?
8. Why is breast milk best for babies?
9. What is the difference between fore milk and hind milk?
10. Explain the advantages and disadvantages of breastfeeding.
11. Explain the advantages and disadvantages of formula feeding.
12. Why is weaning usually introduced at about six months?
13. What should be remembered when choosing clothes for babies and young children?
14. Explain the expected rate and pattern of language development in babies and young children up to three years of age.
15. Explain how baby massage can help develop communication between infant and adult.

References and suggested further reading

Baston, H. and Durward, H. (2001) *Examination of the Newborn: A Practical Guide*. Routledge, London.

Beaver, M., Brewster, J., Jones, P., Keene, A., Neaum, S. and Tallack, J. (2001) *Babies and Young Children*, 2nd edn. Nelson Thornes, Cheltenham.

Bee, H. (1992) *The Developing Child*, 6th edn. Allyn & Bacon, Boston, MA.

Dare, A. and O'Donovan, M. (1998) *A Practical Guide to Working with Babies*, 2nd edn. Nelson Thornes, Cheltenham.

DfES (2003) *National Standards for Under Eights Day Care and Childminding*. DfES/DWP, Nottingham.

Green, S. (2004) *Baby and Toddler Development Made Real*. David Fulton Publishers, London.

Harpley, A. and Roberts, A. (2006) *Helping Children to be Skilful Communicators, from Birth to 3 Series* (ed. S. Green). David Fulton Publishers, London.

Harpley, A. and Roberts, A. (2006) *Helping Children to Stay Healthy, from Birth to 3 Series* (ed. S. Green). David Fulton Publishers, London.

Harpley, A. and Roberts, A. (2007) *Helping Children to be Competent Learners, from Birth to 3 Series* (ed. S. Green). David Fulton Publishers, London.

Harpley, A. and Roberts, A. (2007) *Helping Children to be Strong, from Birth to 3 Series* (ed. S. Green). David Fulton Publishers, London.

Keene, A. (1999) *Child Health: Care of the Child in Health and Illness*. Nelson Thornes, Cheltenham.

Phillips, C. (1996) *Family-Centred Maternity and Newborn Care*, 4th edn. Mosby Publishers, St Louis, MO.

Sheridan, M. (1991) *From Birth to Five Years: Children's Developmental Progress*, NFER Nelson.

Sheridan, M. (1997) *From Birth to Five Years: Children's Developmental Progress*, revised edn. Routledge, London.

Websites

www.babycentre.co.uk
www.pampers.com
www.bounty.com
www.parentlineplus.com
www.nctpregnancyandbabycare.com
www.sandy-green.com

Providing Support for Children with Disabilities or Special Educational Needs

This unit covers:

- understanding how to support a child with disabilities or special educational needs
- understanding how to help the child to take part in activities and experiences
- understanding how to support the child and family according to the procedures of the setting.

This unit will help develop skills and understanding in relation to working with children with a disability or those who have special educational needs.

As some of the conditions discussed are genetic in origin, the unit starts with a brief outline of genetic inheritance before going on to look at the care needs of children with specific conditions. You will then learn about ways of helping children to take as full a part as possible in activities and experiences. Finally, you will read about relevant legislation and the codes of practice to which all early years practitioners currently work, and you will look at ways in which the setting strives in partnership with the child's parents and professionals to support the child's inclusion in society.

grading criteria

To achieve a **Pass** grade the evidence must show that the learner is able to:	To achieve a **Merit** grade the evidence must show that the learner is able to:	To achieve a **Distinction** grade the evidence must show that the learner is able to:
P1 identify a range of disabilities and special educational needs that affect children	**M1** explain how a child with a disability or special educational need can be supported	**D1** evaluate ways of helping a child with a disability or special educational need to take part in activities and experiences
P2 identify current legislation and relevant codes of practice affecting provision for children who are disabled or have a special educational need	**M2** explain how a child with a disability or special educational need can be helped to take part in activities and experiences	**D2** evaluate ways of supporting the family of a child with a disability or special educational need

grading criteria

To achieve a **Pass** grade the evidence must show that the learner is able to:	To achieve a **Merit** grade the evidence must show that the learner is able to:	To achieve a **Distinction** grade the evidence must show that the learner is able to:
P3 outline ways to help children to take part in activities and experiences	**M3** explain the steps undertaken to ensure the effective and appropriate observation of children	
P4 identify ways of interacting effectively with children who are disabled or have a special educational need	**M4** explain what is meant by partnership with parents	
P5 describe the potential effect a child with a disability or special educational need might have on a family		
P6 outline ways in which support can be given to the child and the family		

Understanding how to support a child with disabilities or special educational needs

Genetic effects on development

Genetic inheritance

keyword

Genotype
The complete genetic inheritance of one person that is present in their chromosomes.

The human body is a complex machine; its basis is the 46 chromosomes in each cell. Each chromosome is made up of thousands of genes, and our genetic inheritance (**genotype**) is determined by the combination of genes present in the chromosomes of our parents and handed down to us.

Although the usual number of chromosomes in each of the body's cells is 46 (23 pairs), the exceptions are the sex cells (in males, the sperm cell; in females, the egg), which have only 23 chromosomes each. One pair of chromosomes is responsible for determining the child's sex; in males, this pair is made up of one X chromosome and one Y chromosome, whereas females have two X chromosomes. Conception takes place when the male's sperm cell fertilises the female's egg (ovum), which implants itself into the wall of the uterus. The ovum

keyword

Phenotype
The physical and behavioural characteristics of a person that are visible and are the result of the interaction of genetic inheritance and environment.

contains an X chromosome; the sperm could contain either an X or a Y. Thus, the sex of the conceived child is determined: XX = a girl; XY = a boy.

Genes are not the only factors influencing a person's development; the environment (e.g. diet, social context and habitat) also plays a part. The **phenotype** is the outcome of the interaction between genes and environment; it comprises the individual's behaviour and characteristics and, unlike the genotype, is observable.

Genetic inheritance is also discussed in Unit 1, page 38.

keyword

Autosomal recessive transference
When both parents are carriers of a condition passed on through the genes.

Autosomal dominant transference
When at least one parent is affected by a condition passed on through their genes.

X-linked transference
A disorder found on the X chromosome and passed on through the genes of the parent.

Genetically inherited disorders

Physical disabilities and learning disorders can place limitations on development and require additional support from carers. They occur for a variety of reasons: some are genetically inherited (caused by the genes of our parents); while some are congenital (they exist at birth but are not due to our parents' genes).

Genetically inherited disorders can be transferred to an infant in three different ways:

- **autosomal recessive transference**
- **autosomal dominant transference**
- **X-linked transference**.

Autosomal recessive transference

Autosomal recessive disorders can occur when both parents are carriers of the defective recessive gene. There is a one-in-four chance of offspring being affected, and a two-in-four chance of their being carriers. Autosomal recessive disorders include Batten's disease, cystic fibrosis (CF), phenylketonuria (PKU), sickle-cell anaemia and thalassaemia.

Figure 8.1
A defective recessive gene

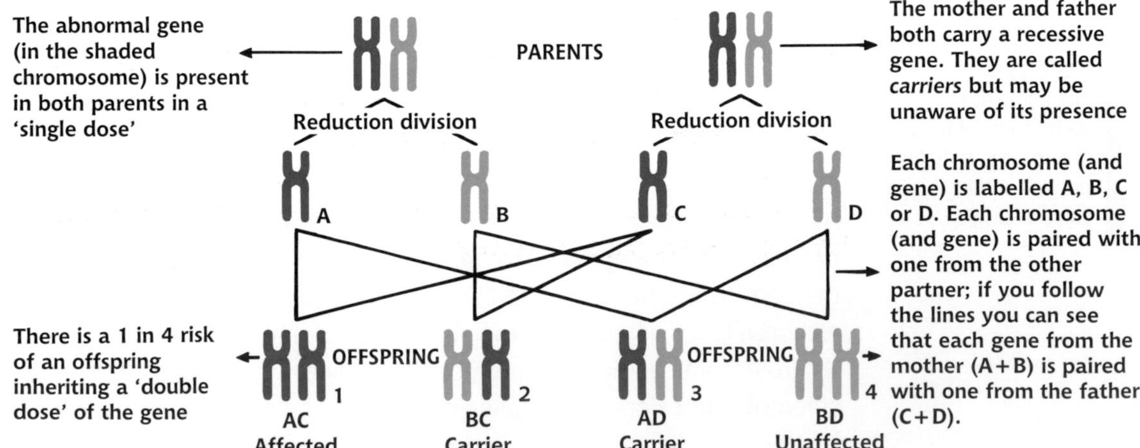

For more on CF, thalassaemia, Batten's disease, PKU and sickle-cell anaemia see pages 362, 364, 367 and 368.

Autosomal dominant transference

Autosomal dominant disorder occurs when the carrier is also affected by the disorder themselves. If one parent is an affected carrier, there is a two-in-four chance of the offspring also being affected. If both parents are affected carriers, the likelihood of incidence rises to three in four. Autosomal dominant disorders include Huntington's chorea (which does not show symptoms until middle age), Marfan syndrome and osteogenesis imperfecta (brittle bones).

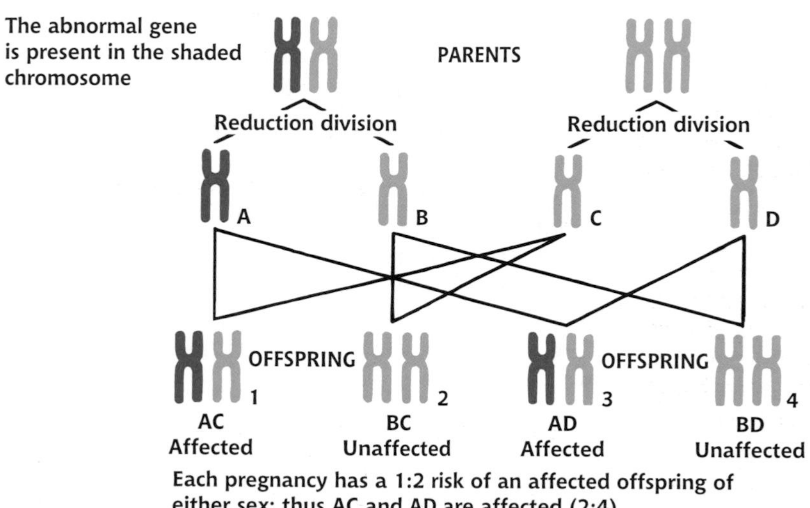

Figure 8.2 Dominant inheritance

For more on Marfan syndrome and osteogenesis imperfecta, see page 368.

X-linked transference

In the case of X-linked transference, the disorders are carried on the X chromosome of the mother. As the mother has two X chromosomes, the defective X acts in a recessive way in female offspring and a dominant way in males; there is therefore a higher likelihood of male offspring being affected than females. X-linked disorders include Duchenne muscular dystrophy, fragile X syndrome, haemophilia and Lowe's syndrome.

For more on Duchenne muscular dystrophy, fragile X syndrome, and haemophilia, see pages 360–362.

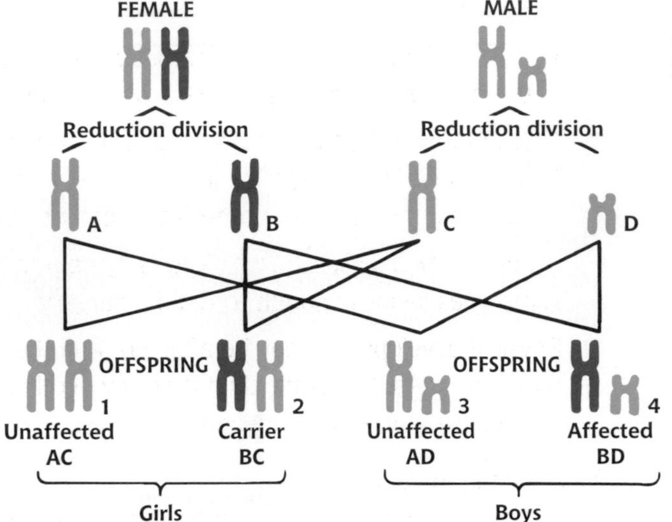

Figure 8.3
X-linked transference

Needs of the individual child

Down's syndrome

The syndrome is easily identified at birth:

- Children have distinct facial features, which include;
  - an upward slant to the eyes
  - an enlarged tongue that often protrudes
  - a shorter than normal neck and slightly smaller head, flattened at the back
  - short, stubby fingers.
- Muscle tone is poor; infants with Down's syndrome are very 'floppy'
- Physical development is noticeably slower than usual.
- Eyesight is often poor.
- Congenital heart disease is often present.
- Respiratory and ear infections are common, sometimes leading to deafness.
- Intellectual development is slow but reaches lower levels of normal in some children.
- Life expectancy is to around middle age, but occasionally people with Down's syndrome can live to be older.

Care needs

A child born with Down's syndrome will have a learning disability and will require educational support. However, while there are many similarities among children with Down's syndrome, each child inherits characteristics from his own family background so there will be significant differences. Such differences will affect the level of care required. In addition, there may possibly be health difficulties, which can include:

- Impaired hearing – vulnerability to frequent coughs and colds makes glue ear more likely.
- Vision problems – there is sometimes a squint or other associated difficulties; in some children there may be lack of peripheral vision.
- Gross motor skills, such as crawling and walking, will probably be delayed. Children with Down's syndrome have a tendency to put on weight; this will need to be monitored and a healthy diet followed.
- Around 40% of children with Down's syndrome have a heart problem; this is sometimes serious enough to require surgery.
- Physical development may be affected, and the child may be smaller than their peers. As the young child is floppy and has poor muscle tone, additional physical support will be needed.

Williams syndrome

Williams syndrome is a rare disorder and like Down's syndrome is caused by a chromosomal abnormality. It is a non-hereditary syndrome which occurs at random and can affect brain development in varying degrees. The incidence is approximately 1 in 25,000 but the figure is rising as publicity about the syndrome spreads. There is no cure and there is wide variation in ability between individuals with the condition.

Physical effects range from lack of co-ordination and slight muscle weakness to possible heart defects; in some cases, there is kidney damage. Hypercalcaemia (a high calcium level) is often discovered in infancy, and normal development is generally delayed. Diagnosis is not easy because effects vary considerably. However, there are certain indications that Williams syndrome may be present, such as:

- The children have similar facial features, sometimes referred to as 'elfin' features, including a wide mouth, with large, slack bottom lip, very retroussé nose (turned up at the tip) with flattened bridge, slightly 'bulgy' cheeks, irregular teeth that are widely spaced, and, in some cases, a squint.
- Early problems can include low birth weight, being 'late for dates', slow weight gain or, sometimes, weight loss; below average growth; very slow feeding; restless sleeping and irritability; hernia; and a squint. Excessive vomiting leading to dehydration and constipation are sometimes seen. A raised calcium level is found in some babies.
- Heart problems – all children with Williams syndrome appear to have a slight narrowing of the aorta above the valve; in many cases this is insignificant, but it may occasionally lead to more serious heart defects.
- Psychological effects include hyperactivity in early years, extreme uninhibited behaviour, excessive talking in an inappropriate and 'adult' manner, over-friendliness with strangers, compulsion to talk to adults while being unable to make friends with peers. There may be an obsessional interest in certain

things (e.g. cars, trains, vacuum cleaners, wheels), and/or fear of heights, open stairs and uneven surfaces. Emotional immaturity is exhibited by over-reaction to events, and exaggerated displays of fear, excitement, sadness, happiness, etc. are common.

- Hypersensitivity to noise – about 90% of children with Williams syndrome show great distress on hearing sudden loud noises (e.g. guns firing, balloons bursting, Christmas crackers, fireworks).

Care needs

Early diagnosis means better understanding of the problems which may arise, leading to a happier life for the child and relief and support for the parents. Affected children have many care needs:

- When hypercalcaemia (high blood calcium levels) occurs in the first year or two of life, a low calcium diet is prescribed.
- Many children with Williams syndrome have renal and cardiac problems. They may also have dental abnormalities, back and joint problems, and raised blood pressure. The rate of growth may be delayed, resulting in low stature and slightness of build.
- Children with the syndrome have an unusual pattern of abilities, and this may give rise to unrealistic expectations in relation to their abilities in other areas. However, comprehension is poor and this should be taken into consideration when instructions are given and activities provided. There is often a short concentration span, which adds to learning difficulties.
- In addition, there may be marked gross and fine motor problems and visuospatial difficulties. There is no one type of school that is ideally suited to these children's needs and finding the most appropriate school will depend on the individual child's level of ability and also on the provision that is available in local schools.

Asperger's syndrome

Asperger's is part of the autistic spectrum. In summary:

- The greatest feature of the condition is lack of interaction with others.
- Children tend not to form relationships.
- Lack of response tends to isolate individuals.
- Facial expressions tend to be inappropriate.
- Body language tends to be stiff.
- Communication 'cues' are missed.
- Children with Asperger's tend to become obsessed with a specific interest.
- Routines can become obsessive and crucial to maintaining normality, with even slight changes causing great distress.
- Some individuals have a good level of intellectual ability.

- Some individuals are able to live independently and hold down regular employment, but more severely affected individuals need sheltered living facilities.

Care needs

Children with Asperger's syndrome may be highly intelligent, especially in certain areas of the curriculum (often mathematics and computer science) and they should be given the opportunity to utilise these skills with a differentiated curriculum if necessary. However, they will still require help with social skills and the use of language appropriate to any given situation. They will need help in knowing what to do in social situations and in acquiring the social skills necessary to make friends and work alongside other people. Often the child with Asperger's syndrome will be fixated on a particular topic, which does not hold any interest for other people. Because of their difficulties with social interaction, they are not easily able to switch to another topic or understand that the person they are talking to is bored with the subject.

Programmes such as Social Stories (by Carol Gray), where pupils are provided with accurate information about social situations, exploit the strengths of an individual with Asperger's syndrome such as good visual/reading skills. Social skills groups, where children are taught the rules of social interaction, can also be very useful.

Children with Asperger's syndrome usually attend mainstream school. As they have language and the disability is not clearly visible, they are often not diagnosed until their other difficulties become more apparent, and they can therefore be the targets of bullying as their behaviour is not understood.

Autism

This is the most extreme end of the autistic spectrum. In summary:

- A child with autism does not seem to understand the need to communicate with other people.
- Imaginative play is almost non-existent.
- Children live in an isolated world.
- Delayed speech is common and children play quietly.
- Many children with autism also have learning difficulties.
- Some children have above-average intellectual ability.
- Hand flapping and other repetitive behaviour is common.
- Routine is important for security; great distress is shown if routine is changed.
- Obsessive interest is shown in minor details of objects, for example the wheel on a toy car.
- Behaviour can be hard to manage and exhausting for parents and carers.
- Lack of understanding of jokes and humour can lead to comments being taken literally.

- Inappropriate social behaviour is common.
- The child's inability to understand how other people feel is evident in inappropriate responses.

Care needs

Many children with autism are educated in mainstream schools although some of the more severely affected children may attend special schools or specialist units attached to mainstream schools. They require social skills training and need many types of support if they are to have access to the curriculum. Children with autism are good visual learners, and a visual timetable can therefore be a great benefit. It is important to incorporate a card denoting a change of routine because such changes can be very difficult for the autistic child to deal with. In whole-group situations such as carpet time, it can be helpful for an assistant or key worker to have a series of cards, which can be held up for the autistic child to see to help them behave appropriately; for example, one might show an ear depicting listening.

Some autistic children have heightened senses; hearing, for example, may be very acute. This can cause distress in noisy, busy places, so it is important to keep the environment as low stimulus as possible.

keyword **TEACCH** Treatment and Education of Autistic and related Communication-handicapped CHildren.

This can be difficult in a mainstream primary school where there are many displays and a very busy atmosphere. Wherever possible, the autistic child should have access to a calm, quiet area possibly with their own 'work station', an approach based on a programme developed in North Carolina for people on the autistic spectrum. The programme, which is known as **TEACCH** (Treatment and Education of Autistic and related Communication-handicapped CHildren), includes language- and behaviour-focused intervention programmes. The five TEACCH concepts are:

- physical structure of the environment
- visual cueing
- the work station
- concept of finish (many autistic children need to learn what this means)
- concept of first work, then play.

Autistic children take language very literally. It is important to speak very clearly and directly and not use idioms such as 'It's raining cats and dogs'. Some children with autism will have speech difficulties and may benefit from using a visual communication system such as the Picture Exchange Communication System (PECS).

Refer back to Unit 3, page 128, for information on PECS and other communication systems.

> **keyword**
> **ABA**
> Applied behaviour analysis.

Other treatments which may be beneficial include music therapy and an intensive one-to-one programme known as applied behaviour analysis (**ABA**). This is an early intensive behaviour therapy approach carried out by a trained team, usually within the home environment. It is, however, sometimes included on a child's statement of special educational need and is continued in the pre-school or school setting.

> **activity**
> **8.1**
> **GROUP WORK**
>
> (a) Design a visual timetable for a morning's activities at a pre-school.
>
> (b) Design a series of visual cards that an assistant might hold up to show to the child with autism, reminding them of appropriate behaviour in the group.

> **keyword**
> **ADD**
> Attention deficit disorder.
> **ADHD**
> Attention deficit hyperactivity disorder.

Tourette's syndrome

Tourette's syndrome is a recognised medical condition which is often inherited. Although there are treatments, there is no cure. It is both a movement disorder and a neurological condition and affects all aspects of life – education, relationships and employability. The syndrome sometimes occurs with other conditions, for example, attention deficit disorder (**ADD**) or attention deficit hyperactivity disorder (ADHD) and obsessive-compulsive disorder (**OCD**).

See page 366 for more on ADHD.

While the cause of Tourette's syndrome has not been established, it involves the abnormal processing of the neurotransmitters dopamine and serotonin. The condition is three to four times more likely in boys.

Symptoms of Tourette's syndrome are tics, repeated movements and speech. These usually start in childhood at around the age of seven and persist throughout life, although they may decrease towards the end of adolescence. Some tics involve movement (e.g. eye blinking, head jerking, shoulder shrugging and facial grimacing, jumping, touching people and things, smelling, twirling). Some individuals may hit and/or bite themselves.

Care needs

Most people with Tourette's syndrome are not significantly affected by their behaviours and so do not require medication. Using relaxation techniques to alleviate the stress that tends to make tics worse can be helpful as can behaviour therapies which teach the substitution of one tic for another that is more acceptable.

It is important that Tourette's syndrome is treated early and that people who associate with the child with Tourette's understand that the actions and vocal utterances are involuntary.

Tics can provoke ridicule and rejection by other children and adults. The child may be bullied, excluded from activities and prevented from enjoying normal relationships; these difficulties may increase during adolescence.

As a group, school children with Tourette's syndrome have the same IQ as the population at large. However, some individuals may have special educational needs such as difficulties with reading and writing and with arithmetic, and perceptual problems. If Tourette's is combined with attention deficit disorders, special educational assistance will probably be needed, perhaps in the form of a teaching assistant, especially in cases where the pupil is being educated in a mainstream school. Tape recorders and computers can be useful aids for those with reading and writing problems. Permitting the child to leave the classroom when tics become overwhelming can be helpful.

Cerebral palsy

- Cerebral palsy can occur before birth, due to infection or placenta problems.
- It can occur at birth, following a difficult delivery.
- It can occur immediately after birth, due to head injury or infection,
- The condition is not reversible.
- It does not change in its severity.
- Cerebral palsy affects physical movement and limb control.
- Speech is often difficult to understand.
- Intellectual ability is unaffected.

Care needs

Cerebral palsy is a condition which affects movement, posture and co-ordination; problems may be seen at or around the time of birth or may not become obvious until early childhood. As cerebral palsy is a wide-ranging condition and can affect people in many different ways, care will depend on the individual needs of the child. Some children have cerebral palsy so mildly that its effects are barely noticeable, while others may be extremely affected and require help with many or all aspects of daily life. Physiotherapy and speech therapy are usually offered.

Some people have a combination of one or more types of cerebral palsy. It is often difficult for a doctor to predict accurately how a young child with cerebral palsy will be affected later in life. Cerebral palsy is not progressive (i.e. it does not become more severe as the child gets older), although difficulties may become more noticeable.

There is no cure for cerebral palsy. If children are positioned well from an early age and encouraged to move in a way that helps them to improve their posture and muscle control, they can be supported to develop and achieve more independence for themselves. Physiotherapists and occupational therapists will advise on the appropriateness of any arrangement for an individual child; these therapists may need to show staff how to handle a child in a way that will help the child to develop the best possible control over their body, and prevent staff from suffering back strain or injury. However, some key points to remember are:

- Try not to move the child suddenly or jerkily as their muscles may need time to respond to changes in position.
- Do not force movements – let muscles tense and relax in their own time.
- Fear can make muscle spasms worse, so give the child as much support as they need when you are handling them, being careful not to give more support than they need.
- Whatever the child's size or level of impairment, make sure that they spend time in different positions.
- Try to position the child so that they can see what is going on around them.
- Many physically disabled children are helped greatly by properly fitting and supportive seating. As a general rule, the child's feet should be flat on the floor, knees bending at right angles, with hips firmly against the back of the seat. Some children benefit from having chairs with arms.

Other difficulties and medical conditions may occur more commonly in people with cerebral palsy, but just because a person has cerebral palsy does not mean that they will also have other difficulties. A setting should, however, take into account any additional needs that a child may have. Difficulties may include:

- Problems with constipation or sleeping – a doctor or health visitor should be able to offer advice.
- Toileting skills – the degree to which a child is ultimately able to be responsible for their own toileting needs will vary greatly. Some children, particularly those with severe or multiple impairments, may never achieve full independence in this area of personal care.
- Speech and associated difficulties in chewing and swallowing – most children will use speech to communicate, but speech may be delayed or very difficult for a few and they will need help to support communication. A speech aid might be the best way forward if it is clear that the child will find speaking very difficult but any child can benefit from using pictures and symbols to support playing and learning. They may also have problems understanding the spoken word. A speech and language therapist will suggest the best way to help an individual child.
- Eating – some children with cerebral palsy cannot suck, swallow and chew easily so eating may be messy. Rubber suction mats can be useful. Eating may also take longer, but it is important to take time to ensure that the child has a healthy diet. Staff can encourage children to feed themselves or to make choices about food and drinks. There are special cups and pieces of cutlery that might be helpful. Brushing teeth is particularly important when children have eating difficulties since food can easily get stuck in teeth and gums, and this can lead to decay and gum disease.

- Hearing difficulties – some children with cerebral palsy might be more prone to hearing difficulties.
- Epilepsy – this is usually well controlled with medication, and the setting may only need a volunteer to administer medication if the child stays all day. However, the medication might affect the child's behaviour, ability to concentrate or need to use the toilet, and these possibilities should be discussed. Where children may have a seizure, staff need to feel confident that, through discussion and training, they are able to deal with it effectively.
- Distinguishing and comparing shapes – difficulties relate to the person's ability to interpret what they have seen (visuospatial perception) and are not caused by a problem with eyesight. In the most severe cases, children with cerebral palsy may appear blind, but many can improve their useful vision with plenty of stimulation and support. Children may have difficulty with pictures, line drawings and writing. We use spatial awareness to work out where we are in relation to objects and people around us, but this is a problem for some children. If a child is walking or using a wheelchair themselves, they may bump into things or move into spaces that are far too small. In bookwork, they may find it difficult to 'see' an object or picture in their heads and may need to use real objects for counting and other maths games for longer than is usual.
- Learning difficulties – these can be mild, moderate or severe. There may be a specific learning difficulty, or there may be problems with a particular activity, such as reading, drawing or arithmetic, because a specific area of the brain is affected.
- Cognitive impairment may be severe, which means they cannot reason well or understand their environment fully.
- Challenging behaviour can be a feature in this group, especially when the child cannot communicate effectively.

remember

Even someone very severely affected by cerebral palsy may have average or even above-average intelligence.

Spina bifida

This occurs when a failure in the development of the neural tube during pregnancy leads to defects in one or more areas of the vertebrae (the bones in the spine). Women are advised to increase their intake of folic acid before and during the first months of pregnancy to help prevent neural tube defects occurring. In summary:

- Minor-type spina bifida (spina bifida occulata) is identified as a dimple or tuft of hair on the lower area of the spine where the vertebrae are not completely joined.
- A slightly more serious version (meningocele) causes a swelling in the lower back, allowing spinal tissue to push through a gap in the vertebrae.
- Mostly, with meningocele the nerves remain undamaged, and disability is therefore minimal;

- The most serious version (myelomeningocele) causes the spinal cord and the meninges (the tissue lining the spinal cord) to push through the gap in the vertebrae.
- With myelomeningocele, infection is common due to the membrane breaking, and the individual will be paralysed from the affected part of the vertebrae downwards.
- Bowel and bladder problems are common.
- Hydrocephalus (water on the brain) is common; varying degrees of learning difficulty are found in individuals with hydrocephalus.

Care needs

Toilet needs, mobility and access, specific health needs, continuation of programmes of care such as physiotherapy and occupational therapy and any special dietary requirements are amongst the care needs that the early years worker must be aware of.

The specific care requirements for a child with spina bifida will depend on how severely affected the child is, and this depends on the position of the lesion. The higher in the spine that the malformation occurs, the greater the effect is likely to be. However, damage in the lower spine is more common. The severity of the condition also depends on how much damage there is to the spinal cord.

In any condition where there is paralysis (loss of movement and sensation), tissues are likely to be deprived of oxygen, resulting in pressure sores or ulceration. The early years worker should look out for these when a child is unable to move about.

Muscles and limbs that do not move of their own accord must be exercised by the carer. A physiotherapist may demonstrate exercises that the carer can follow, involving gentle movement of the muscles and joints that the child cannot move unaided. Carers will also need to be aware that a child who has lost sensation below the waist will have difficulty controlling their bowel and bladder. Whatever method of management is used, for example a catheter, the carer will need to support the child and learn about the techniques and help required. Encouraging the child to become independent in the management of bowels and bladder is very important. A high-fibre diet with plenty of fluids to prevent constipation is essential.

When a child has paraplegia (no movement or sensation below the waist), mobility is primarily achieved by wheelchair. Children who have more control of their movement may be helped by using crutches and frames. Occupational therapists and physiotherapists will be involved in deciding the most effective way of improving mobility and can advise the early years worker on how to ensure that the environment is wheelchair friendly.

The children will need to be taught the skills that will enable them to become wheelchair proficient and manage small steps and uneven surfaces with confidence. While children with spina bifida are more dependent on their upper limbs as they need strength and power for controlling wheelchairs and crutches, some children are less skilful and dexterous manually than their peers of a similar age. Activities to develop fine motor skills are recommended (e.g. manipulating Duplo, pegboards, playdough).

activity 8.2 INDIVIDUAL WORK

You have been put in charge of the role-play area, and the group you are working with includes Ayesha. Ayesha has spina bifida, and one of the targets on her individual plan is to improve her fine motor skills.

What kind of activities could you introduce that would help to address this need?

Professional Practice

- It is always important to keep clearly in your mind that a child is simply a child.
- Their specific care needs should not detract from your providing for them as an individual person with the right to enjoy as full a range of activities and experiences as they are able.

Duchenne muscular dystrophy

Only boys are affected by this condition. In summary:

- The first signs are seen at around 18 months old.
- A delay in walking is common.
- Falls become increasingly noticeable.
- The child will have difficulty in running or climbing due to weakening in the pelvic and leg muscles.
- The muscles become increasingly contracted (tight and restrictive).
- This is a progressive condition, and boys often need to use a wheelchair by the age of 10 to 12 years.
- Chest infections are serious.
- A limited life span is usual, as a result of respiratory or heart failure.

Care needs

The progress of the condition cannot be halted by specific medicines or treatment, but good management can ensure a good quality of life for the child and limit associated problems. The child should be given the chance to develop a wide range of social relationships, experiences, hobbies and interests that can be continued once his mobility is reduced. Muscles need exercise so swimming, ballet, gym clubs and horse-riding should be included in the activities; in addition, these will help prevent the child from becoming overweight, which is a possibility when mobility is reduced.

The child may require up to four hours of planned exercises a day, which you may have to help implement with input from the physiotherapist. Hydrotherapy is often used as a valuable and enjoyable exercise because muscles move more freely in water and are less likely to overstrain. As with other conditions where a child may be using a wheelchair or mobility aids, the environment must be checked in order to enable safe use.

Fragile X syndrome

- This condition most frequently (and more severely) affects boys.
- Girls mostly have a normal level of intelligence.
- Boys' intellectual levels can range from severe to just below normal.
- A long, thin face is a usual physical feature.
- Large ears and prominent forehead are common in boys.
- Life expectancy is normal.

Care needs

The effects of Fragile X syndrome range widely: from specific learning difficulties and subtle learning problems in an individual with an average IQ to severe intellectual disability and developmental delay. Any one child may present only a few of the problems or a whole range of features but in a mild form.

Many children and adults with the syndrome remain undiagnosed because they only have mild learning difficulties, and they may not get the help and support that they need.

Understanding emotions is difficult for individuals with Fragile X syndrome and many children with the syndrome will have autistic-like symptoms and behaviour, so social skills groups and programmes can be helpful. Other strategies used with autistic children, such as PECS, Makaton and the TEACCH programme, are also helpful, especially where speech and language are affected. Delayed development in these areas is one of the earliest presenting features. Receptive language skills are generally better than expressive.

Refer back to Unit 3 page 130, for information on PECS and to page 354 of this unit to remind yourself about TEACCH.

Boys tend to have more behaviour problems, especially problems with concentration, while girls are more likely to be shy and socially withdrawn and to suffer from anxiety and depression. As girls with Fragile X syndrome are less likely to be severely affected, they are more likely to go to mainstream schools, and counselling and training programmes designed to promote self-confidence and self-esteem may be helpful.

Differentiation of the curriculum will almost always be necessary, and the support of a teaching assistant may be required. Particular areas of the curriculum, including mathematics, tend to cause difficulty as conceptual learning is difficult. Handwriting can present problems, while reading and spelling can be relative strengths. Computers are effective learning tools as these allow for endless repetition of tasks, are consistent and have large memories. Computers give immediate responses and are not personally threatening. Social anxiety can be a key feature of children with Fragile X syndrome.

Haemophilia

It is almost exclusively boys who are affected with this condition, which is a bleeding disorder. In summary:

- Severe internal bleeding occurs at the slightest knock or injury.
- There is swelling of joints and bones at the site of injury.
- Deformity and pain are common.
- Minor surgery (e.g. dental surgery) can be problematic without special procedures to restrict the blood loss.
- Sufferers are particularly susceptible to being infected with hepatitis B and need to be immunised against it.
- Pain killers containing aspirin should not be given because these affect the blood-clotting process.

Care needs

The effect of haemophilia on a child's lifestyle, growth and development should be minimal; there should be normal growth and life expectancy, not a life of pain. Normal play and schooling is usual. It is important that over-protection is avoided and that normal handling, cuddling and play take place. When the child is at the toddling stage, sensible protection for knees is essential (e.g. dungarees). Good dental hygiene is necessary. Toddlers with haemophilia may have more bruises than their peers, and false allegations of child abuse have occurred in some situations.

It is good practice to seek medical advice if the child falls and hits his head. Normal safety precautions should be followed (e.g. stair gates, robust toys, no sharp edges, etc.). Exercise helps develop strong joints and muscles, better balance and sharper reactions leading to better avoidance of injury. Swimming is especially valuable, but physical contact sports are not recommended.

Cystic fibrosis

Cystic fibrosis (CF) is the most commonly found inherited disorder in the UK. In summary:

- Sticky mucus is produced in many of the infant's organs.
- Obstruction of the bowel is often found soon after birth.
- The lungs and pancreas are particularly affected.

> **keyword**
> **Percussion therapy** Physiotherapy of the chest to loosen secretions blocking the lungs.

- A high-calorie diet is recommended.
- An enzyme supplement is given shortly before each meal to help with the absorption of nutrients.
- Lung problems are the most serious aspect.
- Physiotherapy (**percussion therapy**) is needed regularly throughout the day to keep the lungs clear.
- Life span is often around 20 years, depending on severity, but this is increasing as treatments improve.

Care needs

> **remember**
> In CF, the cough is not infectious.

The three main areas of care with regard to a child with CF are maintenance of nutrition, prevention and control of lung infections, and physiotherapy to keep airways clear. All staff should be aware of the severity of the condition and the importance of diet and medicine. Time and space for physiotherapy is needed as is good liaison with school health services.

When a child is too large to be comfortably placed over the knees, percussion therapy will have to take place over a foam wedge. Breathing exercises such as blowing games with bubbles and steaming mirrors can be introduced from about the age of two. Trampolining is a good form of exercise. From about the age of five, the child should be encouraged to spit secretions out so that the mucus can be observed for indications of infection, changes in stickiness, etc. Also, swallowing mucus can increase nausea and affect appetite.

The child should be offered full involvement in all activities and wherever possible should make their own decisions about how many strenuous games and activities they can manage. This will depend on the severity of the condition at any one time. Children with CF need to make friends and have the opportunity to succeed in areas where they can compete equally with their peers, such as music and creative activities.

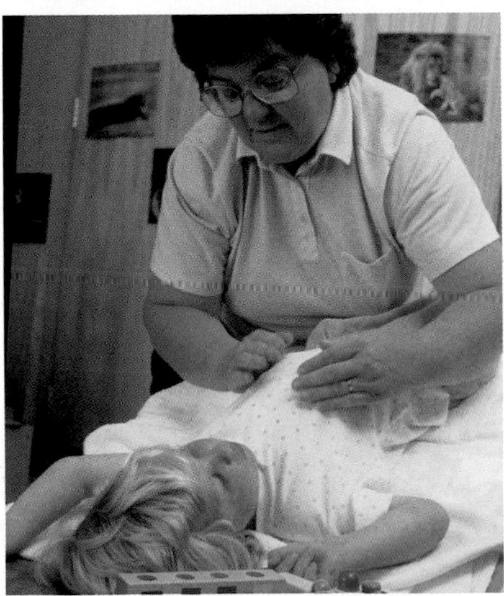

Figure 8.4
Percussion therapy

In order to help the child take full advantage of the learning opportunities available, a childcare worker needs to maintain a balance, being sensitive in their approach and demonstrating understanding, but without being over-protective. Be ready to intervene if a child is picked on because of coughing or expectorating, or because they are underweight or need to take medicines regularly. As with any medical condition there will be absences from school due to infections, so it can be helpful if the key worker or teaching assistant keeps a class diary to help with missed work.

Thalassaemia

This is a life-long condition. In summary:

- There are two different types of the condition, alpha and beta.
- The first signs are seen between three and six months.
- Symptoms include anaemia, lack of interest in feeding, and vomiting after feeds.
- Jaundice is common due to a faster breakdown of the red blood cells.
- Too many iron-rich blood cells accumulate in the body and can cause damage to vital organs like the heart and liver.
- Liver and spleen are often enlarged.
- Diabetes can also occur.
- Life expectancy can be shorter in individuals severely affected by the condition.

Care needs

With effective treatment, a child can attend and thrive in a childcare setting from playgroup to mainstream school. Carers need to be aware that the child is likely to become tired and need extra rest. Symptoms are controlled by regular blood transfusions, and regular, often daily, drugs given by injections under the skin.

Dyspraxia

This is a neurological disorder in which messages are not transmitted in the brain in the normal way. In summary:

- It leads to impairment or immaturity of the organisation of movement.
- In most cases, there is no known cause.
- There are associated problems of language, perception and thought:
  - speech and language – speech may be immature or unintelligible in early years; language may be impaired or late to develop
  - perception and thought – there is poor understanding of the messages conveyed by senses and difficulty in relating to those messages; spatial perception is poor, and children tend to bump into objects and people.
- Dyspraxia is also known as 'clumsy child syndrome, developmental co-ordination disorder, minimal brain dysfunction, motor learning difficulty, and perceptuomotor dysfunction.

- Physical activities are hard to learn, difficult to retain and generalise, hesitant and awkward in performance.
- Symptoms and severity of the condition vary enormously.
- Up to 10% of the population may show symptoms of dyspraxia and 2% are severely affected. Of those diagnosed, 80% are male.
- Many people go through life with the condition undiagnosed and may cope reasonably well – mainly by avoiding situations in which they fail, or by developing coping strategies, such as writing lists to overcome short-term memory problems.

Care needs
Early recognition of dyspraxia enables a child's special educational and social needs to be identified. Action can then be taken to reduce the impact of the condition on the whole family.

It is important that practitioners are sympathetic to the condition and put strategies in place, adapting the curriculum as necessary in order that the child will have a sense of success and self-worth. Very often these children feel a sense of failure and their 'clumsy' behaviour can lead to their being bullied, with consequent frustration and behaviour difficulties.

Sometimes, children with dyspraxia will become the class 'clown' in the hope that others will laugh with them rather than at them.

Poor handwriting is a common symptom, and exercises such as those suggested by Mary Nash-Wortham and Jean Hunt in *Take Time* and Ion Teodorescu and Lois Addy in *Write from the Start* can be useful.

Children should have ready access to computers so that they can take pride in written work. Computers also help with reading and spelling (e.g. programmes such as Wordshark). Many children with dyspraxia have difficulties with reading and spelling, as these are adversely affected by their limited concentration and poor listening skills and their literal use of language. A child may read well, but not understand some of the concepts. They may be reluctant to read aloud because of articulation difficulties or because they lack self-confidence.

A child with dyspraxia will be late in reaching milestones such as rolling over, sitting, standing, walking and speaking. Strategies and resources should be put into place to assist the child with their fine and gross motor skills and in learning skills such as dressing, forming a correct pencil grip, running, hopping, catching and kicking a ball, doing jigsaws and completing sorting games.

Young children can be introduced to balancing and co-ordination activities through movement and play. The setting can seek advice from physiotherapists and occupational therapists as to activities for specific individuals. Most children will benefit from non-competitive activities which require them to improve on their own balancing and co-ordination skills, for example doubling the length of time that they can stand on one leg.

Organisational skills will be poor and the older child will need help with these as well as with following instructions; visual cues and other methods used with children on the autistic spectrum can be helpful. As the child with dyspraxia often has difficulty making friends and can appear anxious and distracted, they may benefit from social skills groups.

Attention deficit hyperactivity disorder

Attention deficit hyperactivity disorder (ADHD) is a medical diagnosis given to children who, compared with their peers, have developmental, behavioural and cognitive difficulties. Usually, these are children who have three main kinds of problems:

- difficulty in paying attention and concentrating
- impulsive behaviour
- overactive behaviour (hyperactivity).

A diagnosis is only correctly made when there are problems in these areas over and above those found in the peer group and in more than one setting. It is known that genetic (inherited) factors are important in ADHD but as yet it is not known which genes are involved. Environment also plays a part.

Because they are overactive and impulsive, children with ADHD often find it difficult to fit into school. They may also have problems getting on with other children.

Some children have significant problems in concentration and attention but are not necessarily overactive or impulsive. These children are sometimes described as having attention deficit disorder (ADD) and are frequently overlooked because they may be quiet and dreamy rather than disruptive.

ADHD is not related to intelligence. Children with all levels of ability can have ADHD, but unless the condition is recognised and treated, children may not reach their potential because the characteristics of the disorder mean that learning becomes more difficult.

Care needs

Stimulant drugs such as methylphenidate (Ritalin) and dexamphetamine (Desadrine) are often prescribed for children diagnosed with ADHD. Such drugs work by stimulating those parts of the brain which control behaviour and regulate activity. The drugs seem to help many children to concentrate and regain control over their actions. As children calm down they are able to mix better with others and respond more effectively to teachers and parents. Children may become less aggressive as well as less hyperactive, and their performance at school may improve significantly. It is important to recognise that medication does not cure ADHD, but it can provide a 'window of opportunity' in which children can be helped to manage their own behaviour.

Behaviour management strategies are essential to monitor the child's progress and check for any side effects. For example, some children develop sleep problems, become drowsy, lose weight or become depressed. The sorts of strategies that can be helpful to a child with ADHD include:

- arranging the classroom to minimise distractions as you would with a child on the autistic spectrum
- including a variety of activities during each lesson, alternating physical and sitting-down activities
- setting short, achievable targets and giving immediate rewards when the child completes the task
- keeping class rules clear and simple
- rewarding positive behaviour with teacher attention and praise
- giving the child special responsibilities so that other children can see them in a positive light.

Less common conditions that you may come across during your career

The following brief summaries are based on Gilbert (2000).

For details of Gilbert's book, see References and suggested further reading on page 396.

With each of these conditions, as with those already discussed, specialist guidance will be needed when caring for each individual child.

Batten's disease

- There are four different types of this condition.
- Progressive mental and physical deterioration is seen.
- Convulsions are suffered.
- Eventual loss of vision is usual.
- Life span is usually less than 10 years.

Phenylketonuria (PKU)

This is caused by a build-up of the amino acid, phenylalanine. In summary:

- A routine test called the Guthrie test is carried out on all newborn infants to detect PKU.
- A special diet must be adhered as prevention against:
  - severe vomiting in the earliest days following birth
  - convulsions
  - skin problems – skin can be dry and have the appearance of eczema
  - learning disability, which can be moderate to severe
- Life span and intellect are usually normal if the very restricted diet is adhered to for life.

Sickle-cell anaemia
This is a life-long condition. In summary:

- It is seen in people of Mediterranean countries, African-Caribbean people and in some Asian and Middle Eastern people.
- The first signs are seen at about six months old with swelling in hands and feet.
- It involves an abnormality of the oxygen-carrying substance in red blood cells; the shape of the cells changes (becoming sickle shaped).
- There is severe pain.
- Anaemia is a common and ongoing problem.
- Problems with an enlarged spleen can occur.
- Bone infections and enuresis (bed-wetting) are common problems.

Marfan syndrome

- Children with this condition are extremely tall.
- The long limbs are in proportion to their tall bodies.
- Fingers and toes are often particularly long.
- Problems with the spine often occur (scoliosis).
- Shoulders are often rounded (kyphosis).
- Dislocated joints are common as joints can be very weak and flexible.
- In a small number of children, joints are particularly stiff (contracted).
- A deformed chest is common.
- Poor vision, short-sightedness and detached retinas are common.
- Owing to problems with the aorta (large artery from the heart), life span is reduced to middle age in many sufferers.
- Normal intellect is usual, although visual problems may make learning more difficult.

Osteogenesis imperfecta (brittle bones)
In this condition, small bones are particularly fragile and prone to fracture. In summary:

- Spinal deformities can occur (scoliosis and kyphosis).
- Teeth are prone to cracking or breaking.
- Problems with the small bones of the inner ear can cause hearing difficulties.
- Blood vessels are fragile and bruising occurs easily.

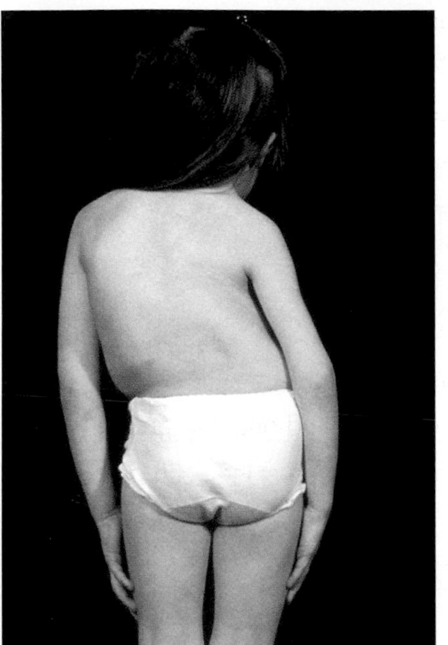
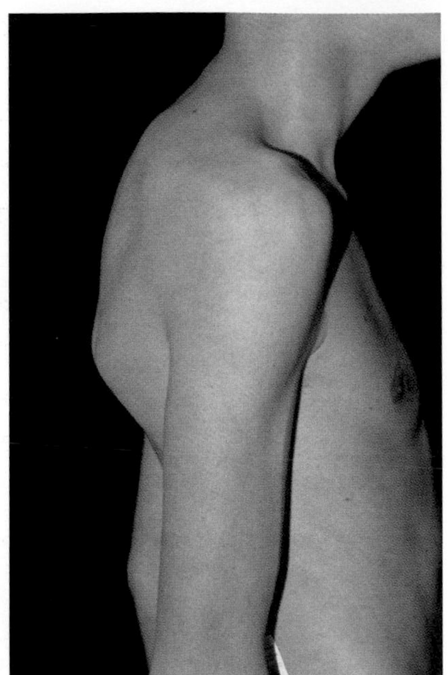

Figure 8.5
Scoliosis and kyphosis

Screening in pregnancy

Some conditions can be identified during pregnancy by one or more screening tests. These antenatal tests include the following:

- blood tests
- ultra-sound scan
- serum alpha-fetoprotein (SAFP)
- the triple blood test
- amniocentesis
- chorionic villus sampling (CVS).

Refer back to Unit 1, page 39 for descriptions of these tests.

Information and care needs

Practitioners, especially key worker staff, should seek information about the individual care and communication needs of a child from:

- the child's parents
- colleagues.

Information from parents

It is very important that professionals working in early years settings involve parents from the start and at every stage during the child's time at the setting. Most parents will have anxieties about their child attending a nursery or pre-school setting, and the anxieties can be much greater for the parent of a child with special educational needs. Many parents of such children may never have left the child with any other carer before, and they need to be reassured that you know as much as possible about how to care for and communicate with their child. Regular communication is essential to ensure that parents are involved and know what is happening. This prevents misunderstandings arising and unnecessary worrying.

A home-link book can be an invaluable source of information both for parents and professionals and provide reassurance for the parent that the setting is doing everything in its power to include the child and meet their needs.

Figure 8.6
Example from a home-link book

13/10/06

Normally, we would have had swimming today but as Sam was persistently tugging at his ear we wondered whether he was suffering from ear-ache and decided that it was best that he stay behind at nursery. As you know, he does not like disruption to his routine but using the visual timetable we explained that there would be a change to his activities. We find the card with question mark on it signifying change very helpful – you may like to try this at home.

Sam enjoyed listening to the 'Spot' story and is now using the Makaton sign for dog.

At lunchtime we introduced broccoli. We made sure that it was not touching the other food (mashed potato and sausage) but he would not try it.

Sam became very sleepy this afternoon. He possibly has an ear infection. Perhaps you could have this checked out?

Sarah (Key worker)

16/10/06

Took Sam to the surgery straight after nursery and he does have an ear infection.
He is now taking antibiotics and is much happier. As a treat for him bought him a soft toy 'Spot'. He won't let go of it but at least it's preferable to that old bit of blanket!

Thought I would try broccoli mixed up into a salmon fishcake. (Isn't Omega 3 supposed to be good for concentration?)

Information from colleagues

When working with a child with special educational needs it is helpful to have as much information about that child as possible in order to include them effectively in the setting. This may involve liaising with a range of other professionals. Other professionals who may be able to share information with you include:

- health visitors
- speech and language therapists
- occupational therapists
- physiotherapists
- Portage workers
- social workers.

If the child has been attending a different setting, maybe an Opportunity group (a pre-school setting for children with special educational needs), then talking to the professionals there can be helpful too.

Portage

Portage is a daily home-teaching programme for children with a particular need in which the Portage worker develops an individual programme for the child and the parents continue to implement it on a daily basis. The Portage worker makes regular, usually weekly, visits.

If a child has been receiving Portage, it can be very useful for the Portage worker/tutor to visit the setting and advise about activities that they have been using with the child and to show you the checklist that they use so that you have a good understanding of the child's level of attainment in the different areas of development.

Following a child's individual plan

Children with special educational needs should have an individual plan. In schools, this is called an Individual Education Plan (**IEP**) and may be issued at the School Action stage of assessment. In pre-school this is called Early Years Action.

keyword
IEP
Individual Education Plans

The purpose of the individual plan is to ensure that activities are set at the correct level for the child to achieve success. If a child succeeds at an activity, they will want to do it again. If they do not succeed, a sense of failure may well be felt and they may not wish to try again. Adapting the curriculum to the individual child's need is called differentiation.

The format of an individual plan varies from setting to setting. Some local education authorities have a standard format for the schools in their area. There should not be too many targets on an individual plan. Sometimes, there will only be one. There should not be more than four or the likelihood of a child succeeding will be reduced.

All targets should be **SMART** This stands for:

keyword
SMART
An acronym for Specific, Measurable, Achievable, Relevant, Time-limited.

- specific
- measurable
- achievable
- relevant
- time-limited.

When setting a target, you should ensure that it is:

- *Specific*. The target is clear and individual; for example, Tom will become proficient in calculating number bonds to 5. He will practise these each numeracy session for one week.
- *Measurable*. It can be tallied or counted; for example, it can be observed that Tom has practised number bonds to 5.
- *Achievable*. This refers to targets that the child has the potential to achieve. In this example, Tom may already be calculating number bonds to 5 but not consistently enough for the teacher to feel that he is able to move on to the next stage.
- *Relevant*. In this example, it could be that the class target is 'knowing number bonds to 10'. It has been recognised that Tom needs to be more secure in number bonds to 5 before he can move on.
- *Time-limited*. The target should be achieved within a given time period that is long enough for the task to be met but not so long that the child loses interest and motivation in achieving the task.

activity 8.3 GROUP WORK

Using a copy of the blank chart on page 373 and the following information, complete an IEP for Sam, a pre-school child. Remember that the targets should be SMART.

Sam's strengths

- Sam can be a very affectionate and co-operative child.
- Sam loves music and responds very well to it.
- Sam has great determination in communicating verbally and non-verbally, despite difficulties of articulation.
- Sam has practical ability which becomes apparent during cookery lessons, washing or drying dishes.
- He is capable of playing well with other children.
- He has a caring attitude towards others.

Sam's needs

- Sam needs to have one-to-one attention to complete most tasks.
- Sam needs to have access to a wide range of activities to develop his tracking and fine motor skills.
- Sam would benefit from a physical programme to develop his gross motor skills and help him gain in confidence.
- Sam needs regular changes of activity, as his attention span is often limited.

Table 8.1 An Individual Education Plan for Sam

Target Number	Targets (this should be a clearly stated, realistic learning or behavioural outcome)	Strategies (this is what will be done that is different from normal class routines – special activities and resources)	Roles and Responsibilities (Which staff will do what, when and how often. Include parents where possible)
1.	The pupil will be able to:		
2.	The pupil will be able to:		
3.	The pupil will be able to:		
4.	The pupil will be able to:		

remember

As a student you should raise any concerns that you may have with your placement supervisor or course tutor, NEVER directly with a parent.

Procedures for referring concerns

Concerns over a child should always be raised with parents. Depending on the concern, for example whether it is a health issue or an educational issue, the appropriate professionals can be consulted. Usually a referral to a paediatric doctor is made through the child's GP. A health visitor can make a referral to a speech and language therapist, occupational therapist or physiotherapist. If the setting requires an assessment by an educational psychologist, they can approach the local education authority (LEA).

Where to seek advice and support to overcome communication difficulties

It may be necessary for a child to be referred to a speech and language therapist. Sometimes, children are seen in a clinic, often in a local hospital setting, or sometimes therapists attend settings especially if they are primarily for children with special educations needs, such as Opportunity groups or special schools. Some therapists will give advice and suggest activities for professionals in settings to follow themselves. Professionals may be able to attend courses to learn Makaton or how to use PECS.

Refer to Unit 3, page 130, for information on the communication systems Makaton and PECS.

Interactions

Communicating effectively

It is important to remember that every child is an individual and that, in order to communicate effectively with a child with special educational needs, a whole range of strategies may be needed.

Verbal strategies

Talking to a child is one of the most important things that you can do. It should be remembered that most children's levels of comprehension are more advanced than their verbal abilities and that they cannot learn language if they are not exposed to it.

Do not be put off if you do not receive verbal replies – some children may signal in other ways that they understand or are responding to what you are saying (e.g. by gesture, smiles or blinking).

Speak in simple terms, especially when giving instructions. Many children can only cope with a very few information-carrying words, and it is better to phrase instructions positively (e.g. 'Sit here' rather than 'Don't sit there'). If a child is using verbal communication but their articulation is not very clear, resist the temptation to ask them to repeat themselves; instead, you should repeat their words clearly for them. This way, they are hearing the correct pronunciation without undue pressure being brought to bear on them. Of course, you may not have interpreted their verbalisations correctly but, hopefully, you will have made an educated guess!

Autistic children often use language very literally, and you should therefore be extra careful to ensure that there are no misunderstandings. For example, when the children are coming in from outdoor play, you may say to them, 'Wipe your feet'. A child with autism may take his shoes and socks off and wipe his feet rather than his shoes on the mat.

Non-verbal strategies

Successful communication can take place without verbal exchange. Many deaf people use British Sign Language (BSL) and consider this their first language. As practitioners, we can gain a great deal of information from people's expressions and gestures. When you are using gesture with children with special educational needs, you should use speech alongside it. You may want to exaggerate gestures and expressions in order to convey your meaning. Pointing is a very important gesture; lack of pointing is sometimes used as one of the indicators that a child may be on the autistic spectrum.

Some children can become lazy if their non-verbal signs are easily understood, and they should be encouraged to verbalise whenever possible. A way of encouraging verbalisation is to offer choices, for example 'Is it the teddy or the car you want?'

The signing system Makaton was based on BSL but adapted for people with learning difficulties. Many children, for example those with Down's syndrome, benefit from this system. As a signing system alleviates some of the frustration that children with delayed speech can experience, it may sometimes be helpful in reducing temper tantrums which, in some children with delayed development, can continue into the school years.

PECS usually uses photographs of familiar people and objects. This makes identification by the child easier than if drawings are used. If you are taking photographs yourself, ensure that the background is blank. Many children benefit from having an album of photographs of family members, pets, favourite toys, etc. A box of objects is another useful stimulus. Pictures and objects can be useful starting points for a dialogue, even if there is no verbal contribution from the child.

activity 8.4 GROUP WORK

(a) What kinds of things would you include in a photo album for a child with no speech in order to communicate with them about their home life?

(b) Create an object box on the subject of holidays. What would you put into it to help a child communicate about their holiday?

Giving praise and reward for children's efforts and achievement

If children are rewarded and praised for their efforts, they are far more likely to repeat the behaviour that has pleased us, whether it be stacking bricks or sitting attentively during story time.

Rewards can be non-tangible; for example, a smile, a clap, and a thumbs-up signal are all powerful signs that we are pleased with a child. Verbal praise should be specific to the performance that we are praising; for example, 'Good listening' informs the child why we are pleased. Whenever possible, avoid telling a child that they are wrong if they perform a task inaccurately. If you have asked the child to pick up the red brick and they pick up the orange one, instead of saying, 'No, that's wrong', you could say, 'Nearly' or 'Good try – have another go'. If a child is told that they are wrong too often, there is a danger that their self-esteem will suffer and they will give up trying because they will be afraid to be wrong again.

Refer back to Unit 1, page 21, to remind yourself how children learn from observing others.

Stickers are an example of a tangible reward. You can now purchase stickers with the reason for the reward on them (e.g. 'I shared nicely today'); these are particularly useful for children with special educational needs who may not be able to tell their parents why they have been rewarded or who may have forgotten. Certificates can be given as rewards, and, if wished, these can be personalised. Items can be collected in a jar for a reward at the end of the day or week (e.g. 'Golden' time, or time on the computer, or an outing to the park).

Group-reward schemes can be useful for fostering a sense of responsibility towards other children, and peer pressure can be a useful way of encouraging children to behave in an appropriate way. However, it must be remembered that many children with special educational needs (and, of course, young children in general) have difficulties with short-term memory. This also applies to children with dyslexia who may otherwise be very able. Any reward will therefore be much more powerful if it is instant.

Professional Practice

- It is better to give attention to a child when they are behaving appropriately and to try to ignore mildly inappropriate behaviour which may be attention seeking.
- Praising other children who are behaving appropriately often has the desired effect on the child who isn't, as they can see that the others are getting positive attention (a reward).

Sensitivity to children's age, needs and ability

All children are individuals, and all children with special educational needs should be viewed as such. You may have two children with Down's syndrome in your setting and, while they will have certain physical attributes in common, they will be as different in other ways as any other two children. It is important to be aware of an individual child's stage of development and not to make assumptions about their ability in different areas. While you do not want to have unrealistic expectations, neither do you want to exclude children from activities that they may wish to attempt with appropriate support.

Having realistic expectations

Being aware of an individual child's capabilities in all areas of development is very important.

At the Foundation Stage, stepping stones are used to ensure that the Early Learning Goals are achieved. Some children will need additional support and may have an individual plan. The important thing to remember here is that each task should be reduced to the stage where a child will achieve and therefore be encouraged to move onto the next stage, thereby raising self-esteem.

For example, there are several ways in which you could adapt the task of stacking bricks to make it possible for a child with a special educational need to achieve:

- You might use larger bricks.
- You might only aim for one brick to be stacked on top of another.
- You might use Velcro or similar on the bricks so that they do not fall off so easily.
- You might use hand-over-hand to achieve the task.

Look back at the approach used by Portage workers, which is described on pages 371–372.

Figure 8.7

The Portage checklist

Age levels: 0–1 (1–14); 1–2 (15–24); 2–3 (25–40); 3–4 (41–64); 4–5 (65–86); 5–6 (87–108)				
	BEHAVIOUR	ENTRY BEHAVIOR	DATE ACHIEVED	COMMENTS
1	Removes cloth from face, that obscures vision		/ /	
2	Looks for object that has been removed from direct line of vision			
3	Removes object from open container by reaching into container			
4	Places object in container in imitation			
5	Places object in container on verbal command			
6	Shakes a sound-making toy on a string			
7	Puts 3 objects into a container, empties container			
8	Transfers object from one hand to the other to pick up another object			
9	Drops and picks up a toy			
10	Finds object hidden under container			
11	Pushes 3 blocks train style			
12	Removes circle from form board			
13	Places round peg in pegboard on request			
14	Performs simple gestures on request			
15	Individually takes out 6 objects from container			
16	Points to one body part, e.g. nose			
17	Stacks 3 blocks on request			
18	Matches like objects			
19	Scribbles			
20	Points to self when as 'Where's (name)?'			
21	Places 5 round pegs in pegboard on request			
22	Matches objects with picture of same object			
23	Points to named picture			
24	Turns pages of book 2–3 at a time to find named picture			
25	Find specific book on request			
26	Completes 3 piece formboard			
27	Names common pictures			
28	Draws a vertical line in imitation			
29	Draws a horizontal line in imitation			
30	Copies a circle			
31	Matches textures			
32	Points to big and little on request			
33	Draws (+) in imitation			
34	Matches 3 colours			
35	Places objects in, on and under on request			
36	Names objects that make sounds			
37	Puts together 4 part nesting toy			
38	Names actions			
39	Matches geometic form with picture of shape			
40	Stacks 5 or more rings on a peg in order			
41	Names big and little objects			
42	Points to 10 body parts on a verbal command			
43	Points to boy and girl on verbal command			
44	Tells if object is heavy or light			
45	Puts together 2 parts of shape to make whole			
46	Tells what happens next in simple, repetitive story			
47	Repeats finger plays with words and action			
48	Matches 1 to 1 (3 or more objects)			
49	Points to long and short objects			
50	Tells which objects go together			
51	Counts to 3 in imitation			
52	Arranges objects into categories			
53	Draws a V stroke in imitation			

activity
8.5
INDIVIDUAL WORK

You want to encourage self-help skills in the children you are working with. How could you break down into stages the task of putting socks on? Look at the example below, the first stage is set out for you:

- Put the sock on over the ankle of the child but ask the child to pull the sock up. With some children you may need to model this hand over hand or by demonstrating on one leg of the child or on a doll.
- ...
- ...
- ...
- ...

No labelling of children

Children develop at different rates. Sometimes, children may give cause for concern at a certain stage of development because they are not achieving the milestones that would be expected of them. Of course, this may indicate that there is an underlying condition, but it may just mean that there is a delay in a particular area of development, such as speech, which will right itself, sometimes with intervention but often with maturity. This is one of the reasons why local education authorities are often reluctant to issue statements of special educational needs to pre-school children.

Giving a child a label can lead to stereotyping on the part of professionals and others involved with the child, and assumptions may be made about the capabilities of the child that may deny them opportunities. On the other hand, if labelling equals diagnosis of a condition, this can be beneficial if the child receives the necessary input from educational and health services and the family benefits from financial support and such services as respite care.

Sometimes, families actively welcome a diagnosis as this allows them to access support groups and enables them to explain a child's condition and behaviour to others. This may be particularly so in the case of the so-called 'invisible disabilities' such as autistic spectrum disorder and ADHD where parents may have blamed themselves for the child's lack of ability to conform.

remember

Remember to use positive terms at all times.

In order to develop a positive attitude towards the capabilities of children with special educational needs, we need to ensure that the language we use in describing the child is also positive. Terms such as 'handicapped' are unacceptable as these suggest a dependency on others. Neither should a child's condition become their main form of identification, for example 'the Down's child'. Using the phrase 'a child with Down's syndrome', for example, demonstrates that the child is a person first and foremost; the fact that they have Down's syndrome is secondary.

Alternative communication using the senses

Some senses are underused. Where children have sensory impairment of any sort, it is helpful to incorporate senses such as touch and smell. Many special schools use smell to alert pupils who may have multi-sensory impairments; for example, fragrant plants may be used to indicate the positioning of areas in a garden. Times of the day and of activities can also be denoted by scent. Key workers may be identified by their scent – they will need to ensure that they wear the same perfume daily if this is to be the case! Similarly, music and sounds can work for children with visual impairment, and these children also enjoy tactile books and other resources which use a range of different textures. An activity that uses as many senses as possible will enhance the memory and therefore learning. SENSE, the national deaf, blind and rubella organisation provides resources for deaf-blind and multi-sensorily impaired children and their carers.

Legislation and codes of practice affecting provision for disabled children and those with special needs

Background

Until the middle of the last century, most children with disabilities, now termed special educational needs, were not considered in need of education. It was thought that they would not benefit and, although there were some special schools, for example for the blind and the deaf, many children with disabilities were not catered for until the Education Act 1944 which made provision for children with 11 different categories of disability to be educated in special schools not alongside their peers.

In 1978, Mary Warnock was asked by the Government to chair a committee of enquiry into the 'education of handicapped children and young people'. The recommendations that the committee made formed the basis of the Education Act 1981. The belief that all children are entitled to an education whatever their disabilities, with the stress on the importance of focusing on a child's educational need rather than on their disability, was a new one. Warnock's enquiries led her to believe that the majority of children with special educational needs could be educated in mainstream school with extra provision but that about two per cent would need the protection of a statement of special educational need.

Recent legislation

The following Acts and their accompanying guidance are the backbone of the Government's education policy. The legislation expects mainstream schools to include all pupils fully. This means making changes to accommodation, organisation, curriculum and teaching methods. The law places a duty on schools and LEAs to ensure that this happens. There are still special schools throughout the country but some are closing as the number of pupils on role drops as a result of inclusion. The expertise and resources are shared with mainstream schools. Some pupils with special educational needs spend part of the week in a special school and part in a mainstream school.

keyword

Code of practice
The procedures (usually written down) by which a setting or profession operates.

SEN
Special educational needs.

Education Act 1993
This Act reviewed the whole area of special educational needs and replaced the 1981 Act. It set out, in a **code of practice**, the duties of the LEAs with regard to special educational needs (**SEN**). The SEN code of practice set out the key principles for identifying, assessing and reviewing special educational needs.

A new code of practice became effective from 2002 and has replaced the 1994 Code (see below). Schools were required by the 1993 Act to have a special education needs co-ordinator (SENCO) and a special educational needs policy.

Education Act 1996
This Act brought together the existing legislation on special educational needs. It stated that a child is considered as having special educational needs if they have a learning difficulty which requires special educational provision (that is more provision than is needed by the average child) to be made for them. Many children have learning difficulties, but the important points are:

- The learning difficulty must be significantly greater than those experienced by the majority of others of the same age.
- The disability prevents or hinders the child from making use of the facilities provided for other children.

SEN children should be educated in mainstream school provided:

- they are being provided with the education that they need
- it will not interfere with the education of others
- there is efficient use of resources.

The board of governors should:

- make sure that all SEN pupils receive the education they need
- make sure all those who are likely to teach them are aware of their needs.
- ensure that teachers are aware of the importance of identifying and providing for SEN pupils.

Disability Discrimination Act 1995
This Act placed new duties on schools. Schools are not to treat disabled pupils less favourably than others and should make 'reasonable adjustments' so that these pupils are not disadvantaged.

keyword

SENDA
Special Education Needs and Disability Act 2001.

Special Educational Needs and Disability Act 2001 (SENDA)
SENDA strengthens the rights of children to attend a mainstream school. Unless their parents chose differently, or there were no 'reasonable steps' that the LEA or school could take to make that choice compatible with 'efficient education for other children', children with special educational needs have the right to attend mainstream school.

Revised code of practice

A revised code of practice, which took effect in 2002, emphasises early identification. Although very similar to the original, this version of the code also takes account of the new rights and duties of SENDA 2001. It sets out five main principles:

- Children with SEN should have their needs met.
- Their needs would normally be met in mainstream schools.
- Children should be asked for their views and have them taken into account.
- Parents have a vital role in supporting their children's education.
- Children with SEN should be offered full access to a broad and balanced curriculum.

The revised code stresses the importance of progress in learning, and new Action stages have been introduced:

- *School Action or Early Years Action* if in pre-school settings. This happens when it is felt that a child needs support additional to that provided as part of the usual curriculum. This action will be interventions agreed by the SENCO and the child's teacher or playworker in consultation with parents.
- *School Action Plus or Early Years Action Plus*. At this stage, outside support services or more specialist advice is sought to aid a child's development.
- *Statutory Assessment*. If the stages above are not sufficient to meet the additional needs of the child, a request for a statutory assessment may be made so that a statement of special educational needs may be considered. The assessment is a detailed multi-professional examination to find out exactly what the child's special educational needs are. Parents are also asked to give a report and, wherever possible, the assessment should include the views of the child. Requests for an assessment can be made by the parent, or professionals that have contact with the child.
- *Statement of Special Educational Needs*. This is a document issued by the LEA, detailing the specific and exceptional provision needed after gaining information about the child from a statutory assessment and taking into consideration that the required extra provision can only be met in this way. It is a legal document, which is reviewed once a year, and the school receives additional funding to ensure that the provision for the child is put into place.

Parents do not have to agree with a proposed statement if they are unhappy with any part of it. They can receive help at any point in the process from an Independent Parental Supporter provided by the Parent Partnership Service. An Independent Parental Supporter supports parents by, for example, attending meetings, encouraging parental participation and helping parents to understand the SEN procedures.

Figure 8.8

Proposed statement

The Proposed Statement The statement is split into six parts:
Part 1 – Introduction gives the child's details.
Part 2 – Special Educational Needs outlines any areas of difficulty the child experiences.
Part 3 – Special Educational Provision should give details of all provision to be made directly relating to all needs listed above and the arrangements for monitoring progress.
Part 4 – Placement School, or other educational provision, the child will attend, to be left blank in proposed statement.
Part 5 – Non-educational Needs, those which are agreed by social services, health or other agencies and the LEA.
Part 6 – Non-educational Provision gives details of non-educational provision, e.g. by health, social services or other agencies, and how it will be met.

Table 8.2 Key documents

Special Educational Needs Code of Practice 2001	This document published by the Department for Education and Skills (DfES) gives guidance on special educational needs. Early years settings, schools and LEAs must have regard to it when considering a child's special educational needs.
SEN Toolkit 2001	This provides additional guidance for teaching staff and should be read in conjunction with the Code of Practice (DfES).
Special Educational Needs – A guide for parents and carers	This short guide provides information on the levels of assessment and the statementing processes as well as details of all the Parent partnerships in England (DfES).
Inclusive Schooling – Children with Special Educational Needs	This provides guidance on the statutory framework for inclusion. It gives examples of the reasonable steps schools must make in ensuring children with statements are included (DfES).
Removing Barriers to Achievements – The Government's Strategy for SEN	This strategy sets out the Government's vision for enabling children with SEN to realise their potential.

The importance of following the above codes

The legislation and guidance outlined above are known as the 'inclusion framework'. It takes time for inclusion policies to be fully effective, and during the process there has been a great deal of debate about what inclusion should mean for pupils in both mainstream and special schools.

It is very important that codes of practice relating to children with special educational needs or disabilities are adhered to. The codes have been introduced to ensure that these children have equality of opportunity educationally and socially. All establishments need policies to address discrimination, plans to include possible as well as actual pupils and strategies for becoming increasingly inclusive.

remember

Make sure that you read your setting's special needs and equal opportunities policies and ensure that you abide by them.

According to the Disability Code of Practice, discrimination is treating a child less favourably where the less favourable treatment:

- is substantial
- is related to the disability
- cannot be justified.

Understanding how to help the child to take part in activities and experiences

Methods

Observing sensitively to identify any barriers to participation in activities

Direct and indirect observation of a child can enable us to identify any barriers to participation in activities. If possible, it should not be obvious to the child or to other children that they are being assessed in any way. Once a barrier has been identified, it is important to think of ways to overcome it, whether by extra staffing, such as a one-to-one assistant, or resources such as electronic aids, or by adapting equipment and furniture.

Refer to Unit 1, pages 43–58, for information on methods of observation.

Offering alternatives as required in consultation with others

Sometimes alternative activities will need to be offered to the child with special educational needs. It may be that a risk assessment has been carried out and it has been deemed unsafe for a child with a specific educational need or disability to participate in a certain activity. In such cases, an alternative activity should be offered in consultation with parents. In order that the child is not isolated from their peers, that activity could also be offered to other children.

To remind yourself about risk assessments and how they are carried out, refer back to Unit 4, page 148.

Adapting activities, experiences and environment

When mobility is restricted

A child with restricted mobility will need more space to move about in than children with full mobility. Points to consider include:

- providing plenty of space between activities and tables
- allowing plenty of space for wheelchairs to turn easily
- having a table that a child in a wheelchair can use, ensuring integration with others at mealtimes as well as in play
- providing suitable seating for a child who needs additional support (e.g. chairs with arms)
- providing wedges to support a child who needs to lie on their front (prone position)
- providing a mobility stand to support a child who cannot stand unsupported
- ramps to help independence when using steps into the garden or other areas of the setting

- lifts (if setting is on more than one floor)
- wide doorways
- a large toilet to accommodate wheelchairs and walking frames
- low-level hand basins to encourage independent personal care
- handrails at child and adult heights where necessary
- sloping boards for writing etc.
- press buttons, door handles, etc. at the right height.

Many children with special educational needs will be slower at becoming continent, and changing facilities will therefore be necessary. A shower may be a necessary piece of equipment for children who are incontinent.

When hearing is impaired
Children with hearing impairment require an environment that is well insulated, i.e. with:

- carpeted floors
- low ceilings, possibly tiled
- covered walls.

When vision is impaired
Children with impaired vision will need to have lighting assessed according to their specific needs; they may require the use of:

- a lamp
- a low-vision magnifying aid.

A constant layout will help a child with visual impairment to develop confidence and personal independence. They will also benefit from:

- plenty of natural light
- plenty of space to move around
- floors clear of clutter
- raised edges on surfaces to prevent objects falling off, thereby spoiling the enjoyment of activities and making floors hazardous.

To help visually impaired children identify where they are within the setting or outside, provide:

- textured surfaces at the edge of areas, such as the sandpit
- bright colours or visual clues to help them identify doorways, steps, and so on.

Figure 8.9
'Come on, Andy. Join in!'

When children are on the autistic spectrum
Children on the autistic spectrum respond best to an uncluttered environment and may benefit from their own individual work-station, separated off from others to prevent distractions.

To support a child with an autistic spectrum disorder:

- keep the routine as constant as you can
- try to minimise unnecessary noise and over-excitement
- give opportunities for playing alongside a main group, if group play appears to be overwhelming for them.

Professional Practice

- Children need to become as independent as possible, and the purpose of using additional resources is to promote that independence and with it a child's self-esteem and sense of worth.
- The environment needs to be assessed in order to best meet the needs of children with particular needs.

Play equipment and toys

For children with physical difficulties, suitable examples are:

- ball pools to stimulate the whole body
- large beanbags to offer supported movement
- soft-play areas to offer opportunities to explore, reducing risk of injury
- trikes and other ride-on toys with straps for feet
- trikes with a trailer to take a friend
- push-along toys with additional weighting to aid balance
- large balancing ball to lie on and roll.

For children with generalised sensory loss, provide:

- safety mirrors offering concave and convex reflections
- sensory balls, quoits, etc. made from textured rubbers and plastics
- Braille blocks, with textured letters and numbers
- resources offering sound, such as rainmakers, music boxes, etc.
- resources offering visual experiences, such as bubble tubes, wind horses and mobiles
- resources made from natural materials to help children explore taste, texture, etc.

activity
8.6
INDIVIDUAL WORK

Find out about some other examples of toys for children with physical difficulties and sensory loss.

activity
8.7
GROUP WORK

Danny is a child with athetoid cerebral palsy. Owing to his involuntary movements, items often end up on the floor when he plays with table-top activities, causing him a great deal of frustration.

How could you adapt furnishings or the environment to prevent this happening?

Encouraging positive behaviour

remember

Not all adaptations cost a great deal of money. Sometimes, imagination is all that is required.

Positive behaviour can be encouraged in children with special educational needs in the same way as with any other child. Praise and reward for appropriate behaviour is important, as are clear guidelines so that the child knows what would happen if they behave inappropriately (e.g. withdrawal of a privilege or time out). Children respond best to clear expectations and boundaries and above all to consistency. While the individual requirements and developmental stage of the child with special educational needs must be taken into account, positive behaviour should be encouraged at all times.

Some people make the assumption that all children with special educational needs will have behavioural difficulties. This is not so, although there are some special needs which by their very nature mean that a child may experience difficulties in this area, for example children on the autistic spectrum and those with ADHD and associated conditions.

Sometimes, these behavioural difficulties are due to a lack of understanding about how to behave appropriately in certain situations, and we may occasionally need to make allowances and to adapt the curriculum in order to ensure that the child is able to cope with a particular situation. For example, many children on the autistic spectrum feel great levels of anxiety in noisy, crowded places, so the potential benefits of a trip to the local supermarket would have to be weighed against the potential distress to the child.

Some children with special educational needs will at times feel very frustrated, often because they cannot understand why they are frustrated. They may well turn to attention-seeking or disruptive behaviour or avoidance tactics. The more that professionals are aware of individual needs and capabilities and can adapt the curriculum to suit individual requirements, the less likely this is to happen.

Children with special educational needs often experience bullying, usually as a result of the bullies' ignorance of their condition. It can be helpful (with parental permission) to educate other children in the setting about a child's disability, as this may reduce the likelihood of bullying. For example, if other children are aware that a child with dyspraxia has problems with motor co-ordination that make it hard for him to kick and catch a ball accurately, they may have a better understanding of his difficulties and make allowances for him. The introduction of a persona doll may also be useful.

Refer to Unit 5, page 194, for a description of persona dolls.

Understanding how to support the child and family according to the procedures of the setting

Partnership

Importance of parental and family knowledge of a child

Parents are the people with the most knowledge of their child and should always be consulted. The parents of a child with a rare special educational need are likely to have sought out relevant information and to be far more knowledgeable about the condition than the GP who may never have come across the disability before. Communication with parents should be regular and confidential. Sometimes, parents are not known to the setting because the child may be brought by another person, for example grandparents. However, they still need to be informed about what you do and how you help their child. A home visit might be appropriate, or an invitation to meet socially with other parents in the setting may work well.

Impact of having a child with a disability or special educational need within the family

The impact of having a child with a special educational need within a family should never be minimised. Most parents are not expecting to face this situation. They are expecting a 'normal' child, and the feelings that are usually associated with the news that their child has special educational needs are like those that people experience following bereavement:

- shock
- disbelief
- anger
- sorrow
- a feeling of numbness.

Most parents come to terms with the fact that they may have to reassess their hopes and expectations with regard to their child's future, but this takes time and varies within each family. In addition, the way in which the news is broken to parents can have a lasting impact on the way in which families deal with the situation.

Depending on the nature and severity of the special educational need, there are many implications for the family; for example:

- the requirement for 24-hour care, which may necessitate both parents giving up their jobs
- adaptations to the home
- financial problems; there are sometimes grants, but not always
- additional stress on the marriage or partnership (although families are sometimes brought closer together)
- negative impact on siblings (It is important that they do not feel left out. Their needs must be met too.)
- difficulty in having the friends of siblings to the house
- not being able to go on family outings
- children being bullied because they have a sibling with a disability
- children being expected to take on responsibilities at home beyond their years
- lives taken over by hospital appointments
- feelings of isolation; support groups can be invaluable.

Parents should consider respite care for their child with special educational needs, not only to give themselves a much-earned break but also to spend time with their other children, enabling them to do the things they would not otherwise be able to do because of the demands of looking after the child with special educational needs. (Usually, the child will be cared for during the respite period by a specially selected family or they may be admitted to a residential setting.)

A very positive finding is that many siblings are extremely caring and responsible and often enter the 'caring' profession as adults.

Integration/inclusion in placement settings

What is meant by inclusion?

According to the website of the Centre for Studies on Inclusive Education (CSIE), inclusive education means 'disabled and non-disabled children and young people learning together in ordinary pre-school provision, schools, colleges and universities, with appropriate networks of support'.

Inclusion means 'enabling pupils to participate in the life and work of mainstream institutions to the best of their abilities, whatever their needs'.

The CSIE believes that because children – whatever their disability or learning difficulty – have a part to play in society after their school years, an early start in mainstream playgroups or nursery schools followed by education in ordinary schools and colleges is the best preparation for an integrated life.

Many parents require a mainstream placement for their child with special educational needs. As long as there is an adapted curriculum and the environment is suitable for the child's particular disability, then successful inclusion can be achieved. However, staff must have the requisite training, and the resources necessary to manage the inclusion successfully must be in place. Not only will children with special educational needs be learning from their peers but the other children will be learning about different needs and abilities and the fact that a special educational need is not a barrier to a fulfilling life. Some of the fear and ignorance that surrounds special educational needs will be lessened with the inclusion of more such children.

activity 8.8 GROUP WORK

List six possible advantage and six disadvantages of including children with special educational needs in mainstream settings. Think about:

(a) possible advantages for the child with SEN in a mainstream school
(b) possible advantages for the child with SEN in a special school
(c) possible advantages for other children if the child with SEN is educated in a mainstream school
(d) the effects on families if a child is included
(e) the effects on families if a child is segregated.

case study 8.1

Annie

Annie, a three-year-old child with Down's syndrome, is due to start at the pre-school where you are working. Coral, the planned key worker for Annie, has liaised with the Portage worker who has been supporting Annie and her family and has been given the following summary of Annie's abilities and needs:

- Annie was late starting to walk and to use language.
- She has a few single words but mainly communicates with gestures or vocalisations. She is beginning to use some Makaton signs.

- She has immature social skills and finds sharing with other children difficult.
- She enjoys physical play but can be rather rough with other children.
- Her fine motor skills are immature.
- She responds well to praise.
- She is toilet trained but does have the occasional 'accident' when she is involved in activities.

activity
GROUP WORK

How could Coral ensure that Annie is included in the pre-school curriculum?

You may want to consider activities that she could work on and any extra resources or staff that might be necessary to support Annie.

Integration/inclusion in the community

In order for inclusion in the community to be successful, more children with special educational needs should be encouraged to join community groups and activities such as Cubs and Brownies as well as having the opportunity to attend social groups, such as those run by Mencap (e.g. the Junior Gateway Clubs).

Libraries encourage children with special educational needs to use their facilities by including some or all of the following:

- collections of story tapes with a wide range of stories, poems and songs
- books reflecting the special needs of children with disabilities
- large-print copies of books to read alongside tapes and CDs
- books in Braille and 'touchy-feely' books for blind or partially sighted children.

The National Centre Co-ordinating Agency for the development of disability sport in England provides support and advice to anyone wanting information on sporting opportunities for disabled children. Some local authority leisure centres operate a policy of 'helper goes free', which means that one parent or helper with a disabled person can get in free for casual sessions such as swimming. Many local authorities also run swimming clubs for disabled people. They may also run play schemes during the school holidays where children with disabilities and those without can enjoy a wide variety of activities such as arts and crafts, music, play activities in the sensory room or soft-play zone, sports and trips.

Some playgrounds now provide equipment which is suitable for children with disabilities. Soft-play centres can be beneficial for many children with additional needs. Another valuable activity is horse-riding: the Riding for the Disabled Association offers horse-riding sessions for groups from schools and residential centres and for individuals.

Planning for each child's individual requirements with colleagues and parents

The new code of practice emphasises, alongside the Children Act 2004 and the Education Act 1996, the role of parents of children with special needs and that parents and professionals should enter into a partnership of support and co-operation. Parents should be consulted when the child's needs are being discussed so that they can feel part of the decision making and can support the child at home, for example by working on an IEP target.

Multi-professional assessments are sometimes necessary, involving professionals from several different areas of expertise, such as physiotherapy, occupational therapy, speech and language therapy, and health visitors. All these can contribute to planning for a child's individual requirements.

Support

Helping family members to take part in activities

Family members should be involved in the activities of their child with special educational needs in order that they feel empowered and included. Schemes such as Portage and Opportunity Play Groups are very good at empowering parents. Often family members, including grandparents, will need to be shown activities so that they feel confident in carrying them out; for example, they may need help in communicating effectively with the child. They may also need advice on how to include the child in activities outside the home so that they can be confident when accessing recreational activities in which the child's siblings can be involved.

Giving feedback about the child's progress

A child with special educational needs may make slower progress in certain areas of development than other children. Progress is sometimes very slow, and it is important that feedback given to the child and other adults, especially parents, is as positive as possible. The 'feedback sandwich' is a useful guide:

1. Begin with something positive.
2. Continue with an area which can be developed, with clear strategies as to how this can be achieved.
3. Conclude with a positive statement.

It should be remembered that low self-esteem can be an aspect of many special educational needs and that, for a child to feel positive about themselves, they have to feel successful. Parents too may be lacking in confidence and may feel some guilt that their child has special educational needs. They also need encouragement so that they can support their child in a positive way.

case study 8.2

Peter

You are to meet with Peter's mother and report on his progress.

Peter is four years old and has Down's syndrome. He has recently begun to use several Makaton signs and is enjoying story time and music time. Peter has now mastered stacking rings on a peg in the correct order, and he is able to identify the colours red and blue. However, he often refuses to stop an activity when it is time to do so and tends to have a temper tantrum if asked to clear away with the rest of the group. Peter is also inclined to snatch toys from other children.

activity
INDIVIDUAL WORK

Using the 'feedback sandwich' approach, how would you report on Peter's progress and on your concern to Peter's mother?

remember

Every pre-school setting or school will have methods of recording progress that should be adhered to.

Recording progress of a child according to procedures

An advantage of having an Individual Education Plan is that there is a built-in review which should take place at least every six months. A statement of special educational needs has to be reviewed at least annually by law. The child and the parents are invited to review meetings as are all the professionals that have been working with the child. The review meeting is usually chaired by the Special Educational Needs Co-ordinator (SENCO).

Often, pre-school settings will have a system of key workers, and in schools there may be teaching assistants working with the child with special educational needs. They may be asked to complete observation forms and target sheets for particular areas of the curriculum or for self-help skills.

Seeking help from others when information and support are needed

If a child has been born with a disability such as Down's syndrome, parents will have been given advice and guidance on the management of their child and will usually have been put in touch with local support groups and national ones, such as the Down's Syndrome Association, by paediatricians and other professionals at the hospital where the child was born. These groups can be a very valuable source of information and support for families and for professionals working with the children.

When a child's disability is not apparent at birth and is not diagnosed until much later on, it may be part of the role of the early years practitioner to seek out information and support for the family and for others working with the child. This may be in collaboration with health visitors or social workers. These professionals can also be invaluable when respite care is needed by a family.

Specialist local and national support and information for children and families

Local support

As knowledge of special educational needs becomes more widespread and the need for education and support is recognised, many more local support groups have been formed. Every area will have its own services for children with special educational needs and disabilities; many of these have been set up by parents of children with additional needs. There are also local branches of national organisations, such as the National Federation of Gateway Clubs (affiliated to Mencap). The Federation's clubs provide a range of community-based activities covering leisure and social education; there are Junior Gateway Clubs for the under-18s. The local branches of such organisations as the Down's Syndrome Association and the National Autistic Society can be invaluable to parents who feel isolated.

Parents and carers can support each other by sharing experiences, information and ideas. Through a self-help or support group, parents and carers can:

- talk to people who understand the day-to-day issues of raising a child with special educational needs
- get the benefit of other parents' experience, moral support and practical tips
- organise social events and speakers to discuss certain topics
- become involved in other focus groups in the area to perhaps influence local policies.

activity 8.9 GROUP WORK

Find out what support there is in your local area for a child with special educational needs and their family. Your local education authority may have a directory of services for children with additional needs.

National support

There are now support groups for most special educational needs. These give information and highlight the implications for the education and care of the child. Most national groups and many local ones have websites, and information is easily accessible. Examples of national organisations which it can be useful to know about are:

- *Contact a Family*. This national charity works across the UK to support families caring for disabled children or children with special educational needs (a learning difficulty, physical disability, medical condition, rare syndrome, life-threatening condition or behavioural difficulty). It publishes a quarterly newsletter called *Share an Idea*. Local parent representatives offer a local sign-posting service to parents and professionals.

- *The Down's Syndrome Association*. This is a national support group.
- *The National Autistic Society*. This is a national support group.
- *SCOPE*. This national organisation supports people with cerebral palsy.
- *The National Parent Partnership network*. This is a statutory service, providing impartial advice, information and support for parents of children and young people with special educational needs. Local branches will be able to put parents in touch with other organisations in the area. Parent partnerships also have a role in making sure that parents' views are heard and understood and that their views inform local policy and practice. Some parent partnerships are based in the voluntary sector; the majority, however, are based in the local education authority.

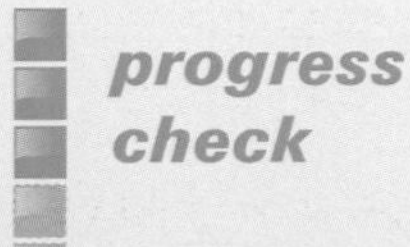

progress check

1. What is meant by the term 'genetic inheritance'?
2. What is the difference between autosomal recessive and autosomal dominant transference?
3. Give two examples of a condition due to autosomal recessive transference.
4. Give two examples of a condition due to autosomal dominant transference.
5. Give two examples of a condition due to X-linked transference.
6. What is TEACCH?
7. What is the difference between the conditions ADD and ADHD?
8. Explain the role of a Portage worker.
9. Why are home-link books so useful?
10. What are SMART targets, and when are they used?
11. What is an IEP?
12. Explain (a) what is meant by inclusion and (b) how inclusion benefits all children.

References and suggested further reading

Birkett, V. (2004) *How to Support and Teach Children with SEN*. LDA Publishers, Wiltshire.

Dare, A. and O'Donovan, M. (1997) *Good Practice in Caring for Young Children with Special Needs*. Nelson Thornes, Cheltenham.

DfES (2001) *Special Educational Needs Guide for Parents and Carers*. DfES, London.

DfES (2004) *Removing Barriers to Achievement*. HMSO, London.

Family Information Service (2006). *A Directory of Services for Children with Additional Needs*, 2nd edn. B&NES.

Gilbert, P. (2000) *A–Z of Syndromes and Inherited Disorders*, 3rd edn. Nelson Thornes, Cheltenham.

Gray, C. and White, A. L. (eds.) (2001) *My Social Stories Book*. Jessica Kingsley Publishers, London.

Halliwell, M. (2003) *Supporting Children with SEN: A Guide for Assistants in Schools and Pre-schools*. David Fulton Publishers, London.

Nash-Wortham, M. and Hunt, J. (1994) *Take Time*. Robinswood, Stourbridge.

Tassoni, P. (2003) *Supporting Special Needs: Understanding Inclusion in the Early Years*. Heinemann, London.

Teodorescu, I. and Addy, L. (1996) *Write from the Start*. LDA, Wisbech.

Wall, K. (2003) *Special Needs and Early Years: A Practitioner's Guide*. Paul Chapman Publishers, London.

Websites

www.downsyndrome.org.uk
www.dyspraxiafoundation.org.uk
www.tsa.org.uk
www.williams-syndrome.org.uk
www.cafamily.org.uk
www.parentpartnership.org.uk
www.scope.org.uk
www.direct.gov.uk/educationandlearningschools/sen
www.special-educational-needs.co.uk
www.drcorg.uk/yourrights
http://inclusion.uwe.ac.uk/csie

Glossary

ABA – applied behaviour analysis.

ABC of resuscitation – a sequential emergency first aid process: open the airway; breathe for the injured person; help circulation to be restored.

Accident book – a book in which staff record all accidents or injuries that occur in the workplace.

Active listening – ensuring that you are focusing on what you are listening to.

ADD – attention deficit disorder.

ADHD – attention deficit hyperactivity disorder.

Apgar score – score denoting the health of a baby at birth.

Associative play – children play with the same activity, watching what others are doing, but are not yet playing co-operatively.

Attachment – an emotional bond that develops between a baby and their carer.

Autosomal dominant transference – when at least one parent is affected by a condition passed on through their genes.

Autosomal recessive transference – when both parents are carriers of a condition passed on through the genes.

Barrier to communication – any obstruction to understanding between individuals.

Bond – the close relationship formed between a child and one or more of the child's main carers.

Boundaries – rules that guide behaviour and ensure consistency.

Challenge – an experience that will help develop a skill or aspect of learning.

Child assessment order – a legal order applied for in court when a child is considered to be at risk or already suffering significant harm.

Child protection register – a computerised list, kept by a local authority, of children who are considered to be 'at risk'.

Children Act 2004 – a major piece of legislation, bringing together a range of laws to do with the rights and well-being of children; it builds on the Children Act 1989.

Code of practice – the procedures (usually written down) by which a setting or profession operates.

Cognitive development – the development of knowledge through thinking and problem solving.

Communication – the means of passing and receiving information.

Communication cycle – a reciprocal form of passing and receiving information.

Confidentiality – not passing on information inappropriately; keeping information to yourself, thereby respecting the privacy of others.

Co-operative play – the stage of play when children play with each other, sometimes taking on simple roles or making simple rules for their games.

COSHH – Control of Substances Hazardous to Health Regulations 2002.

Culture – beliefs, customs and values of people from a similar background.

Custom – usual practice.

Dehydration – state in which the water content of the body falls dangerously low.

Development – the changes that take place as an individual grows.

Direct discrimination – telling an individual that they cannot do something because of their race, sex, situation or disability.

Discrimination – the unfair treatment of an individual, group or minority, based on prejudice.

Diversity – being different or varying from the norm.

Dysfluency – being unable to speak words fluently, stammering. This is a common (temporary) occurrence in young children.

Early Learning Goals – the aims of the six areas of learning that make up the Foundation Stage curriculum. Most children achieve these goals before they enter key stage 1 of the National Curriculum.

Eczema – a dry, scaly, itchy skin condition.

Emergency protection order (EPO) – an order of law, applied for through the courts to help protect children from harm.

Emotional disturbance – is evidenced by behaviour that causes concern and needs professional intervention (when serious or long term) or sensitive handling by parents and carers (for temporary or common problems such as tantrums).

Equality – the state of being equal, of having an equal opportunity.

Evaluation – reflecting on and giving consideration to a past event, action or project.

Exploratory play – play in which a child is able to find out by experimentation and discovery.

First aid – the emergency actions taken following an accident or sudden illness.

Fontanelle – the area of an infant's skull that allows flexibility during the birth process.

Foundation Stage curriculum – a Government-led curriculum for children from the age of three years.

Genetic inheritance – features passed down to an infant from their parents; this may involve the passing on of a condition or disorder through the genes of one or both parents.

Genotype – the complete genetic inheritance of one person that is present in their chromosomes.

Growth – increase in size, height, weight, and so on.

HASAWA – the Health and Safety at Work Etc. Act 1974, 1999.

Health – the state of well-being.

Hygiene – good practice regarding cleanliness, handling food and personal care.

IEP – Individual Education Plan.

Institutional discrimination – the policies or practice of an organisation, which systematically discriminates against a minority group or groups.

Interpersonal skills – communicating with others in a positive (with good skills) or negative (with bad skills) manner.

Lactation – the production of milk by the breasts.

Laissez-faire model – an approach involving unrestricted freedom or indifference; e.g. the adult lets the child play without restriction and with little or no guidance.

Language disorder – a problem that may cause difficulties in speech and communication.

Legal framework of child protection – laws and procedures to protect children and vulnerable young people.

Listening skills – different ways of really listening.

Local Safeguarding Children Board (LSCB) – a group of professionals who meet to discuss individual child abuse or protection cases.

Marginalised – treated as insignificant or unimportant; placed at the edge (of importance).

Milestones – significant events linked with stages in development.

Minimum space requirements – legal requirements concerning the space needed for the numbers of children being cared for in any one place.

National Curriculum – the curriculum followed by children in all state schools.

Neonate – an infant under one month old.

Non-participant observation – observation where the observer does not actually interact with the person or activity being observed.

Non-verbal communication – the messages that are given through body language and facial expression.

Objectivity – observing without any pre-judgement or bias.

Parallel play – the stage of play when children play alongside other children without interacting.

Parental consent forms – forms in which parents give written permission for something, e.g. for emergency medical treatment to take place.

Participant observation – observation where the observer is involved with the person or activity being observed.

Partnership with parents – active involvement of parents by the setting.

PECS – Picture Exchange Communication System, a system for signing language.

Perception – the organisation and interpretation of information received from the sensory organs; gaining insight or awareness.

Percussion therapy – physiotherapy of the chest to loosen secretions blocking the lungs.

Persona dolls – dolls designed to represent children from various cultures and/or with a range of disabilities.

Phenotype – the physical and behavioural characteristics of a person that are visible and are the result of the interaction of genetic inheritance and environment.

Portage – a daily home-teaching programme specified for the individual child.

Prejudice – an opinion formed in advance, a pre-judgement.

Pre-pubescent – before the onset of the development of secondary sex characteristics, such as periods, body hair and breast development in girls.

Prerequisites for language – what is needed in order for successful language development to take place.

Pre-term – born before 37 weeks of pregnancy.

Primary socialisation – the impact of immediate family and social groups on a child.

Primitive reflexes – automatic responses seen in newborn infants that are not generally observed in older children and adults.

Recovery order – a legal order enabling the police to take into their possession a child who is the subject of police protection or an emergency protection order, if the child is missing, has run away, or has been abducted from the person responsible for their care.

Reflection – the process of giving something thoughtful consideration.

Reflective listening – where the listener echoes the last (or most significant) words spoken by the speaker.

Reflex – an involuntary response to a stimulus, for example blinking.

Religion – a person's belief in a god or gods.

RIDDOR – Reporting of Injuries, Diseases and Dangerous Occurrences Regulations 1995.

Rights – our entitlements as individuals.

Risk assessment – the identification of potential hazards and guidance on managing the risk of accident or incident.

Role model – a person who is considered to be setting an example to others.

Routines – set procedures that should meet the needs of all concerned.

Safety marks – national standards with regard to safety, printed on the packaging of such objects as toys, baby equipment and electrical appliances to guide consumers as to their suitability for the intended use or recipient.

Screening – the process of examining a whole population to identify who is showing signs of a disease or may be predisposed to develop it.

Secondary socialisation – the impact on a child of social contacts outside the child's immediate family and social group; these would include teachers, early years professionals, and so on.

Self-concept – an understanding of our own identity that includes how we are seen by others.

Self-esteem – feeling good about oneself, feeling confident.

SEN – special educational needs.

SENCO – special education needs co-ordinator.

SENDA – Special Education Needs and Disability Act 2001.

Signed language – forms of language in which signs replace speech.

Small world play – play with toys that are a scaled-down version of real life.

SMART – an acronym for Specific, Measurable, Achievable, Relevant, Time-limited.

Social constructivist model – an approach to learning that emphasises the importance of exploring a range of experiences and objects from everyday life.

Social learning theory – the theory proposing that children learn by observing and copying the behaviour of others; this theory was supported by Albert Bandura's Bobo doll experiments.

Solitary play – playing alone, a normal stage of development in young children.

Stages of play – the changes in how children's play develops, usually linked to age.

Standard attainment tasks (SATs) – tests carried out at regular intervals during formal schooling.

Stereotyping – categorising, taking away individuality.

Sterilising techniques – methods of ensuring that utensils (bottles, teats, etc.) used for babies are free from bacteria.

Supervision order – a legal order in which a child is under the supervision of the local authority, but where the authority does not have parental responsibility.

TEACCH – Treatment and Education of Autistic and related Communication-handicapped CHildren.

Teamwork – working co-operatively with a group of colleagues.

Tokenism – making only a small effort, or providing no more than the minimum, in order to comply with criteria or guidelines.

Transmission model – an approach in which the adult controls the learning process, often suppressing the child's own initiative.

Trustworthy – reliable, honest, dependable.

UN Convention on the Rights of the Child – this 'national constitution' was adopted by the United Nations assembly in 1989 to uphold agreed rights for children whenever possible.

Values – moral standards.

Weaning – the introduction of solid food to an infant's diet.

X-linked transference – a disorder found on the X chromosome and passed on through the genes of the parent.

Index

Page references in *italics* indicate figures or tables

Index